FROM THE WAR ON POVERTY TO THE WAR ON CRIME

FROM THE WAR ON POVERTY
TO THE WAR ON CRIME

The Making of Mass Incarceration in America

ELIZABETH HINTON

Harvard University Press

Cambridge, Massachusetts, & London, England

2016

Publication of this book has been supported through the generous provisions
of the Maurice and Lula Bradley Smith Memorial Fund.

Third printing

Library of Congress Cataloging-in-Publication Data
Names: Hinton, Elizabeth Kai, 1983– author.
Title: From the war on poverty to the war on crime : the making of
mass incarceration in America / Elizabeth Hinton.
Description: Cambridge, Massachusetts : Harvard University
Press, 2016. | Includes bibliographical references and index.
Identifiers: LCCN 2015039012 | ISBN 9780674737235 (alk. paper)
Subjects: LCSH: Criminal justice, Administration of—Political aspects—
United States—History—20th century. | Urban policy—United States—History—20th century. |
Crime prevention—United States—History—20th century. | Crime—Political aspects—
United States—History—20th century. | Imprisonment—United States.
Classification: LCC HV9950 .H56 2016 | DDC 364.973—dc23
LC record available at http://lccn.loc.gov/2015039012

For Big Papa

CONTENTS

FROM THE WAR ON POVERTY TO THE WAR ON CRIME

INTRODUCTION

Origins of Mass Incarceration

Since President Lyndon Johnson first called for a "War on Crime" some fifty years ago, prisons, jails, and law enforcement institutions have functioned as a central engine of American inequality. It is one of the essential ironies of American history that this punitive campaign began during an era of liberal reform and at the height of the civil rights revolution, a moment when the nation seemed ready to embrace policies that would fully realize its egalitarian founding values. The year 1964 witnessed the passage of the Civil Rights Act and the launch of the federal initiatives that constituted the "War on Poverty." The next March, Johnson sent to Congress the Voting Rights Act, which provided African Americans in the southern states the opportunity to participate in the electoral process as equal citizens. Yet President Johnson hoped that 1965 would be remembered not only for this momentous victory but also as "the year when this country began a thorough, intelligent, and effective war against crime." On March 8, Johnson presented to Congress the Law Enforcement Assistance Act. Coming a week before the Voting Rights Act and after a summer of urban unrest in Harlem, Brooklyn, Rochester, Chicago, and Philadelphia in 1964, the punitive legislation offered a response to the threat of future disorder by establishing a direct role for the federal government in local police operations, court systems, and state prisons for the first time in American history.[1]

A new era of American law enforcement had begun, one that would soon shift the country's progressive policy trajectory. Following the passage of the Law Enforcement Assistance Act, the federal government began to retreat from and eventually undercut many of the Great Society programs that are often heralded as the Johnson administration's greatest achievements. Republican and Democratic policymakers alike instead mobilized to fight the War on Crime and, later, President Ronald Reagan's more aggressive "War on Drugs." This long War on Crime would eventually produce the contemporary atrocity of mass incarceration in America, distinguished by a rate of imprisonment far above all other industrialized nations and involving the systematic confinement of entire groups of citizens.[2]

The capstone of Johnson's Great Society was the Safe Streets Act of 1968, which invested $400 million worth of "seed money" in the War on Crime. To promote the modernization of law enforcement and to help each state build its respective criminal justice apparatus, the legislation created the Law Enforcement Assistance Administration (LEAA) to administer this funding. Housed within the Department of Justice, the LEAA became the fastest-growing federal agency in the 1970s, its budget swelling exponentially from the $10 million Congress allotted to the War on Crime in 1965 to some $850 million by 1973. When the LEAA was finally disbanded in 1981, during Reagan's first year in office, it had funded roughly 80,000 crime control projects and awarded 155,270 grants amounting to nearly $10 billion in taxpayer dollars—roughly $25 billion in today's dollars. No less than three out of every four dollars the LEAA dispersed during its fifteen-year life span went to police operations, for a total outlay equivalent to some $15 billion today. The states dedicated hundreds of billions of dollars more to criminal justice and law enforcement during the same years, stimulated by the programs national policymakers subsidized and designed.[3] The result was a significant expansion of America's carceral state: the police, sheriffs, and marshals responsible for law enforcement; the judges, prosecutors, and defense lawyers that facilitate the judicial process; and the prison officials and probation and parole officers charged with handling convicted felons.[4]

The mission that the White House and Congress effectively assigned to the LEAA was to expand supervision and control in low-income urban communities. Across political and ideological lines, federal policymakers shared a set of assumptions about African Americans, poverty, and crime that in time became a causal and consensus-building force in the domestic urban policy following civil rights legislation.[5] Even if their legislative language never evoked race explicitly, policymakers interpreted black urban poverty as pathological—as the product of individual and cultural "deficiencies." This consensus distorted the aims of the War on Poverty and also shaped the rationale, legislation, and programs of the War on Crime. The seemingly neutral statistical and sociological "truth" of black criminality concealed the racist thinking that guided the strategies federal policymakers developed for the War on Crime, first in the 1960s, then through the 1970s and beyond.

Although the Reagan administration is generally credited with spearheading the domestic policy shift toward confinement and urban surveillance, the national crime control programs it developed in the 1980s were hardly a sharp policy departure. The targeted deployment of such crime control programs in urban areas began during the civil rights era with John F. Kennedy's "total attack" on delinquency in 1961. The Kennedy administration's antidelinquency programs were intended to provide low-income citizens in sixteen cities with counseling, job training, remedial education, and other social welfare programs as a strategy to prevent youth crime. Johnson expanded Kennedy's intervention on a national scale and reframed it as a "War on Poverty," while also introducing more aggressive and exhaustive supervision in the black urban areas previously targeted by the Kennedy administration. When Richard Nixon took office in 1969, he disinvested from his predecessor's more progressive programs and seized upon the punitive impulses of Johnson's domestic policies, introducing draconian sentencing reforms, supporting the targeted deployment of aggressive local, state, and federal undercover police squads on the streets of American cities, and incentivizing prison construction. Roughly a decade into the crime war, as it became clear that the white "youth in trouble" were also entering the justice system at alarming rates due to the punitive climate generated by national law enforcement programs, Congress intervened to decriminalize certain offenses that policymakers associated with white children and teenagers. Simultaneously, new legislation placed the label "potentially delinquent" on any urban youth of color who had family members with arrest records, attended public schools, lived in public housing, or received welfare benefits. Shifting the purpose of the crime war from restoring "law and order" to ensuring "domestic tranquility" when he took office in 1974, Gerald Ford established urban policies that sought to rapidly process and confine targeted "repeat offenders" in jail for long terms. With a robust national law enforcement program under way at both the state and local levels, Jimmy Carter moved to dissolve the federal LEAA and place crime control measures at the center of the national government's broader urban policy, framing his punitive policies as security precautions, rather than crime control measures.

Relying on the strategies, institutions, and bureaucracy developed at the state and local levels during the War on Crime's first fifteen years, Reagan made the national law enforcement program far more punitive by the end of the 1980s. His administration brought to fruition some of the most controversial legislative proposals of the Nixon and Ford era, further centralized federal law enforcement in the institutional vacuum Jimmy Carter had created by disbanding the LEAA, and opened up what had previously been a domestic War on Crime to the military by extending surveillance and patrol to the nation's borders. But the extraordinary expansion of the urban police forces, court cases, and prison populations during the War on Drugs should be understood as the culmination of the domestic policies described in this book, rather than their beginning. In full historical context, the policies of the Reagan administration marked merely the fulfillment of federal crime control priorities that stemmed initially from one of the most idealistic enterprises in American history during the era of civil rights.[6] Waged over the past half-century, since it emerged from within the War on Poverty and alongside it, this long War on Crime has today positioned law enforcement agencies, criminal justice institutions, and jails as the primary public programs in many low-income communities across the United States.

MAKING MASS INCARCERATION

In the century between the end of the U.S. Civil War in 1865 and Johnson's call for the War on Crime, a total of 184,901 Americans entered
state and federal prisons. During just the two decades between the
passage of the Law Enforcement Assistance Act and the launch of
Reagan's War on Drugs, the country added 251,107 citizens to the prison
system. The American carceral state has continued its rapid growth ever
since, so that today 2.2 million citizens are behind bars—representing a
943 percent increase over the past half century. Home to the largest
prison system on the planet, with a rate of incarceration that is five to
ten times higher than that of comparable nations, the United States
represents 5 percent of the world's population but holds 25 percent of its
prisoners. This prison system costs taxpayers $80 billion annually, and
has become such a paramount component of domestic social policy that
states like California and Michigan spend more money on imprisoning
young people than on educating them.[7]

The rise of mass incarceration over the past fifty years has disrupted
millions of American families, nearly all of whom are low-income.
However, policymakers' decision to expand the punitive arm of the state
has had especially severe consequences for racially marginalized Americans. Black Americans and Latinos together constitute 59 percent of
the nation's prisoners, even though they make up roughly a quarter of
the entire U.S. population.[8] Although in recent decades Latino Americans have entered the nation's carceral institutions in greater numbers,
and they are disproportionately ensnared in the growing system of
immigration detention, African Americans have in the long term been
hit the hardest by the punitive transformation of domestic policy.

Regardless of socioeconomic status, African Americans are more
likely to serve prison or jail time than any other racial group in the
United States. Odds are 50–50 that young black urban males are in jail,
in a cell in one of the 1,821 state and federal prisons across the United
States, or on probation or parole. And assuming punitive programs continue in their present form, African Americans born after 1965 and
lacking a high school diploma are more likely to eventually go to prison
than not.[9]

Arguably the most important question facing American society today is why, in the land of the free, one in thirty-one people is under some form of penal control. Scholars, activists, policymakers, and advocates have come up with a range of answers since the outset of the War on Crime. The first and most forceful explanation reiterates the rationale that Johnson and other federal policymakers offered at the time: rising crime rates in the 1960s and 1970s demanded that the federal government intervene in what had been a state and local matter for the previous two centuries of American history. As Senator Strom Thurmond put it in 1967: "No country has ever incurred as much crime as America is enduring today." But contrary to the sensationalized media coverage and fear-mongering political rhetoric at the time, when Johnson began the national law enforcement intervention, violent crime had in fact steadily declined after peaking in the interwar period, and crime levels had remained relatively stable since the repeal of Prohibition in 1933. When crime began to rise sharply in urban centers, it rose as federal policymakers invested in state and local law enforcement programs that aimed to modernize police departments. Many previously hidden crimes suddenly came to light as reported crime rates determined the extent of national crime control funding. For example, the number of recorded robberies and burglaries in New York City skyrocketed from a combined total of 48,000 in 1965 to 143,000 the following year. This threefold increase resulted not from an actual upsurge in crime, but from the crime reporting reforms Mayor John Lindsay implemented when he took office in 1966. The development of crime statistics, a new technology of knowledge production, alongside early federal law enforcement measures, meant that rising crime rates in New York City and elsewhere correlated directly to rising crime reporting, a fact that skewed perceptions of violence.[10]

The Federal Bureau of Investigation (FBI) provided a national portrait of these distorted figures in its Uniform Crime Rate, which has stood as the nation's primary measurement of crime since 1930 despite its known inaccuracies. One year after the FBI began collecting these statistics, a report warned of "the danger of having law enforcement agencies responsible for collecting and disseminating crime data because of their vested interests." At the outset of the crime war in the 1960s, congressional representatives raised questions about the utility of the FBI data and the extensive and systematized manipulation of the national crime rate in the past. Yet the very problem—impossibility, even—of precisely measuring crime ultimately served as a rationale for providing additional criminal justice resources. Moreover, leading social scientists have been unable to establish a strong correlation between incarceration and crime rates, debunking the idea that the threat of imprisonment serves as a powerful crime deterrent. When Reagan called the War on Drugs and prison populations went on to soar, the crime rate had decreased from its high levels in the mid-1970s. Politicians and officials have explained mass incarceration as a seemingly natural policy response to a surge in criminality and violence among specific sects of the citizenry, but scholars have pointed to the ways in which mass incarceration and the justice disparities within it expressed changes in law, budgetary allocations for crime control, and punitive practices at all levels of government.[11]

A common account relies on party politics to explain why Johnson and other national representatives pursued this punitive domestic policy path. The story usually begins with the "law and order" rhetoric Barry Goldwater introduced into political discourse during the 1964 presidential campaign that Nixon went on to appropriate in the 1968 contest. The wars on crime and drugs then appear as shrewd electoral strategies developed in reaction to the upheavals of the 1960s and the uncertainties of the 1970s that carried over into the 1980s. From Nixon's "Silent Majority" to the Reagan Democrats, Republican policymakers employed the racially coded politics of crime control to appeal to disenchanted white voters.[12]

Electoral ambitions and special interests certainly help explain the federal government's commitment to enlarging the carceral state beginning in the mid-1960s, but Republican Party strategy is not a satisfactory answer alone. Without question, the rightward turn of the American political system played a role in the appearance of anticrime legislation. Segregationists in Congress such as John McClellan, Sam Ervin, and Thurmond emerged as some of the most outspoken crime control proponents in the early stages of the federal government's law enforcement program even as they opposed other social programs. Yet the

Republican coalition that emerged in the postwar period did not engineer the War on Crime and the rise of the carceral state. As the product of one of the most ambitious liberal welfare programs in American history, the rise of punitive federal policy over the last fifty years is a thoroughly bipartisan story. Built by a consensus of liberals and conservatives who privileged punitive responses to urban problems as a reaction to the civil rights movement, over time, the carceral state and the network of programs it encompassed came to dominate government responses to American inequality. Indeed, crime control may be *the* domestic policy issue in the late twentieth century where conservative and liberal interests most thoroughly intertwined.[13]

In addition to focusing too narrowly on the tactical dimensions of crime control politics, scholars have underestimated the federal government's active role in revolutionizing American law enforcement before the 1980s. Although state and municipal governments retained control over their respective criminal justice systems, the creation of the LEAA made national policymakers meaningful partners in law enforcement and criminal justice at all levels. Groundbreaking studies have recently emphasized the distinctive role of states in supporting the proliferation of crime control and punitive programs, examining the actions of state legislatures and the networks of state officials and local law enforcement authorities that formed an effective criminal justice lobby beginning in the 1970s.[14] The focus on state-level factors illuminated developments that precipitated mass incarceration across the country, but it has also diverted attention from the profound national dimensions of crime control, which have yet to be fully examined. After all, in the absence of the policing, juridical, and penal programs federal policymakers imposed, it is entirely possible that state and local governments would have decided to invest in an entirely different set of priorities. At a time when the harms of mass incarceration are increasingly recognized by policymakers, political candidates, and growing sectors of the public, national action is needed once again if we are to move toward solutions.

Most recently, political scientists and historians have begun to highlight the black politicians, community leaders, and clergymen who responded to disorder by demanding tougher crime control measures in urban communities. Their work has revealed new dimensions of the politics of crime control and the diversity of opinion within African American communities.[15] In these depictions, however, the range of ways black activists and leaders responded to policing, crime, and drug abuse often gets obscured. During the 1960s and 1970s in particular, the version of the War on Crime that many black activists imagined involved community control, oversight, and inclusion in the development and implementation of urban law enforcement programs. The version of crime control that federal, state, and local authorities imposed was far different. The emergence of black and Latino activist groups that called for armed self-defense, from the Black Panthers to the Revolutionary Action Movement to the Young Lords, can be seen as a response to the expansion of police and surveillance in targeted low-income urban communities after 1965. These groups drew upon a long tradition of direct-action mobilization against police brutality and aggressive law enforcement that took on different approaches over the course of the 1970s and that continues to this day.

By the 1980s, when the social service centers that had been established during the War on Poverty were nowhere to be found in some of the most vulnerable and isolated neighborhoods in American cities, residents had no one else to call *but* the police and law enforcement authorities when their children engaged in criminal activity, and when friends and family members robbed them in order to fuel a drug habit. For those neighborhoods lacking comprehensive rehabilitative or social welfare programs, when law enforcement and criminal justice institutions became the last public agencies standing, the police were the service that could be summoned when help was needed. Some African Americans made the conscious decision not to involve law enforcement and the criminal justice system in their lives and the lives of their neighbors—what today is referred to as the "stop snitching" movement. And according to polling data, the majority of African Americans remain suspicious of law enforcement and cynical about the criminal justice system.[16]

Police officers have always served as the first line of contact between citizens and the justice system, yet most existing accounts of mass incarceration leave out the law enforcement channels that facilitate the entry of citizens into prisons. This omission often hides the full depths of the carceral state's racist dimensions. We cannot fully account for how mass incarceration happened or why black and Latino citizens are overrepresented in the nation's penal system without examining the transformation of American policing in the last fifty years. In her groundbreaking *The New Jim Crow: Mass Incarceration in the Age of Colorblindness*, Michelle Alexander traced the dynamics between federal and state priorities, police departments, and black communities that created severe racial disparities in the criminal justice system. Alexander brought much-needed attention to the policing practices that emerged during the War on Drugs and the way federal policies assigned urban police forces to the task of searching for and apprehending as many suspects as possible.[17]

Although Alexander masterfully synthesized two decades of political science and sociological research focusing on connections between mass incarceration and the War on Drugs, fully accounting for this remarkable transformation in late twentieth-century domestic policy requires beginning much earlier. The federal government sought to control the flow and use of narcotics well before the Safe Streets Act of 1968, establishing the Treasury Department's Federal Bureau of Narcotics to focus on regulating drugs in the 1930s, an approach that became more punitive during the War on Crime in 1973, when the Nixon administration created the Drug Enforcement Agency.[18] It also requires looking beyond drug enforcement policies alone. The records of the LEAA, internal memoranda, previously confidential reports, and public speeches make clear that the concern Nixon and other federal policymakers shared about drugs was very much rooted in their fears about crime in general. Narcotics enforcement had been a federal responsibility since the early twentieth century, and the Nixon and Reagan administrations launched antidrug campaigns partly as a strategy to generate a larger sphere of influence for the national government in low-income urban communities.

The War on Drugs should be considered one component of a much larger set of domestic anticrime policies that focused primarily on black youth and their families but have increasingly come to ensnare millions of Americans regardless of their race. Before the 1980s, national law enforcement programs introduced various forms of surveillance into social welfare programs, labeled entire groups of Americans as likely criminals and targeted them with undercover and decoy squads, ran sting operations that created underground economies, and combated gangs with militarized police forces and severe sentencing guidelines. Together these practices helped to fuel the phenomenon of mass incarceration and to bring the nation to a fiscal and moral crossroads.

MAKING THE WAR ON CRIME

The roots of mass incarceration had been firmly established by a bipartisan consensus of national policymakers in the two decades prior to Reagan's War on Drugs in the 1980s. Thus the expansion of the carceral state should be understood as the federal government's response to the demographic transformation of the nation at mid-century, the gains of the African American civil rights movement, and the persistent threat of urban rebellion. Between World War I and Vietnam, more than 6 million rural African Americans escaped the exploitation and terror of southern segregationist regimes and moved to northern cities, a mass migration that transformed the nation. Black civil rights activists and labor leaders began organizing at the start of this migration and eventually pushed President Franklin D. Roosevelt to desegregate defense and government industries in the context of World War II. The marshaling of federal resources to challenge discrimination during the New Deal grounded unrelenting calls for integration that eventually led the Supreme Court to endorse the desegregation of southern public schools in 1954's *Brown v. Board of Education* decision. With Jim Crow's "separate but equal" principle destabilized, the African American protest movement flourished, using direct-action tactics, petitions, and class-action lawsuits to demand an end to racial inequality. Young activists came to play an increasingly important role in these local and national struggles, which had evolved to demand economic justice for African Americans nationwide and galvanized hundreds of thousands of protestors to participate in the March on Washington for Jobs and Freedom in the summer of 1963. As black citizens continued to relocate to the urban north amid the burgeoning civil rights movement, the ongoing exodus of primarily white, middle-class residents from cities to suburban areas required new approaches to the problems municipalities faced with tax bases in decline.[19]

In response to these transformations, federal officials now made the entwined goals of remedying racial discrimination, ending poverty, and fighting crime in American cities central to domestic programs. Most African Americans had been excluded from Aid to Dependent Children, the GI Bill, and many other social welfare programs associated with the New Deal, making the Kennedy administration's "total attack" on delinquency one of the federal government's first responses to the impact of the Great Migration in American cities. Kennedy's creation of the President's Committee on Juvenile Delinquency and Youth Crime in the spring of 1961 began a series of direct government interventions in cities with high concentrations of black citizens.[20]

The President's Committee set the strategies and established the partnerships with local municipalities and private organizations that Johnson expanded into a "War on Poverty." With the specific purpose of promoting socioeconomic mobility in the nation's most devastated low-income areas, in March 1964 Johnson sent the Equal Opportunity Act to Congress, legislation that vastly increased the scale and the potential power of the federal government's urban intervention. Concerns about controlling crime in black urban neighborhoods, however, limited the range of possibilities of New Frontier and Great Society programs alike.[21] Although federal policymakers and officials did acknowledge unemployment and subpar urban school systems as factors contributing to both poverty and crime, incidents of collective violence during the second half of the 1960s moved liberal sympathizers away from structural critiques of poverty and support for community action programs.

From the ashes of the Watts "riot" in August 1965, a growing consensus of policymakers, federal administrators, law enforcement officials, and journalists came to understand crime as specific to black urban youth. They concluded that only intensified enforcement of the law in black urban neighborhoods, where contempt for authority seemed widespread, would quell the anarchy and chaos on the nation's streets. Increasingly, federal policymakers treated antipoverty policies less as moral imperatives in their own right and more as a means to suppress future rioting and crime. The Johnson administration quickly combined the existing education, health, housing, and welfare programs aimed at eliminating crime's root causes with the police training, research programs, and criminal justice and penal reforms intended to suppress criminal activity.[22]

Even as the equal opportunity efforts of the War on Poverty only feebly attacked the underlying structural and historical factors that caused mass unemployment, deteriorating housing conditions, and failing public schools, federal policymakers supported the influx of more police officers and military-grade weapons on the streets as riot prevention measures. Yet the uprisings only increased in their fury and frequency, with destructive incidents of collective violence in Newark and Detroit in July 1967. The Johnson administration believed that African American men between the ages of fifteen and twenty-four, influenced by civil rights activists increasingly advocating for self-determination and community control, were primarily responsible for the unrest.[23] This group quickly emerged as the foremost target of federal policymakers. It seemed that antipoverty programs had failed to reach the "hard-core" black urban youth who appeared particularly susceptible to collective violence and, by extension, crime. Without evoking race explicitly, the White House and Congress then built a set of punitive policies that focused on controlling this group by expanding the field of surveillance and patrol around them.

President Johnson saw urban police officers as the "frontline soldiers" of the War on Crime, and, as such, law enforcement authorities received new military-grade weapons and surveillance technologies, along with new powers in the direction and administration of urban social programs. Beginning in the late 1960s, police departments began to establish themselves in the spaces that had been vacated by War on Poverty programs. With federal funding, the police force in Washington, DC, started an after-school program for black youth in a center that had been left behind by a community health clinic almost immediately after it closed in 1967. And in Baltimore, police officers delivered food and toys to African American families.

When issues of crime control, sentencing, and confinement moved to the center of domestic policy, the strategies federal policymakers adopted for the urban intervention yielded new possibilities for supervision in the halls of urban schools, in the elevators of housing projects, and in the reception rooms of welfare offices. Soon, federal policymakers required employment initiatives, public schools, and grassroots organizations to partner with juvenile courts, police departments, and correctional facilities in order to receive funding, an act that was perhaps more consequential in the long term than the modernization and militarization of American police forces. The result was a vast and ever-expanding network of institutions responsible for maintaining social control in post–Jim Crow America. Born from the fusion of law enforcement and the community action, job training, and public housing programs within the Great Society, this network metastasized into the modern carceral state.

When Johnson introduced a comprehensive antipoverty program in low-income urban communities for the first time while simultaneously launching an anticrime intervention, the balance tilted from social welfare to punishment as the national law enforcement program crowded out the goals of the poverty war. By expanding the federal government's power in the pursuit of twinned social welfare and social control goals, Johnson paradoxically paved the way for the anticrime policies of the Nixon and Ford administrations to be turned against his own antipoverty programs.[24] After 250 separate incidents of urban civil disorder—what policymakers, journalists, and most of the public at large called "riots"—that occurred in 1968, nearly half of them in the aftermath of Martin Luther King Jr.'s murder in April, Johnson signed the Safe Streets Act in June.

This law introduced block grants into domestic policy, a new approach to federalism that placed nationally funded programs under the control of governors rather than localities and community groups. Using block grant formulas, the White House and Congress urged state governments to create criminal justice institutions and dedicate resources to increasing the nation's punitive and carceral capacities. Directives from the executive branch propelled the revolution in American law enforcement and criminal justice, but block grant formulas allowed states to develop crime control strategies as they wished, as long as they matched or contributed to congressional allocations.[25] States from New

York to California increasingly turned to the LEAA and block grant funding to administer job training programs and community centers that had been funded by the Office of Economic Opportunity during the War on Poverty.

Indeed, in deciding to bring punitive measures into urban policy, channeling funds through block grants, and inviting private sector participation in public social programs, the Johnson administration helped to lay the groundwork for subsequent federal action generally associated with conservatism. The Law Enforcement Assistance Act of 1965 and the crime control legislation that followed it underscore the extent to which, even at the height of the liberal welfare state, the seemingly opposing domestic policy approaches put forth by liberal and conservative policymakers were in fact complementary. The fact that federal crime control programs criminalized racially marginalized citizens and perpetuated inequality does not make those programs inherently conservative. After all, Democrats controlled both chambers of Congress from the Johnson administration through the final years of the Carter administration. Across party lines and working together during and between political campaigns, representatives increased urban patrol forces, enacted harsh and racially biased sentencing laws, and endorsed new penal institutions that made mass incarceration possible.[26]

Emphasizing the significant spheres where conservatism and liberalism overlapped is not an attempt to argue that conservatives and liberals had no policy innovations or distinct agenda of their own. The civil rights movement had led to a shift in the popular and political consciousness during and after World War II that increasingly viewed racial discrimination in housing, employment, and education as pernicious. In line with the changing national mood on "the crisis of race relations," liberal political rhetoric of the 1960s consistently emphasized the harms of prejudice in American society. Kennedy's "total attack" on delinquency and Johnson's War on Poverty were seen by federal policymakers as attempts to address finally the racial inequality that had stained American history and promote opportunities for citizens who had been systematically excluded from civic life. Conservatives cited a belief in limited government in opposing the partnerships that liberals forged between the federal government and local organizations, and they immediately cited the extension of civil rights and the franchise as a cause of crime and lawlessness. Johnson and Goldwater both called for "law and order," but Johnson saw his approach as a complement to the Great Society programs that his opponent and other conservative politicians sought to invalidate. The issue of civil liberties also produced ideological rifts between liberal and conservative policymakers that played out in debates over the Safe Streets Act and later policies of the Nixon administration.

The New Frontier and the Great Society had expanded the granting powers of the president and Congress for social programs, creating a new degree of federal influence that conservatives led by Nixon seized on to transform the revolution in law enforcement and criminal justice in their own image. During the 1970s, the diffusion of crime control techniques into the everyday lives of low-income African Americans intensified as all urban social programs were increasingly integrated into the bureaucracies, institutions, and industries at the heart of the carceral state. The ongoing imposition of separate and overlapping methods of surveillance, a process that fostered what historian Heather Ann Thompson has described as "the criminalization of urban space," came to define everyday life for low-income urban Americans on the ground.[27]

As Nixon acted to weaken programs of the War on Poverty, his administration led Congress in revising the block grant formulas and funding incentives to reflect its own priorities, including prison construction. Although states had relative autonomy in how they spent money designated for crime control purposes, block grants firmly established the goal of expanding incarceration in the early 1970s. Building from the wiretapping provisions that Johnson reluctantly endorsed when he signed the Safe Streets Act, new crime control policies advocated by conservative policymakers led to some of the gravest civil liberties violations in American history. The punitive priorities of the right wing of the bipartisan consensus included the extensive surveillance unleashed by FBI agents and local police against black radicals and the militant left, thousands of raids conducted by officials representing Nixon's Office of Drug Abuse and Law Enforcement, and a series of reforms of the federal criminal code, adopted in haste by the states that increased opportunities for the arrest and supervision of entire low-income urban neighborhoods.

In blatant contradiction of his own stated commitment to states' rights, Nixon assumed even greater control of the discretionary portion of the crime control budget to ensure the federal government's investment reached black urban communities. Indeed, the mobilization of law enforcement resources, the growth of the American prison system, and the high concentrations of low-income men of color behind bars can be gauged most clearly in federal policymakers' use of discretionary funding. During the Nixon and Ford administrations, discretionary allocations, which offered the White House and the LEAA a means to institute law enforcement initiatives of their own choosing, supported the extensive deployment of militarized special police units at the federal and local levels, the use of electronic surveillance, and the reliance on decoy and undercover strategies that often blurred the distinction between entrapment and sound police work. Carter appropriated discretionary funds to improve security in public housing projects, creating new links among the entire spectrum of executive agencies responsible for domestic social programs. All of these measures ensured that the programs of the War on Crime would remain focused on segregated low-income communities.

Although members of the broad political consensus that mobilized the War on Crime and, later, the War on Drugs differed over the contours of government surveillance and civil liberties in general, their determination to police low-income urban citizens proved to be a more powerful unifying force. Both liberals and conservatives worried that collective urban violence would become a permanent feature in American life, and they could not envision prevention and crime control strategies outside of creating a more central role for law enforcement in vulnerable neighborhoods. Even Johnson's attorney general Ramsey Clark, considered one of the most liberal federal officials of his era, clearly articulated the main objective of this broad political consensus in his testimony during House hearings on juvenile delinquency in 1967. For Clark, his colleagues in the Johnson administration, and their conservative and liberal allies in Congress, the merger of social welfare with

The drastic escalation of police forces in black urban communities during the War on Crime often led to confrontations between residents and officers, such as this scene from Harlem in June 1970.   *Photograph by Jack Garofalo. Paris Match Archive, Getty Images*

punitive programs and the focus on black youth in domestic urban policy seemed "the best way to protect society, because for better or for worse, these people are going to be with us, and we had better get them straightened out."[28]

MAKING BLACK CRIMINALS

Bolstering this consensus were new ways of understanding and responding to black urban crime that emerged during the 1960s and 1970s, based on new research into the problem of urban crime that was supported with federal funding and grounded in cultural interpretations of racial inequality. By consistently reinforcing the urgency of the crime issue, the new data and the new policies together became a self-perpetuating force that deeply shaped domestic policy and encouraged the continual flow of law enforcement resources into low-income African American communities.

The research of the postwar period extended a long tradition of racially biased understandings of crime. In the decades following Emancipation, scholars, policymakers, and social welfare reformers had analyzed the disparate rates of black incarceration as empirical "proof" of the "criminal nature" of African Americans. The publication of the 1890 census and the prison statistics it included laid the groundwork for popular and scholarly discussions about black Americans as a distinctly dangerous population. Coming twenty-five years after the Civil War and measuring the first generation removed from slavery, the census figures indicated that African Americans represented 12 percent of the nation's population but 30 percent of its prisoners. The high arrest and incarceration rates of African Americans served to create what historian Khalil Gibran Muhammad has called a "statistical discourse" about black crime in the popular and political imagination, and these data deeply informed ongoing national debates about racial differences. Statistical discourses rationalized the expansion of the American prison system, sustained harsh sentencing practices, informed decisions surrounding capital punishment, and endorsed racial profiling in general. Although the problem of crime among poor white and immigrant communities also concerned elected officials and academics, it was often explained as the product of socioeconomic factors rather than biological traits, and by World War II, Irish, Italian, Polish, Jewish, and other European ethnic groups had for the most part shed associations with criminality. The perception that crime and violence were a hereditary problem among citizens of African descent has long endured.[29]

Considered an objective truth and a statistically irrefutable fact, notions of black criminality justified both structural and everyday racism. Taken to its extreme, these ideas sanctioned the lynching of black people in the southern states and the bombing of African American homes and institutions in the urban north before World War II, both of which were defended as necessary to preserve public safety. In the postwar period, social scientists increasingly rejected biological racism but created a new statistical discourse about black criminality that went on to have a far more direct impact on subsequent national policies and, eventually, served as the intellectual foundation of mass incarceration.[30]

The theory behind the juvenile delinquency programs developed by the Kennedy administration came from liberal criminologists Lloyd Ohlin and Richard Cloward, who, like earlier social reformers targeting European ethnics, saw crime among urban black and Latino youth as the product of social forces rather than of individual behavior. Ohlin and Cloward's "opportunity theory" sought to change the relationship between young low-income urban Americans and the social institutions around them in order to break the community pathologies that Ohlin and Cloward believed perpetuated poverty and, in the process, to prevent delinquency. This conception of urban problems emphasized the "systemic barriers" that contributed to inequality and crime, yet the antidelinquency initiatives Ohlin and Cloward went on to develop for the Kennedy administration in the early 1960s targeted the behavior of individual children and teenagers, rather than systems and institutions.[31]

As assistant secretary of labor during the Johnson administration, Daniel Patrick Moynihan also promoted the idea that poverty could be alleviated through strategic interventions in black communities and families. In March 1965, just after Johnson began the War on Crime, Moynihan circulated *The Negro Family: A Case for National Action* as an internal document to his colleagues in the Department of Labor. The memo, now known as the Moynihan Report, argued that the combined impact of a long history of racial discrimination and "cultural deprivation" had produced a "tangle of pathology" in black urban families and communities, evidenced by high rates of illiteracy, single-parent households, and delinquency.[32] The Johnson administration accepted Moynihan's view of pathology as the root cause of poverty while recognizing poverty as the root cause of crime.

Backed by the theories and new statistical knowledge of black families produced by Moynihan and others, federal officials proceeded to develop a blueprint for the national law enforcement program. The available figures indicated that people under the age of twenty-five committed roughly three-fourths of crimes, and that nearly 2 million of the 2.8 million crimes reported to the police occurred in cities. White men had the largest number of arrests, but the FBI statistics suggested that black men had a higher rate of arrest in every category except "offenses against public order and morals." This led policymakers to conclude: "The common serious crimes that worry people most—murder, forcible rape, robbery, aggravated assault, and burglary—happen most often in the slums of large cities. . . . The offenses, the victims, and the offenders are found most frequently in the poorest, and most deteriorated and socially disorganized areas of cities." The FBI data supported the Johnson administration's perception that "most crimes, wherever they are committed, are committed by boys and young men, and that most crimes, by whomever they are committed, are committed in cities."[33] Federal policymakers had a specific locale (urban centers) and a specific group (young men approaching adulthood) at which to aim the reconstitution of American law enforcement.

As urban civil disorder escalated, the overall focus of domestic policy shifted even further from fighting poverty to controlling its violent symptoms. In the wake of Newark and Detroit's uprisings in 1967, Moynihan grew increasingly pessimistic, as did many of his fellow liberals, about the ability of the War on Poverty to reach the most "hardcore" youth. Moynihan joined conservative political scientists Edward Banfield and James Q. Wilson in advocating divestment from community action programs and other social welfare initiatives. As rates of reported crime increased alongside the federal government's investment in police forces and research programs, all three came to see black poverty as a fact of American life and crime and violence as somehow innate among African Americans. With Moynihan serving as special advisor to Nixon on urban affairs, and with Banfield and Wilson working as consultants on various presidential task forces, their ideas helped push the Nixon administration toward an understanding of black cultural pathology, rather than poverty, as the root cause of crime.

The aims of the crime war began to change in the 1970s. Although the merger of social welfare and law enforcement programs was never disentangled from federal policymakers' commitments to social control, the Kennedy and Johnson administrations launched their antidelinquency and law enforcement interventions in an attempt to improve American society. In the long term, the shared notions about race and crime underlying the bipartisan consensus supporting national punitive policy in the 1960s would give rise to what sociologist Bruce

Western has deemed the "mass incarceration generation," composed of children born after the civil rights movement.[34] But even if the law enforcement policies themselves were built on a set of racist assumptions, this result was largely unintended initially. The Nixon administration, in contrast, increasingly treated crime as a problem that domestic policies should seek to contain, rather than eliminate. Instead of constituting one aspect of a larger program of social reform and uplift, Nixon's War on Crime sought to offer all by itself a means to solve (or at least to manage) the symptoms of historical inequality and African American poverty. Marred by racism, many of the consequences of the punitive urban programs developed by Nixon and subsequent policymakers were fully intended.

In the 1970s, the deliberate arrest and incarceration of young African American men became a strategy to prevent future crime, rationalized by the new theoretical and scientific approaches to understanding black criminal behavior. Wilson attributed the increase of violent crime in the 1960s to the nation's growing youth population and urged policymakers to develop crime control programs based on demographic realities. "The only sure way we know of fighting crime is birth control," he concluded. For Wilson, to curtail crime rates "short of locking up everyone under 30 years of age," urban police needed to make "the scene of the prospective crime" more secure.[35] And since black urban neighborhoods, statistically speaking, were the most likely scene of prospective crime, the federal government anchored the national law enforcement program in those neighborhoods with the purpose of rounding up potentially serious criminals. The calculated decision to remove low-income youth of color from their neighborhoods was justified and reinforced by new data on African American crime that appeared in the early 1970s—data that were the product of the modernization of police departments and the new state criminal justice bureaucracies established during the prior decade. National law enforcement programs focused on black neighborhoods from the outset heightened the chance of arrest for young African American men, and fostered the rise of a statistical apparatus primarily concerned with measuring street crime. All of these reinforced the association between black neighborhoods and criminality.

Research initiatives and punitive projects grew more tightly integrated still as the Nixon administration pursued its strategy based entirely on the anticipation of *future* crime. In St. Louis, for instance, growing numbers of low-income youth entered the criminal justice system as a result of a computer identification project launched by the police department with federal crime control funds. Police catalogued demographic information on suspects gathered by officers during voluntary interviews with teenagers, who were targeted due to their race, class, and age and who were largely unaware of their right not to answer questions. Law enforcement authorities used the compiled information to map young residents' relationships and associations and target individuals for arrest. "If a youth persistently stays in a group of questionable purpose," the St. Louis program manual stated, "charges of behavior injurious to his welfare by loitering may be brought against him." Utilizing new methods of statistical analysis, such research programs relied upon racial profiling to remove "questionable" youth who might go on to engage in illegal activity. "It is expected that the predictive techniques will enable the police to better anticipate criminal activity and act to prevent it," an LEAA administrator wrote to a White House colleague, a theory that continued to shape law enforcement measures and eventually evolved into CompStat and other preemptive statistical programs that police departments across the United States use today, with far more sophisticated computer algorithms than their forerunners in the 1970s.[36]

Some federal officials were wary of the inherently discriminatory dimensions and ethical problems of the St. Louis project. As Geoff Shepard, a Nixon official who observed the St. Louis program, noted, "one immense difficulty here is that the computer files do not consist of convictions or even of records of arrests, but rather of opinions by police officers on individuals. Civil Rights is not my bag . . . but this stuff scares me to death." Writing to his colleagues in the White House, Shepard continued, "What you have here is the compilation of policemen's opinions, without court tested evidence or proof, which turns people into suspects for future crimes. It seems to me that this could amount to computerized harassment, since the police will begin picking up suspects from their computers and the suspects will have no way of removing themselves from the computer files unless they can convince policemen that they are not likely to commit crimes." Shepard highlighted serious questions about the constitutionality and the inherent racism of the program. Yet he wrote in closing: "What troubles me the most is that the project is probably very effective."[37] Either Shepard's assumptions about race led him to believe that all of the youths profiled by the St. Louis program would eventually engage in some form of criminal activity, or he saw the apprehension of young black residents, whatever the reason, as "effective" in fulfilling the evolving objectives of the War on Crime. Indeed, by the end of the decade, as the work of conservative thinkers reached policymakers and the general public, a growing consensus argued that "nothing works" in reducing black crime, save incarceration.[38]

Throughout the 1960s and 1970s, flawed statistical data overstated the problem of crime in African American communities and produced a distorted picture of American crime as a whole. The FBI's Uniform Crime Report failed to measure beyond the point of arrest, and thus did not account for whether or not suspects were ever eventually convicted. In the 1970s, African Americans had the highest rate of arrest for crimes of murder, robbery, and rape, but these crimes also had the lowest percentage of arrestees who eventually faced prosecution and trial.[39] If police arrested a group of black teenagers for stealing a car, even if they were released without charges, their encounter with the criminal justice system factored into the national measurement of crime and the subsequent policy decisions. But arrest rates depended crucially on the extent of police force in a given community. The FBI data also emphasized street crime to the exclusion of organized and white-collar crime. As such, the figures federal policymakers referenced as they developed the national law enforcement program reflected the crimes committed by low-income and unemployed Americans.[40]

However flawed, statistical data on crime deepened federal policymakers' racialized perception of the problem, informing strategies for the national law enforcement program that sought to prevent crime before it occurred—in specific spaces and among specific groups of Americans. Acting on future and potential crime did little to actually reduce crime, which drastically increased both in statistical measures and as a reality in low-income urban neighborhoods after Johnson began the national law enforcement program and which peaked at the height of the crime war in the 1970s. Instead, such preemptive strategies normalized the presence of law enforcement authorities and crime control technologies in the everyday lives of young Americans living in segregation and poverty, drastically increasing the specter of their arrest and incarceration.[41] In turn, the penal confinement of disproportionate numbers of young African American men during the 1970s often transformed first-time offenders and drug addicts into hardened criminals. Even Nixon referred to prisons, often overcrowded and inhumane, as "colleges of crime." And given state and federal policies that excluded former prisoners from participation in civic life (through felon disenfranchisement) or the formal economy (by permitting employers to ask about a prospective employee's felony record), this expanding system of incarceration led overwhelmingly to recidivism.

The federal policies described in this book escalated both violence and imprisonment but failed to prevent crime and improve public safety. What is remarkable is that these policies' lack of success seemed fundamentally irrelevant to national, state, and local officials as those officials prosecuted the War on Crime. The fact that much of the rationale for the War on Crime was based on faulty statistics mattered little to federal policymakers in the end. As Nixon's "crime guy" Egil Krogh concluded to domestic counsel John Ehrlichman in 1971, "The crime problem is more apparent than real."[42] The scope of the riots of the 1960s and the threat of collective violence in the future, the reality of black poverty and segregation, and social science research all underscored the very real fact of urban crisis. Crime control and punitive measures directed at black urban Americans seemed the most politically astute and economically viable way to solve that crisis. Ultimately, policymakers were determined to police urban space and eventually to remove an entire generation of young men of color from their communities.

The long mobilization of the War on Crime was not a return to an old racial caste system in a new guise—a "New Jim Crow." Rather, the effort to control and contain troublesome groups with patrol, surveillance, and penal strategies produced a new and historically distinct phenomenon in the post–civil rights era: the criminalization of urban social programs. In the two decades preceding Reagan's War on Drugs, this phenomenon laid the groundwork for the continued rise of mass incarceration and its deep racial injustices into the twenty-first century.

[1]

THE WAR ON BLACK POVERTY

In March 1965, President Lyndon Johnson sent three bills to Congress that epitomized the federal government's ambivalent response to the civil rights movement. The Housing and Urban Development Act subsidized private homes for low-income renters, the Voting Rights Act gave black Americans in the South the opportunity to participate in the electoral process as full citizens, and the Law Enforcement Assistance Act established a role for the federal government in local police operations. It was the apex of the civil rights revolution and a landmark year for liberal reform, with Job Corps, Head Start, and other community action programs up and running. In addition to launching these social welfare policies, Johnson told Congress "the Federal Government will henceforth take a more meaningful role in meeting the whole spectrum of problems posed by crime," and ordered his fellow policymakers to begin a "thorough, intelligent, and effective war against crime."[1] Thus the beginning of the federal law enforcement program coincided with the height of progressive social change; from this point on, the focus of national punitive measures would be primarily directed at black Americans living in urban neighborhoods that had high rates of reported crime.

Unlike Johnson, President John F. Kennedy recognized the parallels between the demands the federal government confronted following the

Civil War and the challenges that faced Kennedy's own administration—even if the historical tendency to respond to the expansion of civil rights with punitive measures escaped him. At the centennial commemoration of the Emancipation Proclamation in September 1962, Kennedy proclaimed from the steps of the Lincoln Memorial that the Reconstruction era was the most "impressive" chapter in American history. The president hailed not only the extension of citizenship and the franchise to black men during this period but also the establishment of the Freedmen's Bureau and other federal social programs that sought to foster racial equality and socioeconomic opportunity for 4 million former slaves by providing access to food, clothing, and education. Roughly a century later, as the United States increasingly preached freedom abroad but had failed to "eradicate the vestiges of discrimination and segregation" at home, Kennedy hoped his administration would "move to complete the work begun by Abraham Lincoln," by "fully emancipating" the descendants of enslaved Africans, who were "not yet freed from the bonds of injustice." Five months after his address, as part of his pledge to "fulfill finally the promise of the Declaration of Independence," Kennedy became the first American president to commit to desegregation when he sent the Civil Rights Act of 1963 to Congress.[2]

That legislation would eventually bring an end to Jim Crow, but it did little to address the impact of centuries of racism and structural discrimination. Although characterized by the expansion of the middle class, the decades after World War II witnessed slow economic growth, frequent recessions, and the displacement of untrained and unskilled labor through automation. These developments hit African Americans harder than they hit the rest of the U.S. population, and the numbers of black citizens unable to secure a decent living rapidly grew during the postwar period. In 1940, black and white Americans experienced comparable levels of unemployment, at 11 percent and 9 percent, respectively. By the 1960s, these figures had diverged significantly: unemployment rates of African Americans were more than double those of their white counterparts. The AFL-CIO estimated that at just 12 percent of the total U.S. population, black workers represented some 36 percent of long-term, or "relatively permanent," unemployed Americans.[3]

Declining job prospects for African Americans during the second half of the twentieth century exacerbated segregation and poverty in the neighborhoods where displaced southern agricultural workers congregated.[4] As 2 million white residents left cities for suburban areas, 1.5 million black Americans migrated to industrial centers in the North and West, joined by Latinos and white Appalachians, and moved into the neighborhoods previously occupied by European immigrants and their children. By the early 1960s, 31 percent of African Americans lived in twelve northern cities, their living conditions characterized by the isolation, marginalization, and exclusion that stemmed from segregation.[5]

Policymakers and public figures worried about the concentrations of African American citizens in cities like Cleveland, Detroit, New Orleans, Philadelphia, Baltimore, and St. Louis, where African Americans represented at least a third of the total population, and in the nation's capital, where African Americans were already a majority. "The building up of a mass of unemployed and frustrated Negro youth in congested areas of a city is a social phenomenon that may be compared to the piling up of inflammable material in an empty building on a city block," Harvard's president-emeritus James B. Conant told a group of federal policymakers and businessmen at a conference on unemployed, out-of-school urban youth in May 1961. Conant went on to describe this demographic as "social dynamite," a phrase that was picked up by the mainstream press to generate support for new federal programs intended to remedy the situation. "The growing hard core of those in urban communities," the nationally syndicated columnist Ralph McGill warned, "are, indeed, potential social dynamite . . . requiring emergency attention." For Kennedy officials too, the lack of jobs available to black urban youth was "potentially the most dangerous social condition in America today," as Secretary of Labor Arthur J. Goldberg put it in the spring of 1961.[6] President Kennedy hoped the radical new social programs his administration developed that targeted low-income urban African Americans would effectively defuse the "social dynamite" before it exploded into chaos.

Kennedy and his advisors recognized the limitations of civil rights laws alone to address historical inequality. Acknowledging the shortcomings of his own proposed civil rights legislation, Kennedy argued before Congress in 1963: "There is little value in a Negro's obtaining the right to be admitted to hotels and restaurants if he has no cash in his pocket and no job." In the tradition of the Freedmen's Bureau, which the federal government established in 1865 to foster the inclusion of former slaves in public institutions and improve social conditions in the former confederate states, Kennedy called for a "massive upgrading" of public schools and created programs that would stimulate literacy; provide vocational training programs; and improve access to secondary education, health care, and public benefits.[7] These measures would focus explicitly on African Americans and other groups who had been largely excluded from Social Security provisions and the federal housing and education programs that primarily benefited white veterans and their families under the New Deal and the terms of the GI Bill.

Instead of implementing various job training, education, and equal opportunity programs as such, the Kennedy administration framed its urban social programs as antidelinquency measures. In the spring of 1961, Kennedy convened the President's Committee on Juvenile Delinquency and Youth Crime, chaired by Attorney General Robert F. Kennedy and including the secretaries of Labor and Health, Education, and Welfare and a selected group of advisors. With funding and broad discretion under the terms of the Youth Offenses Control Act of 1961, the President's Committee focused its programs almost explicitly on black youth, emphasized prevention as a key goal in controlling crime, and included social scientists in policy discussions.

The Kennedy administration's delinquency prevention programs departed significantly from previous initiatives at all levels of government and laid the groundwork for the social welfare and community uplift programs that the Johnson administration went on to initiate. Among other novel social programs the President's Committee developed, its early childhood education and manpower development programs evolved into Head Start and the Job Corps during Johnson's "War on Poverty." Whereas the Kennedy administration launched these social welfare measures as crime control initiatives, Johnson presented his administration's attempt to suppress the "social dynamite" in African American urban neighborhoods as a larger, more expansive fight against poverty.

Yet in a moment of possibility for both racial and economic justice, the unprecedented changes at the federal level that were born during the launch of the War on Poverty and the enactment of civil rights legislation created a seedbed for an increasingly punitive orientation in domestic urban policy. Amid a growing civil rights movement, at a time when scientific racism had been discredited and public racism was no longer tolerated, the widely accepted view that cultural and behavioral deficiencies—what leading social scientists called "social pathology"—caused poverty emerged as an intellectual framework through which policymakers launched a major national urban intervention. By articulating urban problems through the discourse of this perceived pathology, policymakers presented inequality as a problem of individual behavior. Federal officials and planners believed that consciously addressing the impact of racial discrimination within African American communities would reduce the structural dimensions of poverty, but this approach removed fundamental socioeconomic change from the domestic policy agenda. In other words, the Kennedy and Johnson administrations aimed to change the psychological impact of racism within individuals rather than the impact of the long history of racism within American institutions.

Although the federal government's new commitment to racial minorities and the poor started out with sincere intentions, the notions of black cultural pathology that concealed policymakers' own racism prevented their vision for a more egalitarian America from achieving its larger aims. Highly flawed in their intellectual foundations and design, the policies of the 1960s that created a new role for the federal government at the local level left open the possibility that the only way to manage the problems facing urban centers was to aid law enforcement authorities who were charged with the task of keeping segregated urban communities under control.

This punitive turn in domestic policy did not emerge out of nowhere. The programs of the New Frontier and the Great Society were never independent from federal policymakers' desire for social control, or from their concerns about crime. An effort to combat inequality that the Kennedy administration framed as a youth crime control intervention evolved into a more comprehensive effort that sought to "eliminate the paradox of poverty in the midst of plenty" via the Economic Opportunity Act of 1964. Together, the earlier antidelinquency and antipoverty programs set the precedent for the Law Enforcement Assistance Act of 1965, legislation that marked the beginnings of a more lasting War on Crime. These entangled antipoverty and crime control measures further reinforced the idea, rooted in policymakers' own assumptions about the fundamental causes of black poverty and crime, that conditions in low-income neighborhoods were the result of individuals' shortcomings rather than structural factors. As a result of these assumptions, the White House and Congress sought to monitor and regulate the behavior of individuals in order to change that behavior and, in the process, fight poverty and the scourge of American racism with civil rights reform. The legislation federal policymakers enacted in earnest over the course of the 1960s moved domestic programs further and further away from fostering fundamental changes in American social and economic institutions that might have eradicated the poverty and segregation in black communities.

Thus the War on Poverty is best understood not as an effort to broadly uplift communities or as a moral crusade to transform society by combating inequality or want, but as a manifestation of fear about urban disorder and about the behavior of young people, particularly young African Americans. The Youth Offenses Control Act of 1961, the Economic Opportunity Act of 1964, and the Law Enforcement Assistance Act of 1965 represented the federal government's tepid answer to the civil rights movement and the fact that policymakers could no longer ignore the material consequences of historical inequality as these consequences had developed in the century after Emancipation.

A "TOTAL ATTACK" ON DELINQUENCY

On May 11, 1961, the same day President Kennedy established by executive order the President's Committee on Juvenile Delinquency and Youth Crime, he sent to Congress a bill that would begin an unprecedented level of federal involvement in areas that policymakers had begun referring to as the "inner city." Vague in its language and ambitious in its call for a "total attack" on delinquency, the Juvenile Delinquency and Youth Offenses Control Act of 1961 sought to address the problems of "youth unemployment, poor housing, poor health, inadequate education, and the alienation of lower-class communities and neighborhoods," as Attorney General Robert F. Kennedy explained. He and other federal policymakers believed that the racial discrimination black families confronted within school systems and workplaces was the root cause of this "alienation." The preamble to the act itself argued that "delinquency and offenses occur disproportionately among school dropouts, unemployed youth faced with limited opportunities and with employment barriers, and youth in deprived family situations."[8] As a result, the national antidelinquency program would focus on youth who had come into contact with law enforcement or criminal justice authorities, as well as groups of young people whom federal policymakers believed to be susceptible to delinquency.

In late September, Kennedy signed the legislation into law, and the committee could then begin planning and supporting antidelinquency programs in major urban centers. With an initial allocation of $10 million a year for three years, the act supported demonstration projects (highly experimental programs that, if proven effective, would be administered on a national scale), a major training measure for social service personnel, and general assistance to local organizations and governments. In order for their areas to qualify for funding, municipal authorities needed to form separate nonprofit organizations with welfare professionals, juvenile courts, churches, and other local institutions to collaborate on grant proposals. This strict planning process both made youth crime control a local priority and unified law enforcement and social welfare services. Because the act had established a direct channel between the federal government and local organizations, the President's Committee had a strong degree of oversight over the planning and implementation of programs.

Almost immediately after World War II, when the "teenager" emerged as a formidable political and cultural category, state and local governments began to enact delinquency policies that expanded the surveillance of black urban youth. Urban police departments from New York City to Houston started to increase patrol in targeted low-income neighborhoods as a means to control unruly teens. Juvenile delinquency programs in Oakland, for instance, brought police officers into public schools to monitor and arrest youth identified as "troublemakers" by school and social service staff. The Oakland Police Department aggressively enforced misdemeanors—both on and off school grounds—just as it began to offer recreational programs for this same group of "troublesome" young residents. As a result of such antidelinquency measures in Oakland, Houston, New York City, and other urban centers with concentrations of African American youth, the number of young people who were under some form of criminal justice supervision nationwide grew 2.5 times between 1949 and 1957.[9]

At the federal level, concern about juvenile delinquency emerged alongside changing racial demographics in American cities and increasing media coverage of youth crime. As the number of African Americans in the North continued to rise, the 70 million "baby boomers" born after 1947 were beginning to transition from childhood to adolescence. In 1957, the Senate Subcommittee to Investigate Juvenile Delinquency formed to examine the youth crime problem as a first step toward national action. Although policymakers continued to let state and local governments control young offenders independently from federal authority during the 1950s, by the time Kennedy took office in 1961, juvenile delinquency had become generally understood as "a national problem calling for national action," particularly in the low-income urban centers that distressed White House officials the most.[10]

Even as the Kennedy administration and Congress endorsed new urban interventions in the name of fighting delinquency, youth crime was more of a moral concern rooted in long-held racial fears than it was a measurable problem. The most reliable sources on delinquency trends during this period come from the FBI and the Children's Bureau, yet each organization used different methods of reporting, making it difficult to accurately determine the extent of delinquency in the nation or whether or not the problem was in fact increasing. Crime data indicated that juvenile arrest rates were rising in the 1960s, but this was a result of the evolution and modernization of data-gathering methods more than a reflection of actual changes. Moreover, although a number of federal researchers pointed out that youth crime was common across racial and class lines, the fact that low-income and racially marginalized youth were more likely to encounter criminal justice authorities skewed the data such that it seemed as though the problems were concentrated among them. "Whether there was in fact any more juvenile crime committed during this period than in the past is difficult to say. Probably there was not," wrote Daniel Patrick Moynihan in 1968 in *Maximum Feasible Misunderstanding.* "But it did at this time assume a more threatening character," he noted, in reflecting on his days as assistant secretary of labor.[11] As Moynihan's comments indicate, national policymakers and planners lacked concrete statistical measurements of youth crime but carried underlying racial assumptions about its character. The federal government viewed the problem as specific to low-income Americans (and black urban Americans in particular), and its initial response to civil rights demands and ongoing debates about the place of racially marginalized citizens in American society first emerged in an attack on youth crime.

However tainted it may have been by officials' assumptions about race and crime, the administration broke with previous approaches at the state and local levels that had tended to respond to the problem of delinquency with punitive measures. Instead, the President's Committee sought to reform the social conditions that gave rise to delinquency. This ambitious undertaking was based on the "systemic barriers" conception of urban problems that Lloyd Ohlin and Richard Cloward described in their 1960 book *Delinquency and Opportunity.* Both scholars had previously worked with prisoners in the mid-1950s (Ohlin as a researcher for the Illinois Parole and Pardon Board while pursuing a doctorate in sociology at the University of Chicago; Cloward as a social worker at an army prison in Pennsylvania), and both had been strongly influenced by sociologist Frank Tannenbaum's theory of delinquency.[12]

In *Crime and the Community* (1938), Tannenbaum suggested that law enforcement programs should focus on social systems rather than individuals in order to be effective. He argued that when authorities treated actions such as playing games in public or playing truant at school as criminal or delinquent, they further isolated already marginalized youth from mainstream society, increasing the resistance of that marginalized group to formal social institutions and exacerbating delinquency. For instance, ten teenagers in East St. Louis were arrested for cursing, shouting, and throwing various objects in June 1961. Under Tannenbaum's theory, the decision to arrest these teenagers under charges of delinquency, and their subsequent description in the press as "hoodlums," reflected more the failings of traditional social welfare systems and public institutions than the behavior of the teens themselves. Labeling as delinquent activities that the "hoodlums" themselves likely saw as adventuresome began a process Tannenbaum called the "dramatization of evil" and inadvertently encouraged future criminality among them. "The person becomes the thing he is described as being," Tannenbaum wrote.[13]

Building from Tannenbaum's ideas about the sources of crime and the impact of criminal labeling, Ohlin and Cloward devised "opportunity theory" at Columbia University, where they both taught in the School of Social Work beginning in the late 1950s. They argued that criminal "pathology" did not stem from culture or individual traits, but was inculcated by inadequate resources for neglected children and punitive responses to their everyday behavior, making it more likely that low-income youth would fail in school, be unable to gain employment, and eventually engage in criminal activity. Thus, effectively controlling delinquency meant changing "opportunity structures" by strengthening the institutions in which poor young people interacted with education, training, and development programs. Paraphrasing Tannenbaum, Ohlin and Cloward explained: "The target for preventive action should be defined, not as the individual or group that exhibits the delinquent pattern, but as the social setting that gives rise to the delinquent."[14] These preventative measures could effectively break the cultural pathologies that seemed to breed delinquency.

Kennedy officials considered opportunity theory a significant breakthrough in understanding and responding to urban problems, and executive director David Hackett immediately brought Ohlin onto the President's Committee as an advisor and promoted him to chief researcher in 1962. The inclusion of Ohlin, Cloward, Moynihan, and other scholars in these policy discussions was unprecedented. Federal officials had previously relied heavily on the opinions of agency officials and bureaucrats in shaping national programs, but the proliferation of academic research after World War II had produced a body of knowledge that could account for trends at the national and local levels by the early 1960s. With these quantitative data in tow, the Kennedy administration could articulate a theory of the sources and solutions to delinquency that was supported by statistical evidence.[15]

In particular, Ohlin and Cloward's comprehensive delinquency prevention strategy opened up two policy domains for the federal government: partnerships with community-based organizations and the plight of racially marginalized citizens. As activist and scholar Frances Fox Piven put it in a 1969 interview: *"Delinquency and Opportunity* made it acceptable for the federal government to do something about poor black people" and "made it possible for the federal government to do something about local problems." Influenced by Ohlin and Cloward's expert thinking, the administration aimed to foster a community transformation, framed as an antidelinquency program, which required a simultaneous attack on "pathological handicaps" and institutional barriers to inclusion. Controlling youth crime itself would be "only a small part of a large and just reward," Hackett explained to members of the Institute of Juvenile Delinquency in 1961.[16]

Neighborhoods where low-income ethnic and racial minorities lived in concentration had suffered from high rates of delinquency historically, yet when areas surrounding the central business district in cities such as Syracuse, New York, and the Hough area of Cleveland transformed from majority white in the 1940s to majority black in the early 1960s, federal officials began to take notice of youth crime problems. National policymakers believed that communities like Hough could "be saved" with significant federal antidelinquency funds, as Health, Education, and Welfare Secretary Anthony J. Celebrezze testified before the Senate Subcommittee on Employment and Manpower in 1963. "We feel we could not have found a better spot in which to test our theories," Celebrezze boasted of the million-dollar federal antidelinquency grant that the President's Committee had awarded the city. Although a modest antidelinquency initiative in Charleston, West Virginia, served a majority white constituency, "most of the programs in action or being developed will affect primarily minority youth—Negroes in almost every city, Mexican-Americans in Los Angeles and Houston, Puerto Ricans in New York, and Indians in Minneapolis," explained Hackett in a 1963 letter to Attorney General Kennedy. "It is the slum areas of our large metropolitan centers which harbor the highest concentration of delinquency, unemployment, school dropouts, family inadequacies and cultural deficiencies," he suggested.[17]

Hackett and other Kennedy officials believed that if the social and behavioral problems they attributed to urban youth of color remained unaddressed, crime and delinquency would continue to escalate, and among black youth especially. In Detroit, Philadelphia, and Cleveland, at least 80 percent of youth served by the federal antidelinquency programs were African American. In Washington, DC, "undoubtedly all the youth involved" were Negro, as Hackett wrote to Kennedy. And in cities like Syracuse and New Haven, Connecticut, where black populations were 5 percent and 15 percent, respectively, half of the participants in the antidelinquency demonstration programs were African American.[18]

Despite the President's Committee's awareness that "delinquency has increased in the suburbs and rural areas," shared notions about residents in the "decaying core of the inner city" strongly influenced the committee's decision to invest the vast majority of juvenile delinquency appropriations in programs targeting African American youth. In the opinion of policymakers, researchers, and professional staff, black urban neighborhoods contained "the most imposing array of social pathology." In Harlem and other segregated black communities with median family incomes well below the national average and with an unemployment rate twice as high as elsewhere in the United States, the committee faced "a challenge and an opportunity" to remedy the "broad, established, pathological base" that appeared to be the source of the community's problems.[19]

Federal officials identified these pathologies—the various cultural and familial patterns in low-income families that experts and policymakers saw as deviant—in racial terms. The officials feared that unless national programs stimulated education, skills training, and empowerment measures in Harlem, Syracuse, Detroit, and other cities targeted by the President's Committee, existing behavioral "problems" would be transmitted—and likely worsen—from one generation to the next. Failing public schools and grim job prospects for urban African Americans had created, in President Kennedy's words, "an atmosphere of frustration, resentment and unrest which does not bode well for the future." This understanding recognized the problems facing black citizens a century after Emancipation and the role of racial discrimination in perpetuating socioeconomic problems. But Kennedy and his advisors believed that cultural pathologies had taken on a life of their own, independent of structural forces, an interpretation that limited the range of possibilities in the solutions they proposed.[20]

Although Kennedy and the President's Committee emphasized the relationship between structural inequality, poverty, and youth crime in their rhetoric, in practice the antidelinquency programs focused on the community pathologies that policymakers viewed as the root cause of crime. Since Hackett and other federal officials believed the combination of poverty and discrimination created "conditions which may breed crime among young people," the President's Committee focused less on overhauling the formal juvenile justice system than on addressing the "social antecedents" officials saw as contributing to delinquency.[21]

In the absence of major socioeconomic reform on the administration's policy mandate, the President's Committee went on to develop a host of antidelinquency programs that aimed to foster equal opportunity and inspire "alienated" youth to become productive citizens. Kennedy officials worked with public and nonprofit local agencies to establish Youth Opportunity Centers and Manpower Development and Training Act programs across the United States, but of all the juvenile delinquency demonstration programs the committee funded, the president called New York City's Mobilization for Youth "the best in the country at this time." The $12 million initiative eventually served as a model for the community action programs at the center of the Johnson administration's War on Poverty. Ohlin and Cloward had been involved with the planning and implementation of Mobilization for Youth from the outset, seeking to put their opportunity theory into action. With funds from the National Institute of Mental Health, the Ford Foundation, City Hall, and the President's Committee, Mobilization for Youth offered remedial education, job training, and social service programs to young black and Latino residents in the Lower East Side of Manhattan.[22]

In theory, Mobilization for Youth and other antidelinquency demonstration programs would encourage the formation of new community-based organizations and produce a generation of "indigenous" social workers. As Ohlin later explained in an interview, "We were old Jeffersonian democrats who said that the people had to be involved." Ohlin and Cloward's opportunity theory blended Tannenbaum's ideas about the impact of criminal justice labeling with Saul Alinsky's organizing methods that emphasized grassroots participation. Ohlin had consulted Alinsky in 1960 as he began working on a draft of the antidelinquency program that would eventually become Mobilization for Youth. Like Ohlin, Alinksy had worked as a criminologist for the state of Illinois, and in the 1950s began organizing black residents in Chicago's South Side. Believing that citizens could best mobilize themselves around local struggles, Alinsky privileged community representation in social service efforts. Ohlin went on to argue that an "indigenous social movement" premised on civic engagement would heighten "the personal investment of members in the established order." He convinced the President's Committee that if traditional social welfare organizations were the primary beneficiaries of new federal grants, the delinquency programs would adopt more conservative approaches and fail to inspire fundamental changes to existing conditions. These "indigenous" workers included the fifteen women Mobilization for Youth paid to act as "troubleshooters" with Lower East Side families, and the skilled black professionals whom staff at the Houston Action for Youth program recruited, by virtue of their skin color, to organize a job training program for African American high school dropouts.[23]

The committee's emphasis on community empowerment and supporting "indigenous social movements" largely overlooked effective community-based efforts that were already working at the time Mobilization for Youth began its intervention. The case of the Boys Brotherhood Republic organization in the Lower East Side provides a telling example. Founded in 1932 for young men between the ages of seven and nineteen, the organization functioned as a "juvenile-run municipality" directed entirely by youth without adult supervision. The Republic's 640 members paid ten cents per month in "taxes" to its own "city council." A "police department" enforced the laws of the organization, and all violators were tried by a "court," which included a judge, a jury, and defense lawyers. The program proved to be a highly effective antidelinquency measure: none of the children and teenage "citizens" of the Republic had a criminal record or had ever been seriously involved with law enforcement authorities.[24]

Although the Boys Brotherhood Republic had effectively prevented delinquency in the Lower East Side, its lack of support from public programs that shared its ultimate aims underscored federal officials' resistance to projects that did not involve trained antidelinquency staff and social workers. At the time the President's Committee formed, the Republic occupied a five-story converted tenement dwelling on Third Avenue between Avenues C and D in the heart of the Lower East Side. With 400 young men on its waiting list, the organization sought to obtain a bigger space and approached New York City mayor Robert Wagner about the possibility. "Not one of our members has ever been arrested," the Republic's "mayor," eighteen-year-old Gus Fassier, informed Wagner. "We are proud of that, and now we need some help." With only $68.40 to contribute, Republic members promised to wash cars and to do other odd jobs to raise additional funds. "Everybody will help," Fassier promised. "That's democratic, isn't it?" Because the Republic had goals that were very much in line with the larger objectives of the Kennedy administration's approach to combating delinquency, assisting the Republic in expanding their programming and membership would have been a fitting project for the President's Committee and Mobilization for Youth to fund. Federal and local officials were hesitant to support an organization operated entirely by and for low-income youth, however, and the Republic retained its dilapidated headquarters on Third Avenue until 1967, when it received a $1.1 million donation from the Vincent Astor Foundation. The private funds enabled the Republic to acquire a new building inside the Lillian Wald Housing Project on Avenue D, complete with an assembly hall, meeting spaces, a library, recreation rooms, two gymnasiums, and a kitchen.[25]

The lack of support the Boys Brotherhood Republic received from federal officials reflected the top-down strategies favored by Mobilization for Youth planners and national antidelinquency programs elsewhere. For all its emphasis on grassroots empowerment, the President's Committee mainly facilitated the influx of social service workers into predominately low-income African American communities. Complementing the modest efforts to include residents and citizens of color in leadership positions within antidelinquency programs, Kennedy and his advisors largely conceived of the demonstrations as a "domestic peace corps." Shortly before Kennedy called the President's Committee, the administration had established the Peace Corps in March 1961 to draw on volunteers to help underdeveloped nations "meet their urgent needs for skilled manpower." Associated Community Teams (ACT), one of the first demonstration programs the President's Committee funded, received a $250,000 grant to bring volunteers into central Harlem—many from outside New York City—and train them to work with youth in schools, settlement houses, and churches. "These young volunteers have, in the past year, brought the spirit of the Peace Corps to the dismal slums of Central Harlem," the committee later said of the program. Like their counterparts working to "assist the needy" overseas, antidelinquency volunteers would promote social and economic development in poor and politically volatile places in American cities.[26]

By providing social services to low-income citizens, this "domestic peace corps" intervention was meant to encourage "hard-core youth" and their family members to adhere to the standards of American living as the first step in addressing socioeconomic isolation. The larger purpose of the services ACT, Mobilization for Youth, and other antidelinquency demonstrations offered was to "channel the anger directed at social injustice *away* from self-defeating behavior and into constructive avenues of constructive action." As stated in the program's objectives, the chief goal of Mobilization for Youth was "to make educationally, culturally, and economically disadvantaged members of minority groups more employable by helping to increase work and work-related skills and helping to develop a suitable 'work personality.'"[27] It was a purpose that was influenced entirely by the intellectual foundations of national antidelinquency programs, which viewed black cultural pathology as the driving force of inequality.

In the Lower East Side community, Mobilization for Youth installed four neighborhood service centers—what the President's Committee referred to as "Mental Hygiene Clinics"—that served entire families in the Lower East Side. In addition to providing fundamental services such as medical and dental care, staff worked with residents to meet welfare eligibility requirements, educate the residents on tenants' rights issues, secure child care, "improve [their] homemaking skills," and resolve family conflicts—all of which a *Washington Post* editorial aptly described as "missionary work." Such counseling programs enhanced traditional therapy treatments with field trips, movie nights, and sports leagues. Staff also helped youth and their families fill out job applications, prepare for interviews, and dress for the professional workforce, tailoring these services to the "individual aptitudes" of youth and their families as determined by the extensive written and verbal tests Mobilization for Youth conducted. High school–age youth received training to become plumbers, electricians, and seamstresses. Some worked in the gas stations and convenience stores that Mobilization for Youth opened to gain experience that might prepare them for the work force and supplement their family income. The organization paid others to pick up trash, plant flowers around the neighborhood, and paint deteriorating buildings. Together, these counseling, job training, and educational programs were "essentially designed to aid in arresting self-defeating modes of behavior," as one researcher explained, not to transform institutions outside the Lower East Side neighborhood.[28]

The educational measures that the President's Committee supported came closer than any other aspect of the administration's intervention to addressing the socioeconomic roots of youth crime. In particular, the pre-kindergarten programs that a number of cities implemented with antidelinquency funding were an early iteration of Head Start. In addition to preschools, Mobilization for Youth staff developed curricular models that they hoped would foster greater academic engagement and participation among vulnerable youth. One initiative focused on improving training for teachers by encouraging them to visit their students' homes in order to gain a better sense of the impoverished conditions in which their pupils lived and to dispel stereotypes and assumptions about low-income families. Most of the educational programs the President's Committee funded, however, focused directly on remedial education needs. In Boston, an experimental reading program brought teachers' assistants into every class at six junior high schools in the antidelinquency target area as a means to improve literacy. And in

Syracuse, a corps of teachers received a federal grant to create a "communications skills" program for sixty children who required extra attention to improve their language and reading abilities.[29]

These efforts to increase educational access and improve the general curriculum in urban public schools were necessary. And they remain necessary. But policymakers and officials' concerns about community pathology shaped the purpose of these reforms in their earliest stages of development. In the words of the director of Mobilization for Youth's education division, the preschool classes the organization offered to low-income families were designed to "head off retardation that most often comes early in these slum areas." A St. Louis public school administrator boasted that the early education program at the highly segregated Benjamin Banneker Elementary School had successfully established "a middle-class environment in a slum neighborhood school," by giving the "deprived child" the tools to become "an able student and later a productive member of society." Philadelphia's pre-kindergarten demonstration hired only male teachers to "offset the predominantly female-centered families the target area children come from."[30] These education programs had been designed not only to teach children to read and write but to expose them to the values, norms, and ways of speaking in dominant society.

Beyond remedial education measures, many of the antidelinquency programs that sought to provide "opportunities [for vulnerable youth] to behave differently" translated to attempts to foster greater discipline among them. Concerned with both the prevention and control of juvenile delinquency, the President's Committee focused on rehabilitating "youth in trouble" and preventing "anti-social activity among all youth in the target area." Following Tannenbaum's argument, Ohlin and Cloward theorized that many youth turned to delinquency and crime out of a desire for fun and adventure. They encouraged the committee to develop programs that would meet this perceived need while simultaneously organizing youth in a "quasi-militaristic" form. "Lower-income youth prefer the rituals, symbols, and activities of a paramilitary organization to the soft, folksy style of traditional recreational programs," the President's Committee explained. In its Adventure Corps program, Mobilization for Youth staff organized fifteen squads with about twenty-five members each, all of whom were between the ages of nine and thirteen. Sporting uniforms, rank insignia, and other "quasi-military symbols of status," the Adventure Corps "cadets" met once a week in the late afternoon to drill, exercise, and engage in various learning activities and community projects—from a marching band to sports teams to movie nights to camping trips—as a means to capture the "zeal and imagination often characteristic of delinquent behavior." Planners assumed that imitating military rituals and symbols would appeal to youth in the Lower East Side "much as the Boy Scouts do in other areas." The committee embraced this militaristic discipline in an attempt to shield low-income urban children from the type of penal discipline they might go on to experience in formal carceral institutions.[31]

Indeed, a major imperative of the federal antidelinquency program was to restructure basic social services so that official agencies could "serve hard-core youth in community settings in which youth are less stigmatized," as federal planners reasoned. These seemingly organic settings offered an important alternative to the "stigmatized isolation" that might result from prolonged interaction with formal criminal justice institutions. Yet even as the antidelinquency programs functioned as a layer of contact between "youth in trouble" and uniformed law enforcement officials, the programs introduced new forms of supervision—what could be seen as soft surveillance—in targeted urban areas. As a community-based alternative to training schools and prisons, Mobilization for Youth opened two coffeehouses to serve youth with gang affiliations and "disadvantaged youths who may become delinquent unless there is a significant intervention on their behalf," as Hackett explained in a 1963 memo to Attorney General Kennedy. Officials believed this group may have resisted the services offered at the neighborhood centers, and the coffeehouses provided a channel through which the "youth in trouble" could receive educational, medical, vocational, and psychiatric services. Posing as "informed bartenders," adults employed by Mobilization for Youth supervised the teenagers as they played chess and checkers, conducted theater workshops, and started photography clubs at the coffeehouses. Beneath the seemingly natural setting of the coffeehouse was a carefully planned neighborhood center that made it possible for staff to watch troublesome teenagers while simultaneously providing social welfare services.[32]

In places like Chicago and St. Louis, where antidelinquency program staff came into contact with delinquents and potential delinquents on the streets, a different form of soft surveillance emerged. Like similar neighborhoods where the President's Committee implemented youth crime control programs, the St. Louis target area was majority African American and suffered from severe rates of delinquency, unemployment, and illiteracy. Near the massive Pruitt-Igoe Housing Project that housed a third of the 108,000 residents in the targeted community, authorities dispatched three college graduates to "expand opportunities for the youth of the ghetto." Their task was to work with two black and one white group of youth between the ages of sixteen and twenty, groups that officials assumed were "probably in an incipient stage of development that would probably result in organized street gangs." Prior to their assignment, the three gang outreach workers received a training course consisting of lectures and question-and-answer sessions conducted by social work professionals. The President's Committee assumed that if placed under adult supervision, "these youth could be guided into conventional activity." A former probation officer was responsible for handling one of the African American groups who, as a federal official observing the program informed Ohlin, had been labeled as "troublesome because of disruptive behavior, drinking, etc."[33] Only a handful of the youth even had criminal records, but their peers were guilty of delinquency by association.

Much like its equivocal stance on the Boys Brotherhood Republic in the Lower East Side and other efforts to fight delinquency that had been organized entirely by residents themselves, authorities felt that the African American group required a separate intervention that followed prototypes of the President's Committee despite the fact that such an outlet already existed for the young men. Well before the former probation officer began his outreach work, these youth spent much of their free time at a confectionary owned by one of their mothers. "This woman was declared to be a very positive influence on the boys," the federal official mentioned in his letter to Ohlin, "when in her presence." Rather than stimulating the kind of "indigenous participation" Ohlin and other officials had advocated (in theory at least) by simply funding an effort that was already working, officials chose to impose the President's Committee's own form of programming under the direction of trained authorities. Acting as a liaison between community agencies and the black youth themselves, the St. Louis social worker hosted activities such as movie screenings and spent time with the young men as they went about their day-to-day activities to "give them a focus on life," as the director of the St. Louis program stated. The idea was that by keeping low-income urban youth under constant adult supervision by public welfare agents such as the assigned social workers of the St. Louis program or the "informal bartenders" of Mobilization for Youth instead of law enforcement authorities or capable adults in their own communities, these youth would, in turn, be more receptive to existing educational and employment opportunities that could change their behavior.[34]

As social workers increasingly performed surveillance and crime control functions, law enforcement authorities, too, increasingly performed social service functions under the auspices of the federal anti-delinquency programs. "Police services need to be more closely related to the community," White House planners argued.[35] Soon, police and other "official control agencies" collaborated with social service providers as part of the joint effort to fight youth crime. In programs such as New Haven's Community Progress Incorporated, youth ranging from minor offenders to those who had served time in prison were referred by various city and state correctional agencies to Neighborhood Service Teams consisting of social workers, juvenile court officials, and police officers.

Aside from forging partnerships between law enforcement and social welfare authorities, the President's Committee encouraged police departments to create juvenile divisions if they had not done so already in order to professionalize the status of law enforcement. Members of the President's Committee considered urban police forces to be "semi-professional," but through their participation in both antidelinquency demonstrations and special youth crime control units, "the professional status of police officers [would] become more firmly established." In places like Cleveland, where federal funds supported the creation of a police unit that formed for delinquency prevention work and counseled almost 700 young residents in the target area, the bureaucratic structure and purpose of law enforcement began to shift. Yet as federal programs changed the role of the police within urban social institutions and communities, they did not simultaneously work to change institutional practices so that officers would be rewarded as much for their social service role as for their effort to enforce the law and foster public safety. Federal planners recognized that "More juvenile officers will produce more juvenile statistics," and worried that "labeling a youngster a delinquent, from this kind of target area, only increases the problem."[36] But if the committee could orient police and criminal justice personnel "to their theoretical framework and to a different way of working," the impact of labeling would be diminished.

Ultimately, the strategies federal policymakers developed to fight youth crime during and after the Kennedy administration only confirmed Tannenbaum's "dramatization of evil" concept—the idea that explicitly punitive responses to troubling youth behavior only perpetuated the very problem—that had inspired opportunity theory and preventative approaches to delinquency in the first place. With the focus of such programs more on reforming individual behavior and less on reforming the purpose of police departments, the delinquency problem not only persisted but drastically worsened, moving the "social dynamite" closer to an explosion.

The Kennedy administration developed its "total attack" on delinquency with the best intentions. Yet officials' own racism, hidden in explicit terms through the discourse of racial pathology, limited the committee's ideas about the types of social welfare services possible in the low-income neighborhoods that members targeted. The desire to improve conditions in the nation's most troubled communities, to empower residents in those communities to take on new civic roles, and to increase the presence of municipal and federal employees evolved into a form of benign social control, imposing soft forms of supervision in segregated urban communities. As Mobilization for Youth and other antidelinquency demonstrations sought to address "systemic barriers" to full civic inclusion, the theory of delinquency that served as a framework for federal programs and the heavy reliance on social workers, "domestic peace corps" volunteers, and antidelinquency police units to foster this inclusion eased the transition to the punitive federal programs that fully emerged during the Johnson administration and within the Great Society.

A "WAR ON POVERTY"

When Lyndon Johnson took office, the "total attack" on delinquency waged by the Kennedy administration quickly became expanded and recast as a "War on Poverty." Kennedy's urban intervention had been a much smaller effort by comparison, one that funded programs in only sixteen cities with a relatively modest allocation from Congress. Given the broad scope of the earlier antidelinquency measures, which had aimed to transform both urban social institutions and individuals, the President's Committee could not fund all the grant applications it received. "The poverty program would be a way of funding the proposals and moving toward the poverty idea, which was implicit with delinquency," Richard Boone explained in a 1969 interview, having worked in the Office of Juvenile Delinquency during the Kennedy administration and the Office of Economic Opportunity during Johnson's presidency.[37] Boone and a number of other former members of the President's Committee on Juvenile Delinquency also worked for the Johnson administration, bringing with them many of the same approaches to urban inequality and, with them, many of the same limitations stemming from pathological assumptions about the causes and cures of poverty and crime.

Despite a growing awareness of the lack of jobs available to unskilled, untrained workers and the social consequences of this problem, federal policymakers continued to skirt the possibility of structural reform and chose to address unemployment by focusing on behavior. Wary of the costs of a major employment initiative, the Johnson administration rejected programs that would have provided actual long-term jobs. Instead, it built from the policies of the Kennedy administration to embark upon a major national program to offer job training to low-income individuals—regardless of whether they could find employment afterward. White House officials argued that an $11 billion tax cut would lead to more private spending, more jobs, and less poverty. With the 1964 presidential contest in mind, Johnson's Council of Economic Advisers drafted a domestic policy package that focused on promoting opportunity in "a relatively *few groups and areas* where problems are most severe and solutions are most feasible," and promoting economic growth as the solution to joblessness in the era of industrial decline.[38]

Drawing on the urban social programs that the President's Committee on Juvenile Delinquency had developed and the strategies that the council suggested, Johnson called for a War on Poverty in his 1964 State of the Union address. The president made a moral appeal that those Americans who enjoyed the unprecedented prosperity of the 1960s were ethically obligated to support reforms that would improve the social and economic condition of less fortunate citizens. Johnson flipped the understanding of poverty that had steered the Kennedy administration's antidelinquency programs, telling the nation: "Very often a lack of jobs and money is not the cause of poverty, but the symptom." The deeper cause, for Johnson, was the denial of opportunity based on race, or "the failure to give our fellow citizens a fair chance to develop their own capacities" in education and training, medical care and housing, and "decent communities in which to live and bring up their children."[39] Framing this effort as a "war" underscored the urgency of antipoverty policy as a major new direction for domestic programs and allowed the president to appear action oriented to voters just before the upcoming election. No one wanted to seem an enemy of the poor. The Economic Opportunity Act of 1964—the first piece of War on Poverty legislation—moved through Congress swiftly and smoothly, and Johnson signed it into law in late August 1964.

The Economic Opportunity Act was the most ambitious social welfare program in the history of the United States, making an investment of nearly $1 billion to fight poverty. Community action programs brought the methods employed by Mobilization for Youth and other juvenile delinquency demonstration projects of the Kennedy years to the national level. The hallmarks of these social programs became official policies and programs for the War on Poverty. The Job Corps supported the development of conservation camps and urban centers to provide training to low-income youth between the ages of sixteen and twenty-one for two-year terms at $150 a month, while the Work Experience Programs helped "unemployed fathers and other needy persons" secure the "capability for self-support or personal independence." In addition to community action and the Jobs Corps, the legislation launched work-study programs to make higher education more accessible and created adult education programs to help illiterate Americans become "better able to meet their adult responsibilities." For small business owners on the verge of bankruptcy, the act provided loans and managerial training. With the Volunteers of Service to America Program (VISTA, later renamed AmeriCorps), the Economic Opportunity Act brought home the spirit of the Peace Corps and the "domestic peace corps" that had been established by Kennedy's antidelinquency demonstration in Harlem. This service effort was paired with an initiative that connected mentors with "needy children." Within its first 100 days under the direction of President Kennedy's brother-in-law and former Peace Corps director Sargent Shriver, the newly created Office of Economic Opportunity (OEO) had spent $200 million fighting the War on Poverty in thirty-three states—from Appalachia to Indian reservations to the "city slums" and everywhere in between.[40]

Congress did not explicitly invoke race in the language of the Economic Opportunity Act, but the broad policy Johnson introduced and the programs that the OEO funded implicitly responded to the changes wrought by the continued exodus of black Americans from the southern states as well as the direct-action protests of the civil rights movement. Robert Kennedy warned Congress as it considered the legislation: "I think that if we do not deal with the problem of poverty and the problem of civil rights very quickly, we will be overwhelmed by them." Kennedy and other supporters argued that participation in formal, institutionalized community action programs would help youth overcome feelings of powerlessness and alienation. For Kennedy there was "no question" that "the Negroes, their lack of opportunity, their need for special attention in our society" was one of the most vexing social issues of the 1960s.[41]

Fifteen percent of the OEO's budget was reserved for demonstration projects, which Shriver could fund directly without approval from local community action agencies. Reflecting the concerns Kennedy articulated during the debate over the bill, these demonstration projects gave special attention to black urban areas for experimental social welfare services, establishing an entirely new set of partnerships—modeled after Mobilization for Youth and other antidelinquency demonstrations—between the federal government and grassroots organizations. The Kennedy administration's notable antidelinquency programs that offered preschool classes "for the culturally disadvantaged" in target neighborhoods evolved into what Shriver called the OEO's "kiddie corps," or Head Start, and it was the most widely implemented of the community action programs. By the end of the summer of 1965, community action agencies had enrolled roughly 200,000 preschool children in the program.[42] Moreover, the Upward Bound initiative the legislation created strongly resembled the Weekend Rangers demonstration program in Boston, a measure supported by the President's Committee that took delinquent and potentially delinquent youth outside their urban settings to a work camp on weekends and school holidays.

Despite the popularity of Head Start and the Upward Bound program, the emphasis on grassroots empowerment that was crucial to the creation of early War on Poverty programs quickly became controversial. Although planners and officials largely resisted grassroots participation in the antidelinquency programs in practice, Ohlin and Cloward's opportunity theory had emphasized that only the widespread participation of local people, working with local agencies supported and assisted by the federal government, could disrupt the culture of poverty. This eventually became the basis of community action. While Ohlin and other Kennedy officials referred to this as "indigenous participation," Congress stripped the concept of its racial undertones and enshrined it in the Economic Opportunity Act as "maximum feasible participation." In practice, this principle meant "assist[ing] the poor in developing autonomous and self-managed organizations which are competent to exert political influence on behalf of their own self-interest," as defined in the *Community Action Program Workbook* the OEO distributed to local agencies in March 1965.[43] The OEO would attempt to remedy the systematic exclusion of the grassroots from urban social welfare programs and simultaneously empower them.

The principle of "maximum feasible participation" did not cause much debate in Congress initially, but it created power struggles over the administration and control of the War on Poverty and tested the Johnson administration's commitment to its own rhetoric about equal opportunity and community representation. For activists, organizers, and residents of segregated communities throughout the United States, "maximum feasible participation" opened the door for radical approaches to disrupting existing racial hierarchies and exercising the claims to self-determination increasingly voiced by mainstream civil rights leaders. For instance, with support from the OEO, Mobilization for Youth confronted public school administrators, unresponsive landlords, the New York City Department of Welfare, and the police department. Similarly, the Syracuse Development Corporation supported low-income residents in protests, rent strikes, and sit-ins. Drawing from the organizing methods developed by Saul Alinksy, the Woodlawn Organization of Chicago received a $1 million development grant to work with youth associated with the Blackstone Rangers and East Side Disciples gangs.[44] It was the first time grassroots organizations received direct federal funding to address social problems in their communities on their own terms.

With federal funds supporting these and other campaigns against mayoral administrations under the auspices of community action, local officials bristled. "Maximum feasible participation" was "fostering class struggle," as Syracuse mayor William Walsh asserted. Disturbed by the OEO's workbook and the general direction of community action programs, mayors, social welfare agencies, and congressional Republicans feared that funds would be used to build a radical base in "unorganized sections" of low-income areas, fueling a major voter registration drive for the Democratic Party.[45] Some charged that communists had infiltrated these groups, just as they had allegedly penetrated civil rights and black nationalist organizations, using federal funds to organize the poor and launch attacks on City Hall. Eventually, the Woodlawn Organization's effort to provide an alternative to gang membership invited sensationalized charges of fraud, revolutionary schemes, and illicit narcotic and contraband trafficking.

Such allegations made community action and the wider War on Poverty, by association, easy targets for critics of Johnson's Great Society and created new alliances between northern mayors and southern

Democrats. Increasing numbers of white liberals linked to urban political machines joined the growing clamor for law and order. Even as criticism of community action mounted among local officials, who were sidelined by the practice, for the first year of its operation, the OEO defended grassroots representation as a primary objective of the War on Poverty. But as the program evolved during the second half of the 1960s, the possibility that the War on Poverty would lead to fundamental social transformations brought about by citizens themselves had diminished.

Like the Kennedy administration's "total attack" on delinquency, Johnson had pledged in his first State of the Union address of 1964 to "not only relieve the symptom of poverty but to cure it, and, above all, prevent it." Yet the vast majority of War on Poverty programs offered a more cautious approach to relieving American poverty, committing to vocational training and remedial education programs in the absence of job creation measures or an overhaul of urban public schools. Despite the administration's rhetorical gestures, the antipoverty programs focused more on fighting the effects of inequality than on combating its root causes. As Congress made clear, "These are not programs to bring about major structural change in the economy, or to generate large numbers of additional jobs."[46] Policymakers did not design or intend War on Poverty initiatives to eliminate poverty itself, then, but to promote the principle of "equal opportunity" to the so-called disadvantaged.

From the President's Committee to the OEO, federal policymakers instead continued to develop policies that would alleviate the individual pathologies they understood to be the chief cause of poverty. "Maximum feasible participation" may have been the theoretical approach Congress initially adopted for community action programs, but it was never their chief goal. Much like the Kennedy administration's approach to urban delinquency, community action programs were designed to institutionalize democratic values in communities where, as far as federal policymakers were concerned, deficient parents and local programs had spawned "antisocial behavior" and "deviance" among urban youth. The federal government responded by providing opportunities for empowerment while simultaneously encouraging discipline among vulnerable groups. "The solution to juvenile delinquency is to give purpose and meaning to aimless young lives," wrote Johnson's task force on the issue.

"When a potential school dropout is encouraged to stay in school . . . a potential delinquent is turned into a potentially responsible and productive citizen. The same is true when . . . order is brought into a disordered, unstable home through constructive social service." Along these lines, the Johnson administration believed that through its War on Poverty programs, "an environment is being created in which young people will find their own ways toward a constructive rather than a destructive life."[47] Breaking the "cycle of poverty" by providing services and increasing the supervision of low-income people became an even more pressing focus of the antipoverty effort during the second half of the 1960s. The participation and empowerment of grassroots organizations and residents to design and shape the programs that aimed to change their life prospects and immediate socioeconomic circumstances proved to be a brief moment in time, as urban uprisings during the summer of 1964 led Johnson officials to rethink the more radical strategies they developed for the War on Poverty.

A "WAR ON CRIME"

Exactly two weeks after Johnson outlawed discrimination and Jim Crow segregation in signing the Civil Rights Act of 1964, on July 16, a demonstration protesting the murder of a fifteen-year-old high school student by a New York City police officer evolved into six nights of disorder in Harlem and the death of one resident. The taunting of police officers, burning, and plunder in department and grocery stores, what policymakers and the general public referred to as "rioting," spread to Brooklyn's Bedford-Stuyvesant neighborhood and touched off similar incidents in Philadelphia and Chicago. The largest and most destructive riot that summer emerged a day after the unrest in Harlem and Brooklyn subsided in the smaller deindustrializing city of Rochester in upstate New York. Four people died in Rochester during the uprising, and approximately 1,000 residents were arrested—nearly double their numbers in New York City—a sign that the social conditions that fomented unrest weren't specific to major metropolitan centers.[48] The civil rights movement brought a long history of police brutality and vigilante violence to the attention of the nation during the 1950s and early 1960s, but the explosions during the summer of 1964 underscored the ways in which discriminatory policing deeply shaped black urban life. The uprisings exposed the tensions that existed between law enforcement officers and residents in segregated urban neighborhoods. They also brought to the fore the unanswered legacy of Emancipation: despite civil rights reform and the unprecedented War on Poverty Johnson had recently declared, monumental federal actions had failed to resolve entrenched inequality and everyday racism within American institutions, North and South. The "social dynamite" that had worried policymakers and officials at the outset of the decade had finally exploded, despite the Kennedy and Johnson administrations' prevention efforts.

Rather than critically examine the deeper causes of urban unrest, Johnson declared that "the immediate overriding issue in New York is the preservation of law and order." Johnson had spoken out against racial violence in the South and was now becoming increasingly concerned with the violence that plagued the Northeast. "The denial of rights invites increased disorder and violence," Johnson told the American Bar Association during its annual conference at the Waldorf-Astoria hotel in New York, recognizing that African Americans who engaged in direct action protest and collective violence shared similar grievances. But ultimately, the president argued that the "fulfillment of rights and prevention of disorder [goes] hand in hand." He pledged his administration "will not permit any part of America to become a jungle, where the weak are the prey of the strong and the many."[49] Although the actions of the black residents who participated in unrest during the summer of 1964 represented a response to discriminatory policing strategies and structural exclusion, Johnson believed that civil rights legislation and equal opportunity programs offered a sufficient cure, and he viewed their actions as criminal.

Eight months after Harlem erupted, in March 1965, Johnson called the federal government's War on Crime. Marking the first national investment in local crime control efforts, Johnson's Law Enforcement Assistance Act of 1965 sought to bring the Department of Justice to a new level of prominence and expand the power and influence of the attorney general at the local level. The legislation proposed a new federal crime control agency, the Office of Law Enforcement Assistance (OLEA), to support training programs and experimental surveillance techniques for police forces serving low-income urban communities. The administration hoped the OLEA's demonstration projects would provide the basis for a permanent national crime control program.

Beginning a federal law enforcement intervention was in part a calculated political move to take possession of the issue from conservatives. "No right is more elemental to our society than the right to personal security and no right needs more urgent protection," the president affirmed in his March 1965 speech to Congress on crime, emphasizing that "one of the most legitimate functions of government is the preservation of law and order."[50] Southern politicians relied upon similar anticrime rhetoric immediately following the *Brown v. Board of Education* decision to oppose racial integration, and Republican presidential candidate Barry Goldwater had introduced the idea of a "forgotten civil right" into national political discourse to attract newly embittered white voters. As commentators observed at the time, and as scholars have since concluded, Johnson vowed to protect the safety of "ordinary" Americans and made his federal law enforcement intervention part of the Great Society to maintain support of this critical portion of the electorate. More than a campaign strategy, however, the Johnson administration's turn to the War on Crime was largely an extension of the assumptions about "culturally disadvantaged" Americans that had emerged in domestic policy alongside the crescendo of civil rights demands.

Rooted in the theoretical frameworks that had shaped the aims and implementation of urban social programs from the Kennedy administration onward, the punitive measures Johnson included in his Great Society built upon the federal government's previous interventions in black communities. Shortly after Johnson sent the Law Enforcement Assistance Act to Congress, Daniel Patrick Moynihan submitted a report on the "crisis of race relations," one intended for a small audience of policymakers and state officials, to Secretary of Labor W. Willard Wirtz. Moynihan had joined the Kennedy administration as assistant secretary of labor after receiving his PhD in sociology from Tufts, and he was the driving force behind the creation of Kennedy's Task Force on Manpower Conservation, its research, and its general conclusions. Kennedy convened the task force in the fall of 1963, with Wirtz as its chairman and with the participation of the secretaries of Defense and Health, Education, and Welfare, out of concern about the alarming numbers of young men deemed unfit for military service. Although Kennedy was assassinated before the task force completed its research, Wirtz delivered its report, *One Third of a Nation: A Report on Young Men Found Unqualified for Military Service*, to Johnson on January 1, 1964. The task force drew connections between poverty, low literacy, and national security, making the case for a federal intervention in urban and rural areas where low-income families were concentrated. According to the task force, the young men who failed the army's mental test had inherited poverty from their parents, and unless job training, counseling, and literacy programs broke that cycle, they would "surely transmit" it to their children. In the absence of immediate federal action, the task force argued, this "third of a nation" would, most likely, "face a lifetime of recurrent unemployment."[51] An outspoken critic of community action programs during his tenure in the Kennedy administration, Moynihan believed the mounting pressure from black Americans—through nonviolent direct action protest and collective urban civil disorder during the summer of 1964—provided an opportune moment to advocate for new federal employment measures once again.

Moynihan came from the postwar tradition of liberal social science that took Gunnar Myrdal's analysis as its starting point. In 1944's *American Dilemma*, Myrdal described black poverty as a "vicious circle" perpetuated by economic inequality, cultural exclusion, and the psychological impact of racism. Myrdal importantly challenged genetic theories of racial inequality with ideas about pathology, a term he borrowed from medical science, to describe the impact of social ills on individual behavior. This pathology could be disrupted if black Americans acquired, in Myrdal's words, "*the traits held in esteem by dominant white Americans*" and assimilated into the mainstream.[52] Building upon Myrdal's ideas, Moynihan argued that what he called the "tangle of pathology" could be alleviated through planned interventions in black communities (as Moynihan declared at a conference on poverty at Berkeley in February 1965: "I think the problem of the Negro family is practically the property of the federal government") but that confronting existing discrimination in American institutions was a critical step in doing so.[53] Like many liberal social scientists before and after, Moynihan grounded his case for systemic reform in behavioral and cultural assumptions.

Further elaborating upon the implications of the data he collected for *One Third a Nation*, Moynihan drew in equal measure on social science research and psychological theory to argue that delinquency, crime, unemployment, and poverty resulted from unstable black families and what he called the "pathology of post-industrial society." According to Moynihan, the submissive "Sambo" and the emasculating "Mammy" figures that characterized the black family during slavery had been transmitted from one generation to the next, producing high rates of unemployment, failing school systems, and neglected housing. Four generations removed from slavery, Moynihan argued that poor African American families were trapped in a self-perpetuating "tangle of pathology" that could "be broken only if these distortions are set right" by federal policies that actively created jobs for black men and, by extension, promoted stable families.[54] Moynihan's research went on to influence the federal government's racial reforms in the post–Jim Crow era, grounding the legislative proposals that laid the basis for not only the War on Poverty but also, as special advisor to President Nixon for urban affairs, the War on Crime.

On March 23, 1965, weeks after the initial "Eyes Only" confidential copies of the report were printed, Secretary of Labor Wirtz sent Johnson a memo summarizing Moynihan's key findings. The memo, drafted by Moynihan himself, warned Johnson that the nation confronted "a second stage, a new crisis" of racial inequality that demanded that the federal government expand upon rights "traditionally associated with *Liberty*" to meet demands for "the democratic ideal of *Equality*." Federal policy aimed at sustaining and creating two-parent households in black urban areas would be a "cornerstone for a new era of social legislation" that focused explicitly on the consequences of racial exclusion. Johnson interpreted Moynihan's arguments selectively, rejecting Moynihan's idea of federal responsibility and his proposal for job creation while embracing his ideas about the black family. Moynihan's

understanding of the urban crisis as rooted in black pathology provided the administration with a rationale for directing domestic programs specifically at the plight of black men while removing itself
from accountability for the de facto restrictions, joblessness, and racism
that perpetuated poverty and inequality.[55]

In his commencement address at Howard University in June 1965,
Johnson did commit his administration to the "next and more profound
stage" of reform Moynihan suggested. The night before its delivery,
Moynihan and presidential assistant Richard N. Goodwin together
penned Johnson's remarks, transforming social science "data" into political rhetoric. "Freedom is not enough," Johnson proclaimed to Howard's graduating class. "Equal opportunity is essential, but not enough."
But the president's tone shifted from the limitations of the nation's
founding egalitarian principles to individual behavior, as he explained
that the disproportionate rate of black American poverty resulted from

Young men of Howard University's graduating class of 1965 witnessing President
Lyndon Johnson deliver their commencement address on June 4. "This is American
justice," Johnson told them. "We have pursued it faithfully to the edge of our imperfec-
tions, and we have failed to find it for the American Negro." *Photograph by Yoichi
Okamato. White House Photographic Office Collection, Lyndon Baines Johnson Presidential Library*

"the breakdown of the Negro family structure." This, Johnson argued, was a problem that flowed "from centuries of oppression and persecution of the Negro man" and "from the long years of degradation and discrimination." Johnson proclaimed that the "deep, corrosive obstinate" differences between "white poverty" and "Negro poverty" lay in the fact that for the latter, historical inequality radiated "painful roots into the community, and into the family, and the nature of the individual." Without a national policy to foster two-parent households, Johnson believed, "the circle of despair and deprivation" in black urban America would never break.[56]

As Congress considered the Law Enforcement Assistance Act that summer, Moynihan's claims introduced black family life into the crime control equation. Liberals drew from Moynihan's analysis to promote social science research on crime and black poverty. New York's noted liberal congressman James Scheuer asserted: "In almost every case behind a delinquent child lies a delinquent parent, and thus I believe that one facet of a national crime prevention program must be an analysis of a parent's role in the prevention of crime and delinquency." For Senator Edward M. Kennedy, too, "many who transgress the law have themselves been transgressed—by their home life, by their environment, by their lack of opportunity." Senator Kennedy pointed out that the behavioral sciences were "entering more and more into determinations of criminal responsibility." By supporting continued psychological and social science research into the problems of crime and black poverty, Senator Kennedy argued that federal policy could "fix" community pathology and the social forces shaping it.[57]

Working together, White House officials and Congress championed a law enforcement strategy that merged the War on Crime with the War on Poverty, forging a network of social service and surveillance programs that first emerged in the New Frontier under the umbrella of the Great Society. These urban interventions provided a foundation for the rise of the carceral state. Scheuer explained during the Law Enforcement Assistance Act hearings that the federal government "[must fight] this battle on two fronts. We must fight crime today and, at the same time, we must prevent the growth of tomorrow's criminal and thereby protect the future safety of our own children and grandchildren."[58]

Social welfare programs fought *future* poverty by providing new opportunities to low-income youth, while surveillance and police patrol programs would manage the immediate effects of racial inequality and monitor *future* criminals.

Johnson led the federal government in making law and order and the restoration of domestic tranquility its primary responsibility. Racism embedded within federal policy and the social science research that rationalized it encouraged officials to embrace patrol, surveillance, and confinement as means of exerting social control in neighborhoods of segregated poverty.[59] Although the Johnson administration had resisted major structural changes in its fight against economic inequality—offering low-income Americans temporary positions and training programs—it did commit to a major job creation program for police and correctional officers by launching the War on Crime. Johnson told Howard's graduates that "nothing in any country touches us more profoundly, and nothing is more freighted with meaning for our own destiny than the revolution of the Negro American."[60] The question remained whether the administration would respond to that revolution with social welfare or punitive programs. Thus in the ashes of Jim Crow, following the passage of the Civil Rights Act of 1964 and the Voting Rights Act of 1965, and at a time of policy experimentation with the launch of the War on Poverty, the expansion of the welfare state coincided with a new era in American law enforcement. The modern carceral state had begun to take hold.

[2]

LAW AND ORDER IN THE GREAT SOCIETY

On August 7, 1965, the day after President Johnson signed the Voting Rights Act, the House Committee on Education and Labor held a special hearing in Los Angeles to find out why the city had failed to implement War on Poverty measures. The Economic Opportunity Act required the creation of community action agencies in major urban centers, and since officials in Los Angeles had refused to do so after nearly a year, federal policymakers wanted to determine how to get the antipoverty program started. More than a thousand spectators came to witness the Congressional proceedings, held in Will Rogers Park Auditorium in the heart of the Watts neighborhood. The hearing became a day-long rally for community action and grassroots representation in shaping the city's antipoverty program, as Mexican American residents of East Los Angeles and African American residents of South Central expressed their grievances and called on Congress to hold local politicians accountable to the specific needs of their communities. Continued resistance from municipal officials to the War on Poverty and the complete exclusion of low-income residents from Mayor Sam Yorty's Economic and Youth Opportunities Board had "aroused the poverty community in a way that it has never been aroused before," as Dr. J. Alfred Cannon, the associate director of the Department of Social and Community

Psychiatry at UCLA, testified. Cannon noted that black residents in South Central and across the country were the "victims of a kind of unrest" due to their continued socioeconomic isolation.[1] The unrest Cannon predicted among Watts residents materialized five days later, when the largest urban uprising in the nation's history up to that point surfaced in the streets surrounding Will Rogers Auditorium.

Lasting for six days in mid-August 1965, the collective violence in South Central Los Angeles was the litmus test for the War on Crime. The proximate cause of the disturbance—an aggressive encounter between police officers and a black family—was itself unremarkable. Similar incidents of police brutality occurred frequently in Watts and other low-income black communities, and indeed had ignited disorder in New York City, Rochester, Chicago, and Philadelphia the previous summer. But the scale of the uprising in Los Angeles was new. Shortly after the initial incident, the 250 to 300 residents who gathered to witness the confrontation began to assail the California Highway Patrol and the Los Angeles police officers on the scene. Small groups formed, vandalizing property, menacing police command posts, and roaming the immediate vicinity until after midnight, when police made twenty-two arrests. The officers believed that by rounding up the remaining residents on the streets they had largely defused the situation. Over the following days, however, some 35,000 individuals joined their neighbors in destroying white-owned businesses, harming police officers and civilians, and obliterating entire blocks while 70,000 others stood by to witness the violence unfold in their neighborhoods. Army tanks rolled through the streets, helicopters hovered above in the sky, and gunshots resounded from the rifles of National Guardsmen at a nearly constant pace.[2] Amid the ashes of the warzone, a critical mass of policymakers, federal administrators, law enforcement officials, and journalists concluded that only intensified enforcement of the law in segregated urban communities like Harlem and Watts, where contempt for authority seemed widespread, would quell the anarchy and chaos.

The strategies that policymakers at all levels of government pursued during the Watts uprising—from the officer who placed his gun on the temple of a young man and thereby set off the disorder, to the military-like occupation of the neighborhood once it had been placed under curfew—demonstrated that excessive punitive force in segregated urban communities often precipitated violence in those same communities. But this was not the lesson that policymakers and law enforcement authorities took away from the disturbance in South Central. On August 19, two days after the unrest in Watts had subsided and as senators prepared for the upcoming vote on the Law Enforcement Assistance Act, Senate Judiciary Committee chair Roman Hruska told Attorney General Katzenbach, "For some time, it has been my feeling that the task of law enforcement agencies is really not much different from military forces; namely, to deter crime before it occurs, just as our military objective is deterrence of aggression."[3] Yet in providing police departments with military-grade weapons and undertaking a major program to professionalize law enforcement via the newly created Office of Law Enforcement Assistance (OLEA), federal policymakers and local officials overlooked the ways in which excessive force in fact contributed to violence and disorder, rather than curtailing it.

Contemporary interpretations of reactions and responses to Watts offer a limited explanation of a much broader phenomenon that involved the shift from a social welfare to a punitive intervention, even during the years of Johnson's Great Society. Indeed, the Watts uprising exposed the existing failures of the War on Poverty and yet ironically became a metaphor that rationalized a further retreat from the more transformative notions of liberal social reform, such as community action programs and the principle of "maximum feasible participation." The reality of urban civil disorder was also used to invigorate the War on Crime, which had been already percolating, both in its "declared" form and in the elements of surveillance and supervision of segregated urban areas that had been underway since the Kennedy administration. Just as the "attacking force" of police and national guardsmen in Los Angeles caused more disorder in August 1965, the federal government's decision to manage urban crisis through punitive measures only intensified the problems of crime and poverty that national officials aimed to prevent. Policymakers chose to respond to collective violence, however rooted that violence was in civil rights grievances, with greater law enforcement penetration. An alternate policy path that might have wrestled with the urban crime control practices and the racial profiling that set off the incidents in the first place or that might have involved a re-thinking of the rationale behind launching a War on Poverty without recourse to job creation and fundamental structural changes, did not present itself to the White House and Congress. Policymakers' own assumptions about pathological behavior and criminality among urban African Americans made escalating the War on Crime and dissolving the autonomous grassroots programs that steered earlier War on Poverty programs the most practical policy path forward.

"PUBLIC ENEMY NO. 1"

Nowhere else in the country did poverty and affluence contrast as sharply as in Los Angeles, and tension had been mounting during the summer of 1965. The city's resistance to community action prompted demands for greater neighborhood power over the federal program at the House hearing in Watts. As the Reverend H. H. Brookins, the popular preacher at the First African Methodist Episcopal Church and the chairman of the Community Anti-Poverty Committee, told the representatives, "We do not want to control the poverty program. We want to share in it." Brookins and other community members, antipoverty workers, clergymen, and labor organizers asked for a degree of influence and inclusion in the implementation of programs that would respond to the myriad needs of their segregated, densely populated communities. Although the Supreme Court had outlawed racially restrictive covenants in the 1948 case *Shelley v. Kraemer*, California voters had repealed the fair-housing law and reinstated the private right to discriminate during the 1964 election. Racial and ethnic groups in Los Angeles remained relegated to particular areas and kept entirely out of others. In most of the city, each square mile was home to about 5,900 residents, but in Watts and other black communities, the figure was as high as 16,400 people per square mile.[4]

The neighborhood was also characterized by the desperate need for jobs. While the unemployment rate nationwide was only 4 percent to 6 percent of the labor force during the 1960s, in Watts, as many as one in three people could not find work. Major corporations were in the midst of a transition toward a highly skilled, highly trained workforce and increasingly relied on suburban, rural, and overseas labor. Federal officials estimated that 160,000 black residents in South Central fell into the category of "sub-employed," or "the hard-core unemployed" in the decades following World War II, as General Motors, Chrysler, and Firestone began to close the factories they had built during the 1930s. Underfunded and lacking other resources sufficient to prepare students for careers in thriving industries like aerospace and engineering, segregated urban schools could not adequately respond to the fundamental employment problems black residents faced. Whereas the previous generation of black migrants from the rural South could secure employment in the industrial sector when Los Angeles was still the "arsenal of democracy," only a single industrial plant remained in South Central by August 1965. Despite these discouraging prospects, many African Americans still considered Los Angeles a city of promise and opportunity, and each month 1,000 southern migrants relocated there in the hopes of creating a better life for themselves and their families.[5]

This mass unemployment, extreme segregation, and poverty set the backdrop for the confrontation between the Los Angeles Police Department (LAPD), the California Highway Patrol, and black residents that precipitated the uprising. As increasing numbers of African Americans migrated to the city during and after World War II, law enforcement authorities patrolled the boundaries of Watts, Compton, and other segregated black neighborhoods within the South Central area to prevent residents from venturing to South Gate, Lynwood, and other surrounding segregated white neighborhoods. When a group of 250 to 300 residents observed the beating and arrest of Rena Price and her twenty-one- and twenty-two-year-old sons by a group of California Highway patrolmen and Los Angeles police officers around 7:30 p.m. on August 11, the residents responded to the relatively unremarkable incident by hurling cement, rocks, and bottles at the officers until just after midnight.[6]

At the first signs of a major outbreak of civil disorder, Brookins and other community leaders knew that excessive police force would only add to the violence, and so they suggested to municipal officials that residents try to subdue the riot themselves. Questionable police practices had prompted residents to engage in civil disorder in the first place, and a strong police response only threatened to provoke them further. An uneasy calm hovered over the city Thursday morning, August 12, but the tension resurfaced at a meeting called by the California Human Relations Board in the afternoon. Brookins advised Deputy Chief of Police Roger Murdock that "there ought not to be any concentration of police power in this community tonight," urging him to withdraw white police officers from the area and replace them with plainclothes black officers. Murdock rejected Brookins's proposal on the grounds that it violated the department's antidiscrimination policy, and at 7:00 p.m., with sirens blaring, six police cars paraded down 118th Street in Watts, where some 500 residents had gathered. "It was just like an explosion," Brookins later said of the scene; "everything just went haywire." As Brookins predicted, law enforcement officers only ignited an already smoldering situation.[7]

Unlike the wartime race riots sparked by white hostility to integration, the collective violence in South Central in August 1965 and in 250 other cities during Johnson's presidency represented an attack on exploitative institutions in black neighborhoods. Schools, libraries, and other public buildings suffered minimal damage during the Watts uprising, while some 261 supermarkets, pawn shops, and department stores—owned mostly by absentee white business owners and proprietors—were severely damaged or completely destroyed. The actions of the riot's participants and the $200 million in property damage they caused seemed to call for an overthrow of exclusionary institutions or inclusion as full economic and social citizens, neither of which the federal government or local officials were prepared to accept.[8] Instead, they responded with law enforcement and criminal justice control.

Sparked by an incident of police brutality, the spontaneity of the disturbance left Los Angeles police chief William Parker outnumbered by inflamed residents and besieged. On the second day of rioting, Parker declared that he could not provide the media with "the slightest idea when this can be brought under control." He and other municipal officials believed a paramilitary response was necessary to regain control of the city. "This is a criminal, a lawless element in which we're confronted," Mayor Yorty explained at a press conference, "and the only thing they understand is force and power." On Friday morning, August 13, Governor Edmund G. "Pat" Brown called out the National Guard for the second time in California's history, and the Guardsmen joined the LAPD and the California Highway Patrol to serve as Chief Parker's 16,000-strong self-described "attacking force." Altogether, this force was larger than the contingent troops Johnson had sent to invade the Dominican Republic four months prior.[9]

Parker treated the uprising in Watts as an insurgency that was, in his words, "very much like fighting the Viet Cong." The police department and the National Guard saw themselves as confronting a new type of "urban guerrilla warfare"—or what Governor Brown characterized as "guerrilla fighting with gangsters"—one that recalled the violent encounters American troops faced during the same years in the Caribbean, South America, and Southeast Asia. National Guardsmen and their display of militarized force only exacerbated the unrest. State troops and local officers quickly established blockades and posted signs throughout the riot zone that threatened to kill residents ("Turn left or get shot," one declared), and the thirty-one residents who perished during the disturbance died at the hands of law enforcement authorities, while a fireman, a deputy sheriff, and a Long Beach policeman also lost their lives. Attempting to injure a police officer or a guardsman, getting caught with a six-pack of beer that had not been purchased, making the wrong turn at the wrong intersection at the wrong time, or simply attempting to protect personal property could end in death. As Fenbroy Morrison George attempted to remove the belongings of his wife and three children from his burning home, for example, he was fatally shot by two Los Angeles police officers.[10]

With the police and the National Guard behaving like U.S. troops in an overseas military occupation, residents, in turn, shifted the focus of the civil disorder from attacking exploitative institutions to driving out law enforcement authorities. On Saturday, South Central became a full-on war zone. Residents used any and every available raw material in their struggle against the police and the National Guard. They broke down the sidewalks to obtain cement. They disassembled vacant factories and used the bricks to smash law enforcement vehicles. They stockpiled rubbish and stones from the railroad tracks to throw at officers. And

A warning sign issued by law enforcement authorities at the boundaries of South Central Los Angeles during the Watts uprising in August 1965. In all, thirty-one African American residents died at the hands of local police and National Guardsmen during the six days of unrest. *Photograph by Keystone. Hulton Archive, Getty Images*

they used household materials and debris to construct bombs, filling glass bottles with gasoline to make Molotov cocktails.

When journalists and photographers from all corners of the globe descended on Los Angeles to capture the violence, destruction, and plunder in South Central, the police department instituted a curfew to provide a legal rationale for the widespread detention of black residents and thereby bring an end to the riot. Previously, Los Angeles authorities had applied curfew laws only to juveniles; now, the curfew enabled officers to apprehend any resident outside his or her home after 8:00 p.m. At 46.5 square miles, the curfew zone was larger than the island of Manhattan and covered all of the sections that had a black majority inside and outside city limits. Chief Parker encouraged his officers to arrest and detain as many residents as possible to quell the disturbance. The tactic succeeded, and the unrest subsided after the LAPD booked more than 4,000 residents for curfew violations—the largest mass arrest during the first half of the 1960s.[11]

The curfew arrests overwhelmed the Los Angeles criminal justice system. In the days immediately following the uprising, most of the police force was subpoenaed in court to testify against the riot participants, and as a result, police protection in the city was at an all-time low. The mass arrests clogged the local courts and left thousands of suspects without adequate counsel and sometimes without any legal representation whatsoever. Although the police department and state officials blamed the violence on "criminal elements" in the community, the vast majority of those arrested during the uprising had no arrest record or had only received a minor citation previously. Most of the cases were tried without juries, and most of the suspects either pled guilty to looting, arson, and vandalism or were found guilty. The district attorney's office boasted that 80 percent of those participants charged with felonies during the riot were convicted. Judges handed down particularly harsh verdicts, for instance, giving sentences of one year to life in prison for looting when shoplifting or burglary charges in the state carried a penalty of fifteen years. Governor Brown had pledged to "continue to deal forcefully with the terrorists until Los Angeles is safe again," and the mass arrests and severe punishments offered the first step in doing so.[12] For many residents accused and convicted of participation in the uprising, especially the first-time offenders, the mass arrests established criminal records and increased the likelihood that those arrested would serve harsh prison sentences—if not right away, then in the future.

Harrowing media coverage of the uprising evoked long-held racist fears about black disobedience and innate violence, and like the criminal records that had been created for thousands of African American residents in the city, had long-term ramifications. The dominant perception of the Watts violence was that young black residents seized control of the city for nearly a week, seeking revenge for historical racism and inequality, terrorizing innocent people with guns, and threatening national security. The evening news programs and national press outlets presented black youth as "public enemy no. 1" in their coverage of the violence, reinforcing the need for militarized policing and social control. The opening line of *New York Times* reporter Wallace Turner's page one story read, "Negroes in a depressed area of Los Angeles were swept up in an emotional tide of hate and bitterness that caused them to beat and burn." The *Los Angeles Times* quoted a group of teenage girls as taunting: "White man, you got a tiger by the tail. You can't hold it. You can't let it go. The next time you see us we'll be carrying guns. Now it's our turn." Popular news outlets further interpreted the collective violence and the threat of continued destruction, or at the very least armed self-defense, as a declaration of war. "This was not a riot," CBS Radio told its listeners. "It was an insurrection against all authority. If it had gone much further, it would have become civil war."[13] The images of the riot—of black residents confronting white police officers— galvanized this perception, especially among the white public.

Indeed, many white residents and officials in Los Angeles expressed strong support for the police department's energetic effort to restore law and order. During and after the outbreak, the police department received 17,000 letters and telegrams, 99 percent of which commended the department for its handling of the disturbance. Other residents armed themselves in anticipation of future outbreaks, spiking gun sales in the suburbs. As officials from the Departments of Justice and Commerce and the Office of Economic Opportunity reported after the unrest: "There is a wide feeling that the Negro community lacks gratitude for recent economic and civil rights advances and its demands will grow." For increasing numbers of policymakers and the general public, the Watts uprising called Lyndon Johnson's antipoverty record into question, and it reinforced arguments about the deficiencies of the New Frontier and the Great Society. Collective violence in Watts fueled claims from conservatives and even some liberals that federal welfare and housing policy helped to cause the "crime menace." Police Chief William Parker asserted in a nationally televised interview that "civil disobedience erodes respect for all law," implying that the civil rights movement had directly contributed to the violence his officers had confronted in South Central. Like many of his peers, Los Angeles district attorney Evelle Younger criticized social welfare measures and liberals for demoralizing black urban residents and sustaining crime and violence. Younger believed that a "national guilt complex" about historic racism paralyzed the liberal state so that "every time a hoodlum throws a Molotov cocktail or shoots a policeman society is somehow at fault."

While Johnson was deeply committed to his national law enforcement program (and even more so after Watts), he worried that these statements would weaken support for Great Society programs and civil rights reform by linking nonviolent direct-action protest to urban civil disorder in the popular and political imagination.[14]

In a sense, the media and government officials were correct in labeling the events in Watts an uprising and interpreting it as articulating political demands. But they characterized those citizens who participated in the unrest as enemies and rejected the rioters' demands as illegitimate. Challenging the view that insufficient civil rights and social welfare measures had caused the disorder, policymakers, law enforcement officials, and journalists increasingly argued that liberal social programs were excessive if not entirely futile.

Subsequent calls for tightening police patrol overlooked the ways in which excessive police force only exacerbated disorder. Long-held notions about black Americans and criminality rationalized the policing strategies that emerged during the Watts uprising. The LAPD and the National Guard approached the situation as a counterinsurgency against an enemy force initially, and residents in turn redirected their violence from property to law enforcement. Residents' reactions to the aggressive law enforcement were then labeled by public figures as further evidence of criminality that merited severe punishment, an assessment that fueled the theory that only excessive force could contain crime. In short, Watts foreshadowed the cycle of policing, surveillance, and detainment that would characterize the War on Crime during its first fifteen years and beyond.

THE RETREAT FROM COMMUNITY ACTION

Under growing criticism from civil rights leaders and a resurgent left wing for his decision to escalate the war in Vietnam—which occupied an increasing amount of the administration's attention and a growing share of the federal budget—President Johnson found himself on tenuous ground. He needed to placate liberals and respond to the riots so that it did not appear that he ignored the problem of urban poverty, but growing conservative reactions to civil rights gains and sensationalized depictions of urban civil disorder meant that the president could not appear to concede to rioters or reward their actions. "Effective law enforcement and social justice must be pursued together, as the foundation of our efforts against crime," Johnson said. For Johnson and other liberals, a long-range solution involved "an attack not only against crime directly, but against the roots from which it springs." Positioning the federal government's crime prevention and antipoverty programs as mutually reinforcing, Johnson urged Congress to grant unprecedented funding to confront employment, education, and housing issues.[15]

The collective violence in South Central served as evidence for policymakers to advocate for the expansion of the welfare state or the carceral state or both. Reacting to a peak in the black unemployment rate in the city, the absence of a community action agency, and staunch opposition to grassroots participation by the local government, residents in South Central had revolted. The best way to prevent future disorder, it seemed, was to step up the War on Poverty. But others saw the uprising as evidence that Great Society programs were incapable of handling the urban crisis, and the reality of collective violence made Johnson's recent call for the War on Crime all the more pressing. Regardless, these assessments drew from Daniel Patrick Moynihan's notion of "post-industrial pathology," a theory that compelled liberals and supporters of the War on Poverty to change their outlook.[16]

Moynihan's key empirical finding in *The Negro Family*, that welfare "dependency" no longer directly correlated to unemployment, was later disproven. But the notion that a self-perpetuating "tangle of pathology" characterized black families nevertheless emerged as a powerful, and malleable, explanation of persisting racial inequality after the passage of the Civil Rights Act and other egalitarian measures. When taken to its extreme, Moynihan's analysis could support arguments that black American pathology ran so deep that black families were incapable of benefiting from expanded opportunity and self-help programs.[17] Initially Moynihan's theories had been used to support the equal opportunity and social uplift agenda of the administration's antipoverty programs, inspiring Johnson's famous speech at Howard University roughly three months before the Watts uprising. During the second half of the

1960s, however, the pathological framework through which Moynihan articulated these ideas increasingly served as a rationale for the escalation of punitive intervention in low-income urban communities.

Rebellion in Watts prompted growing doubts about the War on Poverty, but Moynihan's recommendation of policies to strengthen the black family and the male role within it continued to gain ground politically and publicly through the fall of 1965. *Newsweek* had excerpted Moynihan's report two days before South Central erupted, and almost immediately after the unrest began, White House Press Secretary Bill Moyers distributed copies of the report to any colleague who had yet to read it. And as policymakers and the mainstream press looked for ways to understand the Watts uprising, *The Negro Family* became their primary reference point. Moynihan's conclusions offered reporters critical insight into what the *Wall Street Journal* called the "orgy of Negro rioting" in Watts. On August 16, 1965, five days into the civil disorder, the *Journal* printed a sensational article on its front page: "Behind the Riots: Family Life Breakdown in Negro Slums Sows Seeds of Race Violence; Husbandless Homes Spawn Young Hoodlums, Impede Reforms, Sociologists Say; Racing a Booming Birth Rate." Drawing on Moynihan's theory, the article pointed to the "spreading disintegration of Negro family life" as an explanation for the violence on the streets of Los Angeles. The more liberal *New York Times* echoed the *Journal*'s analysis in less stark terms. "Nearly one out of every four Negro babies born is illegitimate—the result of a breakdown of family life," the editors of the *Times* explained. High birth and unemployment rates created "self-perpetuating poverty and with it delinquency and crime." As a result, "the worst areas of Negro urban poverty have seemed oblivious to the improvement," the *Times* argued of the impact of War on Poverty programs. "The prevailing moods in those sectors have been economic and political apathy, a rankling sense of grievance against 'whitey,' and a pent-up potential for violence."[18]

These and other sensationalized depictions of disorder in Watts extended Moynihan's assumptions about community behavior beyond the administration, suggesting to the public that single black mothers raising illegitimate children not only explained poverty in urban neighborhoods but also caused the riots. The *Journal* warned of the young people it perceived to be leading violent outbreaks: "A growing army of such youth is being bred in the Negro sections of cities across the country by broken homes, illegitimacy and other social ills that have grown steadily worse in recent decades." The *Journal* inferred that growing up in the slums "warped the minds" of black youth and that the reversal of this trend would be a "discouragingly long-term struggle." Civil rights laws themselves "may temporarily—though surely unintentionally— make the situation worse," by cultivating a new, unfounded sense of freedom that encouraged criminality.[19] Increasingly, this type of analysis created a political environment that influenced federal policymakers' choice to mitigate the effects of crime through new police department programs even as some defended and sought to expand the War on Poverty. The alternative policy path, which involved attacking crime's root cause through the employment and guaranteed income programs Moynihan himself had suggested, never received serious consideration within the halls of the White House or on Capitol Hill during the Johnson administration.

In the wake of Watts, federal policymakers did acknowledge unemployment and subpar urban school systems as factors contributing to what they had labeled a national crime problem. But they believed that pathology was the root cause of urban crime in general and new forms of violence—namely, urban civil disorder—that emerged in the mid-1960s. Less than a week after the violence in South Central subsided, Johnson sent Deputy Attorney General Ramsey Clark, Director of Community Action Programs Jack Conway, and Assistant Secretary of Commerce Andrew Brimmer—one of the administration's top black representatives—to Los Angeles in order to develop "the best programs known to wipe out the causes of such violent outbursts." These three officials recommended more jobs, the implementation of community action programs with strong participation and oversight from residents, and a full-fledged Head Start program. According to the task force, however, "The most that can be done is to help the disadvantaged help himself." Heeding the group's recommendation, Johnson approved more than forty-five "self-help programs" in South Central at a cost of $29 million, including neighborhood centers that offered classes on black culture and heritage, adult education classes, and youth-based recreational programs. At the same time, federal policymakers established police training measures and provided local law enforcement advanced military equipment as riot control programs. Together, these social welfare and punitive initiatives would address, as the task force reported, the "calamitous conditions existing in our urban slums peopled primarily by Negroes," in Watts and other black neighborhoods.[20]

As the administration responded to collective violence, it shifted discussions from discrimination, unemployment, and housing to "social disorganization and dependency." Although Johnson's task force acknowledged the socioeconomic conditions that precipitated the riot, it ultimately pointed to "demographic characteristics" as the chief cause, emphasizing divorce rates, single-parent households, illegitimacy, and delinquency in its analysis. The task force noted that contact between police and residents is a "continuing feature of the environment" in Watts, but this was rationalized as a product of high rates of reported crime in the area. The solution was not to examine the nature of police contact and law enforcement methods, but to provide residents themselves with "opportunities for conforming behavior."[21] For the Johnson administration, the Watts riot made finding a solution to the pathological problems that community action programs sought to combat even more urgent. "Self-help" became the War on Poverty's guiding principle.

Moynihan's conclusions about the role of single-parent households in fostering crime and deviance influenced a shift in the overall aims of the War on Poverty following the collective violence in South Central. Shortly after the outbreak, in September 1965, a project in Charleston, South Carolina, that sought to "help delinquent boys from fatherless homes by providing a socially acceptable adult male with whom these youth can identify" was implemented with $100,000 in federal funds. Community action staff and social workers recruited and trained "stable neighborhood men," or residents with jobs and without criminal records, to act as father figures and to spend time with the youth in small groups, offering them vocational training, counseling, and cultural experiences that would "increase the boys' active participation in community life."[22] These and other mentorship programs accompanied existing antidelinquency efforts supported by the Office of Economic

Opportunity (OEO), such as the experimental program administered by the Kentucky Child Welfare Research Foundation in Louisville that targeted "hard-core" male offenders between the ages of thirteen and fifteen. Seeking to "establish a conventional culture with norms and values that will lead the boys to conventional behavior," the program offered weekly parental group counseling and "aggressive intensive family case-work," as well as remedial assistance and group activities with $99,551 in federal funds.[23] The Johnson administration hoped these sorts of opportunity programs, like similar programs created by President Kennedy's Committee on Juvenile Delinquency, would break the "cycle of poverty" in black families and effectively prevent future unrest in the process.

Social welfare and antipoverty agencies increasingly referred to cultural deficiencies in low-income black communities, rather than employment figures or other economic indicators, in order to generate support for the administration's self-help programs. For example, George Esser, a North Carolina antipoverty official, told the Annual Meeting of the American Library Association in December 1965 that libraries should begin to use techniques that would "help the underprivileged help themselves." He encouraged the association members to partner with community action agencies and "[modify] traditional library operations to meet the needs and capacities of underprivileged people by fostering a better understanding of cultural deprivation on the part of the library's most prosperous patrons."[24] Initially a staunch advocate for "maximum feasible participation," Esser now advocated not for empowering residents to directly shape antipoverty programs, but instead for groups of professionals—whether from the community or not—to set the course of action and lead "culturally deprived" Americans toward conventional behavior.

As support for community participation waned in the months following the Watts uprising, the Johnson administration largely conceded control of community action programs to local officials. In the spring and summer of 1965, the OEO had moved to secure for low-income Americans at least one-third representation on local poverty boards. But almost immediately, the Bureau of the Budget pressured the OEO to stop involving low-income residents in the policy-making decision process. Community action was "organizing the poor politically," as Director Charles Schultze wrote to Johnson in September, and national policymakers were supporting activities of Mobilization for Youth, the Syracuse Development Corporation, and other "radical" groups. In the months following Watts, the federal government began to withdraw further its funding to community-based and grassroots agencies. The OEO issued new regulations restricting independent financing of community action programs and moved its own focus toward comprehensive planning and programs such as Job Corps and Head Start that had been designed at the national level. By December, new rules required every organization that received community action funds to obtain final approval from municipal authorities in order to receive federal grants, and Congress slashed the discretionary portion of the community action budget in its 1966 allocation, further severing the ties between the OEO and local organizations.[25]

Urban civil disorder moved liberal advocates away from the idea of "maximum feasible participation" during the second half of the 1960s. Meanwhile, although Johnson could not have anticipated the extent of violence and destruction in South Central when he first called for the War on Crime in March 1965, the riot reinforced the new importance of crime prevention on the domestic policy agenda. Images of black Americans throwing rocks, beating white civilians, and setting fire to property bolstered popular perceptions that crime was at an all-time high in the United States, although in reality violent crime was lower than in the interwar period.[26] Believing that urban civil disorder in South Central manifested the most violent effects of black familial pathology, the federal government began to retreat from its support of grassroots community action programs to fight the War on Poverty even as it initiated new law enforcement programs to fight the War on Crime.

PLANNING THE CRIME WAR

Roughly a month after the Watts uprising, on September 22, 1965, Johnson signed into law the Law Enforcement Assistance Act, marking the official start of the War on Crime. The act made its way through

Congress without controversy or prolonged debate—much like the Economic Opportunity Act did the summer before. The House authorized the legislation by a 326–0 roll call vote on August 2, before the Watts uprising, and the Senate approved it on September 8 without opposition. The appropriations were relatively modest compared to the burgeoning social welfare apparatus, and just as no congressmen wanted to be seen as enemies of the poor, none wanted to appear opposed to the restoration of "law and order." Undoubtedly, this was a strong vote of confidence for the president's War on Crime. Many policymakers and law enforcement officials shared the view of William Johnson, chairman of the Michigan Association of Chiefs of Police, who believed the legislation was necessary to "arouse a national concern for a situation which, unless checked, will develop into internal disorder and decay, and ultimately anarchy itself." The administration remained supportive of the housing, employment, education, and social welfare programs of the War on Poverty, but "because the anchor of society must be an abiding respect for law and order," as Johnson said in his remarks on signing the act, the crime issue occupied an increasing amount of the administration's attention during the final years of his presidency. Launched as a complement to the War on Poverty and under the umbrella of the Great Society, Johnson's framing of the crime control issue linked law enforcement measures to social programs already in operation in black urban areas. The president told state law enforcement planners in 1966: "If we wish to rid this country of crime, if we wish to stop hacking at its branches only, we must cut its roots and drain its swampy breeding ground, the slum." As the foremost national priority after 1965, when it came to Johnson's crime war, "Nothing short of total victory will be acceptable."[27]

Establishing a Crime Commission on July 23, 1965—officially, the National Commission on Law Enforcement and Administration of Justice—was Johnson's first move in the crime war. Johnson expected the nineteen-member commission to conduct the most comprehensive investigation of crime ever undertaken, surpassing that of President Herbert Hoover's 1929 Wickersham Commission, a more modest endeavor than its successor whose recommendations largely focused on ways to enforce Prohibition and to improve the soon-to-be-repealed Eighteenth

Amendment. Chaired by Attorney General Nicholas Katzenbach, the new Crime Commission was charged with evaluating projects administered by the recently formed Office of Law Enforcement Assistance (OLEA) and designing a rational, well-researched national law enforcement program that would be amenable to Congress. Congress initially granted Katzenbach and his research team $1.1 million, but by the time the commission finished its work, the total cost of its research endeavors—250 law enforcement and academic experts were consulted— nearly doubled this initial allocation. The Department of Justice covered this surplus by transferring funds from the OLEA to the commission.[28]

The Crime Commission essentially functioned as the research arm of the OLEA, also directed by Katzenbach. It evaluated crime control demonstration projects, assessed census data, and conducted cutting-edge research on the problem of crime and its root causes. Unlike Hoover's marginal role within the Wickersham Commission and other previous associations between presidents and their task forces, the relationship that Johnson maintained with Katzenbach and his team was an intimate one as the commission worked to develop a blueprint for a national law enforcement program. Among the many Crime Commission recommendations that continue to shape Americans' interactions with law enforcement, the national emergency phone number the commission conceived became the basis for the 911 system.

Johnson carefully chose commission members to avoid controversy or the appearance of partisanship. As Max Freedman of the *Los Angeles Times* wrote, "The committee is characterized less by experience and knowledge than by the blandness that makes for acceptability to all interested parties. The typical member is the safest of all creatures, a former or retiring official." The most notable and active members included Johnson's friend (and later Watergate Special Prosecutor) Leon Jaworski, lawyer and future Supreme Court Justice Lewis Powell, Judge Charles D. Breitel of the New York Court of Appeals, and federal district court judges James Benton Parsons of Chicago and Luther Youngdahl of Washington, DC. From the law enforcement community came California attorney general Thomas C. Lynch and San Francisco police chief Thomas J. Cahill (Los Angeles mayor Sam Yorty wrote to Johnson in outrage that he overlooked William Parker, who commanded the police force during the Watts riot). Noted legal scholar Herbert Wechsler of the American Law Institute was the commission's corrections expert. These penal and juridical representatives were joined by *Los Angeles Times* publisher Otis Chandler; Julia Davis Stuart, the president of the League of Women Voters; and Yale president Kingman Brewer. The executive director of the National Urban League, Whitney Young, was the commission's only member of color.[29]

Top administrators within the Department of Justice dominated the commission and steered many of its policy suggestions. Katzenbach chose Harvard Law School's James Vorenberg to serve as executive director. Vorenberg had previously worked as a part-time director at the department's Office of Criminal Justice, where he drafted a code of police procedures for the American Law Institute with a grant from the Ford Foundation. That code included a highly controversial "stop-and-frisk" law that Vorenberg continued to advocate as the commission director, writing to White House officials in 1966 that the preemptive patrol practice "probably would not reduce crime since police everywhere stop and frisk now, but it would be welcomed by police and would have the advantage of regulating present practices." Vorenberg also supported provisions that allowed police to question suspects without a lawyer present in certain circumstances and advocated a broader definition of the "reasonable cause" required for arrest so that officers could apprehend suspects with greater ease.[30]

Vorenberg hired his colleague at the Office of Criminal Justice, Henry S. Ruth Jr., to work directly under him. Both men would figure prominently in the development of American law enforcement into the 1970s in both national and private institutions: Ruth went on to serve as the director of the National Institute of Justice during the Nixon administration before joining Vorenberg as attorney in the Watergate Special Prosecutor's Office. In addition, the commission's associate director, Lloyd Ohlin, was already well known for his "opportunity theory," which had inspired community action programs during the Kennedy administration and influenced the design of the War on Poverty. Long after the commission finished its task, across presidential administrations, as law enforcement measures displaced social welfare initiatives, a core group of figures who had come together on the Crime Commission continued to shape the strategies that federal policymakers and law enforcement institutions had adopted as the War on Crime unfolded.

By bringing together experts from the law enforcement, academic, civil rights, and corporate worlds who shared moderate political orientations and were deeply committed to preserving order, Johnson anticipated his Crime Commission would produce a balanced national law enforcement bill to place on the agenda for the upcoming congressional session. In early September, one week after the Law Enforcement Assistance Act of 1965 passed in both chambers of Congress, the staff and members of the Crime Commission held their first series of meetings. As members enjoyed a catered lunch at the White House, Johnson promised to make every effort to get the commission's highly anticipated plan through Congress. "When you find the answers I will try to see that corrective action is taken," he vowed, encouraging members to "be daring and creative and revolutionary in your recommendations." Johnson went on to make dramatic statements about the state of crime in the United States ("Crime is a menace on our street. It is a corrupter of youth") to underscore the significance of the commission's historic role.[31]

Following Johnson's welcoming remarks, FBI director J. Edgar Hoover opened the meeting by turning members' attention to the crux of the crime problem as he saw it: violence and pathology in black urban communities. Earlier that morning, a report reached Hoover's desk detailing a recent meeting between bureau agents, federal criminal justice officials, and, as Hoover described them, "leaders of the colored gangs that have been termed delinquent, unprivileged, and so forth." Hoover had believed many black youth were "on the brink of rioting" in Chicago's South Side, which would foment riots "possibly similar to those riots which occurred in Los Angeles" several weeks earlier. Bringing the leaders up to FBI headquarters was a ploy to prevent unrest in the waning weeks of summer, but it also provided local agents an opportunity to "try to find out exactly what [the leaders'] problem was and why they were in gangs." The field agents reported to Hoover that the lack of parental supervision, coupled with excessive alcohol consumption at young ages, drove black men to violence and crime. "Young boys at seven, eight, nine, and ten years of age start to drink. So, therefore, the example is set," Hoover concluded. "Many of them are from broken homes." First and foremost, the FBI director encouraged the Crime Commission to "dig into" the behavioral problem at hand.[32] Reinforcing the conclusions Daniel Patrick Moynihan had reached, Hoover directed the Crime Commission to focus its energies on the pathological behavior that he believed was concentrated in black urban areas.

The commission began its fieldwork in the fall of 1965. During their eighteen-month investigation, members focused their energies on crime control needs in African American neighborhoods that seemed vulnerable to disorder. They actively observed more than 200 police chiefs and consulted with more than 2,200 law enforcement agencies to "learn where and when certain kinds of crime are committed, and which people are most likely to become victims" in urban areas. In cities like Chicago, New York, Philadelphia, Washington, and Boston, the commission members took an ethnographic approach, riding in patrol vehicles with officers on the high crime beat.[33]

Although the commission was primarily interested in law enforcement problems in black urban areas, it did not seek the views of residents themselves. Aside from a few amenable academics who provided input, the criminal justice and law enforcement community almost exclusively shaped the commission's perspective, an oversight that concerned some members of its staff. In a memo to Vorenberg, Assistant Director Bruce Terris pointed out, "The Commission's job is, in part, to confront the problem of crime committed by the poor, particularly the Negro poor, in our large cities. Yet, the Commission members have had, with a couple of exceptions, virtually no contact with the poor, especially the Negro poor, and little more than an intellectual interest in their plight." Terris suggested holding neighborhood hearings so that the testimony of black residents and their experiences with the justice system would be taken into account, but this effort never materialized. Rather than involve low-income urban residents in the development of crime control programs soon to be implemented in their neighborhoods, the commission instead turned to law enforcement authorities to evaluate the experimental projects financed by the OLEA, from tactical antiriot squads to street lighting initiatives. Members were most interested in the advice of these professionals regarding the best ways to improve urban patrol and surveillance methods, and they crafted what Katzenbach called a "battle plan against crime" that ended up perpetuating many of the existing flaws in American law enforcement programs.[34]

Extending the assumptions that had shaped the national understanding of delinquency and crime during the postwar period, the commission ultimately developed its crime control strategies with the same views about black Americans and community pathology that had steered urban social programs from the Kennedy era onward. The fact that segregated urban neighborhoods received a disproportionate amount of police attention led to an increased number of reported arrests and continued to skew the national crime rate accordingly. The resulting statistical inaccuracies posed a challenge to the Crime Commission. During one of the commission's final meetings in December 1966, members took issue with a description of the composite adult felon in Washington, DC, as a poorly educated, unmarried black male, without dependents, approximately thirty years old and a lifetime resident of his community. Judge Parsons warned of the dangers of this type of assessment, pointing out that because the population in DC was 61 percent black at the time, "if crime were equal among Negroes and whites in Washington, it would turn out that way," meaning that a prototype felon would be black in a black majority city. Still, the commission relied on these misleading portraits of "representative adult felons" to develop its strategies for the War on Crime. Moreover, the commission knew the statistics it used to write delinquency policy were highly flawed as a result of the concentrated deployment of police forces in low-income urban areas. Members recognized delinquency as a problem among white middle-class youth but offered few prescriptions for addressing it. As Vorenberg pointed out: "All of the data we have been able to find really bears on the delinquent in the slum area."[35] This result was in no small part due to the focus of Kennedy's antidelinquency programs and the federal government's research agenda on low-income black urban communities. Even though members were conscious of the shortcomings of the data, they went ahead with the flawed statistics they had to work with in order to deliver a blueprint for the War on Crime. The choice to target research studies on "slums" and to use it to argue for the escalation of patrol and surveillance in those "slums" was in line with the portrait of American crime the commission wanted to depict, a narrative that reinforced the Johnson administration's view that community behavior was the root cause of black poverty and, by extension, crime.

The sentiment among Johnson and other liberal policymakers was that the social conditions of the inner city furnished a breeding ground for crime, which demanded new law enforcement techniques and institutions to break the "tangle of pathology." At the commission's first meeting, Hoover had suggested that it make recommendations that would "face up to the problems of the declining role of the family . . . and what kinds of substitutes you have for parental discipline, parental responsibility." The commission's final report did just that, describing the "typical delinquent" as a boy "15 or 16 years old (younger than his counterpart of a few years ago), one of numerous children—perhaps representing several different fathers—who live with their mother in a home that the sociologists call female-centered. It may be broken; it may never have had a resident father; it may have a nominal male head who is often drunk or in jail or in and out of the house." Building from Moynihan and other social scientists who shared this general outlook, the Crime Commission attributed a "resentment of policemen and teachers" to growing up in a home with a single mother receiving government assistance. The commission also critiqued parents in black urban families as either too permissive or too stern. "Many inner city parents express at once a desire to keep track of children, and keep them out of trouble, and a resignation to their inability to do so," the commission charged.[36] Urban disorder and crime were symptoms of black pathology and familial disorganization, federal officials argued, and in order to contain these problems—which could not be remedied quickly—a punitive intervention that increased surveillance and patrol in segregated urban areas was a necessary complement to the existing self-help and development programs of the War on Poverty, both of which were part of a decisively long-term set of policies. In the meantime, punitive measures would control the symptoms of crime, and the Crime Commission would continue to assist the Johnson administration in drafting the major piece of legislation that would lead to a more permanent crime war.

THE RISE OF POLICE ACTION

After Watts, Johnson and other national officials thought that providing urban police departments with federal funds to increase their manpower, professionalize their force, and arm their officers with military-grade weapons would make an immediate impact on crime rates. "We are today fighting a war within our own boundaries," Johnson told a group of state-level criminal justice planners that formed in the wake of the Law Enforcement Assistance Act. "This nation can mount a major military effort on the other side of the globe. Yet it tolerates criminal activity, right here at home, that costs taxpayers far more than the Vietnam conflict."[37] The OLEA instituted by Johnson's landmark 1965 crime control legislation financed public and private programs that enhanced the surveillance of black urban Americans and, in the process, modernized American law enforcement with advanced weapons and technology. Alongside the Crime Commission's evaluation of these programs and exhaustive deliberations, these early crime war strategies set the course for the development of the national law enforcement program through the Carter administration.

The president liked to call local law enforcement officers the "frontline soldier[s]" in the War on Crime, and his administration believed urban police departments should receive the great majority of the initial three-year, $22 million allocation Congress gave to the OLEA. "It is the policeman on the corner who is our traditional symbol of personal security," Attorney General Katzenbach argued, and the Law Enforcement Assistance Act had enabled the federal government to "provide the leadership, the research, and the experimental assistance which can help preserve that symbol." J. Edgar Hoover had set the precedent for this federal role in local law enforcement beginning in 1961, when the FBI's National Academy in Washington opened its doors to state and local officers, providing them with equipment, training, and services. The Law Enforcement Assistance Act established a more integral role for Department of Justice officials in the realm of local law enforcement.[38] Concerned with the spectrum of crime control problems, not just training needs alone, the OLEA worked to rapidly provide federal law enforcement grants to local police departments.

The grant structure of the OLEA strongly resembled that of the OEO, yet direct federal funding of private criminal justice organizations attracted far fewer objections than did community action programs. As the OLEA sent the money to local officials directly, mayors welcomed the crime control assistance and raised few questions about the level of discretion OLEA director Katzenbach enjoyed, which paralleled the powers of OEO director Shriver. In fact, the National League of Cities praised the flexibility the Law Enforcement Assistance Act gave to the attorney general in fostering "innovative solutions" to the crime problem.[39] Where groundbreaking approaches to community empowerment were met with trepidation, radical new approaches to crime control were encouraged.

Perhaps in reaction to criticisms the OEO encountered, Katzenbach's OLEA relied on professional planners to develop crime control and prevention measures and excluded grassroots activists and social service professionals from leadership roles in these efforts. Katzenbach told the Senate Subcommittee on the Judiciary during its hearings on the Law Enforcement Assistance Act: "I would like really to deal with the professionals on this," and the earliest grants the attorney general awarded closed law enforcement discussions to the residents living in the communities where the OLEA supported new crime control programs.[40] Drawing on a model of business management, the OLEA encouraged the reorganization of local law enforcement institutions and professionalization of the field, funding projects through a channel staffed by people with training and expertise and consciously restricting community participation. Federal policymakers considered crime control a matter for law enforcement professionals only, ultimately rejecting planning proposals that would have instituted community review boards on a national scale or supporting efforts that would have made grassroots representatives and law enforcement officials equal partners in planning and creating police-community relations programs, which received scant funding compared to manpower training and equipment-based measures.

Katzenbach focused his agency on building up the weapon arsenal of local (and particularly urban) police departments by providing them with direct federal assistance. "Not only must we reinforce the public's respect for law and order," Katzenbach believed, "we must restore the public's confidence that law enforcement agencies have the means and equipment to meet crime head on." The OLEA worked actively with governors to organize long-range crime control and prevention committees at the state level. Even if Kaztenbach preferred to directly fund local and private agencies, the state-level planning ensured that the states would follow the federal government's lead in modernizing penal and juridical institutions and increasing patrol. State and local law enforcement officials strongly supported these new national measures, "an inspiration to all who have been waiting patiently for just this kind of federal leadership to bring about effective change," as the executive director of Philadelphia's Crime Commission, Ephraim Gomberg, proclaimed.[41] States received grants to institute planning committees, while municipal authorities suddenly added military-grade rifles, tanks, riot gear, walkie-talkies, helicopters, and bulletproof vests to their stockpile.

Katzenbach channeled 49 percent of the first federal law enforcement grants to private, nonprofit institutions: to universities to conduct research and law enforcement training programs; police organizations like the International Association of the Chiefs of Police and the California Peace Officers; think tanks like the Kellogg Corporation, the Vera Institute, and the National Institute for Crime and Delinquency; and local groups of community businessmen eager to contribute resources to the larger crime-fighting effort. These private groups often acted as consultants for local police departments, evaluating existing programs and training officers in police-community relations and the proper use of new, cutting-edge military technologies on the streets of American cities. In all, the OLEA funded a total of 359 separate projects under 426 grants and contracts that advanced what federal officials believed to be promising new directions for law enforcement.[42] The office also established an information clearinghouse to instruct major metropolitan areas in modern crime control techniques.

The OLEA invested heavily in technological innovation for weapons development, and the agency often turned to private groups for additional support in such efforts. The Institute of Defense Analyses received the largest single grant from the OLEA in fiscal year 1966. The half-million-dollar outlay funded a comprehensive study of the ways in which scientific advances in defense and military contexts could be utilized by the police "soldiers" in the War on Crime. The institute proposed the development of net guns, whereby police officers would fire off a net and trap a suspect, as one might catch a wild animal, as a means to prevent police from resorting to deadly force. Although net guns did not come into frequent use by local law enforcement until the 1980s, these and other earlier strategies were widely embraced during the wars on drugs and terror, and the OLEA warmly received other proposals that officials believed would reduce high rates of reported crime, and particularly in segregated urban neighborhoods where residents had rioted or appeared likely to riot from the perspective of national policymakers.[43]

In Los Angeles, Mayor Sam Yorty's ongoing resistance to community action and his blatant disregard for the Economic Opportunity Act did not prevent the sheriff's department from receiving the second-largest OLEA grant, which supported a helicopter plan for Los Angeles called Project Sky Knight. Previously used only for traffic control and rescue operations, helicopters and fixed-wing aircraft began to be deployed for crime control purposes during the Watts riot. This equipment had performed strongly in managing the unrest, confirming for federal and local law enforcement officials that air patrol offered a quick, technologically astute, and cost-effective solution to surveillance needs. Helicopters could enable law enforcement to "abate the crime problem by enhancing the patrol unit's opportunities for apprehension and repression, without a significant increase in police manpower." Seen as the most important crime deterrent vehicle available to law enforcement, helicopters enabled the LAPD to "see more, travel further, and respond with speed and directness heretofore impossible," the grant proposal boasted. With additional support from the Hughes Tool Company Aircraft Division, following the substantial grant from the OLEA, eight cities within Los Angeles County contracted with the sheriff's department to secure helicopters.[44]

Los Angeles quickly emerged as a pioneer of surveillance and patrol measures that would later be used in other major cities and would come to characterize American policing in the late twentieth century. Federal officials pointed to the early success of Project Sky Knight to demonstrate the benefits of federal-local law enforcement partnerships and to promote the crime war in general. For Los Angeles County sheriff Peter J. Pitchess and the Johnson administration, the project represented a "major step forward in gaining recognition and positive support for law enforcement," and the federal government funded similar hardware projects in fifty other cities in subsequent years.[45]

In addition to increasing the weapons that local police officers employed on the frontlines of the War on Crime, the OLEA helped police departments develop their surveillance capacities as another important element of their modernization process. American police were falling behind their counterparts in London, who carried portable communications devices and had the ability to monitor troublesome streets with hidden cameras, and the OLEA worked to upgrade antiquated crime control methods in urban areas. A demonstration project in St. Louis used computer technology to determine effective police deployment. Law enforcement personnel fed statistics into a machine to "show where and when particular types of crime are likely to occur and help police decide where patrols should be concentrated." The Philadelphia Police Department received a similar computerized crime prediction program to deploy the force based on *anticipated* crime, while Cleveland used OLEA grant funds to install a mobile surveillance unit with a closed-circuit television and video recording capability. In California, the private think tank RAND teamed up with the state government to develop ways in which systems analysis techniques—previously used for defense and national security purposes—could similarly be applied to local law enforcement.[46]

To give the nation's capital, in Johnson's words, "the best police force in the United States," a substantial federal hardware grant awarded to Washington, DC, combined elements of the crime control demonstration projects that were underway in cities such as Los Angeles, St. Louis, and Cleveland. The Washington police received $1.2 million from Congress to add more officers on the streets in black neighborhoods and equip them with modern weaponry, a communication system that brought multiple radio channels to both marked cars and the personal cars of law enforcement officials, and a computer network to consolidate record keeping. The substantial federal grant bought Washington police six-teen new station wagons, three patrol wagons, twenty-five motor scooters, thirty-four scout cars, walkie-talkie radios for patrolmen on foot, eighty new detectives, and 271 additional police officers. The scooters went to a special roving tactical squad implemented by the OLEA for neighborhood patrol. They enabled police to move to crime scenes quickly while maintaining a closer physical relationship to residents than wagon patrol. And at the end of July 1966, IBM held a three-day class in computer concepts for twenty-one senior law enforcement offi-cials in the Washington Police Department. "We're not going to tol-erate hoodlums who kill and rape and mug in this city," Johnson said of his effort to revitalize law enforcement in the district.[47]

A number of special police training and community relations pro-grams complemented the technological boon to local police in the na-tion's capital and elsewhere. Police officers who patrolled high crime areas in Washington, DC, participated in a course on "current social problems and the psychological factors involved in personal relations with people in the community" run by the International Association of Chiefs of Police with a $48,000 grant from the OLEA. The OLEA of-fered a three-week management seminar to fifty police chiefs at Har-vard Business School. Federal crime control assistance also promoted law enforcement curriculums in public schools. In Cincinnati, educa-tors developed law enforcement and criminal justice lesson plans for ju-nior high school students.[48]

Across the country, police departments took on a more central role in public schools and after-school programs with OLEA assistance. The Tucson Police Department received a $67,377 grant from the OLEA to support the School Resource Officer Program, whereby police patrolled six junior high campuses. After the Watts riot, uniformed police offi-cers in Los Angeles appeared in an average of fifteen schools daily to "dispel fear and unfamiliarity," according to the LAPD's Community Relations Program Report. The presence of police officers in inner-city schools functioned to "create a sense of concern for orderly behavior and a sense of responsibility for the maintenance of law and order." On the weekends and during the summer months, the LAPD provided grand outings for some 25,000 "youngsters predominantly from the city's lower socio-economic areas" to sporting, professional, and entertainment venues. Such youth programs "afford opportunities for police officers and young people to engage in non-punitive relationships while working and competing in sports, and numerous other positive educational character building activities," the program report stated. The Los Angeles Housing Authority also paid off-duty LAPD officers to organize and supervise sports leagues and field trips to "reach youth within the housing projects where concentrated populations present inordinate living complications." Similarly, during the summer of 1966 in New York City, the Police Athletic League instituted a "Playstreet Program" with additional support from the National Recreation and Park Association and the sports equipment manufacturer AMF. The program offered bowling, golf, punching bags, tetherball, dome climbers, and horseshoes to low-income urban youth.[49] These examples begin to demonstrate that over time, the health, housing, education, and training programs of the War on Poverty gave way to recreational activities under the auspices of the War on Crime. Instead of seeking to provide these services in their own right, federal policymakers saw recreational programs as a means to improve police-community relations.

From the perspective of policymakers and experts who advocated for a national law enforcement program in the Johnson administration, the crime war was off to a promising start. When Katzenbach was reappointed to the State Department in November 1966, Ramsey Clark, who served as Katzenbach's deputy attorney general and helped to draft the Law Enforcement Assistance Act, took charge of the OLEA. Clark had inherited a booming office: Congress amended the Law Enforcement Assistance Act of 1965 and extended its grant-making authority until 1967, dedicated $15 million to the OLEA for that year, and doubled its budget to $30 million for 1968. Although FBI figures did not indicate that the first year of federal law enforcement programs had reduced crime—the president himself called criminal statistics "incomplete and unreliable"—policymakers believed that pouring money into police departments would eventually restore law and order.[50] Convinced that poverty was the root cause of crime and that community behavior was the root cause of poverty, policymakers turned to crime control to manage the symptoms of Moynihan's "tangle of pathology" while they worked to resolve the socioeconomic problems facing low-income Americans with social welfare programs.

As the new federal law enforcement demonstration programs hit the ground and the Crime Commission worked with national officials to develop the groundwork for the War on Crime, the OEO and other Great Society programs dwindled during the remainder of the Johnson administration. Municipal officials had succeeded in pushing the federal government toward a more limited definition of "maximum feasible participation," and as uprisings in Newark and Detroit in 1967 surpassed the Watts unrest in the scope of their destruction and violence, crime control became the foremost urban issue. The trajectory of funding for the President's Council on Juvenile Delinquency is indicative. During its first year of operation, in 1961, the council was funded entirely by the Department of Labor and the Department of Health, Education, and Welfare. In fiscal year 1963, the committee's budget more than doubled to a total of $231,555, and over the next two years, as the Department of Justice assumed responsibility for a greater proportion of juvenile delinquency program funds, the Department of Labor no longer contributed any money toward the delinquency prevention effort.[51] The committee disbanded in 1965 when the OLEA formed and assumed many of its previous responsibilities.

Community action, secondary education programs, and housing and urban development far surpassed crime control in terms of their proportion of federal expenditures during the Johnson administration, but assistance to law enforcement was more sustained and more consistent. While Congress vastly expanded the OLEA into the Law Enforcement Assistance Administration (LEAA) within three years of its creation, the Office of Economic Opportunity never evolved into a larger, more permanent agency. The LEAA's allocation grew thirteen-fold during the Nixon administration, from $63 million in fiscal year 1969 to $871 million in 1974—the same year the OEO was terminated.[52] A federal employment drive to create jobs for black men never materialized, but the Johnson administration did, effectively, support a job creation program for police departments with nearly all-white forces. Despite the lip service the Nixon administration paid to black representation in police departments in the late 1960s and early 1970s, the federal government continued to provide law enforcement assistance to police departments found guilty of grave civil rights violations and discrimination charges. Alternative domestic policy options escaped federal policymakers, who decided to manage the criminal symptoms of poverty and inequality rather than fundamentally disrupt the racial and economic status quo.

[3]

THE PREEMPTIVE STRIKE

President Johnson devoted part of his January 10, 1967, State of the Union address to outlining his administration's latest plans for the War on Crime. No American president had ever discussed crime and law enforcement at length in the annual message, and none had so boldly committed himself to these issues as Johnson when he declared, "This nation must make an all-out effort to combat crime." The administration had taken the first steps in this effort by sending the Law Enforcement Assistance Act to Congress and appointing the Crime Commission to research the problem and to "carry that attack forward" for the following two fiscal years. With the Office of Law Enforcement Assistance (OLEA) set to expire, Johnson requested that Congress replace it with a new federal agency to fund broader, more advanced research and experimental programs. This institution would require state and local governments to develop "master plans" to modernize their respective police, court, and corrections operations. And it would introduce "the latest equipment and techniques" to local law enforcement "so they can become weapons in the war on crime." Although the Crime Commission's recommendations had not yet been made public, Chairman Nicholas Katzenbach had frequently reported its findings to the president. His updates made Johnson eager for the Crime Commission's final report, which the president expected to be "one of the major documents of our time." Based on the foundations provided by the OLEA's demonstration programs and the soon-to-be-public recommendations of the Crime Commission, Johnson announced to the nation in 1967 that he was "ready to move" after a two-year process of consolidation.[1]

The Watts uprising and its aftermath produced growing doubts about ambitious antipoverty programs while generating enthusiasm for anti-crime policies and aggressive law enforcement. As urban disorder only worsened in the era of Johnson's War on Crime, with Newark and Detroit's disturbances during the summer of 1967 leading to an unprecedented number of casualties and property damage, policymakers continued to militarize police forces without seriously examining the behavior of police, National Guardsmen, and federal troops during the incidents. Lacking adequate training, these authorities tended to respond to the rioters with excessive and often deadly force, actions that foreshadowed the consequences of bringing large numbers of mostly white law enforcement officials into black communities. Rather than develop alternative riot prevention and crime control strategies that sought to reform these abrasive policing practices within departments, Johnson and his advisors fixated on the growing numbers of radical black activists who they believed had incited and exacerbated the uprisings as the Black Power movement emerged on the national stage.

In the final year of Johnson's presidency, the administration developed a set of strategies that encouraged police forces to actively seek out potential criminals in low-income urban neighborhoods. To accomplish this task, the administration encouraged law enforcement authorities to initiate interactions with residents in targeted areas. Whereas in the rest of the country police most often came into contact with civilians in response to emergency calls or specific incidents, in low-income African American neighborhoods, law enforcement authorities would become a ubiquitous part of the social and political landscape as a measure to prevent both rioting and crime. From the Kennedy administration's "total attack" on delinquency onward, antipoverty programs staffed by social workers had been developed as a means to control crime. Now police officers were expected to take a more active role in the fight against poverty. Based largely on the findings of the Crime Commission, neighborhood police stations were installed inside public housing projects in the very spaces vacated by community action programs. Social welfare measures that provided education and training opportunities to poor people were increasingly replaced with police department programs that provided entertainment and recreation.

When federal policymakers and local police departments implemented this preemptive crime control strategy, they accelerated the trend, already in progress, toward giving law enforcement and criminal justice officials new degrees of power over the planning and administration of social welfare provisions. The federal government started to withdraw its financing of grassroots organizations following the Watts riot in August 1965, and during Johnson's last years in office, it consolidated War on Poverty programs in new community-based institutions that made possible the rapid entry of police and law enforcement functions in urban social welfare programs.

The process of combining the programs of the War on Poverty with the programs of the War on Crime began just as the Crime Commission finalized its legislative proposals, when Congress revised the Economic Opportunity Act in the fall of 1966 and redirected federal antipoverty funding from community action programs to government-run social service institutions. The 1964 Economic Opportunity Act had empowered local organizations to develop antipoverty measures to suit their immediate needs. But in the wake of the disorder in Watts, and the riots in forty other cities the following summer, federal policymakers sought to consolidate the various programs administered by grassroots organizations and local welfare agencies into formal, community-based service institutions. The 1966 amendments encouraged state and local governments to organize "all relevant programs of social development" under the umbrella of neighborhood centers in low-income areas. Local governments were to include any initiative that aimed to "have an appreciable impact in such communities and neighborhoods as arresting tendencies toward dependency, chronic unemployment, and rising community tension" within the programming of the service institution.[2] By 1967, the Department of Labor began to establish "Youth Opportunity Centers" in accordance with this new policy direction.

The centers targeted the "hard-core youth" who seemed disinterested in the equal opportunity and self-help programs of the War on Poverty and who troubled administration officials. Thus the agencies provided counseling, education, training, and job placement services in 129 low-income neighborhoods to "those who do not seek, but nevertheless need, assistance," in the words of Secretary of Labor Willard Wirtz.[3]

The consolidation of community action programs in the Opportunity Centers and other new, federally funded urban institutions facilitated the ongoing merger of antipoverty and anticrime measures. Soon, the provision of fundamental social services, particularly for black urban youth, became increasingly tied to crime control institutions in the form of Youth Service Bureaus. The cornerstone of the Johnson administration's strategy for the War on Crime, the bureaus channeled youth who had not committed any crime at all but were seen as susceptible to delinquency into community-based crime control agencies staffed by social workers, municipal employees, and local law enforcement officers. Although these institutions remained outside the formal criminal justice and penal systems, they normalized the presence of law enforcement authorities and crime control technologies in the everyday lives of young Americans living in segregated poverty. The bureaus and similar hybrid agencies were meant to prevent crime by identifying youth whom policymakers labeled as "in danger of becoming delinquent"—not because they were poor but because they were seen as potentially criminal.[4] Preemptive contact between police and residents became routine. Instead of community action workers, police officers emerged as the government's chief representatives in low-income black urban communities.

Policymakers believed that cultural pathology explained the high rates of reported crime in African American neighborhoods, and as a result of these racist assumptions, positioned crime control as the primary social service provided to segregated communities suffering from high rates of poverty and unemployment. By shifting power within domestic urban programs from social workers to law enforcement authorities, federal policymakers introduced far more punitive forms of social control in neighborhoods that had experienced unrest or that seemed vulnerable to rebellion.

THE CHALLENGES OF CRIME IN A FREE SOCIETY

Four days after Johnson's State of the Union address, Chairman Nicholas Katzenbach submitted the Crime Commission's final report, called *The Challenge of Crime in a Free Society*. After fifteen months of investigation, the release of the report in early 1967 advanced the punitive turn underway since 1965. The commission's research made clear that the current criminal justice apparatus "was not designed to eliminate the conditions in which most crime breeds. It needs help." In 340 pages, the report offered the legislative proposals that laid the groundwork for a revolution in American law enforcement, linking crime control and antipoverty policies in new and innovative ways. The commission made some 200 recommendations, spanning the areas of police, courts, corrections, juvenile delinquency, organized crime, and narcotics and drug abuse.

Johnson's State of the Union address had provided a preview of the commission's most important proposals. First, they recommended the creation of criminal justice planning agencies at the state and local levels, as well as a major new federal agency that would enable the attorney general and the Department of Justice to coordinate the law enforcement bureaucracy and guide the War on Crime at all levels of government. Second, the commission encouraged the federal government to invest in the professionalization and modernization of police departments, both by improving the weaponry available to law enforcement and by standardizing crime reporting methods. Finally, the commission urged federal policymakers to support community-based crime control institutions staffed by social workers, municipal employees, and law enforcement officers that provided social welfare services and that operated outside of the formal criminal justice system, such as Youth Service Bureaus. The Crime Commission hoped these policies, taken together, would "assur[e] all Americans a stake in the benefits and responsibilities of American life," a goal that required "strengthening law enforcement and reducing criminal opportunities" above all else.[5]

The Crime Commission's report also defended the Great Society's effort to address the structural factors that contributed to the nation's crime problem. "Warring on poverty, inadequate housing, and unemployment is warring on crime," members wrote. "A civil rights law is a law against crime. . . . More broadly and more importantly every effort to improve life in America's 'inner cities' is an effort against crime."⁶ Accordingly, the commission trumpeted many of the ongoing War on Poverty initiatives, including job training, housing, and early childhood education programs. It also suggested that the federal policymakers actively work to reduce racial segregation, provide a guaranteed income, and reform welfare regulations to encourage both parents to remain in low-income households.

Yet despite the Crime Commission's discussion of the socioeconomic problems at the root of crime—which led *Life* magazine to declare, "The report can only be called liberal, even adventuresome"—conservative pressure from within its own membership and larger policy circles produced a set of recommendations that did not include remedies for those problems. Instead, the commission focused on the "institutional vacuum" they perceived in segregated urban areas. Members condemned black urban families, schools, churches, and other social institutions for failing to "give young people the motivation to live moral lives," concluding: "The social institutions generally relied on to guide and control people in their individual and mutual existence simply are not operating effectively in the inner city." Although the commission acknowledged that "young people today are sorely discontented in the suburbs and on the campuses as well as in the slums," it asserted "there is no doubt that they more often express this discontent criminally" in black urban neighborhoods. Drawing from the research of Daniel Patrick Moynihan and other social scientists, commission members believed that this criminality arose from a generation of young people "who have not received strong and loving parental guidance . . . [who] tend to be unmotivated people, and therefore people with whom the community is most unprepared to cope." Even as members mentioned racial discrimination and inequality as factors that contributed to the crime problem, the commission was not immune to the widely held notions about race and criminality that undergirded both liberal and conservative responses to the plight of black urban Americans. This set of racist assumptions influenced the "battle plan" Crime Commission members went on to develop for the administration, which were limited in the socioeconomic realm and which focused explicitly on ways to improve federal, state, and local governments' surveillance of and patrol capacity in black urban communities.[7]

Based on its evaluation of the demonstration projects funded by the Office of Law Enforcement Assistance involving additional marked and unmarked patrol vehicles, alarm boxes, detection equipment, and street lighting in low-income urban areas, the Crime Commission adopted the popular law enforcement theory that "the widest patrol coverage is the most deterrent coverage." "Increasing patrol force in an area, through use of special tactical patrols," the commission concluded, "causes a decline in crimes directed at citizens walking the streets in the heavily patrolled area."[8] Crime could be contained, then, by saturating a targeted neighborhood with police officers and surveillance equipment. Despite the effects of these practices—in today's terms, "overpolicing"—the Crime Commission asserted that only increased patrol in segregated urban communities could prevent crime. According to this theory, preemptive contact initiated by police instead of residents themselves could effectively control crime in "problem areas."

When the Crime Commission considered the potential impact of these urban patrol practices and the issue of police-community tensions, members emphasized the perspectives and even the feelings of the police, rather than those of residents. Placing blame on black urban Americans for neighborhood disorder, the commission argued: "Ghetto residents will not obtain the police protection they badly want and need until policemen feel their presence is welcome and that their problems are understood." The negative attitudes black Americans seemed to exhibit toward police actually "stimulate crime," the commission argued, as officers could not effectively perform their function in an "angry neighborhood." Thus improving police-community relations required changing black Americans' perception of racism within local police departments, not altering police behavior. To this end, the Crime Commission suggested that special programs emphasizing the "humanism" and "friendliness" of officers could assure residents that police were committed to reducing crime and restoring safety.[9] The commission believed these types of programs were particularly necessary in order to soften the impact of the increased patrols it recommended in black urban neighborhoods.

In order to prevent future crime, the Crime Commission advocated for a long-range federal plan that would reconstruct urban social institutions by integrating law enforcement into existing government agencies. To restore law and order at a moment of "increasing crime, increasing social unrest, and increasing public sensitivity to both," the commission defined a role for police in all public programs.[10] Specifically, members suggested creating planning boards that drew on both police and the community so that officers would "formally participate in community planning in all cities," by placing law enforcement officials in positions of leadership within housing, parks, welfare, and health departments.

The Johnson administration embraced these recommendations and proceeded to restructure War on Poverty programs accordingly. By August 1966, Katzenbach, Crime Commission Director James Vorenberg, and Deputy Attorney General Ramsey Clark argued that "since the social causes of crime cannot be removed very quickly, it is necessary to proceed with a program of criminal justice," and suggested to Johnson's top domestic policy advisor Joseph A. Califano and other White House staff that the administration establish a "middle ground" between community action, manpower development, and other social programs and improvements in law enforcement and courts.[11] With the Crime Commission's suggestions in mind, the administration implemented new, community-based centers—often directed by law enforcement officials—to operate as an umbrella for Great Society programs and to provide a range of services for black urban youth.

The blueprint for a national crime control program the commission described in *The Challenge of Crime in a Free Society*—backing up the relatively abstract "War on Crime" Johnson had endorsed with impressive research and specific, detailed proposals in its final report—helped the administration build a critical mass of support among political and economic elites for a national punitive intervention that would fully merge with the War on Poverty. Not surprisingly, Johnson and White House officials characterized the report as a "major work of scholarship" and "an outstanding piece of work." Officials also circulated early drafts to mainstream civil rights leaders, intellectuals, and policymakers, who for the most part endorsed the plan. Local Urban League directors like

Edwin Berry, for instance, appreciated the recommendations as one more example of welcome attention to the federal government's larger focus on social conditions in low-income African American neighborhoods. For Berry, the Crime Commission's "very important recommendations" were "long overdue." The conservative columnist William F. Buckley Jr. viewed some of the conclusions the Crime Commission reached as left-leaning, but he ultimately praised it in the *Los Angeles Times*. "Said to be distinctively liberal, the commission strikes me as having done excellent work by no means uncongenial to conservatives," Buckley wrote.[12]

The proposals presented in *The Challenge of Crime in a Free Society* became the basis of the Safe Streets and Crime Control Act of 1967, the legislation designed to realize the initiatives Johnson described in his State of the Union address. Originally titled the "Safe Streets and Homes Act" by White House officials, an early draft of the legislation declared that it was "not a substitute for longer range programs . . . to attack the root causes of crime. It will, however, strengthen our first line of defense—our city police forces and the design of the city's landscape. It recognizes as well that there must be a tie-in between police departments and other activities of the whole metropolitan area." As suggested by the Crime Commission, the Safe Streets and Crime Control Act offered a "middle ground" between the Great Society's social welfare and punitive dimensions. As far as officials in the Johnson administration were concerned, the Safe Streets Act would be the "primary method for implementing the National Crime Commission Report," as Attorney General Ramsey Clark wrote in a telegram to the president.[13]

Meanwhile, the Johnson administration also worked to promote the Crime Commission's recommendations outside the legislative realm. The commission sponsored a series of conferences at which judges, sociologists, and specialists were introduced to cutting-edge law enforcement techniques. One meeting brought scientists and businessmen together to consider ways to improve crime control technologies, another meeting focused on legal manpower needs, and a final gathering of law enforcement personnel brought together state-level Crime Commissions. The White House also expected cabinet members to familiarize themselves with *The Challenge of Crime in a Free Society* and to modify their departments' programming accordingly. One of the Crime Commission's chief consultants, Arnold Sagalyn, was appointed public safety adviser to the secretary of Housing and Urban Development, charged with encouraging the design and provision of safety and security features in public schools, parks, and housing projects based on the commission's proposals. Four months after the Crime Commission delivered its report, in June 1967, the Department of Health, Education, and Welfare brought together 400 youth and social service representatives at a conference to discuss crime control programs for young Americans.[14]

Many of the executive agencies responsible for fighting the War on Poverty saw their work as an extension of the social reforms suggested by the Crime Commission. The Department of Health, Education, and Welfare already collaborated with the Office of Law Enforcement Assistance (OLEA) to provide training programs to police as well as to young offenders. Because the goals of juvenile delinquency programs were to "strengthen families, to upgrade education in the slums, to fashion model neighborhoods and decent housing for the poor," in the words of Secretary of Health, Education, and Welfare Wilbur Cohen, then the department was already working to prevent crime. And from the outset, the Office of Economic Opportunity focused its attention on "the poor and disadvantaged" who "often turned to crime."[15] Now these efforts would need to specifically incorporate police-community relations programs and antidelinquency measures into their programming as mandated by the Crime Commission. In practice, this meant that funding for equal opportunity programs was diverted to crime control concerns.

By enthusiastically blending social welfare and punitive programs within the Great Society, the Johnson administration drew together its two separate but related urban policies: the War on Poverty's effort to combat crime by remedying its root causes and the War on Crime's assault on the immediate manifestations of crime. Neither approach offered a structural solution to the employment, educational, and housing problems that policymakers were aware perpetuated historical inequality. "For decades the conditions that nourish crime have been gathering force," Johnson said. "As a result, every major city harbors an army of the alienated—people who acknowledge no stake in public order and no responsibility to others."[16] But despite policymakers' profound concern regarding this "army of the alienated," the strategies they developed in the final years of Johnson's presidency inadvertently exacerbated both poverty and crime in black urban neighborhoods, as the wave of unrest in the summer of 1967 marked another turning point, two years after Watts, in the development of liberal social programs.

"PROGRESS OF JUSTICE OR EQUALITY"

Incidents of urban civil disorder increased in frequency and scope following Johnson's call for a "War on Crime" and alongside the launch of the War on Poverty. During the summer of 1967, two events in particular indicated to policymakers and the public that the federal government's equal opportunity, job training, and community development measures had failed to stem the tide of unrest. As Congress considered the Safe Streets Act, Newark exploded for six days, from July 12 to July 17. Less than a week later, beginning on July 23, Detroit residents engaged in five days of collective violence after police raided a bar in the heart of the predominately black neighborhood of Paradise Valley. The riot— what many Detroiters still refer to as the "Great Rebellion"—halted automobile production in the city for three days and thereby disrupted the American economy to a far greater extent than any other incident of urban disorder in the 1960s. By the time the disturbance subsided on July 27, forty-three people had died—including thirty-two African American residents, one police officer, and two firefighters—and more than 7,000 residents had been arrested. Johnson's entire cabinet agreed during their first meeting after the unrest that this latest episode of collective urban violence was "the worst in our history."[17]

The duration and proximity of the Newark and Detroit uprisings coupled with a mounting student protest movement against the Vietnam War reinforced the Johnson administration's sense that the United States was under attack from within. As one White House official wrote of the disorder in Newark in a letter to the president, "It suddenly seemed as if the whole country had come unglued." After Detroit residents caused an estimated $100 million worth of damage during the first night of unrest—described by the Associated Press as a "Negro rampage of burning and pillaging"—Michigan Governor George Romney wrote a frantic telegram to Ramsey Clark, informing the attorney general that 4,000 National Guardsmen, 1,500 Detroit police officers, and 500 state troopers were "unable to contain this massive outbreak of violence, fire, theft, and general disregard for law and order." Hoping to suppress the rebellion before it evolved into "an organized state of in-surrection," Romney appealed for federal troops, and Johnson deployed 5,000 soldiers to assist the local police department and the National Guard. The presence of federal law enforcement authorities in Detroit made an already explosive situation worse, in much the same way as the addition of the National Guard to the streets of South Central during the Watts uprising. With a combined 17,000 police, Guardsmen, and troops on the scene, shooting at suspected snipers and arresting residents en masse, burnings and gunfire afflicted the city for three more days.[18]

As it had during the Watts riot, Johnson's public response to the dis-turbances in Detroit and Newark stressed the long-term potential of War on Poverty programs to address conditions in those cities while reiterating that "preserving civil peace is the first responsibility of government"—implicitly, a more important duty than ensuring eco-nomic opportunity and social welfare. On the second night of the Detroit uprising, Johnson addressed the nation. "The apostles of violence, with their ugly drumbeat of hatred, must know that they are heading for disaster," the president declared in his televised remarks. "Every man who wants progress of justice or equality must stand against them and their miserable virus of hate." Johnson concluded his message by attempting to distinguish the actions of the rioters from the direct-action protests of the mainstream civil rights movement and the reforms of his own Great Society: "There is no American right to loot stores, or to burn buildings, or to fire rifles from the rooftops," Johnson said. "That is crime."[19] The possibility that the uprisings were a violent expression of civil rights demands, rooted in similar concerns about unequal access and socioeconomic exclusion, escaped the president and his advisors. Linking race, violence, and crime in his rhetoric, Johnson implied that the rioters' actions with their demonstrated "hate" should be taken as an example of reverse racism, or black Americans' hatred of whites, that was nothing short of criminal.

At the first cabinet meeting after the July disturbances, on August 2, Ramsey Clark cautioned his fellow members about the urban law enforcement strategies the administration pursued both within the specific context of the unrest and more broadly. For Clark, the actions of residents and police in Newark and Detroit demonstrated that a haphazard, undisciplined, and aggressive police response only spawned an ever-more-violent reaction. Molotov cocktails were the weapons of choice during the Watts riot in 1965 and the disorders of 1966. By the summer of 1967, however, "sniping was a new and deadly development." Clark explained that police and other state forces tended to respond to sniper fire by randomly firing their own guns, which led to hundreds of civilian casualties and created "the danger of a riot degenerating into a guerrilla war." A suspected sniper in Detroit was shot thirty-eight times, Clark told the cabinet. He warned them that this type of aggressive policing could backfire by "starting guerrilla war in the streets," as evidenced by the climate of sniper fire in Newark and Detroit.[20]

Although charges of sniping were inflated (White House representative Cyrus Vance counted fifty-three reports of sniping in Detroit, yet only two could be confirmed), the constant blasts from rifles and machine guns from law enforcement authorities and residents alike gave police license to act without regard to basic legal principles or human rights. Acting alone or in small groups, the snipers killed very few people, targeting instead precinct stations, firehouses, and other symbols of police power. Residents fired at buildings instead of police and firefighters themselves. On the other hand, when local officers and National Guardsmen in Newark weren't mistakenly engaged in gun battles with one another, they took it upon themselves to randomly shoot at civilians. Most of the police, National Guardsmen, and federal troops responsible for suppressing the unrest had little previous contact with African Americans and lacked adequate community-relations or riot prevention training. They often came into the volatile situations fearing for their own lives and blatantly disregarding black ones. "If we see anyone move," a National Guardsmen said in Detroit, "we shoot and ask questions later." In practice, this strategy produced devastating outcomes. "We heard these shots and figured they was firin' in the air to stop the looters," the brother of twenty-two-year-old Robert Lee Martin explained to a reporter. "They wasn't firing over our heads." Martin was killed by a bullet to his forehead. Newark police always claimed they were returning sniper fire from rooftops or apartment windows, but when officers spotted residents gathered together, they immediately began firing. Sniping, in other words, created an environment that made possible a new threshold of brutality.[21]

In the popular and political imagination, the rioters were assumed to be violent criminals who victimized those law enforcement authorities acting in their own self-defense and in defense of the American social order. Yet black residents made up the vast majority of the rebellions' casualties. During the uprising in Newark, for example, a white police officer and a fireman lost their lives, but the remaining twenty-four victims were black residents. A group of National Guardsmen in Newark shot and killed twelve-year-old Michael Pugh as he took out the trash in front of his house after curfew. Michigan state police opened fire on an apartment after a resident lit a cigarette in the dark, killing four-year-old Tonia Blanding. When Newark police and National Guardsmen pursuing snipers killed fifty-four-year-old grandmother Hattie Gainer, an officer blithely explained to her daughter: "We made a mistake. We shot the wrong person." Gainer's death was rationalized as an unfortunate consequence of police work in a violent community, and in this and hundreds of similar cases during the uprisings of the 1960s alone, police rarely faced the consequences for the lives they took.[22]

Despite the evidence of police misconduct during the events in Newark and Detroit, the administration refused to take the reality of these abrasive policing methods seriously. At a 1966 Crime Commission meeting, Deputy Director of the FBI Cartha DeLoach argued that bureau investigations "proved overwhelmingly that matters of police brutalities, for the most part, have little merit," based on the 3 percent conviction rate of officers accused of such charges. The Crime Commission also downplayed police brutality, viewing any tension between community members and police as a result of citizen hostility. "Most policemen treat minority-group citizens in a nondiscriminatory manner," the commission reported. And among policymakers, law enforcement officials, and many public figures, the general consensus was that violent police behavior was a myth. "In the Negro community in Los Angeles they are convinced there is a brutality," *Los Angeles Times* publisher Otis Chandler told his fellow Crime Commission members, implying that black residents exaggerated the extent of the violence they experienced from law enforcement authorities.[23]

From the perspective of black residents who already faced exhaustive and often antagonistic patrol on a daily basis, police violence was a constant threat and a proximate cause of nearly every uprising during the 1960s. In a federal study of 500 black men arrested during the Detroit rebellion, discussed by the cabinet at their August 1967 meeting, nearly all of the participants answered "police brutality" in response to the question of "what caused the trouble" in Detroit. In Newark, growing animosity between white patrolmen and the city's black majority was the immediate cause of unrest in 1967, and that tension had been mounting for some time. "We ain't rioting agains' all you whites. We're riotin' agains' police brutality," twenty-four-year-old participant Billy Furr Jr. explained to a reporter. "When the police treat us like people, 'stead of treatin' us like animals, then the riots will stop." The next day, when police spotted Furr with a stolen six-pack in front of Mack Liquors, he dropped the beer and fled the scene. Police shot Furr in the back, the impact of the bullet spinning his body around so that a second fatal blow hit him in the face.[24]

By neglecting the brutal encounters that occurred between black residents and the officers who patrolled their neighborhoods, the administration could comfortably encourage the widespread implementation of the policing tactics that had been used to suppress rioting on an everyday basis. Indeed, the experience of fighting urban uprisings deeply shaped the strategies White House officials embraced as they developed the national law enforcement program.

Instead of discussing the police behavior that worried Clark, Johnson linked the riots to "poisonous propagandists" who "posed as spokesmen for the underprivileged and capitalized on the real grievances of suffering people" during the cabinet meeting. Although the president sensed that the riots were not entirely spontaneous events and that they were somehow political in nature, he refused to believe that the majority of residents had been inspired to rebel against their everyday social conditions. Rather, Johnson and his advisors concluded that outside influences, whether communists or black militants, had mobilized the community. The fact that Clark reported the Justice Department had "no hard evidence" that outside agitators were involved mattered little to the president. "I don't want to foreclose the conspiracy theory now," Johnson told the cabinet; "I have a very deep feeling there is more to that than we see at the moment." The potential links between the uprisings and black radicals were not lost on FBI director J. Edgar Hoover, either, who ordered the FBI to include "Black Nationalist Hate Groups" in the covert FBI unit charged with monitoring and disrupting domestic political organizations, known as the Counter-Intelligence Program, or COINTELPRO, less than a month after the Detroit rebellion. Understanding the riots, in part, as the work of "a group of men whose interests lay in provoking—in provoking—others to destruction," in Johnson's words, obscured the alternative possibility that they represented a mass response to the violent conditions that resulted from economic and social isolation.[25]

Convinced that the riot was an attack on existing American institutions rather than an appeal for inclusion within them (concerns that might be addressed by the state if it were more open to change), the cabinet discussed the ways in which the black political sphere seemed to be growing increasingly volatile. Johnson shared a letter he received from Harold Cruse, the editor of the black nationalist *Liberator* magazine and author of *The Crisis of the Negro Intellectual* published that fall. But most of the cabinet's conversation centered on the direction of the Student Nonviolent Coordinating Committee (SNCC) under the leadership of Stokely Carmichael, who was an increasing concern to White House officials and the Justice Department. Carmichael had popularized the phrase "Black Power" at a rally in the fall of 1966 and emerged as the spokesman for the movement thereafter. On July 25, 1967, in the middle of the Detroit rebellion, he had arrived in Cuba to meet with Fidel Castro. Clark read highlights from the speech Carmichael delivered at the First Latin American Solidarity Conference in Havana, interpreting Carmichael's remarks as a threat to the lives of senior government officials and the president. "In Newark we applied war tactics of the guerrillas," the *Washington Post* quoted Carmichael as saying. "We are preparing groups of urban guerrillas for our defense in the cities." ("Don't we have a remedy for these people?" asked Secretary of State Dean Rusk.)[26] Even though Johnson refused to credit the substance of the critiques of Cruse, Carmichael, and other prominent figures who advocated for community control, he was completely open to the idea that SNCC and other groups were actively preparing for guerrilla warfare.

The cabinet worried that black nationalists and revolutionaries were gaining ground and that the government's existing urban social programs had failed to address the community pathology they believed was behind the disorders, an "alienation" that seemed to be growing more receptive to the ideas of revolution. By linking urban uprisings to rising black militancy and demands for self-determination, Johnson and the cabinet could avoid fully coming to terms with the failure of the administration's urban policy to address the underlying causes of unrest and could focus instead on individual, "pathological" behavior and a kind of black politics that, from the perspective of federal officials, must be opposed.

The president was anxious that urban rebellion and the burgeoning Black Power movement would compromise the great potential of the War on Poverty. "We need to gather our forces to keep our [poverty] programs from being cut," Johnson told his cabinet during their August 2 meeting.[27] Yet even as the White House and its allies in Congress continued to defend the federal government's housing, education, and training programs, the unprecedented destruction and the paramilitary response of residents to police and other state officials in Newark and Detroit increased support for the War on Crime among previously ambivalent liberals. In the view of these liberals, the federal government's existing social welfare and punitive interventions had failed to achieve many of their stated objectives and may have even made militant appeals more attractive to young people living in segregated poverty. Across the political spectrum, federal officials and policymakers feared that unless something changed in the administration of urban social programs, militants would organize residents into full-scale rebellion.

The Johnson administration, seeing police departments as vulnerable in this volatile political climate and seeing urban police officers as combatants in war, made its first and foremost objectives to modernize local law enforcement and to upgrade the equipment of routine patrol officers. The administration presented its commitment to militarizing urban police forces as an extension of anti-riot efforts. "If we were to send our Armed Forces into combat ill-equipped, underpaid, undertrained, and underappreciated, it would be a national scandal," Johnson wrote to Senate Majority Leader Mike Mansfield in 1967. "Yet, we accept such conditions as a way of life for the brave city policeman in whose hands rest the lives and security of 200 million Americans." As the "major emphasis" of the national crime control program, the Safe Streets Act allocated 75 percent of its funding to police departments, rather than the courts, corrections, or an entirely new approach to urban law enforcement that might have entrusted residents themselves to keep their own neighborhoods safe, as advocated by increasing numbers of civil rights and Black Power figures.[28]

To facilitate the intensification of police patrol in "ghetto areas," the Johnson administration sought to give law enforcement authorities a new role in social welfare programs, which the Crime Commission had recommended as a means to relieve the tensions between low-income urban residents and officers. Yet even as police departments, the Crime Commission, and national policymakers paid lip service to improving police-community relations and sensitivity training programs, these measures largely translated to public relations efforts to improve the image of law enforcement. The chief duty of urban police forces, even as they increasingly contributed to social welfare programs, remained identifying criminals and removing them from the streets. Thus, as police departments emerged as a major social service provider in the segregated urban battlegrounds of the War on Crime, this federal strategy did not necessarily promote public safety. Instead, such measures brought residents into frequent contact with the punitive arm of the state, increasing the likelihood of their eventual incarceration.

In practice, community relations programs resulted in a further expansion of police presence in black neighborhoods as War on Poverty programs diminished in scope and ambition. With federal funding, police departments established "mini-stations" in storefronts and housing projects. In Washington, DC, for instance, the police department opened neighborhood stations inside the National Capital Authority Projects in the southeast side of the city beginning in late 1967. One center moved into what had previously been a health clinic operated by the DC Health Department with federal funding, providing services to residents in a first-floor suite of the housing project. Open eight hours a day, five days a week, the new recreational center gave youth access to a pool table, a record player, and a library filled with police pamphlets and medical literature left behind by the previous occupants. As Officer Isaac Fulwood explained, the police who supervised the youth in this informal setting acted as "referees, advisers, and father confessors to this community" in order to "prove we aren't the enemies." For DC Public Safety Director Patrick Murphy, the housing project force marked a "step toward communication" between residents and black youth, which would "reduce tension and diminish the possibility of disorder."[29]

As the 1960s waned, law enforcement would fill the void left behind by the Capital Authority Housing Project Health Clinic and many other promising War on Poverty programs that closed their doors while the Johnson administration and Congress continued to scale back the funding of autonomous grassroots organizations and community action programs. Conveniently located in storefronts or public housing projects and staffed by city antipoverty employees and police officers, the new neighborhood centers connected residents to local social service agencies, often with the assistance of law enforcement authorities. For instance, the police officers who participated in the Store-Front Community Relations Program in Fort Worth, Texas, were expected to "help people in the community to solve some of their problems." Residents could now turn to law enforcement authorities, rather than community action workers, if they had complaints about garbage pickup or their landlords, and police would advocate on their behalf. Meanwhile, the police officers involved in the program assisted illiterate residents in filling out government paperwork and obtaining drivers' permits. The more expansive Concentrated Employment Program of the Los Angeles Police Department (LAPD) worked with local community action agencies to provide counseling, job training, and remedial education classes in South Central. Law enforcement officials recruited enrollees to help the department "maintain liaison with hard to reach elements of the community and make personal appearances as speakers before community groups." The aim was not to encourage more resident participation within the LAPD, but to offer services to residents in exchange for their cooperation with law enforcement.[30] As police action eclipsed community action in offering the prevailing public services in Fort Worth, Los Angeles, and other designated urban areas, an entirely new approach to both urban law enforcement and social welfare quickly emerged.

THE "INSTITUTIONAL SUBSTITUTE" FOR PARENTS

The rebellions in the summer of 1967 confirmed a view that had been building among federal policymakers and the nation's top law enforcement officials: that the success of the crime war largely depended on the surveillance and control of low-income urban youth. Criminal justice officials and policymakers broadly defined delinquents as "a class of children who are incorrigible, ungovernable, or habitually truant" and who therefore appeared to be "in need of supervision." This group had been the focus of urban intervention since the Kennedy administration, but beginning with the Watts uprising, officials across the political spectrum took rioting as evidence that antipoverty programs had been misdirected and that existing efforts had failed to reach the most "disorderly" youth. "Looking at the riots," Secretary of Labor Willard Wirtz pointed out during the cabinet meeting shortly after the Detroit disturbance, "I worry that we might be reaching the wrong kids, not the hard core." In Wirtz's view, the disorder had nothing to do with unemployment, but rather with the unsuitability of this group for the jobs available. In fact, in response to assessments of disorder that pointed to high rates of black unemployment as a factor, Wirtz argued that it "oversimplifies the situation to say lack of jobs is the root of the trouble." "If anything," he said of the riot's causes, "it is the lack of training, not jobs. Many Negroes remain unskilled and unable to fill available jobs." The War on Poverty had been successful "with youngsters susceptible to reason and within reach of persuasion" but not with "the rioters deep in the ghettos." Wirtz concluded that this "hard-core" group, the most vulnerable and troubled young people who seemed quick to engage in collective violence, were "unprepared to participate in programs of opportunity." The conduct of "the so-called hard core, disadvantaged youth—the one whose behavior—in rioting and crime—poses the greatest concern to our society," needed to be confronted.[31] Rather than expanding the War on Poverty to fully tackle the areas of unemployment, failing public schools, and deteriorating living conditions, federal policymakers introduced punitive programs into youth-based social institutions, which they believed could have a more immediate impact on suppressing the perceived lawlessness in black urban communities.

The Crime Commission had focused on strategies that would reach this "hard-core" group of black urban youth. As it studied the juvenile courts, training schools, and detention centers funded by the Office of Law Enforcement Assistance for demonstration purposes, members came to the conclusion that, as the Missouri Democratic congressman James Symington put it, "most of the socializing institutions in our society have systematically rejected a hard core of 'troublemakers.'" Lacking sufficient resources and incentives, neighborhood centers and many of the special education and training programs of the War on Poverty tended to "treat delinquency as someone else's problem."[32] Johnson officials and the Crime Commission sought to implement youth-based law enforcement programs as a means to remedy the exclusion of the most concerning young people from social welfare opportunities and fundamental services.

Symington, the executive director of the Crime Commission's Subcommittee on Juvenile Delinquency and the former executive director of the President's Committee on Juvenile Delinquency and Youth Crime during the Kennedy administration, believed that dysfunctional family life caused crime. Symington argued shortly after the Watts uprising in 1965 that it was the federal government's responsibility to provide "institutional substitutes for parents." Influenced by the arguments of Moynihan and other federal researchers regarding youth crime, Symington concluded: "When parents fail to give the child everything he needs psychologically as well as materially for balance and direction, then he must get it somewhere else." In more affluent communities,

Symington and the subcommittee suggested, the local school system should be charged with encouraging youth responsibility. But in segregated urban neighborhoods, where "the risk of delinquency is highest," and where community pathology inculcated crime, it was up to the federal government to provide the "supervision" that delinquents were believed to require. "We are in a War on Crime," Judge Parsons reminded his fellow Crime Commission members. And in order to fight it effectively, "we have to capture these youngsters at the earliest stage."[33] The long-held assumption that low-income youth of color were prone to crime made contact with police inevitable in Parsons's view and in the view of other Johnson administration officials. Federal programs could effectively prevent future crime by ensuring that delinquent youth had access to the remedial education and vocational training programs of the War on Poverty and that potential delinquents were known to law enforcement authorities even before an initial arrest was made.

As an alternative to detention centers, juvenile prisons, or training schools, the Crime Commission sought to put law enforcement into various social services so as to target "troublemakers" before they ended up in the juvenile courts and to rehabilitate formerly convicted youth in their own communities. Following the Crime Commission's model, federal officials merged existing training and remedial education programs with public safety and delinquency programs to provide a community-based form of supervision. These measures, which were widely implemented during the late 1960s and early 1970s, brought the police to both the "hard-core" and "potentially delinquent" youth, rather than waiting for these "troublemakers" to come to the attention of police through various delinquent acts or—at worst—rioting. The result was social welfare programs with a distinctly punitive form.

At Symington's suggestion, the Crime Commission devised Youth Service Bureaus to operate as an "institutional substitute for parents," and to merge smoothly with the programs established as part of the War on Poverty. Indeed, the federal government's social welfare intervention had already "laid the ingredients" for the creation of the Youth Service Bureaus. Although the bureaus strongly resembled the Youth Opportunity Centers and neighborhood service agencies that were supported by the Departments of Labor and Health, Education, and Welfare, the

Department of Justice financed far more of these community-based institutions under the auspices of the crime war, with smaller contributions coming from the Office of Economic Opportunity and the Department of Housing and Urban Development. By the early 1970s, the federal government supported some 170 bureaus nationwide, the vast majority in black urban neighborhoods with high rates of unemployment. The bureaus' average participant was a black fifteen-year-old who had not had contact with the formal justice system; only a quarter of the 200,000 participants nationwide had arrest records.[34]

As the president explained to Congress in the February 1967 address proposing their creation, the bureaus would "assist delinquent and potentially delinquent youth to become productive citizens."[35] Specifically the program was geared toward locating children and teenagers who had not committed any crime but were seen by law enforcement and social service officials as predisposed to delinquency, and keeping them under informal supervision within neighborhood centers, YMCAs, settlement houses, and other social institutions. The bureaus would rein in potential lawbreakers and assist young people in what policymakers believed was their "precrime" stage. In many ways, the bureaus shared the goals of the Kennedy administration's antidelinquency programs, but under the command of the Department of Justice, the Johnson administration increasingly treated delinquency as a criminal problem instead of a social welfare concern.

Federal policymakers and law enforcement officials hoped the social services available at the bureaus, and the voluntary nature of participation in their activities, would facilitate the acceptance of this new crime control agency in urban communities. The Crime Commission felt it necessary to make participation in bureau services voluntary, for "otherwise the dangers and disadvantages of coercive power would merely be transferred from the juvenile court to it." Following this recommendation, federal policymakers sought to strategically place the Youth Service Bureaus outside the formal juvenile justice system to avoid the stigma that might attach to participation and the potential community outrage that policymakers acknowledged would likely accompany the placement of new law enforcement centers in black neighborhoods.[36]

Essentially, in crafting the Youth Service Bureau program, the Crime Commission developed a new approach to identifying worthy recipients of public social services: relying on law enforcement institutions to supply "clients." The bureaus would be required to take referrals from police departments and the court system, but in return, social workers and volunteers sent to the courts youths with whom the bureaus could not "deal effectively."[37] Although existing organizations, schools, and parents could refer youth to the bureaus, police and juvenile courts supplied the bulk of participants. Now, community centers with funding and personnel from law enforcement institutions provided recreational, educational, and employment programs to "delinquents" with criminal records as well as "potentially delinquent" youth who previously received such services from autonomous social welfare institutions.

The first legislation that required states to develop specific plans and programs to address the problem of youth crime—the Juvenile Delinquency Prevention and Control Act of 1968—enshrined the community-based approach of Youth Service Bureaus as a model domestic program. Based on the outline provided by the Crime Commission, the legislation defined the "primary target client group" of the bureaus and similar antidelinquency agencies as "those youth in danger of becoming delinquent."[38] Because the bureaus were designed to prevent crime by identifying future criminals, in order to qualify for services in many cases, youth had to be designated by professionals and social workers as "potentially delinquent." At the same time, the bureaus functioned as a diversion agency, easing an overburdened juvenile justice system by placing youth charged with minor offenses under community supervision and ostensibly shielding them from the official label of delinquency.

The bureaus quickly became an important route for state and local governments to obtain funding for social service efforts. Authorities could establish the bureaus in a short period of time and in conjunction with other community service centers, and they provided visibility of action on both the antipoverty and anticrime policy priorities. As congressional appropriations for the national law enforcement program ballooned during and after the late 1960s, crime control funding became an important means to offer various services to young people

A policeman playing cards with residents at a neighborhood teen center in Washington, DC, April 1968. Federal policymakers hoped that bringing together law enforcement and social welfare services in community-based institutions would improve police-community relations while simultaneously providing law enforcement authorities with opportunities to identify "potential criminals." In practice, the strategy increased the general surveillance of black urban Americans as they went about ordinary, everyday activities. *Photograph by Stan Wayman. The LIFE Picture Collection, Getty Images*

in low-income areas. Facing budget shortages, many agencies operating in targeted urban neighborhoods embraced the newly available delinquency prevention grants by incorporating crime control provisions into their programming and criminal justice officials into their leadership.[39]

One of the best examples of the transition from a neighborhood center to a Youth Service Bureau program model occurred in the troubled city of Bridgeport, Connecticut. On the city's East Side, where dilapidated buildings, vacant lots, empty stores, and low-income housing composed the landscape, the Neighborhood Hall House had served African American and Puerto Rican residents for some fifty years. Almost immediately after the enactment of the Safe Streets and Juvenile Delinquency Acts of 1968, the Hall House began to accept federal grants from the Department of Justice, which converted it into a Youth Service Bureau and a program of the War on Crime. Staff, most of whom also lived on the East Side, began to attend juvenile court proceedings to recruit young people to the center, and began to fund recreational programs and cultural field trips with grants from the Department of Justice.[40]

Other bureaus sought to address the various pathological problems federal policymakers believed contributed to the high rates of reported delinquency among low-income youth of color. The "Roving Youth Leaders" Service Bureau in the segregated black municipality of Fairmont Heights, Maryland (directly adjacent to Washington, DC), offered training programs to "direct juveniles toward acceptable standards of social conduct" as well as arts and crafts activities, college application assistance, and drug counseling. Meanwhile, the bureau in Jackson, Mississippi—called the "Tri-County Community Center"—sought to "teach delinquents good grooming habits, effective use of language, and respect for others," as means to prevent crime.[41] Such paternalistic approaches had been important components of the Kennedy administration's antidelinquency programs and the self-help measures of the War on Poverty. Dismissing structural change as impractical in the segregated urban communities where deviant pathologies appeared to be ingrained, the various disciplinary mechanisms advanced by the Roving Youth Leaders and the Tri-Country Community Center, among other bureaus, could effectively cure poverty, crime, and delinquency.

Beyond efforts to teach low-income urban youth "acceptable" behavior standards, the bureaus provided new outlets for recreation, training programs, and after-school activities to reach youth who appeared to be "in danger of becoming delinquent." This allowed criminal justice and law enforcement authorities to supervise "hard-core" offenders in their own neighborhoods. Under a single roof, youth who had been convicted of a crime could meet with their probation or parole officer, while police and social workers together monitored children and teenagers as they played ping-pong, received help from tutors, and participated in group and individual therapy sessions. In Louisville, Kentucky, the Russell Youth Service Bureau targeted thirteen- to sixteen-year-old first-time or minor offenders as well as "those children who are on the verge of getting into trouble or who have school problems." Yet even though its chief purpose was the control of youth crime, the Louisville program functioned "as a local drop-in center for the neighborhood," where children would "stop by and use the pool table or engage in other recreational activities" after school. Similarly, the Youth Service Bureau in Kansas City, Missouri, called the "Youth Intercept Project," included counseling, foster home placement, work, recreation, and special education programs for "less seriously delinquent juveniles." However, its primary function was "individually tailored work with troublemaking youths." While working in tandem with the courts, the bureau would "handle many troubled and troublesome young people outside the criminal system," offering a community-based form of supervision and providing necessary services to vulnerable residents.[42]

Bureaus that did not attach themselves to existing social welfare organizations tended to focus explicitly on providing comprehensive services to "hard-core" youth. For example, in the South Bronx, where some 250,000 mostly African American and Puerto Rican residents lived within twenty square blocks and the unemployment rate approximated 60 percent, the Neighborhood Youth Diversion Program (NYDP) was established in November 1970 with a grant from the Department of Justice and with planning support from consultants at Fordham University and the Vera Institute. Every participant in the NYDP, regarded as a model Youth Service Bureau by law enforcement officials, had received a referral from the court system. Operating from a four-story dilapidated building the city once had condemned and slated for destruction, the NYDP was affiliated with the New York Department of Probation and received additional funding from the police department. Local law enforcement effectively set eligibility requirements for the program and concentrated the agency's resources on those children and teenagers under criminal justice supervision.[43]

The Crime Commission designed the bureaus as a means to reach the most vulnerable and troublesome youth, yet the presence of the bureaus in the South Bronx and other cities—functioning as a youth center with the chief goal of reducing crime and preventing future crime—stigmatized even larger numbers of young people and precipitated contact between low-income youth of color and law enforcement officials. Even worse, the label of "predelinquent" was a prerequisite to benefit from fundamental social services that ought to have been universal.

A critical minority did recognize the fundamental danger of labeling young people in a preemptive manner and giving law enforcement and criminal justice institutions new powers in urban social programs. "As soon as we start dealing with the kids in [certain] categories as potential delinquents," Crime Commission Director James Vorenberg warned, "and we put that label on them, we may be creating a self-fulfilling prophecy." Despite recognizing the potential negative consequences of measures like the Youth Service Bureaus, however, Vorenberg and other federal officials nevertheless pursued a crime war strategy that focused on the supervision of black youth "in danger of becoming delinquent" as the most promising, and humane, approach to the problem. Officials' own set of assumptions about race, poverty, and criminal behavior largely blinded them from alternatives or prevented them from deeply committing to responses outside of the punitive realm.[44]

In part because policymakers had targeted black youth in the earliest battles of the crime war, Youth Service Bureaus and similar social agencies that would be created during the late 1960s and 1970s as a middle ground between law enforcement and social services established channels of supervision in low-income neighborhoods. The federal government's interventions meant that black urban Americans were vulnerable to the expanding punitive apparatus and thus criminal justice supervision at an early age, increasing the chances that they would be arrested, accrue criminal records, go to juvenile detention centers, and eventually serve long prison sentences. Over time, preemptive efforts to combat juvenile delinquency realized the prophecy Vorenberg and the Crime Commission identified. Paraphrasing Vorenberg's comment in its final report, the commission wrote, "Inherent in the process of seeking to identify potential delinquents are certain serious risks—most notably that of self-fulfilling prophecy."[45] Rather than making city streets safer from and for urban youth, the bureaus, the storefront police community-relations centers, and the merger of social welfare provisions with anticrime efforts in general resulted in more young people from targeted urban areas being labeled as criminal and leveraged calls for an ever-more-aggressive War on Crime.

"SEPARATE AND UNEQUAL"

During his televised remarks to the nation as Detroit's Paradise Valley burned in July 1967, Johnson established the National Advisory Commission on Violence and Civil Disorders to evaluate the factors leading to urban unrest and provide law enforcement officials at all levels of government with techniques to manage and avert it. "What we are really asking for is a profile of the rioters," Johnson said, "of their environment, of their victims, of their causes and effects." On July 29, only two days after Johnson announced his intention to form the commission, the president hosted its eleven members for a White House luncheon. In order that their recommendations "affect this year the dangerous climate of tension and apprehension that pervades our cities," Johnson placed the group on a strict schedule, giving members until March 1, 1968, to complete their work. Because the implications of the commission's research would weigh heavily on issues of national security, it was funded in part by a $450,000 grant from the Department of Defense. The rest came from the president's emergency fund, with contributions from the Departments of Justice and Health, Education, and Welfare.[46]

The conclusions reached by this new commission—commonly referred to as the Kerner Commission, for its chairman, Governor Otto Kerner of Illinois—represented an exception to an unpursued alternative by the growing consensus that supported punitive federal policy in the late 1960s. Compared to the distinctly moderate leanings of Crime Commission members and that body's dearth of elected officials, Johnson stacked the Kerner Commission with liberal policymakers and civil rights advocates. Governor Kerner had a progressive civil rights record, service as a National Guardsman, and experience as a prosecutor and a judge. New York's liberal Republican mayor John Lindsay served as vice-chair, and penned the commission's famous warning: "Our nation is moving towards two societies, One black, One white—Separate and Unequal."[47] From the Senate came Republican Edward Brooke of Massachusetts, the first African American to hold such office since Reconstruction. Senator Fred Harris, the liberal Democrat from Oklahoma, secured a spot for himself by being the first to suggest that Johnson bring together experts to study the riots. Los Angeles's liberal congressman James Corman was joined by the more conservative William McCulloch of Ohio, a vocal critic of Great Society programs who had nevertheless played a key role in pushing the Civil Rights Act through Congress and who held a high rank on the House Judiciary Committee. Other commissioners were AFL-CIO president I. W. Abel, executive director of the National Association for the Advancement of Colored People (NAACP) Roy Wilkins, and Litton Industries CEO Charles Thornton. The lone woman, Kentucky commerce commissioner Katherine Graham Peden, had previously served on President Kennedy's Task Force on the Status of Women in 1963. Finally, Atlanta's veteran police chief Herbert Jenkins seemed a natural law enforcement representative for the Kerner Commission's purposes, since no major incidents of civil disorder had occurred on his watch.

Part exposé of the riots, part history of American racism, and part synthesis of postwar social scientific theory, the Kerner Commission's 426-page study, published in February 1968, offered a perspective on the urban violence and how to solve it that was far more interested than the Crime Commission and the rest of the administration in attacking the socioeconomic roots of urban unrest as a prevention measure. Seeking integration as the desired path for future domestic policy, the Kerner Commission recommended the creation of 2 million jobs for low-income Americans by government and industry, continued federal intervention to ensure school desegregation, year-round schooling for low-income youth, the immediate construction of 600,000 housing units in deprived "ghetto neighborhoods," and a guaranteed minimum income. Expanded policing was also part of its prescription, but twinned with an end to American military intervention in Southeast Asia. John Lindsay and other liberal members of the commission led the majority in calling for a massive, $50 billion federal urban police program to be paid for by pulling out of Vietnam.[48] The Kerner Commission report quickly became a bestseller and sold more than 2 million copies to a public eager for insight into why cities were burning and what factors drove citizens to collective violence.

The commission believed the federal government had three domestic policy options to manage the "crisis of race relations" it had identified: it could work to foster separate but equal access to public institutions, it could enact structural reforms such as busing or affirmative action programs to achieve full integration, or it could continue along its current course while the nation hoped for the best. Inspired by the goals of black nationalist organizations and reflecting the preferences of broad sections of the American public, the Kerner Commission's first option—what it called the "enrichment choice"—was premised on the idea that African Americans could achieve "equality of opportunity with whites while continuing in conditions of nearly complete separation." This would reduce the likelihood of future rioting, but only if enrichment programs addressed income, education, and housing inequality. Whereas some might be satisfied with equality and continued separation, the commission saw enrichment programs as only a "means towards a goal," an "interim action," lifting poor Americans from poverty and giving them "the capacity to enter the mainstream of American life" until the Kerner Commission's preferred option, "the integration choice," could be realized. Ideally, taking this path, the federal government would stimulate the out-migration of black Americans from cities to suburbs, promoting greater access to employment, education, and housing opportunities. "The goal must be achieving freedom for every citizen to live and work according to his capacities and desires, and not his color," the Kerner Commission argued. In the absence of a major commitment of resources on the part of American political and economic institutions, "sufficient to make a dramatic, visible impact on life in the urban ghetto," commission members warned that the nation would be plagued by crime, violence, and lasting inequality.[49]

The Kerner Commission believed that the "present policies choice"—simply maintaining the existing community action, manpower development, and housing programs of the War on Poverty—would be most detrimental to the future of American democracy. If the federal government did nothing to address the forces that perpetuated structural exclusion, the Kerner Commission alleged its continued inaction "could quite conceivably lead to a kind of urban *apartheid* with semimartial law in many major cities, enforced residence of Negroes in segregated areas, and a drastic reduction in personal freedom for all Americans, particularly Negroes." Simply maintaining current programs would unleash conditions whereby "a rising proportion of Negroes in disadvantaged city areas might come to look upon the deprivation and segregation they suffer as proper justification" to engage in "large-scale violence, followed by white retaliation." And unless the federal government forcefully intervened to transform the nation's social, political, and economic institutions and the inherent inequalities within them, the Kerner Commission feared that a "spiral" of segregation, violence, and police force would likely emerge, compromising many of the gains of the civil rights movement and the critical reforms of the Great Society.[50]

Despite such dire warnings, the federal government pursued none of the Kerner Commission's three broad domestic policy options—not even the maintenance of existing policies. The Kerner Commission's attention to the role of white racism in perpetuating inequality and segregation made Johnson uncomfortable. Even though the president deliberately chose to stack the commission with liberals, he viewed its assessment of urban social realities as unreasonable and too radical, and the controversial nature of some of its conclusions led some policymakers to distance themselves from the commission. (Johnson himself refused to publically comment on its report.) Although the Kerner Commission received more public attention than any other presidential task force in the 1960s, the group lacked the long-term legislative and policy impact of its predecessor, the Crime Commission. Instead, the Kerner Commission had a more subtle influence, reinforcing the trend toward a focus on crime in federal urban policy that was already ongoing, its recommendations only coming to fruition when the commission championed the strategies developed by the Crime Commission.

The Kerner Commission identified five basic "problem areas" within urban police departments. First, the Kerner Commission encouraged local law enforcement to develop screening procedures in selecting officers to patrol segregated urban communities. Operating on the assumption that "there is more crime in the ghetto than in other areas," the Kerner Commission hoped screening measures, complemented by special sensitivity training programs, would curtail discriminatory patrol practices, promoting positive community relations and preventing violent outbreaks in the process. Second, like the Crime Commission, the Kerner Commission agreed deploying additional manpower to "ghetto areas" would effectively reduce crime, but unlike its predecessor, the Kerner Commission resolved that urban police forces needed to focus on investigating and apprehending suspects involved in serious crimes that threatened life and property, rather than on relatively minor infractions such as loitering or gambling, which seemed to only foster distrust and tension. Third, the Kerner Commission proposed a number of key institutional reforms, including the development of internal and external police review boards. Fourth, the commission argued that departments needed to develop and distribute detailed policy guidelines to regulate contact between citizens and the police in "high crime" urban areas, guidelines that would help officers determine when to break up a social street gathering or to make arrests for "victimless crimes" such as vagrancy. Along these lines, the Kerner Commission suggested that arrest or field interrogation quotas established by police administrators discouraged officers from differentiating "between the genuinely suspicious behavior and behavior which is suspicious to a particular officer merely because it is unfamiliar." In other words, the strategy inadvertently promoted a patrol climate marked by seemingly arbitrary arrests and "stop and frisk" searches. Changing policy guidelines in urban police departments, then, would necessarily involve reducing or removing entirely the "pressure to produce" specific arrest quotas during each tour of duty.[51]

The Kerner Commission's fifth recommendation was the only policy that was adopted on a national basis by the Safe Streets Act, and it reinforced a concern that the Crime Commission and the Johnson administration shared—the effort to "develop community support for law enforcement." In addition to increasing the number of African American police officers—who were severely underrepresented in all of the departments the commission surveyed—the Kerner Commission strongly urged policymakers to rethink the purpose of urban police by emphasizing their community service role. Due to the fact that police occupied a " 'front line position' in dealing with ghetto problems," the Kerner Commission felt it important that social programs "give the police in general the opportunity to provide services, not merely to enforce the law."[52] Bringing police officers into War on Poverty programs seemed to satisfy the need the Crime Commission had also identified—strengthening law enforcement in black urban areas and improving police-community relations.

Although police programs occupied a substantial portion of the Crime Commission and Kerner Commission's recommendations, the two task forces diverged when it came to the specific crime control strategies that had emerged after Watts under the tutelage of the Office of Law Enforcement Assistance. In a rare moment of disagreement between the two commissions on police matters, the Kerner Commission noted that many new patrol measures actually caused much of the tension that resulted in urban outbreaks. Members criticized the trend toward aggressive patrol in segregated neighborhoods and found that law enforcement officers engaged in disturbing post-riot patrol practices. Whereas the Crime Commission argued that "increasing patrol force in an area, through use of special tactical patrols, causes a decline in crimes directed at citizens walking the streets in the heavily patrolled area," the Kerner Commission noted that tactical patrols and roving task forces instituted by some departments subjected entire communities in high crime districts to "intensive, often indiscriminate, stops and searches." The Kerner Commission believed that black residents would endorse an increased police presence in their communities if aggressive patrol involved a strong commitment to reducing crime. "What may arouse hostility is not the fact of aggressive patrol," the Kerner Report warned, "but its indiscriminate use so that it comes to be regarded not as crime control but as a new method of racial harassment."[53] Despite the Kerner Commission's recognition of the punitive social climate that tactical police squads helped to create, the federal government continued to fund these specialized forces, particularly after enactment of the Crime Control and Safe Streets Act.

In line with larger domestic policy transformations, the Kerner Commission strongly endorsed the merger of social welfare and law enforcement functions within Youth Service Bureaus and other urban institutions. The commission lauded the work of police neighborhood service centers, which allowed law enforcement officials to promote public safety by performing social welfare tasks."[54] In one of its most important policy recommendations, the Kerner Commission argued that if police officers were to increasingly perform social service functions and partner with equal opportunity and self-help programs as part of the national fight against poverty, incentives within departments would need to shift accordingly.

Since the late nineteenth century, it has been the purpose of American police to enforce the law, to make arrests, and to build criminal cases. Suddenly, national policies had called upon police officers to deliver turkeys to needy families on Thanksgiving, play pool with troublesome children in after-school programs, and counsel low-income couples during marital disputes. In principle, these programs had the potential to promote public safety in innovative ways. But in practice, as the Kerner Commission recognized, officers had little incentive to dedicate themselves to social welfare goals. Noting that law enforcement authorities measured the performance of rank-and-file cops by their ability to catch criminals and based their criteria for special awards, promotions, bonuses, and selection for elite assignments on the demonstrated heroism or arrest activity of an individual officer, the commission recommended that these reward systems "take equal cognizance of the work of officers who improve relations with alienated members of the community and by so doing minimize the potential for disorder."[55] Yet federal policymakers did not heed this crucial recommendation, proceeding to increase the patrol and surveillance of "ghetto residents" on the streets, in schools and housing projects, and within social welfare services without working to refashion the very definition of and rewards for effective police work in vulnerable neighborhoods. Officers who were expected to build long-term relationships with residents rarely received the kind of recognition as did their counterparts who successfully apprehended suspects during high-speed chases or shoot-outs.

Beneath its liberal rhetoric, in the final analysis, the Kerner Commission supported a massive War on Crime. Its members took for granted the guiding principle of domestic urban policy in the 1960s—that community pathology caused poverty and crime—and following the Crime Commission's recommendations, it identified black urban neighborhoods as the primary targets for the federal government's punitive intervention. The Kerner Report described a situation where "police responsibilities in the ghetto have grown as other institutions of social control have so little authority." Single-parent families, failing public schools, and the declining significance of religious and community-based voluntary organizations meant, as the Kerner Commission claimed, "it is the policeman who must deal with the consequences of this institutional vacuum."[56] The Kerner Commission, like other administration officials, didn't imagine this state of affairs could be altered so as to reduce the police role again. The commission's call for criminal justice officials to directly shape and participate in urban social programs, particularly those serving black youth, was a proposal that policymakers found well worth pursuing.

In defending the turn to police patrol and surveillance in domestic urban policy, the Kerner Commission also affirmed the focus and attention of crime war strategies on African American youth. The commission's outlook was based on data projections indicating that the black youth population—perceived by policymakers and the public at large as responsible for urban disorder—was the fastest-growing group in the United States. Using FBI data and census population trends, the Kerner Commission predicted that black urban populations would increase 72 percent by 1985, reaching roughly 21 million people. The Johnson administration grew especially concerned about the commission's conclusion that the population of young black Americans especially would "grow much faster than either the Negro population as a whole, or the white population in the same age group." (Black men between the ages of fifteen and twenty-four were identified by both the Crime Commission and the Kerner Commission as the group responsible for the majority of the nation's crime.) Although members of the Kerner Commission maintained "in a phrase . . . the problem is white racism compounded by poverty," its alarming population forecasts and policy suggestions reinforced the urgency of the Johnson administration's historic War on Crime.[57]

Shortly after the publication of the Kerner Commission's report, as Congress considered Johnson's Safe Streets Act and the Juvenile Delinquency Prevention and Control Act, Memphis erupted in late March 1968. On the day the rioting began, Johnson was scheduled to speak to representatives from the Police Athletic League. The president turned to Abraham Lincoln to explain the current "atmosphere of lawlessness" in the nation. "There is even now something of ill omen among us," Johnson lamented. "I mean the increasing disregard for law which pervades the country—the growing disposition that substitutes the wild and furious passions in lieu of the sober judgment of courts, and the worse than savage mobs for the executive ministers of justice." Johnson reminded the league, "If our country is to survive, Lincoln said, we must all realize that 'there is no grievance that is a fit object of redress by mob law.' Now this is as true in 1968 as it was in 1838."[58]

Against the backdrop of collective violence, as mainstream black activists shifted the focus of their organizing from the pursuit of civil rights and equal access to the quest for self-determination and community control, federal policymakers and many of their constituents feared continued chaos in the nation's cities. "For all their destructiveness, I can but read the riots as a terrible call," Office of Economic Opportunity Director Sargent Shriver wrote to Johnson in early 1968. "The Negroes want equal access to the fruits of participating citizenship—the opportunity both to earn and to control their destiny."[59] Crime war proponents shared Shriver's sense that racial inequality had reached a boiling point, although they expressed Shriver's view in entirely different terms. At the annual meeting of the National Conference of American Bar Association Presidents in February 1968, James C. Davis—the president of the American Bar Association's Cleveland Chapter—articulated a common fear that mass racial violence was on the horizon:

> Today there are close to 30 million Negroes in the United States. The total population of North Viet Nam is about 19 million or a little over 60 percent of the American Negro population. Yet the relatively small North Vietnamese population has tied down more than one million allied troops, troops that were unable to maintain security in the face of simultaneous disorders in the cities of South Viet Nam. . . . Should the majority of the Negro populations, in these cities alone, move from passive acquiescence in riots to active participation in rebellion, it is obvious what the result would be.[60]

For Davis, the fact of a large black population in American cities was reason enough to fear a race war. This prospect was the fundamental force underlying federal policy-making beginning with Watts in 1965, taken as evidence in every incident of subsequent disorder, providing national policymakers justification for their post–civil rights crime control priorities. In 1968 and afterward, the federal government did not pursue the Kerner Commission's "present policies choice." It instead failed to maintain its commitment to existing urban social programs and moved forward with the major crime control intervention into the nation's cities it had been developing since the spring of 1965, one that contained the seeds of the War on Poverty's undoing. Rather than attacking the roots of structural racism, the White House and Congress decided to cope with the persistence of racial inequality by launching a punitive counterrevolution that brought to an end roughly three decades of progressive legislation. Although the seeds of this transformation had been planted at the outset of the federal government's urban intervention during the Kennedy administration, it built momentum during the second half of the 1960s and fully arrived when Johnson signed into the law the Safe Streets Act of 1968, four months after Memphis and less than a month after the uprisings in 125 cities followed the assassination of Martin Luther King Jr.

[4]

THE WAR ON BLACK CRIME

When Richard Nixon rose to power, promising to "wage an effective war against this enemy within" as he said during his presidential campaign, he was in a position to advance some of the worst, most coercive dimensions of the Great Society.[1] Nixon is often credited with starting the national government's punitive intervention, but "law and order" had already emerged as a permanent fixture on the national policy agenda by the time of his election, and federal policymakers had already begun to retreat from social welfare interventions. By presiding over the introduction of block grants into the national government's first major piece of crime control legislation, the Omnibus Crime Control and Safe Streets Act of 1968, Lyndon Johnson helped restore a critical degree of funding power to the states in the aftermath of Jim Crow. On a deeper level, however, the punitive impulses and preemptive crime control policies of his urban social programs contaminated other Great Society measures fighting racial discrimination and lack of opportunity. This union of two seemingly opposed policy objectives left behind a complicated legacy of social progression and repression in domestic policy. Nixon merely appropriated the regressive aspects of the Johnson administration as his own, pledging both to end the "crime menace" and to decentralize the administration of domestic social programs.

Partnerships between the federal government, local municipalities, and public and private organizations had been the hallmark of postwar liberalism, a relationship the Johnson administration had expanded and a principle that Republicans and southern politicians strongly opposed. Initially, the Johnson administration envisioned that the national law enforcement program would function in the style of War on Poverty programs, whereby federal officials funded local entities directly. Conservative policymakers refused to continue this practice in the War on Crime. They argued that the welfare state and its giant federal bureaucracy could not adequately respond to local needs, and that decisions about social programs should be left to the states via block grants. This proposed funding system empowered states to act as the "middle men" between the federal government and municipalities. With relative autonomy and less federal oversight, state-level officials would award funding to local governments.[2]

Even though Democrats, who initially opposed block grants, controlled both chambers of Congress at the time of the Safe Streets Act's passage, the need to get the national law enforcement program started and to obtain critical support from conservative representatives caused liberal policymakers to concede the point. Johnson too disliked block grants, and waited to sign the 1968 legislation until the last possible day before his inaction would result in a pocket veto. But the larger goal of providing national assistance to police, court, and prison systems took precedence over the specific channels through which that federal funding would flow. The following year, the political strategist Kevin Phillips wrote in *The Emerging Republican Majority* that Nixon's ascendance to the presidency "bespoke the end of the New Deal Democratic hegemony and the beginning of a new era in American politics."[3] Yet it was Lyndon Johnson who sowed the seeds of postwar liberalism's demise, in part by changing the funding structure for domestic social programs, and in part by establishing a wider field of urban surveillance and social control.

What Nixon called the "New Federalism" offered the states a means to preserve race-based hierarchies after civil rights by returning funding power to governors. Although the Safe Streets Act laid the groundwork for both a massive federal investment in crime control with the creation of the Law Enforcement Assistance Administration (LEAA) and the devolution of national social programs, when it came to crime itself, Nixon freely set aside his commitment to states' rights. Indeed, the administration did not hesitate to closely direct the course of policy when it involved punitive programs in black urban neighborhoods.

The Nixon administration's selective embrace of New Federalism was only one aspect of the widespread hypocrisy characterizing its implementation of the national law enforcement program, which quickly became mismanaged. The Safe Streets Act made tens of millions of dollars available to public organizations, private companies, and individual researchers who could develop technology, hardware, and theories that would help the federal government prevent future crime. As consulting firms and corporations emerged to reap the benefits of such funding, the result was widespread corruption that mirrored the criminal behavior of Nixon and his officials exposed by the Watergate scandal. Recognizing the crime control bureaucracy's dysfunction and inefficiency, the administration rapidly moved into direct federal intervention rather than deferring to state officials.

Specifically, White House officials and LEAA administrators soon struggled to address the mismatch between where reported crime was rising (usually in American cities) and where law enforcement block grants actually ended up (usually in rural towns). Based on the recommendations of the Crime Commission, the federal government had designed the national law enforcement program to focus on street crime in the nation's cities. But, as one Nixon official noted, "states are failing to reorder their priorities *now*, irregardless [*sic*] of our consistent prodding them to do so." For instance, Denver received less than 20 percent of Colorado's $1.8 million LEAA grant in 1970, even though the city was home to 30 percent of the state's total population and 70 percent of its crime; and New York City, which claimed roughly two thirds of serious reported crime in the state, received only 39 percent of New York's total block grant.[4]

Under Johnson and Nixon alike, federal policymakers had pursued a War on Crime to target segregated urban areas as a means to dispel civil disorder and manage the effects of the country's urban crisis. The national strategy was not to revamp smaller departments in areas with lower reported crime rates, as some states seemed to prefer. Thus, notwithstanding New Federalism's promise to increase the power of the states, the Nixon administration used the discretionary portion of the crime control budget to fund law enforcement initiatives of its own choosing. Discretionary allocations, the funds requested by the president and appropriated by Congress on an annual basis, provided the White House and the LEAA with a critical opening that allowed them to award grants for whatever purpose they deemed fit while still operating within the confines of the block grant system and the ethos of New Federalism. Just as the individual discretion of police officers, prosecutors, and judges has always been key to the extent of racial disparities within the American law enforcement and criminal justice systems, the federal government's use of discretionary aid provided national policymakers with a degree of power and influence over local programming.[5] Consistently, the Nixon administration's desire to exert greater punitive authority in black urban neighborhoods prevailed over its own commitments to the principles of small government.

In order to ensure federal crime war programs would continue to support the targeted enforcement of patrol and surveillance of low-income black communities, the Nixon administration turned to discretionary programs to steer money to urban areas. Nixon's policies of decentralization and disinvestment fostered the dissolution of War on Poverty programs, and it has been assumed that the relationship between the federal government, municipalities, and poor Americans that had been established by the liberal welfare state diminished along with them. Yet by essentially abandoning New Federalism when it came to the War on Crime, the strategies the Nixon administration enforced maintained an enduring, highly repressive, federal intervention in segregated urban neighborhoods.

The vast majority of the $2.4 billion that federal policymakers invested in law enforcement and criminal justice institutions during Nixon's presidency went to local police departments, whether through block grants to the states or through discretionary spending. In smaller cities with high concentrations of African Americans living in segregated poverty such as Baltimore, Newark, St. Louis, and Cleveland, the Nixon administration launched the LEAA's single largest initiative, the $20 million "High Impact" program, using discretionary funds. Working directly with mayors and local police departments, Nixon officials established criminal justice planning agencies at the local level that would design and implement new patrol and surveillance programs. High Impact failed to prevent crime and may have contributed to it in the communities where it operated, but it did succeed in increasing contacts between residents and police officers, bringing more residents under criminal justice supervision in the process.

The High Impact program continued Johnson's precedent of using federal grants to train and equip the War on Crime's local foot soldiers. But the Nixon administration turned the federal government's attention to elements of the carceral state that the Johnson administration had largely ignored, namely, the court and prison systems. Shortly after taking office, the Nixon administration introduced a new criminal code for Washington, DC, that officials hoped would eventually serve as a model for the nation. Nixon had rejected Johnson's notion of poverty as the root cause of crime. "If the conviction rate were doubled in this country, it would do more to eliminate crime in the future, than a quadrupling of the funds for any governmental war on poverty," Nixon argued early on in his presidential bid. The District of Columbia Court Reorganization Act of 1970 that the Nixon administration would introduce two years later included mandatory minimum sentences for certain crimes, sanctioned the practice of holding suspects in jail without formal charges, and created new categories of offenders in order to ensure that the "enemy within" would be incarcerated for long periods.

Meanwhile, Nixon asserted himself as the first president to undertake a major overhaul of the American prison system. Under the direction of Nixon and his attorney general John Mitchell, national policymakers began to support the construction of hundreds of new prisons at the state and federal levels. As federal officials worked to modernize the penal system and increase its capacity, the nation's incarcerated population transformed from majority white to majority black and Latino. By the end of the decade, the combination of the surveillance, sentencing, and incarceration strategies—the seeds of which the Johnson administration had planted and that Nixon officials seized upon—set the stage for the explosive growth of the American prison system in the final decades of the twentieth century.[6]

THE ELEMENTS OF THE CRIME WAR

Richard Nixon focused his first major policy statement during the 1968 presidential contest on the ways in which he would restore law and order if elected. In a May 1968 treatise titled "Toward Freedom from Fear," Nixon described a general atmosphere of lawlessness. "We are trifling with social dynamite if we believe that the young people who emerge from these brutal societies in the central cities will come out as satisfied and productive citizens," Nixon wrote, evoking familiar metaphors to imply that the changing demographics of cities threatened the safety of "ordinary Americans." The Nixon campaign did not resort to explicitly racist imagery, but it did evoke fears of neighborhood change, urging the electorate to "vote like your whole world depended on it." Taking cues from the law and order political discourse that Ronald Reagan had successfully employed two years earlier in his California gubernatorial campaign, Nixon appealed to Americans who feared the consequences of the great changes they had witnessed during the social movements of the 1960s. By selecting as his running mate Spiro Agnew, the governor of Maryland and a staunch law and order proponent who once commented that the release of the Kerner Commission Report would only encourage more black Americans to riot, Nixon offered his "Silent Majority" a formidable crime control ticket.[7]

During the campaign, Nixon repudiated community action programs and criticized Johnson's law enforcement strategy for subordinating the War on Crime within the War on Poverty. Nixon offered more developed versions of the theories of community pathology that undergirded much of domestic policy during the Johnson administration, describing the urban crisis as a problem not of inequality but of violent behavior. He argued that Johnson focused too much on the social causes of "high crime environments" and did not sufficiently punish perpetrators for their actions. The Republican Party's 1968 platform declared: "We must re-establish the principle that men are accountable for what they do, that criminals are responsible for their crimes, that while the youth's environment may help to explain the man's crime, it does not excuse that crime." (Nixon himself had called excusing crime and sympathizing with criminals "because of past grievances the criminal may have against society" a "socially suicidal tendency" on the part of liberal federal policymakers and public figures in his May 1968 treatise.) Whereas Johnson's Crime Commission stressed that "warring on poverty is warring on crime," Nixon's attorney general John Mitchell would remark of the Department of Justice, soon after his confirmation, "This is an institution for law enforcement—not social improvement."[8]

Given the actual similarities between Johnson's law enforcement program and Nixon's own proposals, Nixon's tough-on-crime stance was to a great extent a matter of rhetoric. Both men were deeply committed to investing in local law enforcement and enhancing patrol and surveillance programs in neighborhoods of segregated poverty. John Dean, a young lawyer who worked for the Republicans on the House Judiciary Committee during the debate over the Safe Streets Act and who then joined Nixon's domestic policy staff, understood the parallels between Johnson and his successor. "I was cranking out that bullshit on Nixon's crime policy before he was elected. And it was bullshit, too," Dean went on to reflect in 1977. "We knew it. The Nixon campaign didn't call for anything about crime problems that Ramsey Clark wasn't already doing under LBJ. We just made more noise."[9] And the noise helped to get Nixon elected.

Nixon's campaign staff linked issues of crime and civil disobedience to discredit their Democratic opponent, Vice President Hubert Humphrey, and the Johnson administration. In contrast to the Republican Convention in Miami Beach, which proceeded peacefully, the antiwar demonstrations organized by the Youth International Party, or "Yippies," during the Democratic National Convention in August 1968 resulted in confrontations between the Chicago Police Department and National Guardsmen. Widely broadcast images of protesters throwing bottles and rocks at law enforcement authorities, coupled with ongoing urban unrest, made it seem as though the nation was quickly descending into utter chaos and destruction. Coverage of urban civil disorder had already been sensationalized for the American public, and the Chicago incident helped Nixon emphasize "crime in the streets" as the overriding domestic policy concern. This posed a powerful challenge to Humphrey's calls for "order and justice" and vice presidential candidate Edmund Muskie's view that the nation "cannot put a wall around black people and buy safety and security for society." Although the election was close (Nixon received roughly 1 million more votes than Humphrey, taking 43.4 percent of the popular vote to his opponent's 42.7), the Republican candidate carried thirty-two states to Humphrey's thirteen and the District of Columbia, recalibrating the electoral map and asserting a new conservative stronghold in the southern and western regions.[10]

After his election, Nixon created an Advisory Council on Crime and Law Enforcement that developed strategies for a major punitive intervention in American cities. The president-elect selected Martin Pollner, a deputy attorney general under Kennedy, to sit as executive director of the council with Los Angeles district attorney Evelle Younger as the chair. In December 1968, the council urged Nixon to "place the crime crisis on par with the urban crisis, with national security" and maintained that the administration should seek to address the problems of "the urban poor, upon whom [crime] is in many ways a heavier cost to bear than poverty." "This war on crime should be declared with righteous rhetoric," wrote the council to the president-elect in its private report, "and it is one that will win support from editorial pages to the cloak-rooms of Capitol Hill." The specific strategies these advisors developed included the creation of a National Law Enforcement Council, a symbolic gesture to reflect Nixon's commitment to "law and order," and the development of a unique crime control program for Washington, DC, which the council viewed as a "golden opportunity" to test various punitive policies that might eventually serve as national models. "If we are to make good on the promise to help the peace forces in our nation," the council wrote, referring to police departments, "we must give the peace forces the proper tools to fight crime." And to do so meant giving the "peace forces" sweeping authority to question, arrest, and detain suspects "upon reasonable suspicion." Such policies would "confirm what has always been thought to be the role of the police officer in society," potential violations of civil liberties and widespread racial profiling aside.[11]

As they laid out these strategies, the administration assumed that the "criminal species" could be "found predominately in the slums of urban America and not in the suburbs." From the perspective of Nixon's Advisory Council, his closest aides, and Nixon himself, at the heart of the crime problem lay the *street* crime problem, seen as a black, urban issue. "You have to face the fact that the whole problem is really the blacks," Nixon's chief of staff, H. R. Haldeman, quoted Nixon as saying in Haldeman's diary entry from April 1969. "The key is to devise a system that recognizes this while not appearing to."[12] In a direct and systematic way, Nixon recognized that the politics of crime control could effectively conceal the racist intent behind his administration's domestic programs.

Almost immediately on taking office, Nixon eagerly followed through on the strategies for national law enforcement that the Safe Streets Act had required. He first began to consolidate the federal law enforcement bureaucracy. "I don't particularly like military metaphors," the president explained, "but if they are appropriate anywhere, it is in fighting crime." Nixon viewed the LEAA as "the primary instrument for our attack on crime" by providing urban police forces with adequate resources and strategies to function as the necessary "change agents" for a revolution in criminal justice. The Nixon administration relied upon the blueprint Johnson's Crime Commission had developed; as the commission recommended and as the Safe Streets Act had stipulated, the LEAA would function as the federal government's law enforcement consultant, promoting a national strategy on crime to the states and, through them, to local governments. As one administrator in the organized crime division put it, "LEAA is needed as the motivating force to tie the system together, not as a national system but as a truly Federal system, whereby we can provide the necessary means and resources." The agency offered and arranged for technical assistance, both directly and through contractors, consultants, and publications produced by its research arm, the National Institute of Criminal Justice. Like its forerunner, the Office of Law Enforcement Assistance, the LEAA continued to focus on improving the technological capacity of police departments and modernizing police operations, a pursuit the agency maintained throughout Nixon's first term. While the LEAA did not operate as a law enforcement agency in its own right, in special cases (usually in response to black activism and protest), the agency engaged in tactical operations on the ground. For instance, an LEAA administrator advised Federal Bureau of Intelligence (FBI) agents and New Haven police officials when they raided the local Black Panther headquarters in May 1969.[13]

States began to create criminal justice planning agencies on their own shortly after the start of the crime war in 1965, and by February 1968, half of the states had implemented such bodies. Federal policy-makers used block grants to empower state planning agencies to develop their own path for the War on Crime by funding local projects and programs of their choice. But the Safe Streets Act forced states, if they had not done so already, to develop long-term strategies for their respective law enforcement programs, providing federal funding for such efforts at 90 percent of their cost. In order to be eligible for LEAA grants, governors had six months to organize local and law enforcement officials to craft a criminal justice improvement plan. Once the LEAA reviewed plans in areas such as training, detecting, and apprehending criminals, and improving prosecution and the courts, each state received a grant of at least $100,000 with additional funds available based on their population. Even though the LEAA guidelines frequently changed over the years that followed, the agency rarely turned down a proposal and thus often funded poorly conceived plans.[14]

Officials within the LEAA saw the agency as a "business" which served a "clientele" on the state level. The president preferred to treat the LEAA as a military enterprise, explaining to a group of state criminal justice planners of their role in the War on Crime: "As the general staff in that campaign, your plans will determine what forces we array, on what ground we stand, and where we attack." In Nixon's view, the planning agencies served as the state-level commanders, reporting to the LEAA generals who guided the course of the war from their offices on Indiana Avenue. LEAA officials could claim that the federal crime control bureaucracy had been kept to a minimum since the planning agencies utilized far more resources and employed far more people than did the Department of Justice in Washington. Indeed, in a number of states, the local law enforcement officers, policymakers, and corporate executives who oversaw the new criminal justice planning offices created substantial infrastructures. California produced the most polished and powerful planning agency, with sixteen separate boards reporting to its twenty-nine-member executive committee, which included two oil company lawyers and a radio station secretary, as well as a small handful of black elected officials from local governments who had demonstrated their strong support for Governor Reagan's aggressive law enforcement strategies.[15]

To preside over the state-level bureaucracies, oversee the disbursement of crime war funding, and manage the agency's 300 employees, Congress in the Safe Streets Act had crafted a new form of leadership for the LEAA, a "troika" model in which three administrators with different party affiliations needed to reach agreement on all major federal law enforcement decisions. Initially, the Nixon administration felt strongly that a Democrat should lead the agency and selected Charles Rogovin, the former head of the Organized Crime Task Force of Johnson's Crime Commission. Rogovin promptly left his position as an assistant attorney general in Massachusetts to direct the LEAA during the Nixon transition. "There can be no progress in a lawless, disorderly society," Rogovin told the National Association of Attorneys General at a conference in St. Thomas in June 1969. "Neither freedom nor any of its tangible benefits can long co-exist with the fear unleashed by widespread crime." A chain-smoker who wore tinted glasses and loved to play golf, the thirty-eight-year-old Rogovin was described by a friend as "basically a cop in a way," in that he "loves cops, he loves investigative work. He can be one of them. They like him and he can talk back to them." As a former public defender in Philadelphia, Rogovin had worked with urban court systems and criminals, conducted major studies on organized crime, and held police forces in the highest esteem. These views and credentials made Nixon comfortable with trusting the Democrat to run his anticrime agency. Richard Velde joined Rogovin as associate director. Also in his late thirties, Velde worked as a top aide to Senator Roman Hruska when the Republican helped create the Office of Law Enforcement Assistance in 1965, and Velde guided the Safe Streets Act through the Senate Judiciary Committee in 1968. Finally, Nixon brought in Clarence Coster, the Republican police chief of Bloomington, Minnesota, to round out the troika. Coster's previous experience as a narcotics officer for the Los Angeles Police Department complemented Velde's knowledge of crime control policy and Rogovin's of organized crime and the judicial system.[16]

By making crime into a science that could be predicted and anticipated, policymakers hoped that federal law enforcement initiatives would identify effective ways to target street patrol and, in the process, reduce crime levels. To lead the National Institute of Justice, established by the Safe Streets Act as the research division of the LEAA, Nixon appointed Henry S. Ruth Jr., the former assistant director of the Crime Commission and a University of Pennsylvania law professor. Ruth treated law enforcement and criminal violence as a rational science. Under his leadership, the National Institute developed police technology and equipment, explored options for distributing nonlethal weapons to police departments, and improved police communications technology. Ruth and other federal officials believed that research functioned as "an integral instrument to management" and that statistics could assist police departments and criminal justice planning agencies in predicting with greater accuracy when or where crime would occur, thus making the national law enforcement program more effective and efficient.[17]

The troika of Rogovin, Velde, and Coster implemented many of the recommendations developed by the Crime Commission and the Johnson administration, integrating law enforcement into diverse facets of domestic policy in order to promote surveillance and training measures. Continuing the merger of antipoverty and anticrime programs, the LEAA forged links between law enforcement and social agencies in urban centers, sharing resources with the Department of Health, Education, and Welfare and the Department of Housing and Urban Development. The emphasis on interagency planning and coordination in the Safe Streets Act also opened up possibilities for defense and intelligence agencies in the domestic law enforcement realm, and in Washington, DC; Montgomery, Alabama; and New York City, the Army and the Central Intelligence Agency (CIA) played a key role in offering seminars to local police on visual street surveillance, bomb disposal, and records filing. These training programs complemented the LEAA's ongoing effort to make law enforcement into an attractive, middle-class profession: the agency funded the tuition for some 50,000 officers enrolled in police science programs at more than 1,000 colleges and universities in mostly small suburban areas across the United States. Finally, the new federal crime control grants bolstered private businesses that had already contributed to improving the technological capabilities in the law enforcement and criminal justice arena and gave rise to new ones.

LEAA funding incentivized the private sector to manufacture cutting-edge equipment such as walkie-talkies and develop technologies such as computerized criminal justice databanks, tasks that the LEAA viewed as crucial to modernizing American law enforcement and making the crime fight successful but that were beyond its own abilities.[18]

These and other programs of the LEAA marked what Attorney General Mitchell called an "auspicious beginning" for Nixon's New Federalism in 1970. As the cornerstone of the administration's domestic policy, Nixon's War on Crime was intended to provide states a general framework to help steer their plans for local law enforcement rather than mandating specific programs. The approach promised to cut down on red tape in Washington by decentralizing programs and building smaller bureaucracies via state criminal justice planning agencies. Yet once the first LEAA grants reached the states, the vast mishandling of funds and states' lack of attention to Nixon's urban police "change agents" called into question the effectiveness of New Federalism and its deregulatory approach to domestic social programs.[19]

THE LEAA AND ITS DISCONTENTS

Nixon had criticized the Johnson administration's management of the national law enforcement program during his campaign. He charged that lack of coordination among the various federal agencies involved in crime control, coupled with what Nixon and his campaigners characterized as a "mass of departments, bureaus and agencies with duplicative staffing, competing responsibilities, poor coordination and correlation, and self-defeating jealousies and suspicions," had made the LEAA under Johnson incapable of effectively addressing crime.[20] Yet these problems proliferated in the LEAA on the Nixon administration's watch and under the block grant system, when inefficiency, contradictions, and corruption within the agency and the crime war measures the agency funded foreshadowed the problems within the Nixon administration that the Watergate investigation would soon reveal.

For example, block grants and the reliance on the private sector to provide law enforcement with weapons, technology, and equipment benefited corporate leaders closely tied to the Nixon administration.

One such corporation was the accounting firm Ernst & Ernst, which was headed by prominent members of Nixon's 1972 re-election campaign. The chief of Ernst & Ernst's Washington office, Julian O. Kay, organized a number of fundraising galas for the "Victory '72 Dinner Committee," and Ernst & Ernst's managing partner, Richard Baker, chaired the volunteer Certified Public Accountants Committee for the Re-election of the President. In all, Ernst & Ernst employees donated $20,000 to Nixon's campaign. Meanwhile, Ernst & Ernst received large subsidies from the LEAA for various law enforcement projects. The company worked on both the state and local levels to report crime rates and to draw up law enforcement literature. It was paid $40,000 to conduct surveys for the Washington, DC, Police Department and the state of New Mexico. In two separate manuals developed for Louisiana, law enforcement planners working at Ernst & Ernst plagiarized significant portions of existing government publications and still collected $30,000. Indiana, ripe with corruption and misuse of federal funds, granted the firm $300,000 in law enforcement contracts without competitive bidding. Other corporations worked with criminal justice planners at the national and state levels and amassed a monopoly over specific crime prevention areas. The Motorola electronics company monopolized the sale of police radio equipment with the LEAA grant it received, in most cases at or above list prices without competitive bidding. Nearly $200,000 in federal LEAA grant funds went to Motorola to supply the equipment in the state of Wisconsin alone.[21]

In some cases, criminal justice planning agencies supported consulting firms that appeared to form for the sole purpose of reaping the newly available federal grants. A TV announcer, a newspaper editor, and an oil company executive in Alabama started the corporation Criminal Justice Systems to design statewide crime prevention plans. The firm received an LEAA contract just shy of six figures on the same day it incorporated. The three men used the funds to draft a proposal that involved spending half a million dollars on a secret state police force. The Justice Department did not accept that plan, but Criminal Justice Systems received funds from the Alabama Law Enforcement Planning Agency. The LEAA sent five inspectors to the state and discovered that Alabama's planning agency funded a police cadet college costing the federal government more than $100,000, mostly attended by the sons, friends, and relatives of high-ranking state officials. Fed up with the misuses of federal funds, Velde met with Governor George Wallace in early 1971, but the LEAA administrator found himself "just charmed by George" during the visit, and the federal government did little to curtail the corrupt crime war–funding practices in the state.[22]

Alongside such examples of corruption in the distribution and use of federal crime-fighting funds, the limitations of the block grant system quickly became apparent to some Justice Department officials. LEAA administrators expected states to dedicate the federal money they had received to police, courts, and corrections, but planners in states like Indiana used action grant funds to send cards to citizens, urging them to pledge their commitment to the Ten Commandments as a crime prevention measure. This was not the national law enforcement program Rogovin and Ruth had in mind when they helped design it as members of the Crime Commission, and both administrators resigned from the LEAA in March 1970. Rogovin had been frustrated by continued disagreements with Velde and Coster over the direction and purpose of the War on Crime and with the restrictions imposed by the troika leadership model, under which all decisions had to be unanimous.[23] The Safe Streets Act stipulated that Nixon appoint a Democrat in Rogovin's place, but the president opted to leave the top leadership position in the administration vacant until Congress amended the law, ending the troika model and permitting Nixon to designate a fellow Republican.

In the spring of 1971, after nearly a year without an official agency head, Nixon selected a candidate to direct the LEAA who was deeply committed to the Republican Party and the ideological principles of the administration. Jerris Leonard, another former aide to Roman Hruska, the Senate's loudest proponent of the War on Crime, lacked any direct experience in law enforcement or criminal justice. Leonard had worked for Mitchell while an undergraduate, and even though Leonard had to resign from three all-white social clubs in Milwaukee before he could be sworn in as deputy attorney general, Mitchell trusted him to head the Department of Justice's Civil Rights Division, the position Leonard held before his promotion to LEAA director. As the Civil Rights Division's leader, Leonard had proven he would consistently follow Mitchell's orders when it came to federal action on civil rights abuses. Leonard had brought Mitchell a suit that he described as "solid" with "good facts" charging racial discrimination within the real estate firm Coldwell-Banker, but the Civil Rights Division quickly backed off the case at Mitchell's insistence. As Leonard explained to his assistants, Mitchell knew "some of the top people in Coldwell-Banker and can't believe that these practices are 'co. policy.'" When given the task of desegregating schools in Mississippi, Leonard delayed the process until he eventually—if reluctantly—forced the state to comply after lawyers within his own division protested their director's inaction on the issue. Leonard also led the investigations of the 1969 murders of the Black Panther leader Fred Hampton during a raid conducted by Chicago police in conjunction with the FBI and a tactical unit of the Cook County, Illinois, U.S. Attorney's Office, as well as the shooting of Kent State University students by the National Guard in 1970. Despite his own discovery that the Chicago police fired at Hampton and other Panthers between eighty-two and ninety-nine times (the Panthers successfully returned one gunshot), and the Guardsmen involved in the Kent State incident shot off sixty-seven rounds of ammunition in just thirteen seconds, killing four students and seriously wounding nine others, Leonard concluded there was insufficient evidence to press charges against either law enforcement authority despite the undeniable display of excessive force in both cases.[24] With a poor record on antidiscrimination, civil rights, and police brutality, Leonard was now in a position to preside over the implementation of crime war programs with little regard for their deeply racist dimensions.

Under Leonard's direction, the LEAA's mismanagement of federal crime control funds grew worse. In keeping with the outlook of Mitchell and White House officials, Leonard was intent to refocus the LEAA on an urgent national effort on urban areas. States began to receive federal law enforcement funds in less than a month, in some instances before the LEAA had a chance to review their grant proposals. It was more important, in Leonard's view, to get federal crime control funds to riot-prone cities. Later, Leonard's response to the increasing scrutiny of corruption and discriminatory practices embedded within the LEAA and the block grant system mirrored that of his counterparts elsewhere in the Nixon administration. Isolating himself, Leonard carefully selected his public engagements and refused to hold press conferences or speak to reporters at length.[25]

During Leonard's tenure at the LEAA, it became clear to journalists and policymakers that in a number of states, federal law enforcement assistance had evolved into a system of political patronage. The director of the Indiana Criminal Justice Planning Agency, entrusted with disbursing half a million dollars' worth of federal law enforcement funds, resigned within the first year of the program, telling LEAA officials that the governor appointed close acquaintances and "people who are publicly somebody but who don't know anything about crime." The city of Gary, considered the epicenter of crime in Indiana, had no representatives on the state planning agency. Similar favoritism took place in other states. The director of the southwest LEAA region notified an LEAA administrator that "New Mexico's Governor is wont to use the SPA [state planning agency] as his personal staff for speech-writing." Florida also used law enforcement funds to enlarge the governor's office instead of the criminal justice planning agency.[26]

In the summer of 1971, even as Leonard prepared a $200,000 renovation of LEAA headquarters, including a redesign of his own office with modernist silver foil walls and a private bathroom, Democrats in Congress who were disenchanted with Nixon's decentralized approach attacked the LEAA, partly to reveal the shortcomings of New Federalism and discredit the administration's policies for their own political gain. The Legal and Monetary Affairs Subcommittee of the House Committee on Government Operations opened an investigation of the LEAA in July 1971. After discovering gross spending irregularities in the federal government's urban renewal program, Connecticut's John S. Monagan moved on to chair the subcommittee, stacking his team with fellow Democrats and setting the climate for the upcoming 1972 election. In a report titled "The Unrealized Promise of Safe Streets," the subcommittee ultimately concluded that the LEAA's block grant program had no impact on crime rates, even as it spent a total of $1.4 billion in three years. On the defensive, the Department of Justice and the LEAA charged that the subcommittee and other critics of the federal crime program only focused on a few problem states and used the LEAA, in the words of Leonard, as a "whipping boy" for opponents of New Federalism.[27]

The subcommittee's investigation unearthed fraudulent and criminal behavior at all levels: governors, members of the boards of criminal justice planning agencies, top LEAA administrators, and corporate executives alike dipped into the growing pot of criminal justice funding to suit their own interests. States could invest and collect interest on block grants, and Louisiana invested more than $13 million worth of anti-crime funds in U.S. Treasury bills, collecting more than $15,000 from the money the state loaned back to the federal government. The LEAA's reliance on private contracting, too, opened up opportunities for corruption. In Arkansas, for example, four state officials bought stock in the Texas consulting firm Interlock just before it received a half-million-dollar LEAA grant to set up a computerized traffic safety information system and draft a prison management program for the Arkansas State Board of Corrections. The House investigation also revealed that many officials misused federal crime-fighting funds for personal purposes. Police officers in St. Paul were given marked cars to take home and drive off-duty, supposedly as a crime deterrent but without any tests conducted first to measure the benefit of the practice. The Illinois Criminal Justice Planning Agency—which rarely used its luxurious Des Plains office paid for by the LEAA at a cost of $20,000 annually—bought a state airplane with federal crime war funds that was used to transport Governor Edgar Whitcomb to various functions.[28]

Despite federal policymakers' knowledge of corruption and inefficiency within the LEAA, the White House and Department of Justice officials remained largely unscathed from Monagan's investigation and the growing criticism the administration received for its handling of the War on Crime, and most of the local officials involved never faced charges. Having served seven terms in Congress, Monagan lost his seat in the House after building a strong case against the LEAA in the 1972 election. His opponent, Republican state representative Ronald Sarasin, attacked Monagan for being soft on crime and endorsing "reckless government spending" on social welfare programs, even though the Democrat had exposed vast mismanagement of taxpayer funds in urban social programs during his final term in office. Nixon went on to a landslide victory in Connecticut and the rest of the country. Leonard, meanwhile, left the agency for private practice, providing legal representation to Republican National Committee chair George H. W. Bush and later serving on Ronald Reagan's presidential transition team and as an advisor to President Bush in 1989, concluding his political career as a consultant on the George W. Bush transition team in 2000.[29]

If the Nixon administration intended the LEAA to demonstrate the efficiency of block grants, it had failed. Instead, several years into the LEAA's existence, the administration was left wondering how to remedy the unforeseeable consequences of planning at the state level, and federal agencies debated "the degree of federal intervention required to achieve national purposes." In an internal document describing the planning process, LEAA officials concluded that "neither state nor local government is presently staffed, organized, or financed in a manner to enable effective planning and coordination." On the whole, the plans the LEAA received from states agencies were "poor." The LEAA generals still believed their direction for the crime war was sound. The problem was inefficiency and misguided priorities at the level of state command. Too much, it seemed, had been given to the states. "Most of the crime in question," Mitchell wrote to House Speaker John William McCormack in early 1970, "is the so-called street crime." Pointing out that Title I of the Safe Streets Act provided the mechanism for federal discretionary aid, Mitchell affirmed "the present Administration is dedicated to an increasingly effective utilization of that Act" to guarantee that urban areas received their fair share of funds.[30] The Nixon administration soon acted to ensure that police departments in cities with high rates of reported crime and high concentrations of African Americans had ample resources at their disposal.

CRIME WAR ZONES

In a 1969 petition called "The Forgotten Cities," sixteen mayors from the urban Midwest complained to Attorney General Mitchell about the way state planning agencies kept law enforcement funds from the places in the state with the most severe crime problems. Instead, crime control block grants were awarded to powerful state legislators representing rural constituencies. These mayors as well as like-minded policymakers contended that urban crime was as much a threat to the security of the United States as was Vietnam. "The forces of lawlessness appear to be alarmingly close to victory over the forces of peace," Indiana Democrat Vance Hartke told his colleagues in Congress in support of the petition. "If positive action is not taken, and taken soon, a crime crisis of unprecedented proportions will soon surely envelop the nation." It seemed to Hartke and many other politicians and law enforcement officials that the LEAA did little more than build criminal justice bureaucracies at the state level. Not only did state criminal justice planning agencies use substantial portions of LEAA funding for other agencies, such as the Federal Housing Authority and the Department of Defense, but planners in Hartke's own state of Indiana used block grants for seemingly foolish programs.[31]

Concerned about the misguided use of block grant funds, LEAA administrators debated "the degree of federal intervention required to achieve national purposes." Even if state criminal justice expenditures failed to address the problems stemming from urban street crime as policymakers had intended with block grants, the White House and the Justice Department shaped the course of the national law enforcement program with novel use of discretionary aid to ensure that "high crime" neighborhoods would be adequately patrolled and that "hard-core" criminals would receive swift and sure punishment. Treating the "all-out war" on black urban street crime as a "military operation," Nixon officials sought to "first establish the machinery that enables us to gain control of the problem before we can hope to solve it," as White House aide Tom Charles Huston put it in a March 1970 memo.[32] This meant not only appropriating more discretionary funds but also creating new opportunities for the arrest and sentencing of the citizens whom the White House held responsible for the nation's crime.

The Nixon administration led Congress in a series of steps that successfully expanded the carceral state at the local level and maintained the War on Crime's intended focus on low-income black urban communities. First, following the recommendation of his Advisory Council on Crime and Law Enforcement, Nixon pledged to launch a special crime control effort in Washington, DC. The administration could channel funds to the District via the "Large City Special Grants" section of the Safe Streets Act in the interim. Under this discretionary program, cities could receive up to $100,000 in federal funds based on formulas that took into account population size and crime rates. Although DC did not meet the same criteria as did New York, Chicago, Los Angeles, Philadelphia, Detroit, Houston, Baltimore, Dallas, Cleveland, Milwaukee, and San Francisco, the District had been a federal concern since it assumed a black majority and received a special grant. Congress gave cities the freedom to spend the funds for "any phase of law enforcement or crime control activity" as long as the program was "targeted at high crime areas and high crime problems." When the legislation came up for reauthorization in 1970, congressional representatives allocated even more funds to "the nation's large cities where high crime incidence and law enforcement projects present the most difficult challenges." Whereas Congress allocated $32 million to discretionary funding in 1969, with a third going to large cities, that figure more than doubled to $70 million the following year, with more than 40 percent going to large cities. Further reflecting the federal government's commitment to fighting street crime, the maximum grant skyrocketed from $100,000 to $1 million during the same period, an allocation that only New York City received. Finally, with the 1972 election approaching and with rates of reported crime continuing to soar, top White House and Department of Justice officials planned the discretionary High Impact program in eight cities with serious crime problems and fewer than a million residents. Although the program was touted as an "across-the-board attack on burglaries, robberies, muggings, assaults and rapes," during the four years in which High Impact operated, these problems worsened in all of the cities involved.[33]

Nixon began to implement the recommendations of the Advisory Council on Crime and Law Enforcement less than a week after his inauguration, refocusing anticrime attention on troublesome urban areas. On January 27, 1969, at a press conference publicizing the $123,524 grant the local police department received from the LEAA that day, Nixon declared a separate "War on Crime" for Washington, DC. The District had evolved into a majority black city with one of the highest rates of reported crime in the nation over the course of the 1950s, as federal employees steadily moved to the suburbs. The president believed that lack of safety in the capital city, where federal officials would not "dare leave their cars in the capital garage and walk alone," was a "tragic example" of the national crime problem. The District had been a testing ground for federal law enforcement initiatives since the antidelinquency programs of the Kennedy administration, and Lyndon Johnson's DC Crime Control Bill of 1967 set the precedent for the federal government's explicit focus on law enforcement in the District.[34]

After receiving a set of recommendations from the President's Commission on Crime in the District of Columbia in late 1966, Johnson sent Congress a legislative proposal for action. Johnson's version of the bill gave police the authority to issue citations to suspects on the streets and in lieu of taking a person into custody, allowed warrantless arrests with probable cause, and instituted "investigative detention," whereby DC residents could be questioned for up to three hours without formal charges. All of these measures enabled law enforcement officials to establish criminal records on a wider range of residents and to easily bring suspects into the criminal justice system. In anticipation of future uprisings, the legislation also included a special riot control law that regulated the gathering of residents in groups of five or more persons. With conservative representatives leading the way, the House overwhelmingly passed Johnson's bill in late June 1967 with a few critical additions. The House version made robbery a crime of violence in the District and attached a host of new mandatory minimums of one to five years for burglary, two years for robbery, and an indeterminate sentence of two years to life for any crime committed with a firearm. Before the bill passed the Senate with these provisions, Iowa's Republican senator Jack Miller introduced an amendment that extended the warrantless arrests for residents who appeared as though they were "about to commit" a misdemeanor. Both the House and Senate accepted this provision by voice vote, as did the president when he signed the bill into law. Foreshadowing the same reluctance he would go on to express in enacting the Safe Streets Act—not because of block grants but because of the questionable wiretapping provisions the legislation included—Johnson signed the DC Crime Control Bill into law despite his reservations about the mandatory minimum sentences the act imposed. Along with northern Democrats and moderate eastern Republicans, Johnson viewed such measures as an attack on judicial discretion and a "backward step in modern correctional policy." Ultimately however, "no more serious domestic problem faces America than the growing menace of crime in our streets," as Johnson said in his remarks on signing the DC Crime Act, regardless of the ethical and constitutional issues they raised.[35]

The Nixon administration built eagerly on this precedent, beginning with the January 1969 grant. Under Nixon, roughly an eighth of the entire budget of the LEAA went to DC, resulting in the largest number of police per capita in the world. With pressure coming directly from the White House, Washington police chief Jerry V. Wilson instructed his captains in 1971 to reduce crime in the city or expect to leave the force. To help the city reach Wilson's goal and the federal government's shared objectives, the LEAA funded a four-person "warrant squad" to arrest parole violators with discretionary "Large City Special Grants" funding. It also supported measures to supervise suspects released on bail in the District, relying on new statistical systems the federal government was funding and developing, including the National Crime Information Center and Project SEARCH (System for Electronic Analysis and Retrieval of Criminal Histories). These initiatives received a $50 million LEAA grant to coordinate criminal information and make arrest histories easily accessible to officers.[36]

Congress expanded the federal government's authority in low-income urban areas with discretionary allocations, whereby national programs could be implemented outside of the block grant funding structure, to enable municipal authorities in Washington, DC, to fight their own crime war complete with an unprecedented criminal code. The Nixon administration's District of Columbia Court Reorganization Act of 1970—the first of the administration's crime control bills approved by Congress—reflected the approach of the most ardent law-and-order policymakers, bureaucrats within the administration, and conservative criminologists, all of whom believed only severe sentences and widespread arrests could make a dent on crime.

The 1970 legislation introduced an entirely new plane of punitive policy. It required a mandatory minimum sentence of five years for anyone convicted of a second armed offense and allowed life sentences for those convicted of a third felony in an early version of the "three strikes and you're out" law later adopted by California and New York. It also reduced judicial discretion by establishing several categories of offenders and requiring standardized punishments for various new classifications. "Dangerous special criminals" who committed "offenses with high risk of additional public danger if the defendant is released," such as bank robbery or narcotics trafficking, could now be confined for longer periods, and "narcotics addicts" suddenly faced prison time. The act permitted judges to increase sentences of habitual offenders by thirty years if the suspects were charged with a third offense, and applied the same formula to first-time offenders if the crime seemed to fit a "pattern of criminal conduct." The act also gave judges the authority to place individuals on probation without a verdict for relatively minor crimes such as disturbing the peace or public intoxication, and established a permanent requirement for formerly incarcerated city residents to submit to drug testing. Finally, the legislation was particularly harsh on youth offenders. It stipulated that any youth age sixteen or above (and in very special cases, fifteen or above) charged with first degree burglary, armed robbery, rape, or murder or with an *intent* to commit one of these offenses should be taken out of the jurisdiction of juvenile court. As a result of this measure, adult courts soon heard more than half of all juvenile cases in the District, and the act effectively increased the likelihood that young residents would be incarcerated for long periods.[37]

Walter Fauntroy, the pastor of New Bethel Baptist Church who would be elected that fall as the first delegate to Congress from DC, characterized the law as "the cutting edge of fascism and oppression in the United States." Indeed, the DC Court Reorganization Act pioneered several measures whose widespread adoption the Nixon administration hoped to encourage. Preventative detention—the practice of detaining suspects without bail for up to two months—appeared for the first time in the American criminal code in the legislation. For Nixon's officials, the preemptive policy offered a "reasonable and necessary approach to the crime problem" by ensuring that accused criminals were behind bars and thus unable to *possibly* commit crime. Because most of the people who were detained as a pretrial measure were too poor to make bail, the opponents of the practice charged that it violated the equal protection clause and prohibitions against excessive bail and cruel and unusual punishment under the Constitution. In addition, the broad wiretapping authority the legislation provided to federal and local police forces, as well as the "no knock" raids it endorsed allowing police to break into the home of a suspect without a warrant or without announcing their purpose, presented a direct assault on the Supreme Court's expansion of defendants' rights and search-and-seizure rulings during the 1960s.[38]

Despite the questionable constitutionality of the legislation, with DC as its "showcase," the administration set a precedent for state and local governments to endorse a more punitive approach to patrol, arrest, and sentencing and the wider adoption of mandatory minimums and preventative detention. Variations of the "no knock" provision were already on the books in twenty-nine states, but immediately following the enactment of the DC Court Reorganization Act, law enforcement officials arrested thousands of residents while conducting thousands of "no knock" raids from New York City to Atlanta. In 1973, New York State revised existing codes and instituted the drug laws favored by Governor Nelson Rockefeller, which called for a mandatory minimum sentence of fifteen years to life for suspects caught with relatively small amounts of heroin or cocaine. Five years later, the Michigan legislature passed the "650-Lifer Law," requiring judges to sentence offenders convicted of the possession of 1.5 pounds of cocaine or more to life imprisonment without parole. Although the federal government and most state governments did not embrace preventative detention practices until the 1980s, when half of all the current laws were enacted, the practice of incarcerating individuals believed to be dangerous to the public went on to become widely sanctioned during the wars on drugs and terror as a mechanism to detain suspects.[39]

When Congress reauthorized the LEAA in 1970, it advanced the federal government's commitment to fighting urban street crime by allocating nearly 40 percent of the agency's discretionary budget to support projects in "the nation's large cities where high crime incidence and law enforcement problems present the most difficult challenges." Ostensibly, the $25 million grant was intended to improve "coordination and understanding" between black residents and police in "high crime" neighborhoods. But in reality, the Nixon administration was increasingly distancing itself from police-community relations programs. Half of the discretionary funds continued to support the hardware and manpower needs of local police departments. Following the pattern that emerged during the early law enforcement programs of the Johnson administration, crime increased after the LEAA placed more police officers with advanced weapons on the streets.[40]

With this substantial raise in discretionary funding from Congress, the Nixon administration initiated the single most ambitious project the LEAA would launch in its short history, costing $160 million (just under $1 billion in today's dollars). Vice President Spiro Agnew, Attorney General John Mitchell, White House domestic affairs assistant John Ehrlichman, and head Law Enforcement Assistance Administrator Jerris Leonard devised High Impact in late 1971 to focus the national government's law enforcement intervention beyond major metropolitan centers. The program sought to "bring sharp, rapid reduction in street crime and burglary—the types of violent, serious crime most prevalent and most feared by the public" in eight selected cities with less than a million residents, the majority with high concentrations of low-income African Americans.[41] The LEAA guaranteed each city $20 million over a three-year period to create local criminal justice planning agencies to design and implement innovative law enforcement programs with extra assistance and oversight from White House and Department of Justice officials.

In January 1972, LEAA administrators announced the High Impact program to great media attention, claiming it would lower rates of serious crimes by 5 percent in the first two years and as much as 20 percent within five years. Martin Danziger, one of the main High Impact planners at the Criminal Justice Institute, later commented on the crime indication figures: "I just made them up. It sounded good. . . . They needed the twenty percent goal for sex appeal. It was an educated guess and it was important to start sending quantified goals in the criminal justice system." Nevertheless, these quantified goals provided Nixon with a powerful talking point during the 1972 campaign if his record on crime came into question, since the problem had worsened under his watch despite the promises of his 1968 campaign.[42]

The administration's selection of High Impact sites had clear electoral and racial implications. Nixon needed to carry Texas, Oregon, and Colorado to secure his reelection. Thus, the administration selected Dallas, Portland, and Denver for the program—High Impact's "advantaged cities," as federal planners called them—despite their comparatively low crime rates and the fact that all three cities had witnessed an increase in both population and manufacturing sector employment during the 1960s. With black populations of less than 10 percent each, the LEAA granted the local criminal justice planning agencies in these southern and western cities relative autonomy in administering the program. In Newark, Baltimore, Cleveland, Atlanta, and St. Louis—High Impact's "disadvantaged cities"—LEAA officials worked closely with municipal authorities to develop guidelines and strategies for High Impact projects. A black majority seemed imminent in these eastern and midwestern sites, and all five faced higher percentages of families living below the poverty level, the loss of tens of thousands of manufacturing jobs, and the decline of middle-class tax bases in the wake of urban unrest during the previous decade.[43]

Reflecting the larger strategies that federal policymakers developed for the crime war, the priority of the program was to improve street patrol and surveillance. The federal funds would support the influx of "more policemen, with better tactics, equipment, and training," as LEAA director Leonard put it. High Impact planners drastically expanded street patrols more than any other facet of the program. In its grant application, Baltimore indicated that it would use High Impact funds to engender a fivefold increase of foot patrolmen by 1973, from just seventy officers to 410. As soon as Baltimore officials received their first grant installment, they used nearly half of their $1.8 million check to add fifty-two policemen to the streets, using the remaining funds for walkie-talkies, helicopters, and the addition of nine special tactical units. High Impact directors could easily get funding for new equipment such as helicopters (which, the Department of Justice averred, had "been successful as a crime deterrent in some areas") and improved radio and dispatch systems to dispatch officers to crime scenes efficiently, and Baltimore officials took full advantage of this federal priority.[44]

Not surprisingly, given federal policymakers' long concern about delinquency and crime among young low-income urban residents, many of High Impact's youth-focused programs continued the strategies that emerged during the Kennedy and Johnson administrations that tied antidelinquency efforts to social services. Planners in Cleveland concluded that "male young adults and juveniles, non-white, uneducated and unemployed" had committed most of the crimes in the city. Local officials turned to the Youth Service Bureau model, spending $6 million to establish a center for young people with criminal records and "potentially delinquent" youth. By comparison, the Cleveland Vocation and Educational Program, providing summer recreation for low-income youths and generating "adequate jobs for the socially disadvantaged and economically deprived," received a paltry $1.4 million in funding from the High Impact pot. Baltimore planners limited the participation in these types of job training programs to juvenile offenders alone. The Port of Baltimore Sea School trained and prepared convicts for maritime careers, providing educational and counseling services for the sixteen- to eighteen-year-old male participants. The Sea School and other such programs in other High Impact cities increasingly made access to social services available only to residents who had criminal or prison records, or who appeared vulnerable to criminal activity. New approaches to juvenile corrections, including alternatives to institutionalization, vocational education for ex-offenders, counseling services, and employment placement, amounted to a meager 14 percent of all High Impact initiatives.[45]

The actual results of the High Impact program exposed the War on Crime's essential misfires, as two separate evaluations of the program concluded—one by the private Mitre Corporation with $2.4 million in LEAA funds, one conducted independently by the National Security Center (NSC)—that the 200 separate anticrime projects launched by the program had no immediate impact. (The NSC characterized the High Impact program in its 1976 report as an "irresponsible, ill-conceived and politically motivated effort to throw money at a social program.") Instead of dropping 5 percent as Attorney General Mitchell promised, total crime in all eight cities rose more than 43 percent from 1972 to 1976. As planners in Baltimore focused on hardware and security in housing projects, spending $200,000 for additional guards, television monitors, and intercoms in public facilities, crime in the city went up nearly 50 percent. In Dallas, which spent more than $50,000 on a program that tied burglar alarms to a helicopter response system, crime shot up 82 percent. Theft and burglary rates did stabilize in some cities, but violent crime grew to be an even more severe problem by the end of the program.[46]

Whether the reported escalation of crime in the High Impact cities was due to the increase in patrol and surveillance technologies the federal government introduced in the targeted areas with discretionary funding, it was clear to the Nixon administration that the national law enforcement program was losing the war against the "enemy within." Instead of seriously reevaluating their own strategies, policymakers and law enforcement officials increasingly came to view the failures of federal crime control programs as evidence that black urban violence was a foregone conclusion. Unsuccessful law enforcement programs, proponents said, were less the result of questionable tactics and misguided strategy and more the consequence of community pathology. In this respect, the War on Crime had not gone far enough. In order to effectively stop crime, the national law enforcement program needed to shift the focus of its urban intervention, deploying its foot soldiers not only in courts but also in prisons.

The unprecedented federal investment into local police departments from 1965 onward during the first stage of the War on Crime produced an increase in arrests that led, in turn, to the overcrowding of urban jails, court systems, and, increasingly, rural correctional facilities. At the same time, the provisions of the DC Court Act and the practices it generated eventually doubled the number of felony indictments, fueling the incarceration of young urban black men during the 1970s, who accounted for half of the increase in the national prison population during what Nixon officials came to regard as a "new era" for penal confinement. The government's response to the perceived crisis of crime in DC and other cities with high concentrations of African American residents had produced a new series of problems in its penal and juridical systems. Accordingly, the Nixon administration led Congress in enacting fundamental changes to the scope and purpose of American prisons. By revising the LEAA's block grant structure yet again, federal policymakers started a new direction for their punitive intervention within the corrections arm of the criminal justice system, a critical complement to the Nixon administration's general use of discretionary funds and the punitive climate officials spawned in Washington, DC, with an ongoing focus on low-income black urban Americans.

THE "LONG-RANGE MASTER PLAN"

When Richard Nixon took office in 1969, he inherited a penal system that had been shedding prisoners. The 1960s produced the single largest reduction in the population of federal and state prisons in the nation's history, with 16,500 fewer inmates in 1969 than in 1950. Despite this trend toward decarceration, under the auspices of the Nixon administration the federal government began to construct prisons at unprecedented rates. A record half million Americans were confined in penal institutions by the end of the 1970s, reflecting an increase of more than 25 percent, or an additional 120,000 incarcerated men and women. A growing prisoners' rights movement argued that this substantial rise in incarceration was the product of racial profiling in policing and draconian sentencing policies put in place by laws such as the DC Court Reorganization Act of 1970. Policymakers and law enforcement officials explained it as the seemingly inevitable result of high rates of reported crime and violence in segregated urban neighborhoods. But both of these explanations missed a crucial reason for the growth of prison populations. Beginning in the Nixon administration, federal policymakers and White House officials used discretionary funding and executive powers to envision and actively plan for the dramatic growth of the penal system.[47]

As Nixon worked with Attorney General John Mitchell to draft the DC Crime Control Act and twenty other law enforcement bills during his first six months in office, the administration also planned to increase the nation's capacity to incarcerate its citizens. In November 1969, Nixon sent Mitchell a long memo on the dismal state of the American prison system, directing him to lead the Bureau of Prisons in making "the federal correction system a prototype for the much needed overhaul of our generally archaic state and local corrections institutions." Nixon predicted that the prison problem would only grow worse in the future, pointing out that while he believed the national law enforcement program would deter crime in the long run, in the short term the policing strategies that policymakers embraced had substantially increased the arrest rate, clogging the court system and leading to overcrowding in the nation's penal institutions that could no longer be ignored by federal policymakers.[48]

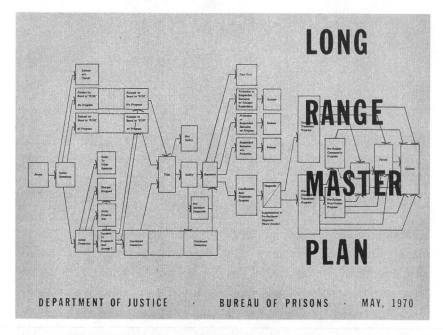

The ten-year "Long-Range Master Plan" Nixon called for in the spring of 1970 remains one of the starkest declarations of policymakers' turn toward managing, rather than ameliorating, racial inequality through confinement in the post–civil rights era. *U.S. Bureau of Prisons, Egil Krogh Collection, Richard Nixon Presidential Library and Museum*

On Nixon's orders, in the spring of 1970, the Bureau of Prisons had devised a ten-year "Long-Range Master Plan" to expand and modernize the American correctional system. The $500 million initially allotted for this expansion—more than $1.5 billion in today's dollars—represented an entirely new phase of investment in federal prisons. The Department of Justice, created in 1870, had operated only three penal facilities for the first fifty years of its existence, although it steadily opened twenty-four more between 1923 and 1950. Mitchell worked closely with the Bureau of Prisons as it set out to construct a dozen prisons for adult men, a dozen reformatories, four women's prisons, four psychiatric facilities, and a special Metropolitan Correctional Center to replace overburdened jails in select "high crime" urban areas by the end of the decade. Nixon had called for a "prototype" at the federal level that would inspire states to follow suit, and the administration's strategies reverberated throughout the entire American penal system.[49]

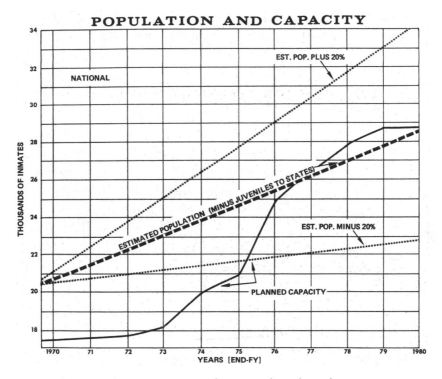

POPULATION AND CAPACITY

Anchored by skewed statistics, crime predictions, and penal population projections such as this one—both a distillate of fears and assumptions plotted as dotted lines along an X/Y axis and a prescription for future governmental responses to poverty and deindustrialization—the remarkable prison construction project launched by the Nixon administration essentially anticipated mass incarceration. *U.S. Bureau of Prisons, Egil Krogh Collection, Richard Nixon Presidential Library and Museum*

The Nixon administration's commitment to a complete overhaul of American prisons all but ensured the future arrest and incarceration of millions of Americans far removed from the meeting rooms of the White House and the Bureau of Prisons. Mitchell and other Nixon officials knew well that their anticrime policies would result in a significant increase in the number of Americans behind bars. The draconian sentencing measures Nixon planned for DC, as well as the heavy-handed policing strategies he and other conservative policymakers supported, were rationalized by the idea that incarceration functioned as a powerful crime deterrent, the value of which could only succeed if punishment was certain. "Deterrence and retribution, many times overlooked in the language of criminal justice, are again being recognized as valid reasons for incarceration," as Norman Carlson, the director of the Bureau of Prisons from 1970 to 1987, testified before the House Subcommittee on Courts, Civil Liberties, and the Administration of Justice in 1975. In embracing the expansion of the prison system and the incarceration of violators for long periods as the only effective means to protect society, Carlson and other Nixon officials believed prisoner rehabilitation was an impractical goal. "The idea that violent offenders can be 'rehabilitated' by some combination of vocational, counseling, and other programs, inside or outside an institution, has yet to be demonstrated," Carlson argued, citing the work of criminologist Norval Morris and political scientist James Q. Wilson.[50] Far from an inevitable process, the deliberate strategy of increasing the number of prisoners that federal officials and law enforcement authorities embraced throughout the 1970s was a critical aspect of the War on Crime.

An internal and confidential bureau document, the Long-Range Master Plan was originally intended only for high-level Nixon officials and Bureau of Prisons administrators. The construction project was "essentially an in-house planning operation," as Carlson explained, and thus its contents did not reach the public until authorities broke ground on the new prisons. Mitchell, Carlson, and the other officials involved in developing the plan failed to include even policymakers in their discussions, instead bringing in a small advising panel with unnamed legal experts and psychologists who served as a "sounding board" for the top-secret team.[51]

When the bureau began working on the Long-Range Master Plan in early 1970, many federal and state facilities had failed to provide each prisoner with a private cell or at least seventy-five to eighty square feet of personal space—the basic standards as determined by the United Nations and the federal government's own National Advisory Commission on Criminal Justice Standards and Goals. The fact that many state and federal facilities had failed to meet these requirements, coupled with severe prison overcrowding in the era of the War on Crime, provided the Nixon administration a strong justification for the reconstruction of the prison system at all levels of government.[52] The bureau and its consultants devised four broad goals for the Long-Range Master Plan: to reduce overcrowding, replace antiquated institutions, establish more humane conditions, and improve general security to increase the safety of both guards and prisoners. The Metropolitan Correctional Centers the bureau designed, for example, were intended to offer authorities in New York, Chicago, San Diego, San Francisco, Philadelphia, and other major cities a replacement for outmoded jails. Even more, the Metropolitan Centers extended the federal penal system from remote areas to the urban "epicenter" of crime.

The Long-Range Master Plan initially called for 2,450 additional prison beds in the Metropolitan Centers and other federal institutions, a figure that grew as the Nixon and Ford administrations worked with the bureau to revise the plan during the 1970s. The bureau estimated a 20 percent increase in the federal population between 1972 and 1982, and as such, the total budget for federal prisons rose from $69.5 million in 1969 to $176.3 million by 1972, of which $60 million alone was designated for the construction of new prisons. Within the first five years of the Long-Range Master Plan, federal prison authorities had successfully added 1,600 additional beds to the system.[53]

The entire rationale for escalating the scale of penal confinement was based not on the reality of crime but on population growth projections based on census estimates. The initial groundings for these forecasts came from the Crime and Kerner Commissions during the Johnson administration. The Crime Commission used census data to estimate that by 1975 prison populations would swell to 558,641 inmates, while the Kerner Commission analyzed census data to predict that young black Americans between the ages of fifteen and twenty-five—the demographic federal policymakers and law enforcement officials believed to be responsible for the bulk of the nation's crime—were the fastest-growing group in the United States. Later, this projection was discounted. In 1973, the National Advisory Commission on Criminal Justice Standards and Goals determined that this same youth population had peaked for the foreseeable future. But the administration nevertheless continued to encourage the tide of prison construction. Based on now-disproven assumptions that the number of black youths would increase and that, as a result of their being black youths, they would contribute to a rise in crime, the Bureau of Prisons planned to add twelve new juvenile institutions in 1970. In the same year that the Advisory Commission invalidated the population forecasts planners relied upon, federal officials proceeded to carry forth the plan, breaking ground on four juvenile prisons in Miami, Memphis, and small towns in Texas and Alabama.[54] Anchored in skewed statistics, crime predictions, and penal population projections, the Long-Range Master Plan that Nixon officials devised set in motion a self-fulfilling prophecy.

To meet the Long-Range Master Plan's ambitious aims, the Department of Justice created a National Clearinghouse of Criminal Justice Planning and Architecture to redesign the carceral landscape. The Clearinghouse recruited faculty from the Department of Architecture at University of Illinois to create new prison designs that would enhance general security while simultaneously fostering living conditions more suitable for larger populations serving longer sentences. The sociologists and architects involved produced an 800-page manual for prison planners that the LEAA used to guide states in designing 300 new facilities and overhauling old ones. While aiming to improve the security of prisons in general, these consultants hoped to upgrade the design of correctional facilities to make the experience of incarceration more humane. The consultants encouraged the substitution of hollow blocks for bars, the glazing of cinderblock walls, and the replacement of long corridors with winding pathways in hundreds of American prisons to foster an improved psychological state among incarcerated citizens. The Wharton School of Business and the Department of Architecture at the University of Pennsylvania provided federal officials with similar plans for juvenile facilities. The Clearinghouse also created teams of technicians, architects, food service specialists, and management experts to provide general guidance and assist state prison authorities with any problems they encountered as the projected influx of convicts entered the system. Meanwhile, as the Long-Range Master Plan triggered the creation of 110,522 new jobs in the punishment sector, federal programs trained a new cadre of staff and guards who, in theory, would be more sympathetic to the needs of prisoners in a changing correctional climate.[55]

This modernization and expansion process was in large part a response to the fact that black and Latino American populations started to approach majorities in many prisons beginning in the late 1960s and early 1970s. The Nixon administration sought to provide federal and state authorities with the tools to control this "new class of inmates" who, in the view of national officials and policymakers, were incapable of responding to rehabilitative attempts and posed a vexing problem to order and control inside prisons. "We must be prepared for this new wave of offenders coming into the prison system—ready not just with added beds and benches, but ready to make the most of an opportunity to reach a larger number of offenders with modern corrections techniques," Mitchell explained to penal administrators as he promoted the administration's strategies at the national conference of corrections in 1971.[56] Although the Long-Range Master Plan mentioned the need to create community-based alternatives for incarceration, officials did not include specific models to stimulate the implementation of these smaller and cost-effective facilities.

The Crime Commission, the Kerner Commission, and National Advisory Commission had encouraged authorities to invest in treatment centers, halfway houses, and other community-based carceral forms as an effective means of rehabilitation, but the Nixon administration was generally uninterested in using public funds to support their development, instead prioritizing the construction of maximum security facilities. In the more punitive maximum security climate, which essentially operated on the basis of a permanent lockdown, prisoners were permitted to leave their cells for only very short periods of time (usually an hour to two per day). This approach to confinement rose as Mitchell and other officials grew increasingly concerned about "offenders who cannot and will not respond to community supervision," as Carlson characterized them. "For these repeat offenders there is a need for some type of sanction, and I think it is incarceration." Framing the underlying socioeconomic issues in pathological terms, Nixon officials believed prison authorities could not effectively "deal with and attempt to rehabilitate this most difficult category of prisoners," or the "violent, aggressive, or disturbed offender." The modern prisons the Nixon administration sought to establish would include separate facilities for "hard-core criminals who require close supervision and particularly secure quarters," as the president wrote to Attorney General John Mitchell. When hunger strikes, fire setting, and formal and informal protests increased within prisons during the administration's early planning stages, and as the rebellion at Attica in September 1971 made national headlines, the apparent need for maximum security facilities became all the more pressing.[57]

For the "new class of inmates" housed in a maximum security setting, behavior modification, rather than rehabilitation, became the ultimate goal for corrections. At the Federal Medical Center in Springfield, Missouri, for example, the Special Treatment and Rehabilitative Training Program (START) placed groups of violent prisoners in complete isolation and subjected them to a lengthy series of experiments. These "tests" included shackling inmates to their steel beds by their arms and legs for days at a time, forcing them to remain in the leather straps and leather chains even as they ate, and humiliating them as they performed basic bodily functions. Framed by authorities and planners as "psychologically beneficial" to the inmates, the degradation, pain, and drug testing measures the START program inflicted came dangerously close to torture. The bureau eventually closed the Springfield facility in the spring of 1974 as a result of an American Civil Liberties Union (ACLU) lawsuit pending against the START program. That summer, the U.S. District Court of Missouri ruled that such programs violated the Constitution and that the purpose of the program was "not to develop behavior of an individual so that he would be able to conform his behavior to standards of society at large," but to make him into a better, more manageable prisoner.[58]

Following the closure of Springfield, prison planners designed "rehabilitation" and "treatment" measures throughout the federal and state systems that were less about providing social services or reintegration back into larger society, and more about regulating inmates who were increasingly committed for long stays in prison. One of 400 behavior modification initiatives the Department of Justice funded in twenty different states after 1974 was the Contingent Management Program developed at the Virginia State Penitentiary in Richmond. As the operations manual of the program stated, the goal was to modify the behavior of "troublesome inmates," to discipline them, so they could "be returned to the beneficial influence of correctional programs." Seven days a week, a white college graduate with a degree in psychology visited the Maximum Security Tier in the segregated C Building of the state prison, armed with a clipboard and a checklist. The inspector was to ascertain whether the mostly black inmates in the unit had tidied their five-foot-by-nine-foot cells, if they had made their beds, and if they were willing to engage in "polite" conversation. For each bit of approved behavior, the incarcerated person would be awarded a point, which was punched into a wallet-sized green credit card to be cashed in later for commissary items or Polaroid snapshots with family members during visitation. A prisoner who scored well and otherwise behaved well could advance to the next stage and move to a lower-security field camp. Many recognized the Contingent Management Program for what it was. "It's a subtle coercion," one of the participants, Antonio, remarked. "They use child psychology on you. You be good and we'll give you a candy bar." (Even the warden at Virginia State dubbed it a "Mickey Mouse Program for ten year olds.") "You think you're gaming on the man," Leon, another prisoner, recognized, "but the man's gaming on you." For others, the program did offer the only hope for, at least, a more comfortable stay in the prison, a way out of maximum security, and, at best, the prospect of early release.[59]

The bureau began to shift further and further away from rehabilitation programs as the policing strategies of the War on Crime, coupled with the federal government's prison construction initiative, brought the nation to the brink of mass incarceration. In line with the larger objectives of the Nixon administration, Carlson led the bureau in "viewing imprisonment as a means of retribution and punishment" rather than correction. Over the course of the 1970s, the bureau retreated from counseling, treatment, vocational training, and other rehabilitation programs, making them voluntary rather than required of prisoners, who now had the option of refusing such services as they wished. The effect was to divert money from rehabilitative programs to construction and general operations. Indeed, by the mid-1970s, only 10 percent of the billions of dollars federal and state authorities spent on corrections went to rehabilitation measures for prisoners.[60]

With the statistical "evidence," the architectural design, and the classification system in tow, the administration went on to impose the offender classifications, management techniques, and construction guidelines it developed on governors while Congress incentivized state prison construction in the 1970 LEAA reauthorization. "These directives and recommendations represent the most determined and comprehensive approach to corrections ever made in this country," Mitchell explained to prison administrators in the fall of 1971. "I refer not only to Federal corrections, but insofar as the Federal Government can provide funds, training and leadership, this approach is a Magna Carta of prison reform for all levels of government." By the end of the decade, as the administration anticipated, Mitchell and the Department of Justice led a nationwide corrections "improvement program" at all levels of government, transforming the American correctional landscape entirely.[61]

At a time when a number of policymakers, criminal justice authorities, and public figures were calling for the termination of prisons amid a growing prisoners' rights movement, emphasizing instead community-based alternatives, the Nixon administration's drive to increase the nation's penal population seemed all the more regressive. "I am persuaded that the institutions of prison probably must end," U.S. district court judge James Doyle reflected in a 1972 ruling in Wisconsin. "In many respects it is intolerable within the United States as was the institution of slavery, equally brutalizing to all involved, equally toxic to the social system, equally subversive of the brotherhood of men, even more costly by some standards and probably less rational." The federal government's own National Advisory Commission on Criminal Justice Standards and Goals, the National Council on Crime and Delinquency, the ACLU, and the Quakers' Friends Committee shared Doyle's general outlook, calling for a moratorium on prison construction. These reformers believed that prisons had no place in the modern world and hoped they would be rendered extinct by the end of the twentieth century. In the absence of a complete abolition, the National Council suggested that nondangerous, nonviolent offenders should be decarcerated as a first step toward this ultimate goal.[62]

Undeterred by these appeals, the bureau continued to plan and build prisons in secret, leading to the rapid proliferation of penal institutions at all levels of government when the Nixon administration successfully persuaded Congress to impose the goals of the Long-Range Master Plan on governors. Part E of the Crime Control Act of 1970 created a new source of block grant and discretionary funding for the purpose of prison construction, renovation, and acquisition. It also required states to dedicate no less than 20 percent of all federal law enforcement assistance grants to corrections programs, with the Department of Justice funding these efforts at 75 percent of their cost. So as not to overstep the bounds of Nixon's New Federalism and the principles of states' rights behind it, as a "block grant within a block grant," Part E expressed national priorities and allowed the federal government to exert direct authority over states while still operating on the premise of decentralization. Even if states hesitated to take the Part E funding and prepare to incarcerate new offenders, the Nixon administration ensured that its relentless prison construction and acquisition plan continued. The state of Wisconsin had used Part E funding to construct a prison at Oxford in 1973. Shortly after the prison opened, criminal justice planners announced they had no need for it, seeking to decarcerate offenders and provide community-based facilities as a sound alternative. The Bureau of Prisons then moved to acquire the Oxford site for the federal system under a lease-acquisition agreement.[63]

From ambivalent states like Wisconsin to enthusiastic partners like California, state-level spending on prisons soared across the board. Whereas in 1969 states allocated 13.5 percent of their law enforcement block grant funding to corrections, by 1970 that figure had more than doubled to 30 percent, and some states chose to dedicate half of their federal funding to their prison system. In monetary terms, the LEAA spent a relatively modest $2 million for corrections and prison programs in 1969. Following Nixon's call for the Long-Range Master Plan in 1970, that figure rose to $58 million. By 1971, Part E funding had increased state spending to $178 million on corrections improvement programs— half of which was allocated in the form of block grants, half of which was granted to the administration as discretionary funding. By 1972, this number had ballooned to nearly $250 million for a 12,400 percent increase in three years.[64]

Backed by the Long-Range Master Plan's half-billion-dollar investment and Part E funding, as states implemented the policing practices and sentencing reforms the administration introduced in DC, the size and racial composition of the American prison population drastically changed—just as Nixon's officials had predicted. The number of federal prisoners increased tenfold between 1895 and 1975, from 2,500 to 25,000 inmates, and the state prison population increased fourfold, from 50,000 to 200,000 inmates, while incarceration rates in local jails more than tripled during the same period. Simultaneously, the number of black prisoners in the nation skyrocketed. African Americans received longer sentences and more punitive treatment in cities like Philadelphia, where the percentage of black prisoners in the county jail increased from 50 percent in 1970 to 95 percent in 1974. In Pennsylvania as a whole, black citizens accounted for more than 62 percent of inmates in the state's jails, even though they constituted less than 10 percent of the entire population. In the southern states, where slavery, convict-lease, and chain gang systems had profoundly shaped the conditions of black lives for three centuries, the expansion of the prison system offered a viable means both to retain segregation and to reassert white control. Black Americans constituted only 15 percent of the population of Florida, but they slept in 55 percent of the state's prison beds. In Alabama, where black residents accounted for only 26 percent of the population, they represented 60 percent of the prisoners in state institutions. And with the largest percentage of African Americans in the country, Mississippi also had a low crime rate but a relatively high rate of incarceration in the 1970s.[65]

Within the federal prison system, black and Latino Americans came to occupy every additional prison bed called for by the Long-Range Master Plan. Between 1970 and 1977, a period in which the percentage of federal inmates who were black and Latino increased from 27.4 percent to over 38 percent, the Bureau of Prisons opened fifteen new prisons for 4,871 inmates. At the same time, federal prisons took in 4,904 new black and Latino Americans. Observing this development at the annual meeting of the National Council on Crime and Delinquency in 1974, corrections expert William Nagel said, "We must conclude, therefore, that the new prisons are for blacks." Once these new inmates of color joined the federal system, they were typically kept between two and five months longer than their white counterparts for assault, burglary, robbery, and embezzlement charges, and a year and a half longer for drug-related crimes. If the bureau had worked to eradicate these sentencing disparities, it would have freed up hundreds of new cells without any construction required.[66] The influence of the Long-Range Master Plan and the implementation of Part E funding sought instead to bring even more offenders into an already overcrowded system, facilitating historic rates of incarcerated African Americans.

The fact that black Americans filled an alarming share of these newly constructed prison spaces was in large part a consequence of the socioeconomic conditions African Americans confronted as the federal government intensified its fight against crime. In 1972, when 42 percent of all Americans in jail were black, 34 percent of black Americans lived below the poverty level, as opposed to 10 percent of the white American population. In Philadelphia, where the jails came to house African Americans almost exclusively in the early 1970s, 40 percent of black youth were unemployed. Access to educational and employment opportunities declined further as the federal government withdrew from its fight against poverty during the Nixon administration, and the absence of such opportunities often determined the likelihood of future incarceration. Of the black Americans detained in local jails in 1972, 70 percent did not possess a high school diploma, and nearly 60 percent earned less than $3,000 annually. Similarly, in state prisons, 48 percent of all inmates were black in 1973. Of those, 64 percent did not complete high school, and 75 percent were under the age of thirty.[67]

Although policymakers, law enforcement officials, and scholars justified the unyielding wave of prison construction by citing the high rates of reported crime during the 1970s, in reality, incarceration rates had little relationship to actual crime rates. Instead, incarceration rates correlated directly to the number of black residents and the extent of socioeconomic inequality within a given state. For example, Hawaii and Colorado had high crime rates but relatively few black and Latino residents, and in both states incarceration rates were low. On the other hand, states with larger numbers of racially marginalized Americans and residents living at or below the poverty level enjoyed lower crime rates but kept larger numbers of citizens in prison and in jail.[68]

Officials had difficulty establishing a sound causal link between incarceration rates and crime, but they knew unemployment rates correlated directly to incarceration. Federal researchers discovered in 1974 that unemployment rates had a "striking similarity" to annual prison admission patterns. National officials used the direct correlation between unemployment rates and incarceration that had been established by the Congressional Research Service not as a means to advance job creation as a viable way to contain crime, but as the basis for further prison population projections. Mixing unemployment and crime rates, the bureau went on to predict that the federal population would increase by a thousand prisoners in 1975.[69] Preoccupied with population projections and assumptions about black criminality, federal planners neglected the poverty, educational attainment, and other socioeconomic factors that fueled both crime and incarceration, using those same figures as the basis for further projections and the subsequent expansion of the prison system.

The central strategies that the Nixon administration developed for the Long-Range Master Plan took on a life of their own even as the president's impeachment cut short his second term. By late 1976, nearly $3 billion had already been spent on 430 new facilities across the country, averaging nearly $7 million for each new prison, with every inmate costing $26,328 in construction dollars. Jails, too, experienced remarkable growth during this period, as an average of twenty-eight new facilities either opened or were placed in the queue on a monthly basis. When the bureau revisited its goals shortly after Carter took office, it worked with state governments to plan for the construction of 2,000 new penal facilities housing half a million new inmates by May 1980, a venture that would effectively increase the institutional capacity of American prisons by 100 percent.[70]

Nixon, Mitchell, Carlson, and other high-level officials in the administration began to actively plan for the remarkable growth of the prison system at a moment when the future of corrections was in question, as policymakers, law enforcement authorities, activists, and prisoners themselves increasingly contested the utility of incarceration. Across the political spectrum, it became evident that fundamental change was needed. Under Nixon's leadership, the federal government engendered that change by removing the earlier goal of rehabilitation. Some officials strongly opposed this new direction. Former warden Martin G. Groder resigned from his position as director of the newly constructed Federal

Center for Correctional Research in Butner, North Carolina, in 1975 to protest the trend he foresaw within the bureau and within the carceral state as a whole: a "hard-line, 'warehousing' approach for prisoners." As the bureau's plan became known to policymakers and journalists in the mid-1970s, Lawrence Meyer of the *Washington Post* similarly observed that it could "only lead to a massive warehousing enterprise."[71] For Nixon's and, later, Ford's officials, however, to be "tough on crime" meant locking up criminals for even the most minor offenses. Warehousing or not, they falsely believed punishment offered the only sure means to contain crime. In the final analysis, the Nixon administration's master plan successfully established the institutional framework that set the United States on the road to mass incarceration.

Using national resources and influence to precipitate a new level of surveillance and a new mode of confinement targeting black urban Americans, the Nixon administration was crucial in the transformation and intensification of the federal War on Crime that began under the Democratic administrations of the 1960s. In the grants that the LEAA awarded to state governments, the increasingly punitive policies that the Nixon administration implemented in Washington, DC, the discretionary programs such as High Impact that facilitated a policing surge in black urban areas, and the prison construction path that revolutionized the correctional landscape and anticipated mass incarceration, a new contingent of conservative Republican policymakers took charge of the bipartisan crime control consensus. By the spring of 1973, when the end of the Vietnam War seemed imminent and Nixon had been handily reelected to a second term, the president further escalated the punitive war at home and the federal government's influence in its day-to-day operations.

This variant of New Federalism restructured the Great Society by directing what Nixon called "narrow purpose aid" programs into revenue-sharing categories. Among other federal programs that emerged in the 1960s, Nixon's revenue-sharing approach touched all of the programs under the Elementary Education Act, including Head Start and AmeriCorps, and the $575 million the federal government spent on Model Cities. "This can be a revolution as profound, as far-reaching, as exciting as the first revolution almost 200 years ago," Nixon said hopefully in his State of the Union address in 1971.[72] Revenue sharing, the legislative name for Nixon's New Federalism, would divert a third of all federal grant programs into massive block grants under broad categories such as urban development, manpower training, education, and law enforcement. The plan matched the $10 billion the federal government already allocated toward social programs with an additional $1 billion to states and local governments to spend as they saw fit, despite the dismal spending record of state planning agencies and the problems the LEAA encountered as it navigated the block grant system. While drastically cutting other public services and what remained of the War on Poverty, the LEAA began assuming social welfare responsibilities. In San Mateo, California, for instance, the agency funded a $75,000 program in the early 1970s that was designed to "aid kindergarten pupils with chronic problems." And in New York City, the LEAA assumed the cost of a $216,000 job training program that the Office of Economic Opportunity had previously supported. With the LEAA's administering both social welfare and crime control services, Nixon proposed in his budget for fiscal year 1974 to increase the LEAA's spending authority. Congress reauthorized the agency in August 1973 with a three-year, $3.25 billion allocation and stronger federal oversight in state and local crime-fighting programs.[73]

The forces of inequality in low-income urban neighborhoods took on new forms as the carceral state grew dramatically during and after Nixon's presidency. Although ascendant numbers of black Americans were imprisoned at disparate rates following the Civil War, until the 1970s they constituted roughly a third of the nation's prison population. Only after federal policymakers started investing in crime control measures, and only after the Nixon administration began to plan and incentivize prison construction, did black Americans encompass roughly half of the nation's incarcerated citizens. Over the course of the 1970s, the set of assumptions shared by a consensus of national policymakers and officials about African Americans and crime, the targeted deployment of surveillance and patrol measures, the ever-more-punitive sentences, and the construction of new prisons that grounded the entire carceral apparatus evolved into a mutually reinforcing cycle. In particular, the construction of new prisons strengthened crime control policies and shaped incarceration trends as these institutions became integrated into the criminal justice system and available for use. (As the saying goes: "If you build it, they will come.") The alternative, a moratorium on prison construction, community-based corrections, or a decarceration process, might have opened up an entirely different set of resources, utilizing the talents of prisoners and social service institutions to create a society that would begin to eliminate the socioeconomic conditions that spawned both violence and crime. Instead, the growing federal law enforcement apparatus successfully channeled punitive resources to states and cities. Americans living in segregated "high crime" neighborhoods grew more isolated from mainstream society as they confronted increased police brutality, increased criminal supervision, and eventually, increased confinement.

[5]

THE BATTLEGROUNDS OF THE CRIME WAR

s the White House Special Counsel on Urban Affairs, Daniel Patrick
Moynihan frequently wrote long-winded memos to Richard Nixon,
commenting on the nation's racial climate and theorizing new urban
policy approaches. In mid-January 1970, as Nixon's first year in office
came to a close, Moynihan felt compelled to provide the president with
a "general assessment of the position of Negroes at the end of the decade." During the 1960s, the plight of black Americans had been "*the*
central domestic political issue.*" At the start of a new year and a new
decade, Moynihan thought, "The time may have come when the issue
of race could benefit from a period of 'benign neglect,'" whereby the "racial rhetoric" that steered domestic policy in the previous decade would
fade. In many ways, inequality seemed to be decreasing: rising incomes
in the affluent 1960s had expanded the black middle class, and black
college enrollment increased 85 percent—with nearly half a million
black students entering universities between 1964 and 1968. The Nixon
administration had little to do with this progress, but Moynihan, ever
the loyal advisor to both the liberal and conservative administrations
he counseled in the 1960s, praised the president's racial reforms. Nixon
had put the "Black Capitalism" rhetoric of his campaign into action by
establishing the Office of Minority Business Enterprise. His "Philadel-

phia Plan" guaranteed fair hiring in construction jobs and laid the groundwork for affirmative action by government contractors. "I dare say, as much or more time and attention goes into this effort in this administration than any in history," wrote Moynihan of Nixon's racial reforms. "But little has come of it." Black female-headed families, which Moynihan had brought to national attention in *The Negro Family*, were still growing in number. And as the freedom struggle shifted its focus from civil rights to economic justice, "socially alienated" black youth had become "quasi-politicized" by groups like the Black Panthers. It seemed to Moynihan that militant protest had mobilized a deeper, perhaps innate, violence among African Americans. He concluded, "Hatred—revenge—against whites is now an acceptable excuse for doing what might have been done anyway."[1] During his tenure in the Department of Labor in the Kennedy and Johnson administrations, Moynihan had urged a "new era of domestic policy" that responded to black male unemployment and attempted to address black familial pathology. Now his call for "benign neglect" implied that the "tangle of pathology" could not be broken after all.

Moynihan's fatalism reflected both the mood of the times and the social science research that guided Nixon's strategies for the War on Crime as the 1960s gave way to the 1970s. Harvard professor Edward C. Banfield, who worked with the administration officials to shape its domestic programs, argued that black poverty and crime were a fact of modern American life. "No matter what we do, we are bound to have large concentrations of the unskilled and the poor," Banfield wrote in a 1968 article, and it was ludicrous to think that government could "eliminate slums, educate the slum child, train the unskilled worker, end chronic poverty, stop crime and delinquency, or prevent riots." Although Banfield acknowledged "most of these people are black," he viewed their problems as a product not of race, but of concentrated urban poverty. "If all Negroes turned white overnight," Banfield pointed out, "the serious problems of the city would still exist." Banfield challenged conventional theories about both race and social programs in his 1970 book *The Unheavenly City*, which established him as an "urban policy maverick" and an "intellectual gadfly par excellence" in academic and policy circles. In the book, Banfield directly attacked the activist state: "Government cannot solve the problems of the cities and is likely to make them worse."[2] Federal policymakers had no business designing social welfare measures, evidenced by the fact that the War on Poverty only exacerbated collective violence and political dissent. Banfield declared that these programs should be abandoned.

In an era of Black Power and militant student protest, when policymakers and the public feared "urban guerrilla warfare" as a very real possibility, Moynihan and Banfield articulated the views of a growing consensus among federal policymakers, law enforcement officials, and many of their constituents. This consensus argued that the focus on the "root causes" of social ills had misguided the domestic policies of the 1960s. It concluded that despite the best efforts of the Kennedy and Johnson administrations, government programs were clearly incapable of making the poor into "productive citizens" or correcting their apparent behavioral deficiencies. If crime was an inevitable condition in low-income black urban communities, a condition that could not be prevented by social welfare programs, this consensus held that domestic urban policy should focus on containing the problems of crime and violence, rather than seeing to eliminate them entirely.

By 1970, a new theory of law enforcement emerged from these ideas. The problem of law and order was seen as resulting from patrol methods insufficient to a growing population, and, in particular, a growing population of black youth living at or below the poverty level. The solution lay in encouraging officers to walk the streets of neighborhoods and to involve themselves in community life. Foot patrol, both in police uniforms and in plainclothes, would allow authorities to identify and remove the "lawless elements" from the community and place them under criminal supervision. This new approach marked a significant shift from the prevailing ideas of the immediate postwar period, when big-city police professionals such as William Parker of Los Angeles and Chicago's police chief O. W. Wilson relied on motor vehicles to give officers mobility and respond to emergencies in haste. The exodus of middle-class families to the suburbs in the 1950s and 1960s left low-income and racially marginalized residents behind in the central city, and now it seemed that motorized patrol had created too much distance between police officers and residents in urban areas. Responding to this perceived problem, the Johnson administration had begun to integrate law enforcement programs into social welfare services by empowering police officers to direct after-school recreational programs, to staff Youth Service Bureaus, and to monitor classrooms as school resource officers. Each of these measures brought officers and urban residents into closer contact and exposed residents to more frequent police surveillance. In the early 1970s, however, such initiatives were complemented by new patrol methods: exhaustive foot patrol and tactical decoy squads.

The federal government was instrumental in the implementation of these new patrol strategies in low-income communities. Undercover and plainclothes operations targeting urban areas expanded upon those used by the Federal Bureau of Investigation's (FBI) Counter-Intelligence Program (COINTELPRO) against the radical left and nationalist groups during the late 1960s, and they relied upon a similar set of assumptions about race and crime. The Law Enforcement Assistance Administration (LEAA) supported new patrol programs that made possible the virtually indiscriminate use of decoy and plainclothes operations in targeted urban areas. After directing the LEAA for its first six months in the final year of the Johnson administration, Patrick Murphy initiated such patrol programs as police commissioner, first in Detroit and then in New York City. Murphy applied these tactical strategies as a means to foster surveillance of communities with high rates of reported crime and to create opportunities to arrest perpetrators. The most aggressive special decoy squad in the history of the War on Crime emerged in Detroit. Known as STRESS (an acronym for "Stop the Robberies, Enjoy Safe Streets"), it engaged in street war and deadly violence that ultimately contributed to a spike in Detroit's homicide rate.

While federal policymakers and private organizations such as the Police Foundation, which the Ford Foundation established in 1970, collaborated to help local police departments like Detroit's to realize new patrol strategies, the Nixon administration created a plainclothes force of its own when the president formed the Office of Drug Abuse Law Enforcement (ODALE) by executive order in early 1972. Applying strategies from the wider crime war to narcotics enforcement and drug abuse, ODALE involved federal agents in similar undercover operations. Like discretionary anticrime funds distributed by the federal government, these antidrug measures largely targeted segregated urban neighborhoods.

Yet unlike the previous crime control programs the federal government supported with discretionary funds, STRESS, ODALE, similar units, and the various new techniques imposed for the purpose of apprehending potential criminals, tended to create peril for both officers and residents and placed entire neighborhoods under surveillance. After ODALE agents mistakenly raided the homes of suburban white families, bringing media attention to the practices that had been ongoing in low-income urban communities, the "White House police force" became a target of controversy and was disbanded, eventually evolving into the Drug Enforcement Agency. Department of Justice officials during the Ford administration revised the tactical plainclothes approach used by such units as ODALE and STRESS, collaborating with the police department in Washington, DC, to execute "Operation Sting" and "Operation Got Ya Again" in the fall of 1975—at that point the largest police sting ever attempted. Soon police departments across the United States looked to the DC program as a model; elaborate undercover investigations made possible mass arrests, and high arrest rates were thought to lead to lower rates of crime. In the process of executing the sting operations, however, federal, state, and local law enforcement officials necessarily encouraged criminal activity, creating informal economies and engaging in crimes themselves.

The strategies that federal policymakers and local law enforcement officials developed to fight crime during the first half of the 1970s had devastating consequences in the cities where they were most energetically implemented. As they unfolded on the ground, these strategies transformed the "War on Crime" from a politically salient, action-oriented metaphor into an actual violent conflict that involved the use of military-grade weapons and dangerous patrol tactics and that resulted in real gun battles and real victims.

THE THEORY OF FOOT PATROL

The retrenchment from the liberal welfare state and the rise of the carceral state during the Johnson and Nixon administrations was profoundly shaped by the ideas of Daniel Patrick Moynihan and his Harvard colleague James Q. Wilson. Moynihan had already made a name for himself in Washington by the fall of 1966, when Johnson appointed Wilson to chair of the President's Task Force on Crime—a nine-member group that worked with White House and Department of Justice officials to refine earlier drafts of the Safe Streets Act based on the initial recommendations of the Crime Commission. During Nixon's first term, Wilson came to the White House on several occasions to visit his colleague Moynihan. Moynihan knew Nixon would appreciate Wilson's fresh perspective on social issues and gave his friend a grand introduction. "Mr. President," Moynihan reportedly said, "James Q. Wilson is the smartest man in the United States. The president of the United States should pay attention to what he has to say."[3] Immediately taken by Wilson and his domestic policy credentials, Nixon appointed him to his Model Cities Task Force in 1969. Three years later, the president entrusted Wilson to help set the course for the Office of Drug Abuse Law Enforcement—the vanguard of the administration's war on street-level pushers—when he appointed Wilson chairman of the Commission on Drug Abuse Prevention.

Wilson's mentor Edward Banfield, also a Harvard political scientist, chaired the Model Cities Task Force, an urban policy initiative that was aimed at creating alternatives to—and that in effect rationalized the dismantling of—the landmark housing program of the War on Poverty. The two men had worked together since Wilson's graduate school days at the University of Chicago, where Banfield supervised Wilson's dissertation on black public life and political leadership. When Banfield left Chicago for the Department of Government at Harvard just as Wilson defended his dissertation in 1959, the mentor brought his protégé along to Cambridge with him. In their 1963 book *City Politics*, the Harvard professors bluntly raised what seemed to be *the* question about the future of urban industrial centers: "Is the central city to become the possession of the lower class and of minority groups or is it to be restored to the middle class?" Although Banfield and Wilson didn't provide a direct answer, it was clear to them that federal policies had forced city governments to follow national priorities and focus on social welfare, which meant municipal authorities increasingly involved themselves "in matters that seem to bear in no relation to it [local government] whatever." Along these lines, on the Model Cities Task Force, Banfield and Wilson found the War on Poverty programs "irrational" and "wasteful." The federal government's social welfare bureaucracy wasn't solving urban issues. Instead, federal housing programs and the Office of Economic Opportunity were "gilding the ghetto," as Banfield put it, by funneling resources to welfare professionals at the expense of low-income residents.[4] The task force urged the federal government to rethink its approach and its general goals in urban social welfare programs by decentralizing control, which translated to funding Model Cities and other urban social programs with block grants, effectively providing municipal authorities greater autonomy in administering the program.

But while Wilson believed Great Society programs were misguided and should be altogether abandoned, he argued that the national law enforcement program remained an essential component of domestic policy. The problem was that Johnson had launched the War on Crime from an untenable premise: that federal policies themselves could eventually obliterate crime. As Wilson concluded in his 1968 study *Varieties of Police Behavior*, the product of research funded by Moynihan's Joint Center for Urban Studies at MIT and Harvard, "The police can cope with their problems, but they cannot solve them." Suggesting that the national law enforcement program shift its emphasis from prevention to deterrence and incapacitation, Wilson argued that the surety of punishment itself was a far more effective means to control crime than social programs. He believed that the role of the policeman in society should be "defined more by his responsibility for *maintaining order* than by his responsibility for enforcing the law." In addition to performing their most basic duty of ensuring domestic tranquility, officers needed to confront *potential* crime. This would discourage residents from engaging in illegal activity and would put officers in a better position to remove from the streets those individuals who exhibited criminal behavior. "The ability of the police to do their job may well determine our ability to manage social conflict," Wilson wrote, "especially that which involves Negroes and other minority groups, and our prospects for maintaining a proper balance between liberty and order."[5] The "proper balance," for Wilson, meant that police needed to take action when confronted with an "ambiguous situation," such as a group of suspicious-looking teenagers roaming the streets in a neighborhood with high rates of reported crime. More likely than not, Wilson asserted, one or more of these youths were breaking a law. Officers walking the streets of high crime neighborhoods—in uniform or in plainclothes— would act as a much stronger deterrent to crime than would simply continuing to increase motorized patrol and stockpiling equipment, as crime war programs during the 1960s had encouraged.

By 1970, when it became widely accepted that the federal government was "losing" the War on Crime, the Nixon administration and law enforcement officials fully embraced Wilson's proposed policing reforms and his emphasis on foot patrol. Wilson joined the board of directors of the Police Development Fund (later the Police Foundation) when it was created by the Ford Foundation in July 1970. With $30 million in private grant funds at its disposal, the Police Foundation instantly became the most powerful crime control interest group in the country. Charles Rogovin had just resigned as director of the LEAA out of frustration over the block grant system and seemed a fitting inaugural chair for the foundation. Whereas the LEAA filtered most of its funds to urban law enforcement authorities via state planning agencies, now Rogivin could oversee the direct funding of police departments from his post at the private foundation, in a manner that seemed to him more responsive to local needs. Rogovin's longtime colleague James Vorenberg, the former Crime Commission director and the head of the Center for Criminal Justice at Harvard Law School, joined Wilson, the executive directors of various police and criminal justice organizations, and a handful of mayors and former mayors on the eleven-member board of directors.[6] Wilson would go on to sit on the Police Foundation board for twenty-three years, chairing the organization from 1984 to 1993, during the height of the War on Drugs.

With Wilson's ideas shaping its programs and policies, the Police Foundation encouraged law enforcement officials to take a more service-oriented approach to law enforcement that centered on extensive foot patrol. The Police Foundation's "Community Policing" strategy marked a return to the earliest methods of American law enforcement. During the first fifty years of professional police forces in the United States—New York City in 1845 created the first such force—officers often lived in the communities where they worked. As a result, police maintained close relationships with their neighbors and assumed a degree of responsibility for their well-being.[7] By the end of the nineteenth century, however, police departments had become entwined with political machines, resulting in widespread corruption and high turnover. Progressive reformers ended the police patronage system and shifted the guiding principle of urban law enforcement from service delivery to crime control. Police work had been a critical source of jobs for unskilled, illiterate men, many of whom had recently arrived in the United States from Europe. Early twentieth-century reforms now required officers to undergo training and adhere to a set of standards. These policies professionalized forces and, by the 1930s, effectively militarized them, but they fostered a new level of disconnect between officers and citizens. Professional law enforcement reformers widened the gulf by strongly encouraging motorized patrol in the postwar decades. By the 1960s, it seemed to many policymakers and law enforcement officials that car patrols had created a chasm between police officers and residents, which was partly responsible for the "atmosphere of lawlessness" they perceived in segregated urban neighborhoods.

One of the first Police Foundation grants went to Detroit Police Commissioner Patrick Murphy in April 1970, to support his radical new approach to patrolling black neighborhoods in the city. Murphy's "Beat Commander System" brought more patrol into high crime zones by having officers walk the streets, hopefully allowing policemen to become acquainted with residents and, over time, build their trust. "If the people become cynical about the police," Murphy argued, "if the people come to believe that the police can't or won't help them, then the people won't help the police fight crime." Putting this theory into action in majority-black precincts in Detroit, Murphy made his beat commanders responsible for a few specific blocks. The officers attended church services, visited schools, and made appearances at block club meetings, creating a new level of intimacy with residents.[8] Murphy left Detroit in September 1970, stepping into the same role in New York City and bringing the Detroit experiment with him. Murphy's roots were in New York, where his father and two brothers served on the New York Police Department (NYPD). From his humble beginnings as an officer on the beat in Red Hook, Brooklyn, in 1945, Murphy quickly rose through the ranks of the force to become one of the most important law enforcement figures in the late twentieth century. During the Johnson administration, he was appointed assistant director of the Office of Law Enforcement Assistance, where he selected and evaluated the earliest crime war demonstration projects. He went on to serve as the first public safety director of Washington, DC, in 1967 and completed his career in the federal government by helping to get the LEAA off the ground in the summer and fall of 1968 before Nixon took office.[9] He would succeed Rogovin as president of the Police Foundation in 1973.

Murphy was as committed to police intelligence programs as he was to police-community relations programs, and he synthesized the two in the foot patrol experiment he launched in New York in the fall of 1970: a 100-man volunteer force of armed plainclothes officers, known as the Citywide Anticrime Section. Although Murphy believed that the police officer functioned as "the best social worker we have" and reestablished uniformed foot patrol to develop trust with residents in vulnerable neighborhoods, he also believed that the American criminal justice system had broken down because "police are not arresting enough violators." The success of any crime control program, he argued, depended on its ability to deliver high arrest rates. Murphy made it clear to the officers who participated in his Anticrime Section that if they failed to increase apprehensions in their districts, they could expect to be dismissed from the force. Luckily for the officers whose employment depended upon meeting Murphy's arrest quota, his strategy yielded promising results: plainclothes officers in the Anticrime Section consistently made five times the number of arrests as their uniformed counterparts.[10]

The Anticrime Section monitored neighborhoods with rising rates of reported crime from 6:00 p.m. to 2:00 a.m. every evening, wearing walkie-talkies so that officers could call for backup if necessary. As Inspector Edmund Joyce explained to the six officers he sent out to duty for the first time from the 71st precinct station house: "The anticrime patrol is expected to increase the theory of omnipresence." The very existence of the special force might discourage residents from resorting to crime, and if the plainclothes officers remained undetected, they could observe illegal transactions and arrest residents with greater ease. As

Murphy put it, a plainclothes officer could "devote his full time and attention to crime prevention and making arrests," operating as either a surveillance or an undercover agent. Joyce sent his small plainclothes team out into the black, Italian, and Hasidic Crown Heights area. "Good luck," he told them. "Good hunting." Within a week, the plainclothes patrol had killed one man and wounded two others in Queens, but this did not prevent Murphy from expanding the size of the force from 100 to 150 officers at the end of its first month of operation.[11]

By the fall of 1972, the Anticrime Section had doubled in size, assumed a headquarters called the "Wheel House," and worked the beat in full-on disguise. Officers dressed as rabbis, elderly women, cab drivers, bums, drunks, and tennis players ("for the Central Park West Crowd," explained the patrolman sporting the costume).[12] Far from Murphy's earlier iteration of the squad in Detroit, which sought to integrate police into segregated urban neighborhoods, his plainclothes strategy was bent on catching criminals—with wigs, wheelchairs, and other props on hand to assist in that process. The undercover approach did not concern itself with more quotidian community-relations matters, and thus could focus squarely on apprehending suspects and potential suspects, which Murphy theorized would restore public safety.

The use of disguises led to confusing and even deadly interactions with residents. In one particularly tragic case, officers killed sixteen-year-old Carnarsie High School student Rita Lloyd shortly after 1:00 a.m. on a Saturday in early 1973. Robert Milano and Edward Roach of the Anticrime Section were riding around Carnarsie in southeast Brooklyn in an unmarked car when they noticed four teenage girls who appeared to be arguing. When the group eventually dispersed, Milano and Roach returned to the site. Lloyd was there with sixteen-year-old Denise Bethel, who was reportedly armed with a sawed-off shotgun. The officers stepped out of their vehicle and drew their revolvers as soon as they spotted the weapon. Unaware that the casually dressed men approaching her with guns drawn were police officers, Denise pointed the gun at her potential attackers. Milano then fired "quick defensive reaction" shots. One of his bullets hit Lloyd in the chest and passed through her back. Lloyd fled to her home a block from the scene, fearing her attackers would continue to pursue her. She died less than an hour later at Kings County Hospital. Bethel was arrested for reckless endangerment and possession of a dangerous weapon, while Milano did not face any charges for his involvement in the shooting. The police department's spokesman told reporters that Lloyd's death was the unfortunate consequence of "police action in the line of duty," failing to acknowledge any wrongdoing on the part of the officers involved.[13]

During its two and half years of operation, the Citywide Anticrime Section involved itself in at least a half dozen such shootings, but it also made a large number of arrests (more than 1,000 apprehensions during its first three months and a total of 3,600 in 1970 alone) and booked 80 percent of its arrested suspects on felony charges that most often led to convictions. Murphy attributed the city's reduction of street crime to the plainclothes program. He also felt it gave a new sense of purpose to frustrated officers who, in Murphy's words, were "losing the war on crime," amid ever-rising crime figures. Although Murphy resigned as police commissioner and his project in New York concluded at the end of Mayor John Lindsay's term in 1973, as chair of the Police Foundation, he went on to support departments elsewhere in implementing similar initiatives. Murphy's hard line on police corruption, his support of gun control laws, and his racially liberal views made him a controversial figure in the law enforcement community, but his tactical squad strategy evolved into a key model for the urban police departments, the LEAA, the FBI, and the White House.[14]

THE "REIGN OF TERROR" IN DETROIT

If Murphy's Anticrime Section in New York became the poster child for plainclothes tactical patrol, the squad that emerged from his Beat Commander System in Detroit became the most violent and notorious example of the strategy in action. "Stop the Robberies, Enjoy Safe Streets" (STRESS) was inaugurated in January 1971 with a $35,000 grant from the LEAA to supplement the $7.6 million the agency had already allocated to the state of Michigan since 1969. Police commissioner John Nichols, Murphy's successor, followed the example of his predecessor and designed STRESS to patrol the low-income, mostly black neighborhoods that had been identified as the epicenter of deviance. Nichols's plainclothes squad yielded far more arrests and a remarkably higher death toll than its counterparts in New York City, Philadelphia, Baltimore, Atlanta, Chicago, Los Angeles, and other urban centers. During the first fifteen months of the squad's operation, STRESS officers killed a young, black male roughly once a month, often in Detroit's Cass-Woodward corridor in the dead of night. In just two years, STRESS made more than 6,000 arrests and killed eighteen civilians and suspects. Of those killed, all but one were black. By the time STRESS was disbanded in 1974, it had become emblematic of the ways in which plainclothes patrol and decoy operations were used by law enforcement officials to anticipate crime and, in some measure, to encourage it.[15]

Numbering somewhere between 100 and 250 members of Detroit's 5,000-man force (the police department refused to disclose specific numbers), STRESS officers policed Cass corridor and other low-income neighborhoods, pursuing a new strategy introduced by Nichols: acting on *predictions* of crime rather than on actual crime. Nichols, who had twenty-eight years of experience on the Detroit police force behind him, was known to his peers as a "policeman's policeman." Shortly after he took office in mid-October 1970, he called for a study of street crime patterns in Detroit, hoping to reduce assault and robbery rates. "If we can predict in which direction the criminal will move," Nichols believed, "we can be waiting for him." The study indicated that robberies usually occurred close to home and that the perpetrators tended to be young, armed, nonwhite males. As Detective Inspector James D. Bannon, the head commander of STRESS, explained, the strategy of committing STRESS units to particular areas based on patterns of prior crime meant that before they began their daily assignments, teams had a sense of "what we are looking for in terms of the general appearance of the culprits and so on."[16] The principle of anticipation meant that anyone who fit the description of a criminal would be subject to additional surveillance and even provocation by the STRESS team.

Commanders of the three- to four-person STRESS crews met at police department headquarters each morning. Together they charted every street crime reported the previous day in order to set patrol routes in the city's "problem areas." Teams were then dispersed to targeted precincts in two shifts, usually from 9:00 a.m. to 5:00 p.m. or from 8:00

p.m. to 4:00 a.m. Murphy's Anticrime Section in New York operated only in the evening, but STRESS members hit the streets nineteen hours a day. The commanders took into account the time a particular crime occurred and the racial makeup of the surrounding neighborhood to plan believable decoy scenarios. Officers chose costumes based on these crime projections, posing as pedestrians, "indigenous residents," cabdrivers, deliverymen, insurance salesmen, bill collectors, and news-boys, aiming to "blend into" Detroit's problem neighborhoods. If a handful of victims reported a purse snatching on a particular block, for instance, then STRESS officers would dress in wigs and skirts to trick potential robbers. Sometimes the decoy or plainclothes tactic worked. Just as often, however, residents would recognize a STRESS crew member and avoid contact, and sometimes residents approached other disguised officers to warn, "Watch out, he looks like a STRESS copper," or to tell them that "the man" was in the area.[17]

For STRESS crew chief Raymond Peterson, who enjoyed posing as a "radical college professor," it was exciting work, and risky too. Goading residents who appeared suspicious left Peterson and other key officers vulnerable to attacks. Before beginning a decoy operation, the officers drove in the squad's inconspicuous cars, surveying the streets where reported crimes had occurred and "looking for a potential robber," Bannon explained. When a probable criminal could be found, the STRESS crew would "drop off a target," or place one of its members on foot near the scene. A delicate balancing act was required of the officers providing cover: backup needed to maintain necessary distance from the target officer but remain close enough to respond within seconds if the operation turned dangerous. The federal government's six-year in-vestment into hardware for local law enforcement provided an extra layer of technological protection, helping to make this kind of under-cover policing possible. Each STRESS officer wore a "second chance" armored vest made of fiberglass, and except for the target posing as a decoy, each carried a "prep radio," or a small, concealable version of a military walkie-talkie.[18]

STRESS officers placed themselves in peril so as to invite robbery and other street crime with the goal of arresting their intended assailants. However, in practice, they weren't innocent victims; they possessed both the violent reflexes and cutting-edge resources that came with being a police officer during the War on Crime. And so, when confronted by the very situations they sought to provoke, they tended to react with force—not infrequently with deadly force. Perhaps more than any other STRESS officer, Peterson was emblematic of the violent patrol culture within the unit. At the time of his appointment as a STRESS crew chief in January 1971, Peterson had compiled a record of more than 1,000 arrests—and nine citizen complaints—during eleven years as a Detroit police officer. Within the first year of his STRESS duty, Peterson had involved himself in a number of shootings that resulted in the deaths of eight black residents and serious injuries to three more. Among the victims was a twenty-six-year-old that Peterson claimed tried to rob him in the spring of 1971, followed by a resident he claimed attacked him at knifepoint just a few days later. Two weeks passed before Peterson killed a twenty-two-year-old he said had also attempted to rob him. In the fall of 1971, he killed a twenty-four-year-old who allegedly tried to resist arrest, followed by a twenty-one-year-old suspect who attacked a member of Peterson's crew with a broom handle. Peterson explained his actions by the nature of the unit's work and its reliance on foot patrol: "I think the reason I've been involved in so many shootings is because we're walking so much," he told a reporter.[19]

In spite of this record, Nichols retained Peterson on the STRESS payroll for two more years, until he was finally caught in a cover-up and faced second-degree murder charges in the killing of twenty-four-year-old Robert Hoyt in March 1973. While driving one night with another off-duty buddy in the force, Peterson noticed the young black man and forced his car to the side of a freeway service drive. Peterson said Hoyt promptly slashed him with a knife, leaving a six-inch tear in his top coat. The STRESS officer fired the fatal shots at his attacker only in self-defense, he claimed. Yet the cat hairs investigators discovered on Hoyt's alleged knife belonged to Peterson's own pet.[20] While Hoyt was the last civilian to die at Peterson's hands, many more residents suffered similar fates from other STRESS officers. Barring the type of forensic evidence that eventually led to Peterson's firing and conviction, law enforcement and criminal justice officials defended STRESS deployments unconditionally.

The assumptions about race and criminality that undergirded the preemptive strategies of the STRESS squad eventually led its members to employ deadly force against fellow law enforcement officers. In March 1972, a five-minute gun battle unfolded between a team of white STRESS officers and four black sheriff's deputies who were playing poker in an apartment on Detroit's west side. The squad's decoy operations produced a good number of arrests, yet most STRESS apprehensions came when plainclothes officers merely witnessed illegal activities while in inconspicuous disguises. In the 1972 incident, a STRESS team spotted the poker game and its players from the street, assumed they had discovered an illegal gambling ring, and burst into the apartment. Since the STRESS officers were dressed in plainclothes, Deputy James Jenkins assumed the intruders were robbers and immediately threw his hands in front of his face, yelling: "We're police officers in here!" The STRESS officers, however, believed the claim was merely an attempt to resist arrest, and quickly fired upon the deputies. Moments before one of the bullets delivered a fatal blow to deputy Henry S. Henderson, he asked his assailants: "Man, you are all wrong, why are you doing this?" Other bullets struck Jenkins in the stomach, temple, and leg, causing him to lose sight in one of his eyes. The STRESS officers remained unharmed. They also managed to avoid legal repercussions. Upon investigation, Wayne County prosecutor William Cahalan concluded that Henderson pointed his gun at the white STRESS officers before they opened fire, arguing that the unit had not resorted to undue force in his murder. Cahalan instead pressed charges only for the injuries the STRESS team caused to Jenkins. All of the officers were eventually acquitted of this lesser charge.[21]

Although the squad had already earned a reputation in the Midwest for the slayings in Cass Corridor and had prompted several anti-STRESS rallies, its role in the death of a fellow officer brought national news coverage and mobilized black law enforcement officials in Detroit. The Guardians, a policemen's organization representing some 325 black officers in the Detroit metropolitan area, used the Henderson killing and the twelve other STRESS-related deaths to demand that Mayor Roman Gribbs abolish the unit. (Meanwhile, young residents continued to die from the squad's bullets. Weeks after Henderson's murder, STRESS officers killed a fifteen-year-old boy and wounded two of his friends. The officers claimed they acted out of self-defense after five teenagers held up a decoy at knifepoint.) For a growing number of Detroiters, Henderson's death indicated that the STRESS unit represented an assault on black residents. Critics of the unit charged that inadequately trained officers "simply draw their guns and shoot instead of trying to catch the suspect without using deadly force." Nichols believed Henderson's shooting was a "tragic mistake," and not the rule, claiming that the 10 percent reduction in robbery throughout Detroit was due in large part to the presence of STRESS.[22] If, as Nichols argued, STRESS was the police department's most successful weapon in the war on crime, then further expansion of the unit was strategically justifiable.

The attention Henderson's killing brought to the STRESS squad did force Nichols to reform its recruitment practices and standards. Initially the Detroit Police Department did not carefully screen or extensively train squad members before sending them out on undercover patrol—the standing grievances against Peterson were clearly overlooked, for instance—but this changed in the spring of 1972. Supervisors took greater caution in the volunteers they selected for STRESS duty, checking into past disciplinary actions and citizens' complaints and subjecting potential recruits to a psychological evaluation. Once accepted to the force, STRESS officers underwent a two-week "indoctrination period," where they learned about state entrapment laws, search-and-seizure rules, and participated in "decision-making training" to help them better determine the situations in which firing shots was an appropriate response.[23]

Despite the reforms, violence continued to prevail within STRESS, and young Detroiters launched what appeared to be a counterattack on the unit's officers. On December 4, 1972, a STRESS team staking out a local drug den in the northwest side of the city engaged in a gun battle with three young black residents that left four officers wounded and one dead. Immediately, the police began to search for the three suspects and raided heroin houses throughout the city, killing a civilian who a STRESS officer claimed began to fire shots as soon as the officers came to his door. Another off-duty STRESS officer lost his life as he tried to stop a bank holdup on December 27. Finally, in early January 1973, a twenty-five-year-old STRESS officer died in what Nichols called an "execution-style" shooting by "mad dog killers." The police department held Wayne State University students John Perry Boyd Jr. and Clyde Bethune and eighteen-year-old high school student Hayward Brown responsible for all three of the deaths. Yet this was another tragic case of mistaken identities. Far from being criminals, the three young men wanted to rid Detroit of drugs in order to improve their neighborhood. "We saw the situation getting worse," Brown said in a statement to police. "More and more dope was coming into the community and making more junkies, and the designated authorities weren't doing their jobs."[24] Taking matters into their own hands, Boyd, Bethune, and Brown had also been monitoring the drug den on the night of December 4. The STRESS squad assumed the three students were drug dealers, chased them, and exchanged gunfire. STRESS officers later claimed they showed the suspects their badges before firing shots, but either way, the three young antidrug vigilantes saw themselves as acting in self-defense.

The STRESS unit launched what black Detroit residents called a "campaign of terror" in the name of bringing the killers of its fellow officers to justice. "We are like one family," STRESS patrolman Ronald Martin said of the camaraderie within the unit. "Whatever happens to one of us happens to all of us." During the ongoing manhunt—the largest in Detroit's history—the unit resorted to harassment and violence against the suspects' families as well as against black leaders, conducting an estimated 500 raids. The police tapped the phones and searched the homes of residents bearing any relation to Boyd, Bethune, or Brown—including friends of one suspect's siblings. STRESS officers broke into the house of Boyd's great-aunt, forcing her son to lie on the floor handcuffed while the officers searched the home and its contents without a warrant. Dressed in jeans and overalls, STRESS officers forced Bethune's cousin to strip to her underwear when the crew received a tip that her family planned to leave Detroit. STRESS officers in plainclothes also smashed in the front door of the pastor of the New Galilee Spiritual Church, who bore no connection to the suspects, holding a gun to his head and warning: "Nigger, if you breathe loud I'll blow your brains out."[25] These searches were completely legal under the "no knock" provisions on the books in Michigan, permitting officers to enter the homes of any resident without a warrant if they had reasonable cause.

The brutal tactics STRESS officers used during the search for Boyd, Bethune, and Brown reinvigorated grassroots campaigns against the unit and placed the Detroit Police Department on the defensive once again. Fearing another large urban rebellion with the 1967 riot still in recent memory, the city council held an open hearing on STRESS at Ford Auditorium in mid-January 1973. For more than three hours, witnesses testified before nearly 2,000 concerned citizens about their encounters with STRESS officers. Afterward, Nichols stepped to the podium before the mostly black audience to read his prepared statement about STRESS's critical role in promoting public safety. The police commissioner acknowledged that his men made "some errors" and promised to investigate the witnesses' charges. He noted that the searches were legal under the "no knock" law, and defended STRESS officers' indiscriminate use of firearms. "The lack of readiness in this case may be a fatal one," Nichols argued, suggesting that STRESS officers needed to have their weapons drawn while conducting searches for their own personal safety. The crowd erupted when Nichols rationalized the unit's violence. "Mad dog killer!" they chanted, appropriating the police commissioner's indictment of the three young suspects. Nichols remained on the stage through the taunts with his arms crossed. Unable to finish his prepared statement, he shook hands with the seven council members and left.[26]

Detroit-based activists saw the meeting as a triumph in their decades-long struggle against police brutality and institutional racism in the city. They also viewed it as a political opportunity. The former labor organizer and League of Revolutionary Black Workers cofounder Kenneth Cockrel used the collective encounter with Nichols as a basis to start an interracial coalition of local organizations. Cockrel collected 100,000 signatures on a petition that called STRESS "a murder squad with an unlimited license to kill and maim." STRESS and the Detroit Police Department had a larger number of civilian deaths at the hands of law enforcement officers than anywhere else in the United States. In 1972 alone, forty civilians were killed by police, while six policemen lost their lives in the line of duty.[27] Again the community demanded the unit's abolition.

The mobilization of Detroiters against STRESS patrols in their neighborhoods compelled law enforcement officers to acknowledge the widespread use of force in African American areas, both to federal policymakers and to the press, but high-level officials in the Detroit Police Department continued to argue that the squad made Detroit a much safer city. When the House Select Committee on Crime called Nichols to testify in April 1973 to explain why his police department had caused an alarming number of fatalities, Nichols brushed off the unit's behavior. "As is the case with most police criticism, the noise comes from a vocal minority," Nichols argued. More importantly, STRESS had become a "nationwide symbol" of a new approach to protecting innocent residents. Even if Nichols could not establish a direct correlation between STRESS surveillance and the reduction of crime, he pointed to the squad's effectiveness by citing its impressive conviction rates, 75 percent on felonies and 94 percent on misdemeanors.[28]

The existence of STRESS made Nichols appear tough and responsive to crime, and Nichols pointed out that many of his constituents appreciated the effort. One woman wrote to the editor of the *Detroit News*: "I beg Detroiters not to be carried away by sympathy for criminals! We need STRESS! The choice is between STRESS and crime!" Nichols shared with the Select Committee a letter he received from a constituent. "I am black and am no law and order man of the ilk of Vice President Agnew, but I am no thief and robber either," wrote the resident in gratitude. "Many other blacks are glad to have policemen around regardless of their race, but for them to say so publicly leaves them open for much criticism and harassment." These endorsements, from white conservatives and black moderates alike, gave Nichols license to maintain aggressive crime control strategies. "As long as the support continues to outweigh the criticism," Nichols testified, "we must continue to use our most effective methods."[29] For Nichols, the tactical squad's crime control ends justified its means, whatever their human cost.

Indeed, Nichols and other law enforcement officials saw the violent methods STRESS officers frequently employed as a regrettable byproduct of police work in segregated urban areas, where community violence demanded an aggressive police response. STRESS commander Bannon remarked to a reporter: "We're involved in a violent business. We just don't walk up and shoot somebody. We ask him to stop. If he doesn't, we shoot. The criminal himself can set the rules of the game."

Nichols also defended the squad in earnest. "It is a traditional dilemma. If you do not police those areas, you're not providing the services," he remarked to a *New York Times* reporter. "If you do come in, you're an occupying army. How do you police a whole community without alienating some elements? You can't do it."[30] For Bannon and Nichols, the criminals "set the rules" and the alternative, to scale down patrol or to patrol less aggressively, would lead only to disorder and more crime.

From the perspective of black Detroiters and their allies, however, it appeared that the very presence of STRESS within an existing climate of violence often sustained and even worsened that climate. In June 1973, William Stevens raised the question in the *New York Times*: "Are the police, in their zeal to make Detroiters safe from criminals, creating their own climate of fear through the tactics they use?" Beyond the unit's everyday decoy operations and the deaths it caused, STRESS officers invaded the homes of black Detroit families and held innocent people at gunpoint. For many residents in the neighborhoods targeted by STRESS, the unit had inflicted "a reign of terror upon honest citizens of the black community." As these incensed citizens noted, the lack of any serious reconsideration of the unit's tactics among law enforcement officials had obvious racial and class implications. In a joint community statement, residents pointed out that "no suburban community would allow for one instant the kind of abuses, intrusions and excesses now being exercised in the city of Detroit." The underlying logic of the STRESS operations, that segregated neighborhoods in Detroit were inherently violent and that this required a similarly violent response from plainclothes police fighting potential crime, had exacerbated the very problems STRESS attempted to solve. In 1972, at the height of STRESS, Detroit's homicide rate peaked, and it became known as the "Murder City" for the remainder of the decade and into the 1980s.[31]

The anti-STRESS campaign did succeed in pushing questions about the practices of big-city tactical squads onto the national radar, and skepticism was brought to bear on similar efforts elsewhere. When the Law Enforcement Assistance Administration awarded the Philadelphia Police Department $1.33 million to start an experimental plainclothes police unit in north and west areas of the city in April 1973, residents immediately worried that the tactical squad would grow to resemble its counterpart in Detroit. The police department's spokesman assured the citizens that his Anti-Crime Team (ACT) was "not a STRESS-type of operation. We are strictly concerned with street muggings and burglaries, and that is all." Although the substantial LEAA grant indicated that the federal government was still committed to funding tactical plainclothes squads (the federal government also gave the city of Baltimore $500,000 to start a fifty-five-man "high crime area" plainclothes team in 1973), the ACT program seemed to have learned from some of the mistakes of STRESS. Forty percent of the 140 officers involved in the ACT program were black, as opposed to the nine black officers working for STRESS in 1972, who constituted fewer than 10 percent of the STRESS squad's rank and file. The ACT officers were less inclined to fire their guns in threatening situations, and the Philadelphia plainclothes squad managed to avoid killing suspects or innocent civilians.[32]

As the Detroit mayoral election of 1973 approached, black candidate Coleman Young used the widespread community mobilization against STRESS to energize his campaign against Nichols, who was also a contender. Young pledged to abolish STRESS, and his supporters saw this vow as a sign that he would reform the Detroit Police Department. When Young won and took office as the city's first African American mayor, he joined a growing cohort of more than a hundred black mayors across the United States who presided over deindustrializing small cities and rural towns as well as major cities like Detroit, where black residents edged into a majority. Young stuck to his campaign promise. In one of his first actions as mayor, in March 1974, he officially disbanded STRESS and moved to increase the number of black officers in the Detroit Police Department.[33]

Despite Young's effort to reduce police violence and increase representation for black officers, however, he could not jeopardize Detroit's share of crime war funds. Such funding had become even more necessary as the federal government divested from other social programs in the city and increasingly tied welfare services to law enforcement. The Young administration replaced STRESS with thirty separate twenty-four-hour police mini-stations in Cass Corridor and other low-income black neighborhoods. Although this marked a return to the kind of surveillance the Kerner Commission had suggested and a clear retreat from foot patrol that federal policymakers and law enforcement professionals advocated, during his five terms as mayor, Young went on to embrace a number of other strategies at the heart of the wars on crime and drugs. Just two years after he abolished the STRESS squad, Young drastically enlarged the police force by recalling more than 400 discharged police officers to duty and imposing a 10:00 p.m. curfew on all Detroiters under the age of eighteen. He was one of the first to set a mandatory minimum sentence for unlawful handgun possession in the early 1980s.[34] Even though Young shared the same racial background as the majority of his constituents, many of the older forms of social control remained.

Although STRESS demonstrated the violent consequences of decoy squads and plainclothes operations, a number of federal policymakers agreed that the methods the squad used were vital. After hearing Nichols, Bannon, and STRESS crew members defend the unit's actions before the House Select Committee on Crime in April 1973, Congressman Sam Steiger of Arizona came to the "inescapable conclusion" that "in spite of the criticism the project is worth the continued effort, because it is clear the simple thing to do would be to abandon it and that way avoid criticism."[35] Steiger and other federal policymakers reasoned that the War on Crime would necessarily raise some resistance from the residents living in the communities it targeted, and even some unfortunate and fatal incidents, but that the crime fight, and the turn to foot patrol and plainclothes operations, should not be scaled back. For the larger criminal justice community, STRESS was an anomaly, and plainclothes surveillance produced impressive arrest rates in the neighborhoods where crime appeared to be escalating. The plainclothes strategy went on to become an even more critical tactic for law enforcement officials in the early 1970s.

THE WAR ON STREET PUSHERS

In January 1972, when the president established a special cadre of plainclothes antidrug agents operating directly out of the White House, the Nixon administration brought the tactical squads pioneered by Murphy and Nichols, and encouraged by the LEAA, together with counterintelligence strategies developed by the FBI. Even though the Office of Drug Abuse Law Enforcement (ODALE) lasted only for a year and a half, it more closely resembled a national police force than any other programs the federal government supported during the wars on crime and drugs. Federal policymakers tended to resist ideas that even *resembled* such a body, as a national force would violate American founding principles that prohibited federal control over state militias.[36] But during the transition from Nixon's first term in office to his second, ODALE placed federal agents on the streets in low-income urban neighborhoods by executive order, unleashing a terror that paralleled what Detroit's black community was confronting at the same time under STRESS.

Just as discretionary funds enabled the president to increase surveillance and patrol in segregated urban neighborhoods, narcotics enforcement provided Nixon a means through which the federal government could claim jurisdiction in local matters. This idea had been circulating in conservative political groups since at least 1968, when the Republican Committee on Planning and Research's Task Force on Crime sent a memo to Nixon's campaign team. "The federal government has abundant jurisdiction in the narcotics field," the Task Force advised, and launching an "all-out war on narcotics trafficking" would "substantially reduce street crime."[37] While law enforcement was always considered a state and local matter, drug enforcement was an issue squarely under the purview of the national government. The 1914 Harris Act gave federal policymakers the authority to police illegal narcotics based on the government's constitutional right to tax, and thus allowed them to intervene in narcotics trafficking. The Nixon administration exploited this rule to shift policing powers to the White House.

In June 1971, White House officials delivered the initial plan for ODALE to Nixon. The special office would operate as a "street-pusher" campaign, targeting citizens who seemed to disproportionately abuse drugs: young Americans and "those in urban ghettos already beset with the serious social ills of urban blight." The purpose of ODALE was not to reduce the supply of drugs, but to police the "'demand' side of the equation." Using various "social indicators" that reflected the "nature" of drug users, ODALE was given "strong directive authority and funding control to carry out a set of specific objectives within a definite period of time." Indeed, White House officials planned for the agency to have a fixed life span, but believed it would nevertheless "build a greater sense of urgency and initiative" regarding the drug abuse that seemed to be sweeping the nation. Nixon hoped that the office would promote a "stronger, better, coordinated set of programs capable of generating permanent solutions" to street crime.[38] Two days after the president received the plans for ODALE, he officially called for a "War on Drugs."

Under orders to "search and destroy" the property of suspected street-level drug dealers and their clients, or as Nixon called them, "the very vermin of humanity," ODALE put the "no knock" raids, wiretapping provisions, mandatory minimums, and new criminal categories of Nixon's DC Court Reorganization Act to use. The Organized Crime Control Act of 1970, which conservative senators John McClellan, Roman Hruska, and Sam Ervin sponsored shortly after the Nixon administration introduced the DC legislation, enabled federal officials to take advantage of the broad investigative powers and harsh criminal codes the White House and Congress favored for the capital city on a national scale. In effect, the Organized Crime Control Act elevated local crimes such as drug dealing and gambling to the status of federal offenses that could be easily enforced by ODALE agents.

With the powers of the 1970 legislation in effect, the strategies White House officials developed for the agency opened up new opportunities to arrest offenders and potential offenders, bringing federal agents into collaboration with local police. Nixon selected Customs Commissioner Myles Ambrose to direct ODALE, with James Q. Wilson and other members of the president's Drug Abuse Commission helping to plan its strategies. Ambrose reported directly to the president. Championing the motto "Caveat Venditor" ("Let the seller beware"), ODALE installed listening posts in twenty-four target cities with funding from the LEAA. A pool of police officers, U.S. attorneys, Department of Justice officials, and agents from the Bureau of Narcotics and Dangerous Drugs (established under Lyndon Johnson in 1968) constituted the agents who were involved in ODALE's everyday operations. With plainclothes agents patrolling urban neighborhoods with high rates of reported crime and interacting with drug abusers and criminals on a daily basis, Ambrose described ODALE operations as "dirty scummy work."[39]

As an undercover, tactical force, ODALE resembled Murphy's Anti-crime Section and STRESS in many respects. It also reintroduced the methods developed by the FBI's COINTELPRO, the program responsible for some of the most devastating incidents of government repression in the history of the United States. Although COINTELPRO emerged in the mid-1950s to monitor the activities of the Communist Party and the civil rights leaders whom the federal government falsely associated with it, FBI director J. Edgar Hoover established a "Black Nationalist Hate Groups" section shortly after the Detroit rebellion in August 1967. The explicit focus on Black Power organizations would carry forth COINTELPRO's larger mission, "protecting national security, preventing violence, and maintaining the existing social and political order," by suppressing militant protest by any means. COINTELPRO used raids, wiretapping, stop-and-frisk methods, and other questionable tactics introduced to "prevent the rise of a 'messiah' who could unify and electrify the black nationalist movement," seeking to incriminate or completely obliterate black political leaders and organizations.[40]

Although many of the tactics COINTELPRO agents used remain a common part of American law enforcement, the most salient of these was the agents' raids on black militant targets. In September 1968, Hoover declared the Black Panther Party the "greatest threat to the internal security of the country." Recognizing that police officers could make a vital contribution to COINTELPRO operations, Hoover suggested that FBI field offices coordinate their efforts with local law enforcement to arrest Panthers and orchestrate raids. Subsequently, in San Diego, Chicago, Los Angeles, and other urban centers with a strong Panther base, COINTELPRO worked with local police departments to conduct raids on the organization and its members. In San Diego and other cities, FBI field officers conducted "racial briefing sessions" for the local police departments to make officers "more alert for black militant individuals." San Diego police used two outstanding traffic warrants as justification to raid the Panther headquarters there in the fall of 1969, leading to the arrest of six members and the seizure of three shotguns, one rifle, four gas masks, and one tear gas canister. In Chicago, the FBI's "Racial Matters Squad" monitored Panther activity and exchanged information with the Panther Squad of the police department's Gang Intelligence Unit. COINTELPRO agents met with the police unit three to five times a week between 1967 and 1969, sharing information and planning an attack that eventually culminated in the raid on December 4, 1969, when police officers murdered local party chairman Fred Hampton in his sleep along with his bodyguard Mark Clark. Hampton and Clark's deaths were but two among many: within a period of roughly three years, ten Panthers and nine police officers lost their lives during raids and various other confrontations across the country.[41]

In Los Angeles, COINTELPRO agents worked with the County Sheriff's Office Intelligence Division and the police department's Intelligence and Criminal Conspiracy Division on a daily basis to track the activity of the Panthers. The bureau targeted Los Angeles specifically, and the Black Panther Party chapter there suffered more assaults than any other nationwide. In September 1969, armed police raided the Panther's breakfast program in Watts, which Hoover identified as "the best and most influential activity going for the BPP [Black Panther Party] and, as such . . . potentially the greatest threat to efforts by authorities to neutralize the BPP and destroy what it stands for." The Panthers were providing much-needed services in segregated urban neighborhoods, from breakfast programs to free health clinics to food drives, and Hoover recognized these initiatives—very much in the spirit of earlier War on Poverty programs—as a critical source of Panther power. Hoover ordered agents to "eradicate [the Panthers'] serve the people programs," and thereafter, Panthers in Los Angeles were arrested on a daily basis, although the charges against most were ultimately dropped.[42]

Four days after the incident that led to the deaths of Hampton and Clark in Chicago, the nation's first Special Weapons and Tactics (SWAT) team debuted at the Los Angeles Black Panther headquarters. The SWAT team was supported by hundreds of thousands of dollars in municipal and federal funds; its existence was made possible, in part, by the technology transfers from the military to civil police which the Law Enforcement Assistance Administration facilitated and by the agency's funding of helicopters and other defense technologies at up to 75 percent of the cost. On December 8 at 5:30 in the morning, a 300-man force descended on the Black Panther Party's Central Avenue base, equipped with battering rams, helicopters, army tanks, and trucks in what the press would deem a "mini-Vietnam." Thirteen Panthers were inside, and the shootout lasted for four hours. Police Chief Daryl Gates at one point sought permission from the Department of Defense to detonate a grenade, but the Panthers surrendered before such drastic actions became necessary, after tear gas seeped into their gas masks. The *Los Angeles Times* elatedly described how the "Panther Fortress" had been "seized," even without the deployment of the National Guardsmen who were waiting in the wings for a dramatic "final assault." By mid-1975, 500 special tactics forces modeled on the first SWAT team had emerged across the country.[43]

COINTELPRO ended in 1971, after the Citizens' Commission to Investigate the FBI exposed its operations, but ODALE and other programs implemented by the Nixon administration kept many of its methods alive. The Racketeering Influence and Corrupt Organizations (RICO) program established by the Crime Control Act of 1970 continued to target radical organizations such as the Weather Underground, Puerto Rican *Independentistas*, and the Black Panthers, but it also moved beyond these groups to focus on low-income black Americans in general. RICO created new categories of federal crimes such as the possession of explosives (associated with militants) and gambling (an offense associated with black Americans who participated disproportionately in the numbers game).[44] RICO provisions also enabled the federal government to convene special grand juries, to seize the assets of any organization deemed to be a criminal conspiracy, and to sentence convicts labeled as "dangerous adult offenders" to a minimum of twenty-five years in prison. Perhaps most importantly, RICO empowered federal agents to interrogate anyone, anywhere, and for just about any reason. The powers secured by RICO gave ODALE agents license to launch a vigorous campaign against street-level drug dealers.

ODALE made COINTELPRO-style raids far more common, focusing not just on political activists in segregated urban areas but on low-level criminals in the same neighborhoods. By March 1972, three months into the ODALE operation, Nixon was already instructing Ambrose to amplify the strike force's attack. "In the whole field of Criminal law, this has the highest priority of this Administration," Nixon said of

ODALE. Following the president's orders, between April 1972 and May 1973, ODALE conducted some 1,439 raids by thirty-eight strike forces. A good number of them proceeded without a warrant. Whereas the Bureau of Narcotics and Dangerous Drugs had conducted four "no knock" raids in the five years before ODALE was established, in its first six months, ODALE officials estimated that the office had been involved in "about 100" "no knock" raids.[45]

During a typical raid, heavily armed officers wearing plainclothes attire would bash down the doors of private apartments and homes in the middle of the night, holding residents at gunpoint while ODALE agents ransacked their belongings. Most of the suspects had been accused of nonviolent crimes, and if agents did not find the drugs they were looking for, they sought other forms of contraband that would allow them to make an arrest. All too often, ODALE strike forces violated the civil liberties of, and even killed, completely innocent Americans. In Los Angeles alone, where the LEAA paid the salaries of local police officers involved in the federal force, ODALE conducted a mistaken raid "once or twice a month." Much like the official responses to the killings of Rita Lloyd in New York and Henry Henderson in Detroit, when innocent people lost their lives at the hands of ODALE agents, officers rationalized the fatalities as "isolated aberrations," or the consequence of "hard-pressed police officers trying to do their job." The demands of undercover work meant police officers increasingly participated in criminal activity themselves, and not without a strong psychological impact. "If you spend weeks undercover, living in a hole and dealing with drug people, your whole life-style changes and perhaps your morals too," an ODALE agent explained. "Sometimes there's a thin line between the hunted and the hunter."[46]

The accurate number of low-income Americans who suffered from ODALE's abuses may never be known, since botched raids were underreported. But when misdirected ODALE raids struck the white suburban community of Collinsville, Illinois, the national media began to take notice. The Collinsville cases, in which ODALE agents dressed undercover as "hippies" terrorized two families, generated sufficient media coverage and public outrage that Nixon eventually dissolved the force. It was never intended to be a permanent entity anyway, but rather a temporary program that would ground future directions of crime control and drug enforcement.

In July 1973, as the Watergate investigation gained ground, the *New York Times* ran a front-page story on the horrors of ODALE. Nixon responded by consolidating ODALE and the Bureau of Narcotics and Dangerous Drugs into the new Drug Enforcement Agency (DEA), a single federal agency that would be responsible for controlling narcotics. Although the White House police force ceased its plainclothes operations, its tactics flourished during the second half of the 1970s, as the LEAA and the FBI supported sting operations by local police departments that focused on entire groups of low-income Americans, rather than individual pushers.

STING OPERATIONS AND THE WAR ON BLACK PETTY CRIMINALS

Despite the negative media coverage and public protest of the brutality of tactical plainclothes operations such as STRESS and ODALE, the federal government continued to support such practices. In the mid-1970s, it also embraced a new battle tactic that moved dramatically beyond the use of individual decoys and enabled federal and local law enforcement to build long-lasting relationships with criminals and make mass arrests.[47] Beginning in 1975, the federal government granted urban police departments money to purchase stolen goods and set up warehouses to fence the black market merchandise. Critics charged that the methods of STRESS came dangerously close to entrapment, but the practice of fencing came even closer. The sting operations, carefully orchestrated by law enforcement officials at the federal, state, and local levels, baited criminals or would-be criminals. Policymakers supported these projects in the name of attacking organized crime. In the main battlegrounds of the War on Crime, however, these methods quickly evolved into an attack on black petty thieves and came to involve the creation of crime itself—a central feature of the rise of the carceral state.

The Washington, DC, Police Department's sting effort was the most elaborate and the most contrived of those supported by this funding. In the summer of 1975, Washington police lieutenant Robert Arscott had set up a small fake fencing operation masquerading as the consulting firm "Urban Research Associates." The undercover officer who manned the operation in downtown Washington sat behind a desk with a hidden camera and a tape recorder, hoping that thieves who had recently lifted office equipment would attempt to sell the stolen merchandise to the Urban Research Associates outfit.[48] But amid the highest unemployment rate since 1941, the façade attracted more job seekers than criminals. The police department promptly shut down Urban Research Associates.

For its next attempt, the DC Police Department used federal and local funds to purchase an unheated warehouse near Langdon Park in the segregated northeast side of the District as a more convincing space for illegal transactions. Beginning in fall 1975, law enforcement purchased $2.4 million worth of stolen property with $67,000 in government funds. The project, called "Operation Sting," involved the FBI, the Bureau of Alcohol, Tobacco, and Firearms, and the LEAA. After only five months, the initiative succeeded in its implicit purpose: to round up hundreds of small-time crooks, nearly all of them unemployed black men. The undercover police officers and federal agents posing as Mafia "dons" gave themselves Italian names straight out of the then-recent *Godfather* films, including "Angelo Lasagna," "Mike Franzino," "Tony Bonano," "Rico Rigatone," and "Bohana LaFountaine." None of the officers were of Italian descent, but they interspersed terms like "Ciao" and "Arrivederci" as they played these roles.[49]

Operation Sting created a demand for crime by providing crooks with a market on which to sell stolen goods. Word quickly spread that the fencing outfit, known to its customers as PFF Inc (for "Police-FBI Fencing Incognito"), was tied to the Mafia and would pay the highest prices in town. The petty thieves furnished PFF Inc with typewriters, adding machines, radios, and television sets, and then went back out to steal more items for the "dons." If no valuable material goods were to be found, the crooks went after their neighbors' mail, bringing stolen housing and welfare checks and credit cards. As their employer, PFF Inc provided the thieves with a steady and continuous source of income as long as they could deliver the plunder.

The officers built criminal profiles of their customers over the course of the sting. To gain permission to enter the warehouse, the crooks called a special number from a phone booth in front of a gas station

The officers and agents involved in "Operation Sting" posing as their "Mafia" characters, March 1976. The federally funded fencing outfit led to the mass arrest of black petty thieves in the segregated northeast side of Washington, DC. Standing from left to right are "Mike Franzino," FBI agent Bob Lill in the car with Washington police sergeant Carl Mattis standing beside him, "Angelo Lasagna," and "Tony Bonano." "Rico Rigatone" and "Bohanna LaFountaine" are kneeling. *Photograph by James A. Parcell. The Washington Post Collection, Getty Images*

down the street, providing basic information about themselves and the items for sale. The distance from the booth to the fencing site gave Detective Patrick Lilly, acting as "Pasquale Larocca," enough time to flash the customer's identity, the date, and the time of the transaction in front of one of the warehouse's many hidden cameras. As each petty thief entered, a two-way mirror hidden by lewd images of naked women captured his identity. To "prove" they were not informants or police, each suspect provided the undercover officers with their Social Security card, driver's license, or birth certificate. Sometimes the PFF Inc agents would provoke the criminals by nonchalantly mentioning the violent mafia crimes they had supposedly committed. Tony Bonano would say in the middle of a transaction: "We gotta stiff in the trunk. Whadda we do?" to which Rico Rigatone would reply: "Tossa him in the freeze." The officers hoped this interplay would make the thieves more comfortable in sharing details about their own crimes. Indeed, repeat customers built relationships with their PFF Inc employers and talked openly about prior crimes and pending court cases. All of the confessions were captured on film. After completing a deal, the officers offered the crooks a glass of Chianti or a shot of whiskey, from which they would promptly retrieve fingerprints of the suspects.[50]

This type of ornate acting offered the fences a welcome break from routine beat work. "We played a game with them," one of the detectives remarked. "We were romance, the mob, the greatest thing that ever happened to them." "Larocca" gained a reputation among the customers for his meatballs, smothered in hot sauce, salt, and mustard. "Have a meatball," the officer might say to a suspect as he entered the warehouse. "You'll hurt Pasquale's feeling if you no have a meatball." Although Lieutenant Robert Arscott, one of the masterminds behind the operation, commented that the crooks "thought they were in Hollywood. It was almost pathetic," perhaps this belief extended to the officers, too, who dyed their hair black to fit the role and drove around in a fleet of limousines. Arscott and his team never questioned the ethical implications of their own actions, but instead delighted in the fact that they had "fooled virtually every hood in town" for the duration of the operation.[51]

When PFF Inc had exceeded its initial budget and considered shutting down the business in late December, the LEAA saved the day and floated the fencing operation for an additional two months. By the end of February 1976, the immense amount of information the officers collected and their desire to act on a number of the recorded confessions brought the fencing outfit to its conclusion. In order to round up the suspects together and save thousands of police man-hours hunting for them one by one, the undercover agents decided to throw a party in honor of their customers, promising door prizes, whiskey, women, and the chance to finally meet the "Big Boss." The tactic had worked for the New York Police Department in a more modest venture, and seemed to be a fitting grand finale for the PFF Inc enterprise. The undercover agents encouraged their customers to attend and spread the word about the event. On the evening of Saturday, February 28, the attendees (referred to as "street hoodlums" by the law enforcement officials) came out in their finest, some even renting tuxedos for the occasion.[52]

Washington police sergeant Carl Mattis, who played guest of honor "Don Corleone," greeted the crooks at the entrance. Soul music blared to prevent new arrivals from hearing the arrests taking place in the back of the warehouse. "Bless you, my son," Corleone said as attendees kissed his ring. "Before you go into the party, I have a really funny thing to tell you. You're under arrest." And arrest they did. The mobsters prepared the handcuffs in advance, with each suspect's name and identification number, bringing seventy of the thieves into custody on the night of the party. Larocca sang "When the Moon Hits Your Eye Like a Big Pizza Pie" as he secured the cuffs on the crooks. The department later issued warrants for the suspects caught on camera, a total of about 120 offenders. Most were released or received light sentences, but all of the suspects who came to the party either took a plea bargain or received a conviction.[53]

When the sting went public, cocktail parties in Washington buzzed with details of the caper. The District's elite expressed varying opinions about the methods PFF Inc employed. For FBI agent Robert Lill, who planned the operations with Arscott, the venture had "succeeded beyond our wildest hopes." Others voiced their misgivings. The journalist Sanford J. Ungar astutely noted in a *Washington Post* editorial, "The very existence of a major fencing operation in Washington's inner city— be it government run or a form of free enterprise—may in effect encourage burglaries and robberies . . . a hazard and a factor that must be considered before LEAA, pumped up with funds by Congress, runs off and sets up a kind of nationwide chain-store fencing network." Residents flooded the DC Police Department with requests to retrieve stolen property and wrote letters to police chief Maurice J. Cullinane expressing their outrage. While many constituents were comfortable with the operation's end result, they found the ethnic stereotypes the police department used to play Italian Mafia dons highly offensive. In an effort to restore the police department's public perception, Officer Lilly thanked "the Italian-Americans for the use of their mythology," and insisted the police did not act in an ethnically insensitive manner. "We meant no harm, except to the thieves," he assured the public.[54] The stings proliferated thereafter, but avoided resorting to ethnic stereotypes as an undercover device when possible.

Federal law enforcement institutions and the DC Police Department found Operation Sting to be so beneficial that they planned and funded another fencing event that summer called "Operation Got Ya Again." The venture marked "a new era in law enforcement," as federal prosecutor Earl J. Silbert noted. This time, police officers courted the thieves and potential thieves by operating under the name H & H Tracking Company. FBI agent Charles E. Harrison handled most of the goods, which again included stolen credit cards, welfare checks, negotiable papers, and personal household items. A more expansive effort than the previous sting, "Operation Got Ya Again" captured 141 suspects—many of whom were out on bail and had also worked for PFF Inc. It involved police departments in Prince George County, Alexandria, and Montgomery County, as well as the FBI, the U.S. Attorney's Office, the Bureau of Alcohol, Tobacco, and Firearms, the General Service Administration, and the U.S. Secret Service. These cross-agency partnerships were unprecedented. As LEAA administrator Richard Velde described it, "The participants have been excited almost to the point of being missionaries about cooperation." These crime war "missionaries" and the interagency and interlevel partnerships they recruited marked a "new chapter in the War on Crime," the *Washington Post*'s Kevin Klose and Ron Shaffer wrote, one in which crime control agencies at all levels of government established new institutions and black markets of their own in the underworld.[55]

Soon, police departments in other cities also wanted to join in fencing stolen goods with federal funds, and the Department of Justice under President Gerald Ford granted twelve urban police departments enough money to arrange twenty separate stings. "Frankly, we've been swamped with requests," Velde said in a press release shortly after Operation Sting, "and we would like to do even more if we could get the money." Even though its proximity to major federal law enforcement centers rendered the capital an opportune site for close collaboration between national and municipal officials, the Ford administration promoted local fencing operations across the United States with a training film made by the FBI and the DC Police Department and $2 million in discretionary grants. Police in Atlanta bought nineteen cars, six trucks, and 1,700 stolen items with $64,000 in federal funds. The effort led to the arrest of 100 thieves, who sold roughly $1.5 million worth of stolen merchandise to fences.[56]

By the end of the 1970s, the federal government focused fencing operations on larger thefts and complex crimes such as "Operation Bear Trap II" in Baltimore. Financed with a quarter of a million dollars from the LEAA, "Bear Trap II" led to the arrest of forty-seven residents at the end of a seventeen-month-long undercover investigation, on charges related to well over a million dollars' worth of stolen property. Law enforcement agents set up an antiques store, an auto parts store, and a brokerage firm that allowed officials to pose as fences to target "career criminals." The stolen property confiscated by Baltimore police included $50,000 worth of silver from the Hampton Mansion, a National Historical Site in the city. As in "Operation Got Ya Again," these criminals faced arrest in the context of an orchestrated law enforcement spectacle, involving 200 state, city, and county police officers as well as a host of journalists and television reporters. In a similar operation in San Francisco in 1978, federal agents opened up what they called "The Store" and moved $721,900 worth of stolen property before arresting nearly 300 people in a single day on charges ranging from car theft to burglary. In Nashville, $300,000 from the Department of Justice bankrolled another "Operation Sting," which led to the arrest of one hundred people in a matter of hours and warrants for 200 more.[57]

With the LEAA allocating $8 million for federal, state, and local joint sting operations in 1978, police departments from Penobscot County, Maine, to Norfolk, Virginia, welcomed the opportunity to hone their acting skills and make sweeping arrests. The Los Angeles County sheriff's department received the largest federal grant for a major sting, called "Operation Tarpit," whereby thirty-three deputies and FBI agents set up fake storefronts at seven locations. For nearly two years, the local police had established a formidable underground economy and had gathered $42 million in stolen property with nearly half a million dollars in buy money. In the four years after the "Got Ya" test case in the nation's capital, police went on to issue arrest warrants for a total of 4,222 people on 6,817 separate charges and recovered $114 million in stolen property throughout the United States. The LEAA was particularly enthusiastic about the operations because of the 98 percent conviction rate for sting-related charges and the high percentage of guilty pleas many defendants accepted.[58] If bringing thousands of black petty thieves into the criminal justice system was the end goal of the fencing operations, then the federal government's enormous investment in the stings made sense.

Ten years into the era of federal law enforcement assistance, as some federal agents posed as mobsters encouraging low-income urban residents to steal from one another, Nixon officials had succeeded in fostering a "massive infusion of police power" and the "allocation of force in high density crime areas" that converted the War on Crime into a self-perpetuating entity.[59] The use of decoy, fencing, and sting operations to identify, arrest, and incarcerate potential criminals would grow even more central to the War on Drugs during the Reagan administration. For the officers who participated in these schemes, the mission provided an appealing alternative to the mundane and difficult aspects of police work. In arresting offenders, police were fulfilling their most basic duty of enforcing the law and promoting public safety. But the operations also gave law enforcement something far more tangible. When it appeared that petty theft and burglary were on the rise, federal and local law enforcement officials believed the stings would help identify a subset of repeat offenders in black urban neighborhoods and arrest them en masse. Capturing residents under legally viable circumstances (however orchestrated) enabled law enforcement authorities to build strong criminal cases against the petty thieves that would assuredly land them in prison.

By the mid-1970s, federal policymakers and law enforcement officials came to see incarceration as a powerful crime deterrent, and the stings offered police an easy means to remove a population they saw as latently criminal from the streets and place them behind bars. From the perspective of criminal justice authorities at all levels, then, establishing an informal economy of their own was a necessary precaution to prevent targets and would-be targets from engaging in further, and perhaps more violent, crime. Due to the draconian sentencing policies that emerged in Washington, DC, and elsewhere during this same period, the suspects arrested in these operations faced an ever-longer period of confinement. In this sense, the federal government's decision to start manufacturing crime via sting operations in the mid-1970s as a strategy for the War on Crime was but one of the numerous forces that fueled the engine of mass incarceration.

When the Senate Select Committee to Study Governmental Operations conducted a full investigation of the federal government's counterintelligence activities in 1976, it concluded: "Although the claimed purpose of the Bureau's COINTELPRO tactics was to prevent violence, some of the FBI's tactics against the [Black Panther Party] were clearly intended to foster violence, and many others could reasonably have been expected to cause violence." Indeed, during the Nixon administration, when COINTELPRO activity was at its peak and when foot patrol and plainclothes policing revolutionized American law enforcement, violent crime in the country nearly doubled, and property crime rose 24 percent.[60] Patrick Murphy's Citywide Anticrime Section in New York, the STRESS squad in Detroit, the White House cadre of "presidential drug cops" in ODALE, and sting operations in black urban neighborhoods across the United States carried forth the legacy of COINTELPRO not only by infringing on the constitutional rights of American citizens but also in heightening the violence of the War on Crime's all-too-often lethal battles.

[6]

JUVENILE INJUSTICE

At around 10:30 p.m. in early 1974, police officers noticed a group of twelve black youths at a popular McDonald's in Watts. It had been nearly a decade since the unrest in South Central, and although no similar incidents of collective violence had occurred in the area since, the sight of black residents gathered together was always enough to arouse the suspicion of law enforcement. The city had recently reinstated its curfew ordinances, which forbade citizens under the age of eighteen from public spaces without a parent or a guardian present. The measure served as an effective pretense to stop, interrogate, and arrest black youth, especially groups of black youth. In this case, the teenagers appeared to be breaking the curfew law as they enjoyed their french fries and hamburgers.

The officers patrolling the McDonald's that evening were part of the LAPD's special CRASH unit, which had been established in 1973 to suppress gang violence in Watts by detaining young residents for minor infractions. The force, whose name was an acronym for "Community Resources Against Street Hoodlums," was an elite cadre of officers who focused their energies on isolating the "troublemakers and repeaters" and "taking them out of circulation," in the words of Captain Dan Sanchez. When police officers spotted the twelve curfew violators, they immediately began to gather information about the youth, cross-referencing their names with the department's own list of repeat offenders in Watts. The officers believed five of the youths, based on their record of previous contact with police, were affiliated with local gangs and arrested them on the curfew charge. All of the young suspects were immediately sent to Juvenile Hall in East Los Angeles, a facility so overcrowded that hundreds of the confined children and teenagers slept on the floor.[1]

Although the LAPD denied that the curfew law was being used to target black youth, CRASH operated under a set of assumptions that linked young African Americans to crime and gang activity. Curfew laws were rarely enforced outside South Central and East Los Angeles, the areas where the city's black and Chicano residents were concentrated. (The CRASH force had been established in the 77th police precinct, the division responsible for maintaining order in Watts.) When police did apprehend white youth for violating curfew, they were most often classified as "youth in trouble" and quickly released to their parents. Black youth, usually labeled by law enforcement authorities as "delinquent" under the same set of charges, were often detained for days or even weeks.[2]

The strategies that guided the previous thirteen years of domestic urban policy fostered the criminalization of such everyday activity as getting a late-night snack in segregated urban neighborhoods. Black youth were more likely to be labeled "delinquent" based on the way in which policymakers, law enforcement officials, and criminal justice authorities evaluated their morality and character. To prevent future crimes that policymakers and officials at all levels of government assumed "delinquent" or "potentially delinquent" youth would go on to commit, the national law enforcement program supported the targeted enforcement of the curfew and similar measures in predominately black neighborhoods. The classification marked young people as ostensibly on the brink of criminality, yet it had little to do with whether these youth had actually broken the law. The result of this early intervention was a statistical portrait of crime that overrepresented black youth, since greater numbers of young black residents had more police contacts and longer criminal records than their white counterparts. In turn, the grim crime figures confirmed policymakers' and law enforcement officials' assumptions about urban youth and fueled the escalation of punitive force to contain the problem. In effect, the cycle of pathological assumptions about African Americans, poverty, and crime, targeted patrol and surveillance, and the resulting skewed statistical portrait of American crime repeated itself, fueling the development of crime war programs and the racial profiling within them.[3]

Beginning in the mid-1970s, after nearly ten years of the national law enforcement program and increasing rates of youth crime, Congress endorsed the local practices adopted by CRASH and other antidelinquency police units and implemented them nationwide when it enacted the Juvenile Justice and Delinquency Prevention Act of 1974. Liberals led this effort, prompted by new research on criminality among black urban youth and concern that "wayward" white youth were being mistreated by the criminal justice system. With an initial $380 million, three-year outlay for delinquency prevention and control programs—an eightfold increase over the Kennedy administration's antidelinquency demonstrations and 2.5 times more than Congress allocated toward fighting youth crime during Lyndon Johnson's presidency—the 1974 act created the modern American system of juvenile justice. The legislation supported the widespread use of juvenile prisons, foster and protective care programs, and shelter facilities. It also established the National Institute for Juvenile Justice and Delinquency Prevention to research and evaluate various programs, acting as a clearinghouse to guide state and local governments as they designed new youth detention and rehabilitation programs.[4]

The debates that emerged in Congress about the purpose and targets of the federal government's youth crime intervention marked a critical turning point in the direction of the War on Crime, unearthing questions that had yet to be fully resolved about whether the federal programs should respond to delinquency as a social welfare or crime control issue. Calling for a major investment in youth crime control required the creation of a permanent executive-level agency to manage the problem and distribute the first block grants for the explicit purpose of fighting delinquency. Although the Department of Health, Education, and Welfare (HEW) had directed federal delinquency programs since the Kennedy administration and liberal policymakers felt the new Office of Juvenile Justice and Delinquency Prevention should remain under its purview, Congress ultimately decided that the Department of Justice was better equipped to handle young criminals. In order to get the national youth crime control program started without prolonged debate, liberals ultimately conceded and located the new office within the federal government's punitive arm.

The shift vastly enhanced the power and influence of the Justice Department. The office was charged with disbursing $600 million in block grants to the states—a striking increase over the initial $14 million Congress allocated for delinquency programs in 1969. Congress proceeded to allocate nearly $900 million to national crime control in 1974, and the department enjoyed its largest-ever operating budget. To make youth crime control a national priority, all fifty states received a minimum of $200,000 to establish juvenile delinquency advisory boards that brought together relevant public and private figures to plan and implement programs—much like the state planning agencies the Safe Streets Act of 1968 had imposed on governors. Since previous experiences in block grant funding demonstrated that states could not be relied upon to follow federal policymakers' preferred strategies for the War on Crime or to focus on low-income urban communities, the office awarded block grants to states based on age and income characteristics alone. States with larger youth populations and citizens living at or below the poverty level received a greater proportion of funds.[5]

On the surface, the 1974 act seemed progressive. Congress deinstitutionalized status offenses, or crimes that applied only to minors (such as curfew violations and truancy), by supporting diversion programs, community-based detention, and foster care. Federal policymakers also encouraged these types of alternatives for nonviolent or minor offenders who they believed could be better rehabilitated outside of formal juvenile prisons. Law enforcement officials and criminal justice authorities could now send "acting out" or "troublesome youth," to community-based rehabilitation programs, which were funded by HEW—the only aspect of the national juvenile delinquency program where the social welfare agency retained its authority. Yet in practice, rehabilitative institutions were widely created in suburban and rural communities, and the "troublesome" label was applied to white offenders on a far more frequent basis than to their black and Latino counterparts.[6]

Indeed, the formal law enforcement system for young offenders that Congress designed in 1974 fractured that system along racial lines. Under the terms of the legislation, while the social welfare arm of the federal government treated white and middle-income youth, the punitive arm handled young people from segregated urban neighborhoods. Policymakers acknowledged that white youth seemed to be growing more susceptible to crime, but shaped by lingering memories of violence from the urban uprisings of the 1960s, they associated the category of "delinquency" in general and "serious juvenile offenders" in particular with racially marginalized youth. For "hard-core delinquents" and "potential delinquents," the 1974 act expanded the formal system of juvenile detention. The policy effectively criminalized black children and teenagers and decriminalized white youth.[7]

Under the terms of the 1974 act, a "juvenile delinquency program" constituted any activity related to "the development of neglected, abandoned, or dependent youth and other youth who are potential criminals." By linking common markers of poverty with perspective criminality, and thereby classifying nearly all youth living in low-income neighborhoods as "potentially delinquent," this clause granted law enforcement officials and criminal justice institutions greater authority in the lives of young Americans whose families received welfare benefits or who participated in urban social programs. This provision, "based on anticipation of future actions," went beyond the strategies federal policymakers had devised during the Johnson and Nixon administrations and opened up a new field of surveillance in segregated urban communities.[8]

By classifying low-income black youth as delinquent *before* they had committed any legal violation, the American juvenile justice regime during this period sustained new forms of supervision in urban public schools, in public housing, and within families receiving public assistance. Attempting to control future crime, the legislation increased opportunities for contact between young residents and police in segregated urban communities, with the result that more youth received criminal justice records, interacted with the courts, and were formally incarcerated. The legislation also led to the sentencing of dispropor-tionate numbers of black youths as adults beginning in the mid-1970s by lowering the age threshold for violent federal crimes so that any sixteen-year-old whom the attorney general deemed to be particularly "dangerous to the community" could be tried as such—a provision that a number of states quickly adopted. As federal policymakers continued to disinvest from many of the social welfare programs that had once been available to "potential delinquents" and their families during the Great Society, the 1974 delinquency legislation critically shaped the rise of the carceral state.[9] In fact, the Office of Juvenile Justice and De-linquency Prevention proved so indispensable to the national law en-forcement program that it remains one of the few federal agencies cre-ated at the height of the War on Crime that persists in the same form today.

THE FRAMING OF BLACK "DELINQUENTS"

A decade of policies that made black youth the primary target of na-tional crime control programs produced arrest and crime figures that supported the continued escalation of law enforcement measures in seg-regated urban neighborhoods. As one local police chief explained this dynamic, "Statistics are used like a drunk uses a lamp post, more for support than illumination." By the end of Richard Nixon's first term, in 1972, crime rates had risen to new highs, and crime committed by juve-niles appeared to grow faster than reported crime in general. Whereas youth crime appeared to increase 144 percent between 1960 and 1974, adult crime had increased 17 percent during the same period. Moreover, throughout the 1960s, juvenile arrests for crime rose about 5 percent annually, but as the War on Crime expanded during the first half of the 1970s, the juvenile arrest rate climbed 19 percent, most notably in 1974, when young Americans accounted for a third of felony arrests nation-wide and almost 50 percent of the arrests in cities.[10] Black youth under the age of eighteen accounted for more than half of all arrests for murder, rape, robbery, and violent crime, while white youths were more than half of those arrested for burglary, larceny, and auto theft in 1974.[11] The assumptions about race and crime that shaped the punitive strategies federal policymakers developed and the statistics driving those strategies had become mutually reinforcing.

The discouraging figures did not necessarily reflect actual crime on the ground as much as they did the flawed criminal justice data-gathering that accompanied the intensification of federal law enforcement programs. Arrests were counted as part of the crime rate regardless of whether they produced a conviction, meaning, for example, that if a group of black youth were arrested for robbing a liquor store, all of those youth would be recorded as burglars and counted as part of the crime rate, even if they were subsequently released for lack of evidence. Since black men under the age of twenty-four had the highest arrest rate in the United States—a result of the targeted law enforcement encouraged by the federal government—they were seen as responsible for the majority of the nation's crime and skewed reported rates accordingly, even though crime was increasing faster in suburban and rural areas in the mid-1970s.[12]

The shift in antidelinquency policy and the emergence of the national juvenile justice apparatus coincided not only with the broader rise of patrol and surveillance programs but also with a rapid expansion of research supported by the federal government—often framed by policymakers, law enforcement officials, and scholars as the "problem of black youth crime." These authorities frequently cited the work of University of Pennsylvania law professor Marvin Wolfgang to argue for the expansion of punitive programs targeting black youth in urban areas. With funding from HEW and the National Institute of Mental Health, Wolfgang studied nearly 10,000 young men in Philadelphia—all of whom were born in 1945—and then looked at who among that group appeared in the records of the Juvenile Aid Division of the police department between their tenth and eighteenth birthdays. Wolfgang found that white youth constituted 71 percent of the overall cohort and only 29 percent of the delinquents. He concluded that the crime problem was essentially one of black and Latino youth, who accounted for more than half of the recorded delinquents, committing a combined total of nearly 10,000 offenses by age seventeen. According to Wolfgang, a small but racially concentrated population of offenders was responsible for a third of the arrests and half of the convictions in Philadelphia, leading him to suggest that since "more non-whites go on after the first offense to more offenses," the federal government's "major concern should be with this racial group."[13]

Wolfgang's findings, released to the public as *Delinquency in a Birth Cohort* in 1972, grounded discussions about youth crime during congressional hearings, among officials in the Nixon and Ford administrations, and in academic circles. His conclusions further convinced policymakers and law enforcement officials that crime was a foregone conclusion in low-income African American communities, where, it was thought, cultural pathologies and inadequate parental supervision fostered delinquency and violence.[14] In reality, Wolfgang's six-year research project captured more the extent of police contact with black youth than a "pattern of criminality"; Wolfgang had labeled as "delinquent" any youth who had come into contact with police for something other than a traffic violation, and the fact that African Americans were more likely to be stopped by police on "suspicion," to be assaulted verbally or physically, and to be arrested skewed the conclusions Wolfgang reached about black criminality. Federal policymakers did not identify the flaws in his research and took Wolfgang at his word when he advised, "We are simply faced with the fact that more social harm is committed by nonwhites, so that the resources and efforts of social-harm reduction should be employed among nonwhite youth, especially the very young."[15]

With Wolfgang's recommendation in mind, federal policymakers reconstituted the American juvenile justice system to in order to "deal with those," as Indiana senator Birch Bayh explained, "who are preying on us within the country." Wolfgang's analysis and the crime figures in general convinced Bayh and other federal policymakers that in black urban areas, the community-based social welfare efforts epitomized by the Youth Service Bureaus had proven, in the words of the 1974 legislation, "inadequate to meet the needs of countless abandoned and dependent children who, because of this failure to provide effective services, may become delinquents."[16] Although the act retained the earlier national strategy of preventing would-be delinquents from committing crime, it shifted focus away from social welfare provisions and instead initiated substantial federal investment into juvenile court systems, detention facilities, foster and protective care programs, and shelter facilities.

"The essential goal is one of delivering needed services or attention in such a way and at a time that may be crucial in preventing the development of a criminal career," officials of the Law Enforcement Assistance Administration (LEAA) emphasized in congressional testimony.[17] As the juvenile delinquency program unfolded under the purview of the Department of Justice, this concept of prevention went on to indict entire communities as criminal.

For Bayh (who authored the 1974 legislation and who called urban delinquency a "matter of internal defense") and for his fellow congressional representatives (who similarly deemed youth criminality "a growing threat to the national welfare requiring immediate, comprehensive, and effective action by the federal government"), the expansion of urban surveillance and increasingly punitive guidelines for social problems could effectively suppress the problem.[18] Framing the delinquency fight as a matter of national security and acting on the forecasts of local law enforcement authorities (such as Kenneth Kirkpatrick, the chief probation officer of Los Angeles, who in 1973 predicted that 100,000 mostly black and Chicano youth would be arrested in 1974), Bayh led Congress in considerably enlarging the national system for young offenders.[19] In order to focus on its intended targets—the low-income children and teenagers who exhibited a "pattern of criminality"—the new punitive program would necessarily need to exclude from juridical and penal institutions the tens of thousands of youth who found themselves ensnared in the juvenile justice system without having committed any crime at all.

Black youth had been the focus of the federal government's attention since the Kennedy administration, when antidelinquency initiatives such as Mobilization for Youth in New York's Lower East Side and Action for Youth in Washington, DC, provided job training, education, and development programs to vulnerable young Americans under the direction of HEW. These early measures, stipulated by the Youth Offenses Control Act of 1961 with an annual budget of $10 million, laid the groundwork for the antipoverty programs that were widely implemented during the Johnson administration. Less than a month after Lyndon Johnson signed the Omnibus Crime Control and Safe Streets Act of 1968 into law, Congress extended the federal antidelinquency program with an allocation of $150 million for three years that mainly targeted "potential delinquents," as Johnson called them in 1967, or young Americans from "broken families, burdened with financial and psychological problems."[20] By endorsing the Youth Service Bureaus and other community-based urban service institutions that Johnson's Crime Commission designed, federal policymakers established a mechanism through which police and the courts could constantly monitor black urban youth while providing social services.

Johnson's youth crime control legislation passed just after the Supreme Court extended the equal protections of the Fourteenth Amendment to young citizens accused of crime via the *In re Gault* decision of 1967. By guaranteeing juveniles the right to due process, the Court's ruling both forced the nation to recognize delinquency as a major problem and required the federal government to support the development of a carceral system for young offenders. With many youth serving time in adult facilities and with still others serving time in juvenile facilities for minor or petty offenses, when the Juvenile Delinquency Act came up for reauthorization in 1974, Congress intervened in an attempt to resolve the impending crisis by extending the scale and influence of youth-focused crime policies.

The formation of the Office of Juvenile Justice and Delinquency Prevention offered the federal government an opportunity to address the problem of crime and violence among young Americans by confronting related problems in urban public school systems, public housing, and low-income neighborhoods. Instead, however, the Juvenile Justice and Delinquency Prevention Act of 1974 shifted the federal government's approach to delinquency toward punishment and managing the symptoms of urban poverty, empowering law enforcement authorities to intervene in public institutions serving youth in segregated urban communities. The decision to place the new agency within the Department of Justice settled a series of ongoing disputes among federal policymakers about the strategies for the War on Crime that had shaped the previous thirteen years of federal urban intervention. In the House, the Committee on Education and Labor sponsored the legislation and proposed that the federal juvenile justice programs continue to provide rehabilitative and preventive social services under the auspices of HEW. The bill passed on July 1 by an overwhelming majority, with 329 representatives in favor and 29 opposing. Most of these detractors were Republicans who wanted the LEAA to direct the program.

The Senate's more punitive vision for the nation's juvenile justice system ultimately prevailed, sponsored by the Committee on the Judiciary. One of the most powerful Democrats on the Senate Judiciary Committee and chair of the Juvenile Delinquency Subcommittee, Bayh had guided the rise of the national youth crime control program from the Kennedy administration onward. As approved by Bayh's subcommittee, the legislation would have retained HEW's authority over juvenile delinquency programs. Roman Hruska, the Republican senator from Nebraska who was strongly influential in the enactment and implementation of the Safe Streets Act, introduced the key amendment that transferred juvenile justice authority to the LEAA. The full Judiciary Committee voted in favor of Hruska's punitive substitute, with Democratic senators Bayh, Michigan's Phillip Hart, California's James Tunney, Massachusetts's Edward Kennedy, and Charles McC. Mathias Jr., the liberal Republican from Maryland, opposing the change.

For the same reason that Johnson reluctantly signed the Safe Streets Act of 1968 with the wiretapping provisions favored by conservatives despite his reservations, Bayh led his fellow liberals in conceding their preferred youth crime control program because of the apparent urgency of the problem and the need for federal action. On July 25, the version of the bill that gave juvenile justice authority to the LEAA passed the Senate with only one vote of opposition, from North Carolina Republican Jesse Helms. Bayh admitted that he had "mixed views" about giving the Department of Justice authority over antidelinquency programs because of its law enforcement rather than preventative orientation. But for Bayh and like-minded policymakers, getting the national delinquency program started "as soon as possible" was more important than upholding previous social welfare approaches.[21] The House agreed, and on July 31 passed the bill with Hruska's amendment attached.

The decision to place the Office of Juvenile Justice within the LEAA and to base the federal crime prevention strategy on identifying youth "in danger of becoming delinquent" before they had been arrested did not pass through Congress without vocal objections. Challenging the

Senate's fear that under the charge of HEW, federal juvenile justice programs would only lead to further fragmentation and "delay the development of needed programs," as the Judiciary Committee wrote in its report on the bill, New York's Democratic congresswoman Shirley Chisholm consistently pointed out that the LEAA itself was characterized by inefficiency and mismanagement. And on the day his fellow representatives conceded HEW as the agency responsible for administering the juvenile justice system, Congressman William Steiger issued a grave warning. "By eliminating HEW," the Wisconsin conservative said on the House floor, "we have done serious damage to our efforts to prevent people from becoming delinquents instead of simply seeing them wound up in the juvenile justice system as it is now." A conservative policymaker from Wisconsin, Steiger represented a minority view within the Republican Party. Steiger's fellow Republican congressman, Missouri's Durward Hall, further argued that the legislation made "vague promises that there has been a technical breakthrough so that we can ascertain those impinging upon near delinquency. . . . I just do not believe it." Finally, Ohio's Republican representative John Ashbrook pointed out that by encouraging the diagnosis and treatment of future criminals, the legislation "can open up a Pandora's box. How do we diagnose and treat a youngster in danger of becoming delinquent? I think anybody with common sense knows that every youth is in danger of becoming delinquent. . . . Where do we draw the line?"[22]

However reluctant some members of Congress may have been about the decision to treat delinquency as a crime control problem rather than a social welfare concern and to act on potential and future crime, the final version of the bill reflected the ideas of an ever-growing consensus of policymakers, law enforcement officials, and scholars that the remnants of the War on Poverty had *worsened* the crime problem, that black youth were responsible for the majority of the nation's crime, and that the focus on rehabilitation and prevention in previous delinquency programs had been misguided. The nation had reached a "turning point in the way we handle children in trouble," the Senate committee reported, and it was the federal government's responsibility to devise new methods of "redirecting behavior that endangers society."[23] Rates of reported crime reinforced the urgency of the problem, leading policymakers to conclude that public programs needed to focus on supporting various punitive measures rather than rehabilitative or preventative services. Despite the clear moral issues and awareness of the impact of labeling young people as potential criminals, policymakers resolved to respond to the problem of urban youth crime with punitive measures, and to base the national juvenile crime control program on assumptions, potentiality, and prediction.

TREATING "YOUTH AND TROUBLE" AND "RUNAWAYS"

Congress enacted the Juvenile Justice and Delinquency Prevention Act of 1974 in part to give status offenders community-based options for rehabilitation and to prevent them from entering penal facilities. The legislation created divisions between "chronic offenders" and "youth in trouble" in order to protect specific groups of youth who had been incorrectly labeled delinquent. The transgressions of young people in the two groups were virtually indistinguishable, but in practice the divergent categories meant that white youth had a better chance than their black counterparts of being punished by their parents or offered community-based alternatives by the courts. One such youth, named Robin, testified before the Senate Committee on the Judiciary as it held hearings on the implementation of the 1974 law. Bayh welcomed Robin's testimony as an example of the problem legislators were trying to fix for white youth who had fallen under criminal justice supervision. Robin was nine years old when she ran away from home for the first time in 1969. The New York Division for Youth removed her from her parents for a time, but once she returned to the same unstable living environment, she continued to leave periodically over the next five years. Beginning in 1974, at fourteen years old, Robin spent nine months at the Spofford Juvenile Center, the secure detention facility in the Bronx, awaiting a more permanent placement. At Spofford, Robin was beaten by guards and given 250 milligrams of Thorazine three times a day, which made her feel like a "zombie." Without a formal adjudication, Robin was classified as a "Person In Need of Supervision," or a PINS, and sent to Tryon, the infamous penal colony for youth an hour northwest of Albany. Robin knew she had not committed a crime, but "being there made me feel like I was a bad person." Her fellow witness Jeff, who was also placed at Tryon in 1975 after being removed from his home for "incorrigibility," got into his first fight just thirty minutes after he arrived at the facility. "It was like living on the streets all over again," he explained. Soon Jeff was sent to solitary confinement, the first time for three months and the second time for five months after he was accused of being one of the leaders of a riot. During that time Jeff slept on a mattress, without a blanket or a pillow.[24]

When increasing numbers of white youth like Jeff and Robin entered Spofford, Tryon, and other juvenile detention facilities across the United States during the 1970s—often for status offenses such as running away, truancy, "waywardness," "disobeying authority," and "ungovernability" and without formal court proceedings—federal policymakers and the general public called for a fundamental change in the juvenile justice system. The urgency was underscored by the fact that Robin and other youth seen as victims of their circumstances were sent to penal facilities like Tyron, where they could be easily influenced by more serious young offenders. "Being in there with juvenile delinquents, and knowing I was a PINS, listening to the stories they would tell of how they had robbed a store—it would seem more or less like fun," Robin said. "I found myself taking place with the juvenile delinquents to fit in with the crowd." Robin's case made clear the danger of housing troubled youth, often from unstable homes, alongside youth convicted of burglary, larceny, or murder in juvenile detention facilities. As Birch Bayh argued, "It is the shame of the entire system of justice in this country that once a teenager is arrested for experimenting with marihuana or stealing a car for a joyride that the treatment he is likely to receive can set him off on a life of crime which might easily have been prevented."[25] The Supreme Court had guaranteed juveniles the right to counsel, to cross-examine witnesses, and to swift proceedings in its 1967 *In re Gault* decision, but the ruling had little practical effect on sentencing practices or on the conditions young Americans confronted in detention facilities and prisons. By turning youth who had been charged with status offenses into hardened criminals, it seemed the conditions within existing juvenile prisons had contributed to the crime problem.

Bayh and other policymakers recognized that the experience of formal detention tended to cause delinquent behavior to devolve into something far more serious. Before the 1974 legislation began to address this issue, judges had no choice but to send young suspects to a detention facility, or to return them with a "stern lecture" back into the environment that had led them to the court in the first place. Congress wanted to give criminal justice authorities a broader set of options in dealing with young Americans. Following the legislation's enactment, thousands of status offenders were successfully diverted from formal correctional institutions. In 1975, 116,000 youth were institutionalized in juvenile prisons for status offenses, but as the federal government supported the establishment of community-based alternatives, by 1976 this number dropped to 103,000, and by 1977 only 59,000 youth were locked up for "crimes" they could not be charged with as an adult. The act succeeded in encouraging states to change their juvenile correctional practices and produced a decrease of nearly 50 percent in detention for status offenses.[26]

But since status offender cases were adjudicated under the broad discretion of judges, race and gender profoundly shaped which youth received this label. Between 1975 and 1977, 70 percent of youth processed as status offenders were white, 20 percent were black, and 8 percent were Latino, Native American, or Asian due in large part to the racial attitudes of the judges who determined their fates. Further reflecting assumptions about demographics and criminality, 70 percent of young women who came before the court system were classified as status offenders, and they were also more likely to be labeled as a PINS—like Robin—or the "Minors" and "Children in Need of Supervision" categories used by other states.[27] Long-held assumptions about gender, race, and crime profoundly shaped the groups who would ultimately benefit from the more progressive juvenile justice reforms stipulated by the 1974 legislation.

Moreover, many of the prevention programs the Office of Juvenile Justice and Delinquency Prevention supported were privately run and catered to a much smaller population of mainly white youth, while the detention programs were publicly run and served a much larger population of low-income urban youth of color. In addition to successfully diverting white youth out of formal court and prison systems and into smaller residential environments, federal officials in the Department of Justice empowered the private sector and local nonprofits to administer the rehabilitative and preventive component of the national juvenile delinquency program. Half of the 1974 law's $168 million investment in community-based programs went to private groups during the first five years after passage, and the national antidelinquency program generated an explosion of privately owned juvenile shelters and community-based custody facilities. By 1978, 90 percent of the delinquency prevention programs funded by HEW were administered by private groups, responsible for some 130,000 youth, or about a tenth of the population of juvenile offenders detained in public facilities.[28]

Much as the drive to deinstitutionalize status offenses primarily benefited white offenders, the private and nonprofit organizations that assumed control over the community-based and rehabilitative crime prevention effort tended to focus their energies on white youth. With funding from the Justice Department, for instance, the Orange County Youth Service Program worked with families in this white suburban area of Southern California to better discipline youth who experienced problems specific to segregated affluent communities. Staff members from the University of California at Irvine helped families to better discipline their children. Parents were encouraged to revoke car privileges if their child was a habitual truant. Teenagers who skipped school some forty miles north in Watts, meanwhile, were handled by the criminal justice system. As one judge put it: "We're not dealing with Tom Sawyer and Becky Thatcher over at Juvenile Hall."[29]

The Juvenile Justice Act of 1974 further bifurcated the justice system along racial lines by establishing the nation's first Runaway Youth Program in Title III of the legislation. This program created local centers that provided runaway youths shelter and counseling while allowing them freedom of movement and, often, the opportunity to remain in school. They were also provided with meals, counseling, clothing, transportation, medical care, legal counseling, job counseling and training, follow-up and aftercare services, placement services, and twenty-four-hour hotlines. Policymakers hoped the Runaway Youth Program would provide more humane and thrifty alternatives for young people like

Kenneth, a white twelve-year-old who testified before the Senate Judiciary Committee that he was thrown "into a cage with a bunch of drunks" after he was picked up for running away. Congress allocated $11 million to support 169 shelters across the United States. But in order to be eligible for the services provided by Title III, young people had to be classified as runaway or homeless youth. Youth who were seen as having mental health issues, drug abuse problems, or violent tendencies—classifications usually associated with black youth—were referred instead to the courts.[30]

The constituency of the Runaway Youth Program shelters matched the gender and racial demographics of the United States in the mid-1970s to a far greater degree than any other crime war measure. Approximately 60 percent of the young people served by the program were women, 73 percent were white, 14 percent were black, and 7 percent were Latino. Still, framing the problem as an issue that primarily affected middle-class young people gravely underserved black and Latino youth, who left home on a far more frequent basis than their white counterparts. Here was an instance where targeting urban youth of color might have been appropriate and beneficial. Instead, the federal government exacerbated existing discrepancies by locating most of the runaway youth programs in rural areas. In Hamilton, Montana, where HEW established foster home programs, juvenile justice officials characterized the "youth problem" as "not one of hard core delinquents, but rather of acting out youth."[31] The lack of these sorts of viable community-based alternatives in segregated urban areas exacerbated the racial disparities in the sentencing and treatment of young offenders. Social service and law enforcement authorities had few options outside of processing young residents of color through the criminal justice system.

For the most part, social service programs that *did* target racially marginalized constituencies often did not provide the same kinds of comprehensive rehabilitative services offered by the shelters. Taking their cue from the Juvenile Justice and Delinquency Prevention Act and an earlier demonstration program supported by the California Criminal Justice Planning Agency in the early 1970s, 350 YMCAs, police departments, boys clubs, and county agencies across the country instituted the National Youth Project Using Mini-Bikes (NYPUM) as a delinquency control measure in 1969. Supported by a $677,688 discretionary grant from the LEAA and 10,000 mini-bikes donated from Honda, by 1976, more than 4,000 "hard-to-reach" mostly black and Latino youth participated in the program. Program officials and funders hoped that NYPUM would help lower recidivism rates and prevent delinquents and potential delinquents from committing future crime, and 75 percent of the participants were referred to the program by juvenile courts, probation officers, police, and school systems. The YMCA required all of the NYPUM participants to set weekly behavioral goals under the supervision of the program director or school authorities. As a reward for meeting these weekly goals, YMCA staff gave the youth opportunities to ride a mini-bike or participate in day trips to the beach or an amusement park, as well as tours of local universities and police departments. Many of these youth had been classified as delinquent on the very same charges lodged against their counterparts in places like Hamilton, Montana. Yet they were far more likely to be sent to juvenile prisons hundreds of miles away from their families and communities than to receive educational, job training, and counseling services—or even a mini-bike from Honda.[32]

Although both white and black youth in the juvenile justice system tended to come from backgrounds marked by poverty, unemployment, and unstable families, they experienced this system in markedly different ways. The federal programs supported by the 1974 legislation focused the majority of rehabilitative and prevention efforts on white status offenders, who had a much greater chance of being successfully diverted from state detention facilities. As the number of young people in private custody increased nearly 10 percent between 1975 and 1977, the population of black youth in penal institutions continued to rise. While black youth constituted only one-fifth of all children under private supervision, they amounted to a third of all youth in public facilities. Due to the targeted deployment of police patrol, black youth were more likely than their white counterparts to have prior criminal referrals, to be charged with violent crimes, to face formal court proceedings, and to be institutionalized in secure, state-run detention facilities.[33]

PUNISHING "POTENTIAL CRIMINALS" AND "DELINQUENTS"

As the Juvenile Justice and Delinquency Prevention Act successfully removed white youth from penal institutions and provided them with
rehabilitative services, it vastly expanded the reach and resources of
urban police in nearly every facet of the lives of black youth. With private and community-based organizations handling "less seriously delinquent youth," federal policymakers relied more than ever on the law
enforcement community to deal with the groups of delinquents and potential delinquents who they felt posed a more serious threat to public
safety. This shift had its roots in the mid-1960s, when punitive programs
first became a major component of domestic social policy. Thereafter,
police received increasing proportions of federal funds and had come
to assume many of the responsibilities that had previously been entrusted to social welfare authorities. By the mid-1970s, federal disinvestment from the public sector and the remnants of War on Poverty
programs meant social welfare agencies in urban centers had little
choice but to incorporate crime control measures in their basic programming in order to receive funding.[34]

The 1974 legislation opened up new avenues of inclusion for law enforcement authorities in the everyday operation of a range of public
institutions—but none more so than urban schools. The federal government approached the problem of school violence as it had other crime
war battles: through planning, patrol, and hardware. In establishing
the Office of Juvenile Justice and Delinquency Prevention, Congress gave
the Justice Department new power within public school systems. Simultaneously, when it renewed the Secondary Education Act in the summer
of 1974, it introduced widespread police patrol in the hallways and
classrooms of schools serving "economically and educationally disadvantaged children." Less than a year after the passage of these punitive programs, officials in the Ford administration in the spring of 1975
proposed various "target hardening" techniques to further increase surveillance and patrol of low-income students by combining electronic
surveillance, improved security of school buildings, and an increasing
presence of law enforcement officials on the campuses of urban public
schools. While some Ford staffers recognized that the approach "may

contribute to a feeling that the school is really under siege," the president and Congress pressed on for implementation.[35] The doubters were right, however, and none of these strategies effectively controlled youth crime as policymakers and law enforcement officials had intended.

School security forces and similar surveillance techniques had been established in a number of urban public schools in the context of urban uprisings during the second half of the 1960s. Yet what started as closed-circuit televisions and groups of city police officers roaming the halls evolved into school police forces in their own right by the mid-1970s as federal policymakers and local law enforcement authorities escalated the war on youth crime. At Crenshaw High School in Los Angeles, for example, four police units patrolled the perimeter of the school grounds while a helicopter flew overhead on the hour. Three armed guards stood at the entrance of the school, which was cordoned off by a steel metal fence with padlocked gates. Teachers at Crenshaw and elsewhere in South Central locked their classrooms from the inside, and social gatherings such as dances and athletic events were frequently canceled due to the prospect of violence. "We have got so we don't refer to it as Crenshaw High School," Crenshaw principal Sid Thompson told the Board of Supervisors, "but as Fort Crenshaw." The students complained that these drastic security measures made them feel imprisoned by their learning environment. Citing an incident in which a group of teenagers from a different school broke into a Crenshaw classroom and terrorized the students and teachers inside it, administrators insisted their purpose was not to criminalize pupils but to "lock the troublemakers out" and improve the general security on campus. A $600,000 grant the LEAA awarded to Los Angeles to install electronic devices on buses, and an additional $400,000 to bring such surveillance equipment inside the schools in the early 1970s helped school administrators realize their immediate security goals. But the surveillance that federal funding made possible did not suppress violence at Crenshaw or at other local schools. As fights broke out on a daily basis, students increasingly carried guns, chains, and knives in their pockets and book bags. "In an atmosphere like that you are not talking about education. You are not talking about learning. Or new curriculum. Or new approaches to teaching," Thompson explained. "You are talking about survival."[36] Keeping students safe at school in segregated urban neighborhoods became a more urgent priority for Thompson, local law enforcement authorities, federal policymakers, and other public officials than providing students with an adequate education.

The security apparatus that federal law enforcement assistance funds helped to put in place at "Fort Crenshaw" spread throughout the nation during the 1970s. As in Los Angeles, law enforcement officials in New York, Chicago, Philadelphia, and Miami fortified schools with monitored entrances, stationed patrol cars, and flying helicopters. In the wake of the 1974 legislation, additional practices proliferated: the widespread use of police-school liaisons to patrol urban junior high and high school campuses, the cameras installed to monitor children on school buses, and metal detectors at the entrances. As early as 1976, at the annual meeting of the National Association of School Security Directors in Alexandria, security companies and law enforcement experts hawked inventions they had produced with federal grants: metal detectors, hidden cameras, ultrasonic alerters, and fountain pens that functioned as communications devices for urban high school teachers.[37]

Even as federal delinquency programs and the growing school security industry created an environment where urban schools were increasingly guarded like prisons, schools nationwide were safer in the 1970s than they were in the 1960s. Senator Birch Bayh had defended the school security measures he introduced into the 1974 antidelinquency law on the grounds that they would manage "a domestic Vietnam occurring in the hallways and classrooms of America." But in the face of these claims, a study conducted by the Department of Health, Education, and Welfare in 1978 concluded that violence and vandalism had not increased between 1971 and 1976. In fact, some urban school systems had demonstrated a marked improvement from the drastic increases in school violence and crime they witnessed during the 1960s.[38]

The rise in surveillance and patrol of students severely compromised educational access for low-income youth, especially because such measures supported the discriminatory application of expulsions. In New York City, for example, a member of the Imperial Dutchmen clique in the South Bronx approached his principal to ask for protection from rival gang members at the school. The administration's solution was not

A police officer at Tilden High School in Chicago's south side chases a group of students after they started throwing rocks on campus in 1975. Federal policymakers had promoted the escalation of surveillance and police patrol at Tilden and other urban public schools with black majorities via the Juvenile Delinquency Act of 1974. *Photograph by Paul Sequeira. Premium Archive, Getty Images*

to work with the students to improve the school's existing climate of violence and hostility, but to encourage all the Dutchmen to drop out of school permanently "in the interest of all concerned." In urban school systems elsewhere, authorities increasingly began to respond to disciplinary problems in this manner. Whereas the Los Angeles Public Schools expelled an average of forty-five students a year in the 1960s, by 1973 that number had reached a record of 225 students. Youth attending the predominately black Washington, Fremont, Crenshaw, and Jefferson High Schools were permanently banished from the city's school system altogether if they received more than one expulsion.[39] Discriminatory expulsions seemed to Shirley Chisholm and her sympathetic colleagues to foster delinquency among undereducated and unemployed youth, a dynamic that further isolated racially marginalized young Americans.[40]

The surveillance of school-age black youth became a gateway to the surveillance of their families as police departments increasingly partnered with social services. Once a "potentially delinquent" youth came to the attention of law enforcement authorities, social services agencies could follow up inside their homes. The "Prevention of Delinquency Through Intensive Supervision" program, or PODTIS, a program administered by the Probation Office in Los Angeles and supported by the Juvenile Justice and Delinquency Prevention Act, handled less serious first-time offenders. PODTIS enabled officers to work within low-income, mostly black families in the Compton neighborhood to "keep the youngster in the community and get the family communications reestablished and get the family problems worked out" by combining crime control with social services.[41] In some instances, these hybrid law enforcement social service workers gave food and clothing to families in need. Other times, if violent or criminal activity seemed evident to the PODTIS official, the encounter resulted in further intervention from child protective services or an arrest.

The diffusion of law enforcement into the everyday lives of black youth and their families via PODTIS and similar programs and the simultaneous decarceration of white youth from formal detention facilities occurred as the demographics of American prisons as a whole shifted from majority white to majority black and Latino. In California, for instance, the penal population in the 1960s was 55 percent white, 25 percent black, and 18 percent Chicano. By 1974, the white population had been reduced to 47 percent, and by 1975, following the enactment of the Juvenile Justice and Delinquency Prevention Act, white inmates constituted 40 percent of the state's prisoners. Meanwhile, the number of black Americans confined in California prisons increased nearly 10 percent during that single year, so that African Americans represented nearly 35 percent of all inmates, with Chicano prisoners coming in at a close second, at 21 percent of all inmates in the state.[42]

In large part, this population shift was due to the influx into penal facilities of black youth, who increasingly found themselves ensnared in juvenile detention facilities, youth camps, and prisons in the years following the enactment of the 1974 legislation. Demographic research linking birth rates to crime rates indicated that as the number of low-income youth in the nation continued to rise, so too would crime. In one of the first major research projects funded by the Office of Juvenile Justice and Delinquency Prevention in 1978, University of Chicago law professor Frank Zimring analyzed birth rates to conclude that "in the 1980s a greater concentration of minority youth will be in the 'at-risk' population, with the potential consequence that an even greater number of minority youth will be handled by juvenile and adult correctional facilities than is currently the case." Zimring went on to warn that in the absence of major reform within American juvenile justice, it would continue to evolve in such a way that disparate numbers of black and Latino youth would find themselves in American prisons.[43]

The Juvenile Justice and Delinquency Prevention Act had stipulated that any sixteen-year-old who committed a crime that would be a felony punishable by a maximum penalty of ten years' imprisonment or more, life imprisonment, or death could be tried as an adult if the attorney general felt that the youth's presence endangered the general public safety, a category of offense that black youth bore disproportionately. Taking the federal government's lead, states such as California, Illinois, Texas, and Florida also lowered the jurisdictional age limit so that children as young as fourteen could be tried as adults in state courts if they were found guilty of a major violent crime and ruled "dangerous to society." By 1997, all fifty states had laws on the books allowing children as young as ten to be tried as adults.[44]

This sweeping reform was largely based upon notions that black urban youth were a particularly violent group who could not be rehabilitated. For example, New York's Democratic governor Hugh Carey had previously opposed trying teenagers as adults. But when Willie Bosket, a fifteen-year-old black Harlem resident, received a sentence of five years after killing two men on a New York subway in the summer of 1978, the governor, who was up for reelection that fall, made juvenile sentencing reform his pet cause. Carey attributed a "small core of violent youngsters" to the urban crime problem, and as Bosket's extreme case made clear to him, the foremost responsibility of law enforcement authorities was to "protect the community from this group of youths who threaten our safety and welfare," as Carey told a *New York Times* reporter. Trying youth as adults seemed to Carey and the New York state legislature the most effective means to do so. Less than two weeks after Bosket's sentence was handed down, state legislators enacted the New York Juvenile Offender Act of 1978—known as the "Willie Bosket law"—that permitted young residents to be tried and sentenced as adults. Anticipating the growth of young black Americans in adult correctional facilities as a consequence of juvenile justice reform at all levels of government, federal policymakers continued to support the dramatic growth of the nation's penal system.[45] Far from a separate program aimed at reforming and rehabilitating the children and teenagers who entered detention facilities, the youth crime control apparatus was the lynchpin of the mass incarceration of black and Latino citizens.

"NOTHING WORKS"

Although the Juvenile Justice and Delinquency Prevention Act of 1974 had labeled virtually all low-income urban youth "potentially delinquent," the single greatest predictor of delinquency was in fact whether a youth had been jailed or detained previously. Within the New Jersey prison system, for example, a 1976 study showed that 75 percent of adult inmates had been in and out of correctional institutions from age twelve. They had spent their lives shuffling from one juvenile detention center to the next until eventually serving time in an adult prison. The young men and women sentenced to juvenile facilities in New Jersey and elsewhere had likely received instruction and insight into techniques that would allow them to go on to engage in extralegal activities within their home communities, which often lacked viable formal economies. Their incarceration as children and teenagers, the absence of any sort of rehabilitation, and their limited job and educational prospects upon release tended to confirm, reinforce, and aggravate their criminal behavior.[46] Recognizing the fact that formal confinement often led young people to a "life of crime," federal policymakers had deinstitutionalized status offenses in the 1974 legislation, but they also paradoxically embraced penal confinement as the foremost crime deterrent. Indeed, federal policymakers and law enforcement officials acknowledged that incarceration itself was a major cause of crime, yet at the same time, they called for more incarceration for certain groups of offenders.

Even as prisons' criminogenic power became better understood, a growing chorus of scholars and law enforcement experts argued that nothing could be done short of more incarceration to control rising populations of low-income black youth. Sociologist Robert Martinson's work, in particular, reverberated throughout criminology classrooms and policy circles in the mid-1970s. Martinson's view that "nothing works" to curtail young violent offenders and that rehabilitation had "no appreciable effect on recidivism" gained traction both politically and publically as crime rates appeared to increase in the 1970s. With $180,000 in funding from the federal government and additional support from the New York State Office of Crime Control Planning, Martinson produced the 800-page volume *The Effectiveness of Correctional Treatment: A Survey of Treatment Evaluation Studies* in 1975, the outcome of six years of research. Summarized in the pages of the *New Republic* and the conservative journal *Public Interest*, Martinson's findings centered on the debate about whether or not rehabilitation was a possible goal for convicted criminals. Martinson argued that educational and vocational training programs only benefited the top 7 percent of incarcerated Americans, who came to prison with an already stronger educational background than the majority of inmates. Even counseling and community-based treatment programs in prisons were incapable of "overcom[ing], or even appreciably reduc[ing], the powerful tendency for offenders to continue in criminal behavior." At his most optimistic, Martinson wrote in the *Public Interest*, "Even if we can't 'treat' offenders so as to make them do better, a great many of the programs designed to rehabilitate them at least did not make them do *worse*." Although Martinson himself committed suicide in 1980, his work went on to shape penal programs long after his death, ultimately influencing the Supreme Court's 1989 decision in *Mistretta v. United States*, which held that sentencing guidelines did not need to include rehabilitation measures of any sort.[47]

Echoing Martinson's argument against community-based alternatives for serious juvenile offenders, the political scientist Charles Murray and the biostatistician Louis A. Cox Jr. concluded in 1979's *Beyond Probation: Juvenile Corrections and the Chronic Delinquent* that only formal supervision reduced arrest rates. To evaluate the effectiveness of rehabilitation programs, Murray and Cox tracked 317 "serious teenage delinquents" in Chicago for seventeen months after they were released from prison, as well as 266 delinquents who had been diverted to community-based programs. Murray and Cox found that 82 percent of those released were eventually rearrested and that those youths on probation, in group homes, or in some rehabilitative facility encountered law enforcement more frequently upon their release than their counterparts who had been incarcerated in state institutions. Based on these findings, Murray and Cox concluded that delinquents who were incapacitated under intensive and institutional supervision, rather than therapeutic programs such as halfway houses or forestry camps, had a lower rate of recidivism. It was an argument that suggested prison was preferable to diversion programs. "For the serious, chronic delinquent, the strategy of minimal intervention—probation, or loosely supervised life in the community—fails to produce any desirable changes," Murray and Cox argued, "whereas tighter, more restrictive forms of supervision (whether in the community or in an institution) may produce some of those desired changes, or at the very least not produce worse delinquency through 'labeling' or 'stigmatization.'" According to their interpretation of the data, the difference between rehabilitation and deterrence was arbitrary, since only punitive carceral programs appeared to successfully suppress future crime. Years later, the criminologist Elliot Currie and others exposed that Murray and Cox had distorted data, and that recidivism was actually lower among those youth who had received counseling services in group homes or forestry camps. But the findings of Murray and Cox, along with those of Martinson, took hold at a critical moment in the development of the American carceral state, just as racially marginalized Americans became majorities within the nation's prisons.[48]

Despite growing consensus that "nothing works" when it came to rehabilitating young urban offenders, however, the federal government in fact funded programs during the second half of the 1970s that proved otherwise. Most notably, beginning in the summer of 1974, Denver's "Project New Pride" provided adjudicated youth between the ages of fourteen and eighteen with vocational training, job placement, and classroom instruction as an alternative to incarceration beginning in the summer of 1974. Founded by Tom James, a black Vietnam War veteran, New Pride was one of the few community-based programs the federal government supported that explicitly served black as opposed to white youth. With more than half a million dollars in matching grant funds from the LEAA, New Pride established itself outside of the formal criminal justice system in Denver's segregated urban neighborhoods that had high rates of reported crime. The program operated under what James saw as a "holistic" approach to juvenile corrections, allowing participants to live at home while simultaneously preparing them for meaningful employment as a means to prevent recidivism. All of the participants in the program had been referred through the probation and court systems and had been classified as "hardcore delinquents" or "chronic offenders"—the same group that Wolfgang, Martinson, and later Murray and Cox studied. A typical New Pride "client" was a sixteen-year-old black male who dropped out of school and had been "extensively involved in the juvenile justice system" or who had come into contact with law enforcement officials at least six times and appeared before a judge on charges of burglary, assault, larceny, or auto theft at least twice. He was likely to come from a single-parent household receiving government assistance, and may have had substance abuse problems. Merging both social services and punitive measures, in many respects New Pride exemplified the process through which earlier anti-poverty programs became tied to the court system and the carceral state.[49]

Much like Kennedy's Committee of Juvenile Delinquency in the early 1960s, New Pride's staff treated youth crime as an educational and employment issue, and one of the chief goals of the program was to help serious young offenders become competitive in the job market in order to fully reintegrate them into their communities. Essentially, New Pride operated from the premise that delinquency was deeply related to school problems and learning disabilities, and thus targeted youth whom program administrators described as "academically deficient, unskilled, [with] unrealistic expectations, no knowledge of the work ethic, and serious behavior problems." To "correct" these issues, New Pride offered adjudicated youth a comprehensive "service delivery system" that included educational testing, life skills classes (in subjects such as how to fill out job applications and perform during interviews), vocational training, and "cultural awareness" field trips to entertainment and sporting events. After receiving training from New Pride staff, youth were placed in furniture and auto repair shops, animal clinics, medical labs, photography studios, and construction companies. New Pride paid each youth for the first three months of his employment at minimum wage in order to give employers an added incentive to hire a young person who had been charged with a crime. These measures were then followed by at least nine months of community-based supervision by an assigned counselor, contact that continued even after the youth returned to school or secured employment.[50]

Within three years, LEAA officials deemed New Pride an "exemplary project" and encouraged its replication. By the mid-1980s, roughly ten years after it opened its doors, New Pride had served more than 1,200 "multiple serious offender youth," helping to ensure that the vast majority—90 percent—remained in the community rather than returning to a correctional institution. Seventy percent of the youth were reintegrated into public schools, and nearly all New Pride "graduates" remained in at least part-time employment. The LEAA's endorsement of New Pride was an important exception to the dominant view on black youth crime and recidivism that a number of policymakers, law enforcement officials, and scholars had reached by the late 1970s. Contrary to these pessimistic assessments, New Pride's record demonstrated that educational programming and job placement offered a viable means of rehabilitation. Even more than the treatment it provided, however, New Pride introduced a cost-effective alternative to incarceration. The state of Colorado expended just under $30,000 annually on every youth it incarcerated, while New Pride spent about $4,500 on each of the youths in its program.[51]

Notwithstanding New Pride's cost effectiveness and its demonstrated success in reducing recidivism among urban youth, some federal policymakers and law enforcement officials criticized its approach as "soft on crime." Although the Law Enforcement Assistance Administration released a major report highlighting the success of the program, there was never an effort to replicate its approach on a large scale with substantial public funding, nor did it ever factor seriously into discussions about rehabilitating so-called chronic young offenders. Similarly un-heeded was a 1976 report by the Task Force on Juvenile Justice and Delinquency Prevention of the National Advisory Commission on Criminal Justice Standards and Goals, which called for rehabilitation efforts. "It seems clear that efforts aimed at the early delivery of ser-vices to young people who may be headed for careers of crime have more promise as a method for reducing crime than attempts to control delinquency solely by strengthening various components of what is nor-mally considered the juvenile justice system," the commission wrote in its report.[52]

When the Office of Juvenile Justice and Delinquency Prevention targeted racially marginalized youth for punitive programs, further increasing the frequency of contact between urban youth and law en-forcement authorities, the crime rate continued to increase during the second half of the 1970s. In the context of these rising rates of reported crime, and particularly violent crime, policymakers increasingly came to agree with the opinion of President Gerald Ford's attorney general William Saxbe that rehabilitation was a "myth." The demonstrated im-pact of New Pride and the federal government's own advisory group's arguments were ignored. Policymakers at all levels of government in-stead decided to spend more money taking in historic numbers of black and Latino prisoners, while cutting rehabilitative programs entirely or entrusting their administration to the private sector. Public authorities would focus on punishing and maintaining control of seemingly vola-tile populations.

The development of the juvenile justice system from the mid-1970s on-ward reveals the ways in which the pathological understandings of race and crime clouded policymakers' attention to other social problems in urban centers, leading them to consistently embrace an increasingly pu-nitive approach. Instead of arresting only actual criminals, the federal government's juvenile justice legislation emphasized a hunt for future and possible criminals. Policymakers' view of juvenile delinquency as the pathological result of welfare dependence, poverty, and racism ra-tionalized the focus on effects rather than insoluble causes, justifying their investment in police departments and court systems to solve social problems. Federal policymakers demonstrated their willingness to attack the consequences of poverty, subpar school systems, and unemployment as those consequences manifested through crime, while they skirted away from the causes. Essentially officials and law enforcement authorities blamed the victim. ·

For example, ambivalence about the potentiality clause introduced by juvenile delinquency policy did not outweigh the general pessimism among Ford officials about the federal government's power to create social programs that could address socioeconomic inequality. Changing employment and educational outcomes, as Public Relations Director Malcolm Barr wrote, "would require massive social and economic reforms in our society which should be pursued or not pursued for reasons more important than the control of crime and delinquency." Barr warned that the potentiality approach "becomes problematic since our ability to predict which youths will become delinquent is not well developed and by identifying certain youths as high risk, we may be creating self-fulfilling prophecies." Yet despite his own reservations, Barr suggested that President Ford "focus on identifying those youths who would appear likely to become involved in delinquency" as a cost-effective approach to juvenile crime control amenable to the American public.[53]

The Ford administration sought to offer the nation a quick response strategy focused on surveillance and swift and sure punishment as a means of "ensuring domestic tranquility"—the hallmark phrase Ford used when he described the aims of his War on Crime to his constituents. "On behalf of the social defense of the citizenry," Ford officials proclaimed of the administration's crime control plan, "the few violent youths can be placed in secure institutions for relatively long terms."[54] As such, public resources and new federal juvenile enforcement, adjudication, and correctional programs concentrated on the relatively small number of young people who law enforcement officials felt should be, as the Ford administration frequently put it, "removed from the community" and sentenced to long terms in prison. Along these lines, the strategies at the heart of the federal antidelinquency program actively promoted the apprehension of young people of color.[55] As the first major piece of domestic social policy Ford signed into law, the Juvenile Delinquency and Prevention Act of 1974 represented an earnest attempt on the part of Congress to remove status offenders from an overburdened, overcrowded juvenile justice system in order to allow prosecutors and judges to focus on incarcerating the "hard-core" offenders, or those youths who had multiple infractions on their criminal records. Federal officials had rejected community-based alternatives for this group, favoring instead the use of detention facilities. The Ford administration exploited this opening, promoting new law enforcement practices and sentencing guidelines that successfully removed a generation of African American men from their communities.

[7]

URBAN REMOVAL

The contradiction between Richard Nixon's pursuit of law and order and the lawlessness and criminal behavior rampant in his own administration came to a head in August 1974, when the House Judiciary Committee voted to impeach the president for obstruction of justice. Nixon's resignation ended his political career, and key figures in the federal crime control program he led, including Attorney General John Mitchell and domestic policy counsel John Ehrlichman, served time in the criminal justice system they had labored to expand and modernize during their tenure in Washington. Gerald Ford, who served as House minority leader when Congress considered the Safe Streets Act of 1968 and introduced block grants into the landmark legislation, stepped into the vice presidency after tax evasion charges forced Spiro Agnew to resign. Like Nixon, Ford was a staunch New Federalist who advocated small government in all things—except for law enforcement. Ford selected as his vice president Nelson Rockefeller, a strong proponent of crime control who came to the White House on the heels of signing laws imposing long mandatory sentences for sale or possession of drugs in his home state of New York in 1973.

Congress had passed the Juvenile Justice and Delinquency Prevention Act of 1974 at the height of the Watergate investigation, and it was the first major piece of domestic policy legislation Ford signed upon assuming the presidency, in early September. Shortly afterward, Ford outlined his administration's War on Crime priorities at the annual meeting of the International Chiefs of Police. In line with his predecessors, Ford was most concerned with "violent crime and street crime in the inner city." He believed that crime in these areas, committed by residents who appeared to survive by participating in informal economies and stealing from their neighbors, "does the most damage to our whole urban structure." Indeed, policymakers, law enforcement officials, and influential social scientists such as Marvin Wolfgang and James Q. Wilson increasingly attributed the national crime problem to this small group of "career criminals." Since previous strategies—militarizing local law enforcement, placing plainclothes officers on foot in segregated urban neighborhoods, and installing surveillance equipment such as video cameras in classrooms—had failed to lower the crime rate, Ford hoped that concentrating on repeat offenders in segregated urban areas would succeed in reducing it. His staffer, Dick Cheney, had summed up the process and its rationale in a memo to the president. "The data points out that most of our violent crime is committed by a relatively small number of individuals," Cheney wrote, "and with the right kind of effort we could substantially reduce the crime rate simply by taking them off the streets."[1] According to this line of reasoning, sending more of the right group of urban residents to prison would prevent future crime and, in doing so, address the numerous other problems urban centers confronted in the mid-1970s. Many of the police chiefs in the audience shared Ford's views of incarceration as the chief crime deterrent.

During the fall of 1974 and the winter of 1975, the administration developed new crime war strategies that sought to refocus the effort on repeat offenders. When Ford delivered the keynote address at the Sesquicentennial Convocation of Yale Law School in the spring of 1975, he used the event at his alma mater as an occasion to preview his plans for the national law enforcement program. The speech marked a rhetorical shift. As Ford's "crime guy," Richard Parsons, one of the most prominent black officials in his administration, observed in a memo to domestic policy advisor Jim Cannon, "the antiquated 'law and order' rhetoric was and is empty—it sets us against one another; it invites us to be careless of our heritage of civil liberty; and, it offers no practical program suggestions." Instead of calling for law and order, Ford described the federal government as responsible for ensuring domestic tranquility. "Have we achieved on our streets and in our homes that sense of domestic tranquility so essential to the pursuit of happiness?" Ford asked his Yale law audience. "Do we provide that domestic tranquility which the Constitution seeks? If we take the crime rates as an indication, the answer has to be no."[2]

While discussing Watergate and "crime in high places," Ford pledged "to restore to the Executive Branch decency, honesty, and adherence to the law at all levels." But white-collar crime was not his emphasis. Instead, Ford vowed that, as president, he intended to focus his energy on combating "street crime, crime that invades our neighborhoods and our homes, murders, robberies, rapes, muggings, hold-ups, break-ins—and the kind of brutal violence that makes us fearful of strangers and afraid to go out at night." Ford blamed the onslaught of these types of crimes on repeat offenders, "the core of the problem." He declared "the rest of the American people have a right to protection from their violence." To provide this protection and ensure "domestic tranquility," Ford believed his administration needed to encourage swift justice and certain punishment of this criminal minority.[3]

The bulk of Ford's remarks that evening thus focused on the related issues of sentencing and incarceration. Officials in his administration argued that crime had surged in the era of the War on Crime because urban courts were ill equipped to handle the historic caseload resulting from increases in surveillance and patrol. In addition to improving police investigations and case management procedures, Ford sought to give court systems tools to intensify and hasten the trial process in targeted urban areas to "ensure that swift and prolonged imprisonment will inevitably follow each offense." For Ford, the case for "prolonged imprisonment" was clear. "The crime rate will go down if persons who habitually commit most of the predatory crimes are kept in prison for a reasonable period, if convicted, because they will then not be free to commit more crimes," the president suggested. To secure this end, Ford's program centered on sentencing restrictions. Anyone convicted of a second felony would serve a mandatory minimum prison term, and first offenses involving a firearm would also carry a mandatory penalty. "I am urging that virtually all of those convicted of a violent crime should be sent to prison," Ford declared.[4]

Although Ford viewed crime as a problem that primarily involved black urban Americans, it was a young middle-class white woman, a follower of the cult leader Charles Manson, who pointed a gun at the president in the fall of 1975, while he was on his way to address the California legislature on the subject of crime. Ford proceeded to deliver his remarks as scheduled after the failed assassination attempt, calling for a nationwide effort to control crime and "the abandonment of partisanship on a scale comparable to closing ranks in war time against an external enemy."[5] Ford maintained his view of crime as essentially an urban problem, one concentrated in the same "disadvantaged" neighborhoods where national law enforcement programs had been unfolding throughout the decade before he took office.

The budget for the LEAA peaked during the Ford administration, at $886 million in 1975, and with it the discretionary funds available for crime control. The Ford administration used this portion of the law enforcement budget to target the young black Americans seen as responsible for the crime problem. With nearly $150 million in discretionary crime control funds at their disposal, White House and Justice Department officials pursued two independent but interrelated initiatives focused on the nation's cities and its "violent repeat offenders": the "Career Criminal program," which targeted citizens with multiple arrests on their records, and "Operation Disarm the Criminal" (which later evolved into "Operation Concentrated Urban Enforcement"). The Career Criminal program created a separate, expedited criminal justice system with mandatory minimum sentencing, while Operation Disarm the Criminal established a federal handgun control squad that operated in urban centers. Following the emphasis set by the Juvenile Delinquency and Prevention Act, both programs focused on young people who "appeared likely" to engage in delinquency or violent criminal activity, as Ford's public relations director Malcolm Barr informed Department of Justice officials in the spring of 1975. Building from the earlier pathological discourse about black Americans and crime, Barr argued that "trends in family structure and in the

divergence of values among Americans" had produced "amoral youths—
youths without remorse for brutal acts, who show no signs of 'conscience'
as we know it." Ford officials were confident that the Career Criminal
program and the gun control measures offered a cost-effective approach
to crime that, by fostering the removal and institutionalization of
"amoral" black urban youth, would restore domestic tranquility.[6]

THE NEW ROOT CAUSE

The mid-1970s were a time of broad cynicism among national policymakers about the federal government's ability to develop domestic policies that could address income stratification, education, employment, and
housing conditions. Crime control programs were increasingly seen as
the most viable solution to urban problems. This certitude was not confined to the ascendant political right. "We can no longer afford the luxury
of confusing social progress with progress in the war on crime. We face
the crime menace now," Senator Edward Kennedy wrote in the *New
York Times*. "Perhaps the social policies we initiate in the 1970's will reduce the crime rate in the 1980's. But that is too long to wait. We fool
ourselves if we say, 'No crime reform until society is reformed.'" Dis-
tancing himself from the approaches to poverty and racial inequality
that had steered the programs of his brother's New Frontier programs
and the Great Society, Kennedy argued, "It is time to fight a more practical, less ideological war."[7]

As Kennedy and other policymakers across the political spectrum
reevaluated previous domestic policy approaches, some came to understand crime as the root cause of urban crisis, and as a problem of individuals that bore little relation to larger socioeconomic issues. Education,
employment, and housing programs, although sometimes defended
on their own terms, were increasingly framed as having nothing to do
with lowering crime. As California governor Ronald Reagan explained
to the Dallas Crime Commission in early 1974, "the problem of crime is
not an abstraction to be debated in some academic tearoom. It is a daily
threat to the lives and safety of our people." Reagan critiqued those assessments of crime that "cast society as the chief villain," rather than
individual perpetrators, since "poverty and unemployment could not

be blamed for the spread of crime." Instead, the domestic policies of the previous decade had ushered in a "golden age of permissiveness" that caused the crime rate to surge. As a result, "the rule breaker and even the lawbreaker is not accountable for his or her individual acts, or the consequences of those actions. Instead, we have been asked to blame 'society,' economic problems, discrimination, anything but the individual act of individuals." For Reagan the criminal justice system had failed to come to grips with the behavioral problems at the root of crime and thus had "become part of the problem."[8] Here a justice system plagued by "permissiveness" could be reformed only by greater punitiveness; otherwise, crime would continue to plague the nation.

White House officials and policymakers at all levels of government agreed that courts themselves were a major source of the crime problem. By the time Ford took office, the federal government had dispersed a combined total of $3.3 billion in crime control grants to state and local governments, most of which supported an influx onto city streets of better-equipped patrolmen under orders to arrest residents, and particularly low-income urban residents, more frequently. Lacking the resources to handle thousands of cases on the docket, court systems took an "assembly-line" approach to justice in the years following the Safe Streets Act. Prosecutors opted to strike plea bargains with suspects as often as possible, leading to the dismissal of charges in roughly half of all felony arrests nationwide in the 1970s.[9] Defense attorneys requested continuances and postponements, knowing they would burden the state further, as a strategy to secure a dismissal or acquittal.

As "assembly-line" justice plagued urban court systems, prison populations began to escalate in the mid-1970s as arrest levels remained high, producing an unmanageable situation for state and local governments. Overcrowding and deteriorating conditions inside prisons compelled authorities to release offenders early, and in some districts, convicts served only half of their sentence.[10] After nearly a decade of federal law enforcement programs launched in the name of modernization and efficiency, it was clear to Ford administration officials that they had inherited a criminal justice system quickly spiraling out of control.

The perceived laxity within juridical and penal institutions produced an environment that policymakers and law enforcement officials characterized as "revolving door justice," one that bred crime and made it profitable for lawbreakers. At a time when the unemployment rate for black youth was between 40 percent and 60 percent and the rate for African Americans as a whole was consistently more than double that of whites, everyday survival in many deindustrializing urban areas during the 1970s depended on engaging in informal and illicit economies. Governor Reagan and other officials may have sought to remove unemployment from discussions about crime, but even in his own state, the strong correlation between the two problems was evident. The same group of youth between the ages of sixteen and twenty-four that policymakers and law enforcement authorities labeled as "chronic offenders" were also chronically unemployed—at a rate of 40 percent, for instance, in South Central, Los Angeles.[11] With few opportunities for formal employment, even within the service sector, residents of economically isolated black urban neighborhoods turned to pimping, prostituting, gambling, fencing stolen goods, stealing, robbing, and drug dealing—employment options of last resort that became known during this period as "hustling." These "hustlers" seemed to accept that their transgressions might have resulted in contact with criminal justice authorities, but they seemed to reason that the potential profit far outweighed the odds of getting arrested or incarcerated.

Federal policymakers and law enforcement authorities believed that petty criminals, deriving much if not all of their income from illicit activity, faced minimal consequences for their actions. Ford officials worried that the courts' "revolving door" quickly released these offenders back into society only to commit more crime. "The fact seems to be that for many unskilled persons crime (with the present low risk of doing time) is *in fact* more profitable than selling their modest capacities for modest wages," Ford's aide Richard Parsons wrote. "In such a cost-benefit context crime, with its excitement and relatively big rewards for time and effort expended, has an unfair competitive edge over gainful employment or training (anti-poverty style) for employment. The edge must be eliminated."[12] Accordingly, Ford hoped to provide the federal assistance necessary to remove this "edge" and effectively process defendants by bringing them to trial and sending them to prison. New sentencing guidelines were necessary to ensure that convicts would serve long terms.

Shortly after Ford spoke at the annual meeting of the International Association of Chiefs of Police in the fall of 1974, pledging to fight violent crime in the "inner city," his attorney general William Saxbe appeared on the CBS morning news program *Face the Nation* to generate public support for the administration's law enforcement agenda. In the face of rising crime rates, Saxbe argued that locking up criminals would bring an end to the pervasive "atmosphere of violence" sweeping the nation. "We do not believe that you are doing them any favors by saying well, he's misunderstood, he's poor, he's black and send him back to the community where he is going to get in trouble again," the attorney general declared. Speaking to a group of urban police commissioners at an event in Chicago, Saxbe offered a grimmer warning, saying that if local court systems failed to sentence criminals to long prison terms, "there is every possibility that crime will inundate us. The nation would then be faced with the prospect of falling apart or devising a national police force in one final effort to restore domestic order."[13] Confident in an emerging new understanding that the root cause of crime was the behavior of a criminal minority that faced no consequences for their actions, the Ford administration promised its Career Criminal program would stamp out crime by increasing opportunities to arrest and incarcerate the group responsible for the problem.

THE CAREER CRIMINAL PROGRAM

In a 1975 interview, John Greacen, the head of the National Institute for Juvenile Justice and Delinquency Prevention that Congress created in 1974 as part of its landmark youth crime control policy, sought to explain the rationale behind the federal government's efforts to encourage incarceration. Fifteen percent of the nation's young offenders, he told the Associated Press, needed to be "locked up because they're dangerous and we don't know what to do with them." Even with the $600 million Congress had allocated to juvenile crime control programs, Greacen lamented, "I don't see any substantial likelihood that the amount of youth crime in the United States is going to go down any substantial degree between now and 1990."[14] If crime was a foregone conclusion among specific sects of the citizenry, as the consensus within the Ford administration held, incarceration seemed the federal government's best option to restore tranquility. In case states didn't share this priority and opted not to spend their law enforcement block grants on improving local court systems, the Ford administration prepared to use discretionary funds to work directly with police, prosecutors, and judges in select cities to implement an accelerated and highly punitive criminal justice program in those cities.

The Ford administration's Career Criminal program in effect established a separate justice system for the new category of "chronic offender" that concerned White House officials. As Ford described it, the discretionary program aimed to "take the criminal out of circulation." The typical defendant selected for the special prosecution tended to be a single, unemployed black man under the age of twenty-four—with limited opportunities in the formal employment sector who had appeared to make crime into a career. Once a defendant had been identified as a career criminal, he or she would be assigned to an experienced local or state prosecutor who devoted all of their energies to ensuring the case was properly prepared and expedited from arraignment to the final ruling, working directly with law enforcement authorities to investigate the suspect all through the trial process. Beginning in 1975, the federal government invested $330 million into Career Criminal units in twenty-two American cities, from San Diego to Memphis, Kalamazoo, and Providence. After only a few months of operation, the program had begun to produce a high rate of conviction and had successfully reduced the average time from arrest to trial by at least three weeks. With a stronger and more punitive criminal justice system in place in key urban areas, Ford argued, "the career criminals now realize that serious cases will no longer simply slip through the cracks in the system."[15]

Local authorities enthusiastically embraced the Ford administration's focus on career criminals and the funding that came with it. The prosecutors who ran career criminal units enjoyed a vastly enlarged operating budget and became the envy of their peers with a special status in their districts. Career Criminal prosecutors tended to have lighter caseloads than their staff prosecutor counterparts, who handled three times the number of trials on a weekly basis. By the prosecutors' focusing on fewer defendants and with no need to juggle between cases, the result was to speed up the sentencing process. Career Criminal cases typically took thirty to sixty days less from arrest to conviction than those of defendants prosecuted under standard court procedure. The additional resources Career Criminal attorneys had at their disposal— enhanced investigative and subpoena powers and close collaboration with police detectives—also led to much higher conviction rates.[16]

For example, in Houston, one of the first cities to receive a discretionary grant for a Career Criminal program, four experienced district attorneys, a statistician, an investigator, several police officers, and a secretary composed the special Career Criminal unit. If the team decided to place a defendant in the program, the judge immediately set bail high enough to ensure the defendant would remain in detention during the accelerated legal proceedings. Soon, the Houston unit was successfully placing 500 offenders in the program annually, sentencing them to an average of thirty years in prison.[17] In an early form of the "three strikes and you're out" law later adopted by California and New York, defendants convicted for multiple crimes under Houston's Career Criminal program received life sentences for offenses including illegal firearm and marijuana possession. But the program did very little to reduce the most serious crimes or to provide the "tranquility" the program was meant to ensure. In 1981, roughly six years after the Ford administration established Houston's program, violence in the city peaked with a record number of 701 homicides.[18]

Despite the Career Criminal initiative's apparent failure to meet their larger deterrence objectives in Houston and elsewhere, the program found strong backers. In a fall 1976 editorial, the conservative columnist James Kilpatrick lauded the initiative as the federal government's first effective law enforcement program. "The purpose is plain—to prosecute the career criminals to the very limit of the law, and to send them to prison for long, long terms. In a word, incarceration," Kilpatrick wrote. "The object is to get these particular criminals on ice, behind bars, where for a number of years they cannot terrorize the people." Kilpatrick defined the career criminal as someone "utterly without conscience, [who] is indifferent to every consideration of right conduct; his animal instincts lead him, without pity to prey on unoffending victims."[19] According to Kilpatrick, formal confinement offered policymakers and justice officials the only means to address the "animal," or, in the words of Ford officials, the "amoral" population of urban criminals who were increasingly held responsible for the problems of cities in general, a group that would become known as "super predators" in the mid-1990s.

Perceptions of conscienceless amorality extended to teenagers and even children, as some Career Criminal programs began to prosecute juveniles as adults, a practice Congress had first authorized in the Juvenile Justice Act of 1974 by specifying that youth as young as sixteen who were deemed "dangerous to the community" could be tried outside the juvenile court system. The District Attorney's Office in Indianapolis, Indiana, had been one of the earliest recipients of discretionary funds for Career Criminal programs. As the program developed, its prosecuting attorney James F. Kelley began to identify young defendants who had a record of previous contact with juvenile court authorities, and Kelley promptly transferred their cases "to felony court to be tried as adult career criminals." After three years, Kelley boasted that "these youthful criminals" and other defendants who were processed by the Indianapolis unit received 50 percent longer sentences than those outside the program. Plea bargaining had decreased substantially, and more youth were now standing trial—both in juvenile and adult courts.[20]

Although Ford officials, policymakers, and law enforcement authorities considered the Career Criminal program a success, some defendants who were selected for prosecution as career criminals appealed their prison terms on the grounds that the program had denied them due process and equal protection. In Ohio, Robert Morton Walker felt he suffered discrimination based on his selection for the program and challenged his conviction on theft and robbery charges in the state supreme court. The court, however, rejected his appeal and ruled that selecting defendants for rapid criminal justice processing and prosecution did not violate the Fourteenth Amendment. When a similar case came before the same court, Judge Edward J. Mahoney defended the initiative in earnest, arguing the Career Criminal program "bears a reasonable relationship to the legitimate interest of the state in the speedy, but fair prosecution of those who have demonstrated a propensity for crime." In order to prove that Career Criminal selection had violated constitutional protections, the defendant would need to prove that his or her selection was based solely on "arbitrary classifications" such as race. Even as these cases and similar litigation came before the courts at the state level, rulings by the U.S. Supreme Court were making the Career Criminal program more difficult to challenge legally, both by raising the bar for proving discriminatory intent within the justice system and by defending prosecutorial discretion to try defendants under various sentencing categories.[21]

Even if the courts denied that race was an "unjustifiable standard" through which prosecutors tried defendants as career criminals, making it difficult to prove that race was a factor in the decision to prosecute a defendant as such, a number of African Americans and civil rights groups recognized the direct impact of Ford's crime war measure within low-income urban communities. The *Baltimore Afro-American* warned of the Career Criminal program, "Unless President Ford looks at those poor people in the inner city ghetto and their relationship to crime in a different way, his crackdown on crime will prove another disaster." Civil rights organizations and criminal defense attorneys similarly recognized the racist dimensions of the policy and went on to challenge the practices of the Career Criminal units. To call for a more equitable career criminal selection process, the National Commission on Law Enforcement and Social Justice endorsed a report released by the conservative American Enterprise Institute that determined that the focus on black youth for special prosecution in New York City and Philadelphia "may result in the discriminatory labeling of minority children." The National Commission warned: "This incompetent and insensitive administration of this program, whether intentional or not, is condemning countless minority youths to misery and failure within the criminal justice system."[22] But while the public statements of White House officials consistently expressed concern about disproportionate rates of black victimization when it came to crime, the disproportionate rates of black criminalization and incarceration did not seem to cause the same level of distress.

Despite the objections to the racial disparities that resulted from the Career Criminal units' work, prosecutors working in the initial programs successfully incarcerated more offenders under Career Criminal auspices than under standard court procedures, and after three years, policymakers and criminal justice authorities moved to establish the program nationally. In the nation's ten largest cities, the initiative had convicted a combined 6,641 "habitual criminals" on more than 10,000 separate charges within its first year. And Career Criminal units receiving discretionary funds boasted a 95 percent conviction rate with the average sentence of fifteen years. Still, FBI data indicated that nearly 250,000 Americans continued to pursue careers in street crime, evidence that justified the expansion of the program even as it demonstrated the program's limited impact on crime itself. In 1978, in the Repeat Offender Prosecution and Prison Improvement Act introduced by New York's Democratic congressman Edward Pattison and Maryland's Republican senator Charles Mathias, Congress moved to make Career Criminal units more permanent and more focused on juveniles and to expand the program to fifty cities. The legislation failed to pass at the federal level, but with LEAA support and on state and local authorities' own initiative, 145 career criminal programs had been implemented nationwide by 1980.[23]

As federal policymakers increasingly framed urban problems as rooted in a crime problem, the Career Criminal program was seen as an important intervention in the crisis. The U.S. Attorney's Office established its own "career criminal" effort in the summer of 1976. Called "Operation Doorstop," its name referred to its principal goal: in the words of Earl Silbert, U.S. attorney for Washington, DC, "to stop the revolving door of arrest-release, conviction-release, rearrest-release, that for too long has characterized the criminal justice process."[24] Silbert saw Operation Doorstop's efforts as "an integral part of our national effort to revitalize our beleaguered cities."[25] As of September 1978, in Silbert's telling, Operation Doorstop had secured a 92 percent conviction rate, had played an important part in removing the source of urban problems from the streets, and thus had made a vital contribution toward improving urban social conditions as a whole.[26] His assessment bespoke the confidence shared by officials who shaped domestic policy during this period—that the crime problem was one of individual behavior and that incarceration was the only reliable solution to continued urban isolation and segregation.

THE WAR ON BLACK GANGS

As federal policymakers in the mid-1970s shifted the focus of the national law enforcement program beyond urban police to the juvenile justice system and courts, a distinct type of crime—"gang violence"—emerged as a source of particular concern. Testifying before the House Judiciary Subcommittee on Juvenile Delinquency in 1974, Los Angeles police chief Ed Davis brought a "new phenomenon in the black community" to the attention of Congress: "killing someone you have never seen before on the street, by a juvenile." Outside of Los Angeles, police departments and researchers reported that low-income youth in Detroit, New York, Chicago, and Philadelphia had organized into groups premised on reclaiming urban space as their own "territory" and battling with rival groups on the streets in segregated neighborhoods with shotguns, rifles, and pistols. Seemingly lacking political objectives entirely, the rise of these so-called gangs coincided with the sharp increases of the federal crime control budget and the doubling of juvenile arrests during the first half of the 1970s. During World War II and immediately after, gangs of racially and ethnically marginalized urban youth mostly engaged in petty thefts and fistfights with a particular emphasis on self-defense. In the oil crisis economy of the 1970s, in the context of high rates of unemployment and school expulsions, young men associated with these groups suddenly began dying on the streets at disturbing rates. For instance, in Los Angeles, the police department attributed 50 to 75 percent of homicides from 1972 to 1974 to gang violence. Even more alarming was federally funded research arguing that black and Latino urban Americans had "the highest potential for involvement in violent and predatory crime," presumably since they comprised 80 percent of gang membership nationwide.[27]

For the Ford administration, the most "obvious solution" to the gang problem was to urge urban street patrols and juvenile courts to "deal more harshly with repeat offenders who are gang members and remove them from the community." White House officials argued in an internal memorandum that "the need for swift and sure punishment of serious violent gang members is apparent. Repeat offenders who are gang members must be prosecuted and removed from the community. . . . This removal from the community would protect the public and the young less hardened members of the gang."[28] The Career Criminal program was already working to combat the gang problem by increasing the likelihood that young urban criminals would pay for the consequences of their actions in juvenile and adult prisons. But the Ford administration believed additional punitive measures were necessary, and so policymakers complemented the efforts of the Career Criminal court programs with an intensive focus on handguns, the weapons these "serious violent offenders" reportedly carried.

The availability and sophistication of handguns had drastically increased beginning in the 1970s, and as with the issue of narcotics and the formation of Richard Nixon's Office of Drug Abuse and Law Enforcement, focusing on the firearms issue allowed federal officials a new avenue through which to intervene directly in local law enforcement matters.[29] In the spring of 1975, with the Career Criminal program underway in its first eleven cities, the Ford administration began to develop gun control policy as a means to identify and remove repeat offenders and gang members from segregated urban communities. In order to curb the manufacture, trafficking, and use of firearms among youth gang members, Ford's proposed Handgun Crime Control Act levied a mandatory minimum sentence of up to three years for unlawful possession of a handgun. Ford officials hoped the measure would blunt the embarrassing escalation of the nation's reported crime rate.

Premised on possession rather than victimization, Ford's proposed law was based on abstract notions of the potential of certain guns to foster crime and violence among low-income urban Americans. The policy targeted black and Latino citizens by proposing a ban on so-called Saturday Night Specials—cheap ($50 or less), low-quality (.32 caliber or less), and easily concealed guns that policymakers associated with urban street crime and gangs. Ironically, although Johnson's Gun Control Act of 1968 aimed to reduce the supply of the low-cost handguns, their availability only increased following the policy's enactment. The 1968 legislation inadvertently promoted a gun trafficking system whereby factories in the southern states assembled the component parts of the Saturday Night Specials and shipped them to urban centers in the North to be sold on the black market.[30]

Unlike the Career Criminal program, the Ford administration's attempt to target racially marginalized youth by imposing a ban on Saturday Night Specials did not receive widespread support on the local level. Police chiefs in Boston, Los Angeles, San Antonio, Atlanta, and Newark argued in separate testimony before the House Government Operations Subcommittee for far broader gun control laws—some even proposing banning all handguns in their jurisdictions. But for these local law enforcement chiefs, the proposed federal measure to attack only the distribution and possession of Saturday Night Specials would guarantee arrests of urban teenagers but would not alleviate the general problem of gun violence.[31]

Ford's attack on low-cost firearms did, however, receive an outpouring of support from ardent gun control *opponents* such as Republican National Committee chairman Bob Dole and Senate Republican leader Hugh Scott, even if the measure seemed to contradict the Republican Party's strong commitment to the second amendment. The legislation carefully distinguished between the rifles, shotguns, and well-constructed handguns that "ordinary Americans" and "sportsmen" possessed for leisure activities from the "shoddy" handguns that offenders carried on the streets of the nation's most poverty-stricken cities.[32] Thirty-seven Democratic and thirty-one Republican senators supported Ford's proposed measure, but the House ultimately declined to pass major gun control legislation in advance of the 1976 election.

Nevertheless, with novel use of discretionary aid, Ford pressed on with "Operation Disarm the Criminal," demonstrating once again the extent to which an administration deeply committed to the principles of New Federalism pursued its own racially motivated policy objectives while still operating through a block grant, states' rights paradigm. Attorney General Edward Levi and other Ford officials even relied upon the 1965 Voting Rights Act to justify the operation's punitive urban intervention, citing that landmark civil rights legislation as the statute most "nearly analogous to a selective handgun control law." Drawing from the Supreme Court's decision in *Katzenbach v. South Carolina*, which empowered Congress to "limit its attention to geographic areas when action seemed necessary," Ford and Levi reasoned the federal government could "prevent excessive localized misuse" of handguns by implementing similar selective controls.[33] The principle that had once been used to allow the federal government to intervene if it determined that public institutions discriminated against African Americans was now being invoked to support a strategy to remove young black men from their communities and incarcerate them.

Yet even in the absence of new legislation, existing federal laws controlling firearms permitted federal policymakers to exert direct influence over designated communities. Relying on the Gun Control Act of 1968 and the Explosives Control Act of 1970, the Ford administration reframed Operation Disarm the Criminal as "Operation Concentrated Urban Law Enforcement" in the summer of 1975, banning the use of Saturday Night Specials in segregated urban areas. The Explosives Control Act of 1970 prohibited "the acquisition of firearms or explosives by certain types of individuals considered to represent potential threats to society," and the Ford administration determined that gang members and career criminals who purportedly carried the low-cost handguns fell into this category. Operation Concentrated Urban Law Enforcement effectively doubled the number of Bureau of Alcohol, Tobacco, and Firearms (ATF) agents engaging in "street work," or acting undercover to purchase guns from illegal sellers in eleven major cities. Using discretionary funds, the Ford administration awarded ATF $15.5 million for the program, using $2 million for hardware that would support the agents in their investigations and the remaining funds to hire new officers. Much like similar plainclothes squads in New York City, Detroit, and Washington, DC, during this period, the teams recruited for the program did not reflect the demographics of the communities where they operated: of 1,674 total agents working for the bureau, only forty-eight were black or Latino, and none of these officials worked in the southeast region where most of the initiative's target cities were located.[34]

To complement the addition of federal gun control agents on the streets of nearly every major American city, Operation Concentrated Urban Law Enforcement conducted a sweeping series of handgun raids in Delaware, South Carolina, Kentucky, Virginia, Maryland, North Carolina, and Ohio. Just as the federally financed fencing operations underway in cities like Washington, DC, used federal funds to purchase stolen goods, ATF agents drew from more than $1.5 million in federal funds to purchase firearms on the black market in cities like Baltimore, Boston, and Chicago. In addition, the bureau worked with White House officials to create what they called the "Significant Criminal Enforcement Program." This program gave federal officials authority to label as a "significant criminal" any "active criminal (even though not previously convicted) with a high potential toward crimes of violence, as documented by specific current and reliable intelligence data." Once a suspect had been classified by the bureau in this manner, he or she would be added to a list of firearms violators much like the FBI's Most Wanted List, except the names of "significant criminals" were not made available to the public.[35] The broad definition the bureau used to identify significant criminals made possible the widespread arrest and federal prosecution of offenders.

In the final weeks of the Ford administration in late 1976, even as the ATF continued its crackdown on gun law violators, the Treasury Department, of which the ATF was part, moved to reorganize its ever-more-powerful law enforcement arm. The reorganization scaled back

New York City police "stop and frisk" a group of Harlem residents for "Saturday Night Special" handguns and drugs in April 1978. *Photograph by Alain Le Garsmeur. Hulton Archive, Getty Images*

field investigations such as Operation Concentrated Urban Law Enforcement, and as quickly as it got off the ground, the federal government's gun control squad came to an end along with Ford's presidency.[36]
But the widespread arrest, prosecution, and incarceration of young
Americans who joined gangs, possessed Saturday Night Specials, or
were seen by policymakers and law enforcement authorities as having
the potential to commit violent crimes had only begun. Operation Concentrated Urban Law Enforcement and the Significant Criminal Enforcement Program had targeted low-income black youth in metropolitan
centers, and as a result, the bureau ultimately concluded that young
urban adolescents used guns with greater frequency than any other
group of Americans. This "finding" led federal policymakers and officials thereafter to conclude that handgun possession was a major cause
of the overall juvenile delinquency problem.

Indeed, the apparent lesson of Ford's short-lived gun control effort
shaped federal policies on youth and crime long afterward. Even as
Congress and the Department of Justice grew to recognize near the end
of the 1970s that "federally funded programs to combat juvenile crime
are perpetuating class and racial segregation," the government nevertheless turned toward greater institutionalization and targeted federal
funding to reach what policymakers now defined as "at-risk" (as opposed
to "potentially delinquent") populations. Although individual Career
Criminal units had used prosecutorial discretion in deciding to charge
youth as adults, the bureau's conclusions about handgun use and broader
research efforts reinforced policymakers' focus on young lawbreakers as a
group. With federal support, the RAND Corporation conducted several
studies examining the repeat offender phenomenon beginning in 1977, ultimately suggesting that the federal government further concentrate its
anticrime efforts on young people, who were entering "the most active
period of their career." RAND determined that criminality peaked before
the age of twenty-four: fifteen-year-olds had the highest arrest level nationwide, followed closely by sixteen-year-olds. Since young people accounted
for the foremost rates of burglary, larceny, and auto theft, the implications
of the RAND study encouraged the federal government to make Career
Criminal programs even more responsive to juvenile offenders.[37]

The Office of Juvenile Justice and Delinquency Prevention also funded
investigations into the "problem of black youth gangs." That funding

reinforced the federal government's decision to target repeat offenders and gang members in urban areas. With $48,000 in federal grants, Walter Miller of Harvard Law School's Center for Criminal Justice set out in 1974 to determine the source and solution to the problem of violence in cities that had gang problems. Miller did not speak with a single gang member during the course of his study, but his understanding of youth crime, one that placed gang activity at the core of urban violence and guns at the core of gang activity, profoundly influenced both popular conceptions of black neighborhoods and the strategies policymakers developed for the national law enforcement program as the War on Crime entered into the late 1970s and 1980s.[38]

Although Miller viewed gangs as historically endemic to urban life, by the mid-1970s, the problem of youth violence was one "of the first magnitude which shows little prospect of early abatement." Miller pointed out that gang members throughout the twentieth century tended to be low-income urban males between the ages of twelve and twenty-one, but the increase in the population of urban young people of color—"a population that currently manifests the highest potential for involvement in violent and predatory crime," in Miller's words— required new federal gang control and prevention resources. The research revealed that the availability of high-quality weapons on the campuses of public schools shaped the nature of gang violence. In Miller's description, public schools evolved into a site where "the gang extorts fees of a quarter to a dollar from students for the 'privilege' of passing through hallways or using school facilities." The situation had deteriorated to the point that one official in Philadelphia called the schools "citadels of fear." Miller's research offered an alarming picture in which youth of color, due to some seemingly innate capacity for violence, made gangs a more serious problem than ever before.[39]

The increasing demographic significance of young black and Latino residents in American cities led Miller to assume that gang violence would continue to worsen over the following decade, a prediction that reinforced the existing objectives of federal policymakers. "Only massive infusions of federal money or massive jailing of gang members [can] stem the coming tide of youth gang violence," Miller concluded. Drawing on Miller's work and his claim that in Los Angeles alone black and Chicano gang members had committed somewhere between 50 and 75 percent of all murders in the city, the American Bar Association endorsed Ford's hard-nosed anticrime strategy in its report on the Juvenile Justice System in 1976. The report commended both the Career Criminal and handgun control programs as necessary interventions to address the seemingly inevitable increase of "youth gangs roaming city streets and terrorizing residents." In the words of LEAA director Richard Velde, Miller's work was both "important and disturbing," and the Department of Justice quickly took action.[40]

Miller's report, released in May 1976, served two political purposes for Ford: it instilled fear in the voting public and supplied figures enabling the president to call for greater social control measures in designated urban areas. The *Chicago Tribune*, for example, covered the report with sensationalized depictions of urban civil disorder: "Gun-toting teenage gangs with such names as 'Savage Skulls' and 'King Kobras' represent a growing threat to schools and communities in the nation's big cities." As national news outlets reported the alarming implications of Miller's research, their coverage built support for the Ford administration's attack on urban youth gangs. Meanwhile, as Ford prepared for a southern tour during the 1976 campaign, he felt comfortable, with Miller's figures behind him, taking an even tougher stance on crime. At an event in Miami Beach, he called for all violent juvenile criminals to be tried as adults. "If they are big enough to commit the crimes they are big enough to go to jail," Ford said. "Too many violent and street-wise juveniles are using their age as a cloak of immunity." When the president proclaimed, "It is time to give the streets back to the law-abiding citizens and put the criminal behind bars," the audience launched into uproarious applause.[41]

PREPARING FOR MASS REMOVAL

Despite the evident racial disparities within the Career Criminal program, Operation Concentrated Urban Law Enforcement, and the juvenile justice system at large, policymakers, law enforcement officials, and scholars during the 1970s consistently denied that racism existed within American law enforcement and criminal justice institutions. The Ford administration emphasized its concern for the black victims of crime, whom the president mentioned whenever he spoke about the issue as an offensive strategy to demonstrate the administration's good intentions. And James Q. Wilson, whose expertise had been instrumental in shaping urban policing practices and crime war strategies from the Johnson administration onward, dismissed the punitive treatment black Americans received in arrest and sentencing practices. "It is wrong, in my view, to say that the system is thoroughly racist from top to bottom, you know, always over-arrest[ing], over-indict[ing], over-convict[ing] and over-punish[ing] blacks or some other minority," he told a group of mostly African American criminologists at a symposium on law enforcement organized by the Urban League in 1977. "I have not seen any evidence to persuade me that either one of those statements, extreme statements, should be taken seriously except insofar as people believe them." Congress and the Justice Department officials eventually acknowledged in a 1978 report that the national war on youth crime had exacerbated segregation and inequality, but nevertheless, they prepared to incarcerate even greater numbers of black youth as the 1980s approached.[42]

Although policymakers refused to confront seriously the existing racial discrepancies within the programs of the War on Crime, they did cite discriminatory juridical practices to support their calls for mandatory minimum sentences. In the San Francisco Bay area, for instance, a citizen convicted of a felony offense in Santa Clara County in 1972 was three times more likely to receive a prison sentence than a citizen convicted on the same charges in the slightly more affluent Marin County nearby.[43] Ford officials argued that standardizing sentencing practices with mandatory minimums would effectively reduce existing discrimination in the criminal justice system, and in 1975 Ford encouraged Congress to include such measures in future crime control policies. "The horrendous sentencing discretion presently exercised by judges gives rise to differences in treatment of similar offenders which are often capricious and increasingly perceived as unfair to the point of scandal," wrote Richard Parsons. Mandatory minimums seemed a means to make the criminal justice system more predictable and equitable by setting uniform standards.[44] The administration was less concerned with racial inequity than ensuring that citizens were treated equally by the criminal justice system regardless of where they lived.

Nixon had imposed mandatory minimum sentences for various offenses in his crime control program for Washington, DC, and Ford continued this project, seeking to establish similar guidelines nationwide. Mandatory minimums were not just a useful means of ensuring uniformity. In line with the goals of the Career Criminal program, Ford officials also believed that high mandatory minimums would reduce guilty pleas and encourage greater numbers of offenders to seek trial. Although Ford's effort did not take hold at the federal level until Congress enacted the Sentencing Reform Act as part of Ronald Reagan's Comprehensive Crime Control Act of 1984—the inaugural legislation of Reagan's "War on Drugs"—states increasingly adopted mandatory minimums during the 1970s. As governor of California, Reagan sponsored a 1974 law that set an automatic mandatory minimum for heroin dealers and for the illegal use of a deadly weapon. Anticipating the measures the Ford administration went on to impose at the national level the following year, Reagan told the California Sheriffs Association: "We feel that if a criminal uses a gun in the commission of a crime, he should go to prison."[45]

Federal policymakers and law enforcement officials may have claimed to support mandatory minimums as a means to reduce discrimination in the criminal justice system, but because they tended to be imposed for drug offenses, gun possession, and other violations associated with street crime, they ended up vastly increasing racial disparities in sentencing. In New York City in 1977, for instance, a twenty-two-year-old African American drug user was charged with selling one eighth of an ounce of heroin. Under the mandatory minimum sentences Vice President Nelson Rockefeller introduced in New York State in 1973, just before he joined the Ford administration, the defendant was sentenced to jail for the rest of his life, unless he received parole, in which case he would be on parole until he died. Meanwhile, across the street at the federal court in the Southern District of New York, a white rabbi who had stolen millions of dollars from elderly residents in a nursing home was sentenced to four months in prison. Unlike the young black defendant, the rabbi never spent a day behind bars. Instead, he served his time in a halfway house during the week and was allowed to return to his home on the weekends.[46] Although mandatory minimum sentences, the Career Criminal program, and Ford's gun control policies operated under race-neutral language, they were informed by racist assumptions that supported policies that consistently reinforced the decision to target crime war measures in low-income urban neighborhoods.

The federal government's decision to manage the urban crisis with policing and sentencing practices that effectively removed hundreds of thousands of African Americans from their communities had created another crisis in the national prison population by the late 1970s. The Long-Range Master Plan for prison construction that the Nixon administration initiated in the 1970s could not keep pace. During the first half of the 1970s, fewer than 200,000 Americans were incarcerated in state and federal prisons. In 1975, this population soared from 208,000 to 228,000, and then by an additional 22,000 inmates by 1976. Inside prisons, populations rose to between 110 and 115 percent of capacity, with some southern prisons at 175 percent of capacity.[47]

At the Southern Ohio Correctional Facility, one of the maximum security prisons constructed under the charge of the Long-Range Master Plan in 1972, the practice of "double celling"—confining two people in a cell that had been originally built for one—quickly became the norm for most prisoners there, who were incarcerated for life for first-degree felonies. Within three years of the prison's opening, it had reached 138 percent of capacity. In 1975, inmate Kelly Chapman filed a case against the prison, arguing that sharing his thirty-two-square-foot cell with another man violated his Eighth Amendment protection against cruel and unusual punishment.[48]

The case made its way to the Supreme Court, which decided in 1981's *Rhodes v. Chapman* that the conditions at Southern Ohio did not, in fact, constitute "cruel and unusual" punishment. With the Court's sole black justice, Thurgood Marshall, offering the only dissenting opinion, the majority ruled that only if prisoners could demonstrate that authorities had subjected them to "wanton and unnecessary infliction of pain" could federal courts take an active role in reforming conditions in state prisons.[49] The Supreme Court's ruling set a precedent that prevented federal policymakers and the courts from intervening if states fostered inhumane conditions inside prisons. Following the wave of penal construction the national government had encouraged during the 1970s, the rulings of the Burger Court in the 1980s granted greater discretion to penal authorities and in doing so worsened the over-crowded and often appalling conditions that characterized mass incar-ceration in the late twentieth century.

Even though the marked expansion of the nation's prison system had failed to halt rising rates of reported crime in the second half of the 1970s, policymakers continued to see incarceration as a powerful crime deterrent. The Ford administration had succeeded in making it a crim-inal justice priority to imprison citizens they viewed as "hardened" and "dangerous" and who appeared to make crime into a career. The strate-gies they developed for the War on Crime sought to make deterrence through incarceration a viable means to both control crime and remove "chronically violent" suspects from the streets of American cities. As state and local law enforcement authorities followed the federal govern-ment's lead and implemented the Career Criminal program, routine "stop and frisk" searches for Saturday Night Special handguns, and mandatory minimum sentences in an effort to control crime, new ap-proaches to domestic social programs emerged in the last years of the 1970s, under the leadership of Gerald Ford's successor, the Georgia Democrat Jimmy Carter.[50]

As Carter pointed out during his presidential campaign, the pro-grams of the War on Crime had made "no contribution to reducing crime," despite the $5 billion the national government had invested in state and local law enforcement. Other federal policymakers and Ford officials saw the Career Criminal program and measures such as Op-eration Disarm the Criminal as highly successful, and as the best means to address the socioeconomic problems of unemployment, failing school systems, and deteriorating housing conditions. But if the concerted at-tack on "habitual offenders" and gang members had not in fact reduced crime, then the purported "success" of these programs rested entirely on the fact that they removed young urban African American men from their neighborhoods. Ford had pledged to protect the victims of crime, but the same group of black citizens most likely to be victimized by murder and other violent crimes was also the same group his crime con-trol policies had targeted for this removal.[51]

In theory, Ford's strategies for the War on Crime concentrated on a small group of offenders the administration saw as responsible for the majority of the nation's crime. In policy terms, federal officials and criminal justice authorities were pursuing "gang members," "habitual criminals," and "repeat offenders." In practice, these labels created new ways for federal programs and the criminal justice system at large to directly target black men between the ages of fifteen and twenty-four who had concerned federal policymakers since the civil rights movement. The set of racist assumptions about African Americans and crime that undergirded the Career Criminal program and Concentrated Urban Law Enforcement, coupled with the labeling of a generation of low-income black urban youth as "potentially delinquent" under the terms of the juvenile justice policy during this period, rendered entire communities criminal. By defining these categories in broad terms, steeped in their own racism, Ford officials knew the likely impact of their policies. Restoring "domestic tranquility" meant incarcerating as many young black men as possible, the group federal policymakers believed were criminal by nature.

8

CRIME CONTROL AS URBAN POLICY

In the summer of 1976, against the backdrop of plant closures across the Midwest and the presidential contest between Gerald Ford and Jimmy Carter, the city of St. Louis removed the final remnants of debris from the site of the Pruitt-Igoe housing project. Pruitt-Igoe was the first public housing development in the nation whose problems—racial segregation, residential abandonment, crime—had become so acute that complete demolition seemed the only antidote. The razing of Pruitt-Igoe's thirty-three high-rises, which once stood as emblems of the city's hopeful future, foreshadowed the fate of similar projects throughout the remainder of the twentieth century and into the twenty-first. Back when the housing authority opened Pruitt-Igoe in the mid-1950s, the project offered desirable living conditions to a generation of African American families. Designed by Minoru Yamasaki, whose World Trade Center towers in New York rose in the moment when his vertical neighborhood started to fall, Pruitt-Igoe and its 3,000 units were clean, modern, and aesthetically pleasing.

Granted, to cut costs, city contractors had built Pruitt-Igoe as cheaply as possible: kitchen cabinets were made of plywood, doorknobs snapped after a dozen turns, and playgrounds, parks, and bushes were nowhere to be found. Even so, Pruitt-Igoe's new tenants saw the project as a vast improvement over the dilapidated housing they had left behind, sometimes voluntarily and sometimes because it had been taken by eminent domain and the land cleared for urban renewal projects. Within fifteen years, however, Pruitt-Igoe had decayed into housing of last resort, its stairwells and galleries a haven for muggings and drug use instead of the community interaction Yamasaki had intended. Residents with the means to escape Pruitt-Igoe's rampant crime and deteriorating living conditions did so, and by the early 1970s only 600 residents remained in a complex originally designed for 15,000.[1] The extreme segregation and poverty that developed in Pruitt-Igoe, and the implosion of its demolished buildings in 1975, raised stark questions about the future of domestic urban programs, laying bare a policy crossroads that Carter would confront when he took office the following January.

Whereas federal policymakers and law enforcement officials during the Nixon and Ford administrations had emphasized individual behavior as the root of urban ills, Carter and his advisors saw federal policy as the root cause of the crime, unemployment, and residential desertion that befell Pruitt-Igoe and similar housing projects in the late 1970s. "The riots have ended," a Carter campaign paper declared, "but the cities have grown more violent. They have become the enclave for the poor and they are becoming less and less able to support a growing demand for social services." Polls during the campaign indicated that most Americans believed "cleaning up social and economic conditions in our slums and ghettos" would reduce crime. As a presidential candidate, Carter offered a domestic policy approach that addressed the structural intersections between high rates of unemployment and crime and committed, if elected, to building more equitable institutions. "We pride ourselves on having a good, fair criminal justice system," Carter told former LBJ aide Bill Moyers in an interview. "Now wealth is a major factor in whether or not you get justice."[2] Carter's attention to the socioeconomic roots of crime during his campaign revived conversations in Washington that had been largely dormant for nearly a decade, since the previous Democratic administration.

Amid a recession, with the estimated unemployment rate for black youth at 40 to 60 percent and with public housing projects deteriorating, Carter acknowledged that black Americans bore the brunt of structural exclusion and crime. Certainly, some indicators seemed to be improving. As a result of electoral gains aided by the Voting Rights Act of 1965, record college enrollment numbers, and a more visible black middle class, African American families earned more money per household in 1974 than they did in 1964. But between 1975 and 1976, 100,000 black families fell below the official poverty level. The number of black Americans without jobs was two times that of their white counterparts. And the black prison population was growing rapidly: a "typical inmate," according to social scientists, was a twenty-six-year-old black high school dropout serving a six-and-a-half-year sentence for a violent crime.[3] Confronting such data, Carter argued for an end to federal law enforcement assistance, a guaranteed jobs program, and an overhaul of public housing. In the context of still-rising reported crime rates and urban crisis, conservatives treated crime as a fact of American life and clung to punishment as the only road to deterrence. Carter departed only so far from this outlook and the broad political consensus that saw crime in black neighborhoods as inevitable and rooted in the individual pathologies of residents. Accepting the need for greater social control in urban areas, Carter and other Democratic policymakers hoped that the socioeconomic factors that they believed contributed to crime could be addressed by keeping law enforcement and criminal justice priorities at the center of a broader urban policy.

Like Lyndon Johnson, Carter linked urban crime to unemployment and poverty, and like Johnson, he believed that only a federal intervention that asserted greater punitive control in areas of segregated poverty could manage the symptoms of urban crisis. Yet Carter's approach to integrating punitive initiatives and urban social programs turned the debate about the root causes of crime on its head. If Johnson officials had argued that "warring on poverty is warring on crime," Carter's attempt to make the first "comprehensive, long-term commitment to the Nation's urban areas" since the 1960s was premised on crime prevention and control as a means to address the issues of poverty and inequality.[4] A belief that crime control measures could be the solution to the problems of housing, unemployment, and subpar urban school systems had been building among federal policymakers, law enforcement officials, and criminal justice authorities across the political spectrum since the mid-1970s. Carter shared their concern for the failures of public programs and the perceived breakdown of social order in areas of segregated poverty, and during his presidency, this idea became more firmly established through new legislative initiatives.

Because Carter viewed crime as a cause, rather than an effect, of urban decay and social inequality, the administration's foremost urban policy priority was law enforcement. Carter believed that only "increased access to opportunity for those disadvantaged by economic circumstance or a history of discrimination" could reverse the urban crisis, but he also suggested that punitive policy was necessary to maintain control in neighborhoods classified as "violent" based on crime statistics.[5] An effort to strike this balance was the Justice System Improvement Act, which Carter sent to Congress in June 1978 and which passed in late 1979. Through this legislation, Carter worked to dismantle the Law Enforcement Assistance Administration (LEAA) and bring an end to the War on Crime and its investment in urban police departments. Yet federal crime control programs continued.

The Carter administration broke with the previous thirteen years of federal crime control policy by empowering the Department of Housing and Urban Development (HUD), rather than the Department of Justice, to direct Carter's Urban Initiatives Anti-Crime program. At the center of Carter's national urban policy, the Anti-Crime program slowly phased out the influence of the LEAA in urban social programs and reframed law enforcement measures as "urban revitalization initiatives." As Urban Anti-Crime program director Lynn Curtis explained, HUD's new role in directing the national law enforcement program was an attempt to bring to an end "the continued Vietnamization of the criminal justice system: more men, more equipment, more incursions, swift and sure punishment to deter a nonwhite enemy whose psychology the white power brokers of this Nation presume to understand."[6] Instead of tactical squads roaming the streets as in earlier crime war programs, improving security and surveillance in neighborhoods of segregated poverty lay at the center of the Urban Anti-Crime program and its redevelopment efforts. Extremely high inflation rates limited the scope and ambition of domestic programs. As a strategy to leverage scarce resources while still improving conditions for low-income Americans, the Carter administration concentrated the Urban Anti-Crime program on housing projects—the places that federal officials in the Carter administration saw as the seedbed of urban crisis.

By fusing together employment, housing, and law enforcement measures and reframing urban policy and crime policy as essentially synonymous, Carter effectively reconciled the ideological tensions at the center of urban social programs. In offering a domestic policy that synthesized the social welfare and social control programs of the New Frontier, the War on Poverty, and the War on Crime, Carter continued to pursue many of the same surveillance and law enforcement objectives sought by his predecessors. The administration's Urban Anti-Crime program brought to fruition the "defensible space" initiative commissioned by Richard Nixon and Gerald Ford, a theory of urban planning that aimed to foster security and crime prevention by redesigning the urban landscape. Carter also reiterated the previous administrations' calls for swift and uniform sentencing while continuing to boost patrol and professionalize the police forces working in urban areas that had high rates of reported crime.[7]

Finally, like his more liberal predecessors, Carter advocated for greater community participation in domestic urban programs. During his campaign and as president, he frequently mentioned the importance of vibrant neighborhoods in a moment when Americans were growing more fearful, more segregated, and more isolated from one another. As Carter framed it publicly, the Urban Anti-Crime program would encourage community involvement by empowering grassroots organizations in and around the targeted housing projects to participate directly in controlling crime in their own communities. But, as in Kennedy's antidelinquency programs and Johnson's War on Poverty, the federal government's idea of such community participation was highly limited. In order to qualify for federal funds, tenants' councils, youth empowerment initiatives, and community centers needed to include both law enforcement and social welfare authorities in the development of programs. And despite his rhetorical gestures to involve citizens in the implementation of the Urban Anti-Crime program, funding for these efforts remained low compared to the funding for cameras, identification systems, fences, and metal security screens that the administration installed throughout the nation's most devastated public housing projects.

Much like his approach to foreign policy and the domestic economy, Carter's urban program laid the groundwork for the privatization, the deregulation, and the "War on Drugs" pursued by his successor, Ronald Reagan, in the 1980s. By the end of the 1970s, conditions in low-income urban neighborhoods had failed to improve significantly: the number of reported crimes increased, drug use worsened, employment remained stagnant, and record numbers of black Americans entered the prison system. The outcome of a broader shift from seeing crime as an anomaly to be combated to seeing crime as an unavoidable phenomenon to be managed, Carter's punitive urban policy firmly institutionalized the carceral state in segregated urban neighborhoods.

THE DISMANTLING OF THE LAW ENFORCEMENT ASSISTANCE ADMINISTRATION

The federal investment in the War on Crime increased threefold from 1965, when Johnson's Office of Law Enforcement Assistance first opened its doors, to 1977, when Carter moved into the White House. The growth was remarkable: the Law Enforcement Assistance Administration (LEAA), which served as the War on Crime's grantmaking and research arm within the Department of Justice, started out with a $63 million allocation in 1969; five years later, the agency received its highest budget from Congress at $871 million. As other domestic programs like Model Cities and the Office of Economic Opportunity either shut their doors or struggled to survive in the context of inflation in the 1970s, the federal government funneled a total of nearly $6 billion ($20 billion in today's dollars) into state and local law enforcement via the LEAA. At the same time, reported crime surged 58 percent over its level in 1965, and rose an alarming 27 percent during Ford's presidency alone.[8]

Believing it to be wasteful and poorly coordinated with little demonstrated success, Carter wanted to end the War on Crime. In order to do so, his administration needed to lessen the power and influence of the LEAA. Under the command of Nixon and Ford, the LEAA had become a "bureaucratic monster," as Carter officials saw it, lacking coherent objectives or strong leadership and incapable of delivering money to the "areas of greatest need." To many White House officials, it seemed that autonomous state-level authority over local programs generated even greater marginalization of Americans living in segregated poverty and crime. Block grant planning spawned corruption and mismanagement, and a direct channel needed to be reestablished between the federal government and local nonprofits outside the confines of discretionary funds. Carter turned back to the categorical funding model the Johnson administration had originally proposed for the national law enforcement program. In the summer of 1977, the Carter administration began to reorganize federal crime control agencies, ordering the Department of Justice to cut a quarter of all of its employees as a means to effectively "streamline" federal crime control. But as much as Carter wanted to avoid the "policy of confrontation with our cities" adopted by the previous administrations, and despite his hints during the campaign that he would abolish the LEAA altogether (calling it "the Republicans' showcase agency"), he quickly discovered that the War on Crime could not be easily dismantled.[9]

The criminal justice community, which had grown substantially alongside the LEAA, partly as a result of the funding the LEAA provided, had a decidedly mixed reaction to Carter's proposed abolition of the agency. The divergent views became evident as the White House began working on Carter's first major crime message in November 1977. Local authorities and liberal organizations tended to be supportive. Law enforcement officials like Baltimore City Police Commissioner Donald Pomerleau and organizations like the American Civil Liberties Union (ACLU) had called for the disbanding of the LEAA and lauded the steps the administration took to scale down the agency. Others wanted to end federal crime control assistance to state and local governments but believed the LEAA could still contribute to crime control by focusing solely on statistical research.[10]

Governors and law enforcement consultants who directly benefited from block grants did not respond as enthusiastically. Carter and Attorney General Griffin Bell fielded complaints from a host of think tanks, state agencies, and businesses that depended on LEAA grants as a critical source of funding. For example, the International Association of Chiefs of

Police, although it had been in existence since 1893, prospered when the agency opened its doors, receiving $12 million in federal grants for fifty-three crime control programs. The states, too, wanted to maintain control over the criminal justice funds they received from the federal government and to keep the focus of national crime control on hardware, since the LEAA provided replacements and upgrades for law enforcement technologies and weapons at up to 90 percent of their cost. In late December 1977, two dozen state criminal justice officials met in Columbia, Maryland, to discuss the federal government's proposed restructuring of the War on Crime. Their consensus statement urged the preservation of the comprehensive planning process in each state, argued for the necessity of block grants, and resisted the Carter administration's gestures toward greater community involvement. Recalling the old debates surrounding Johnson's Safe Streets Act, the planners argued that earmarking crime control funds for specific purposes would compromise the nation's safety. In the hands of local authorities, these state-level policymakers imagined, the national law enforcement program would crumble.[11]

Facing strong resistance from public and private law enforcement and criminal justice institutions, Carter backed off from his proposed abolition of the LEAA. After spending more than a year reviewing the agency, in early 1978, the Carter administration devised a plan that maintained the agency's functions but divided it into three separate organizations that would be phased into existence over a period of several years. The LEAA would continue to provide money to state and local law enforcement agencies, the National Institute of Justice would oversee all federal crime control research, and the Bureau of Justice Statistics would be a clearinghouse for the data that the LEAA and the Federal Bureau of Investigation (FBI) gathered. All three agencies would report to an Office of Justice Assistance, Research, and Statistics, which had been created by Bell in the summer of 1977.[12]

Recasting the federal law enforcement program as a data-gathering enterprise was a way to quietly scale back the War on Crime while also devoting attention to inaccuracies in crime reporting. Ten years after the federal government first required states to modernize their crime reporting systems, it had become clear to policymakers and experts that fundamental inaccuracies in crime-related data had created systemic flaws in the execution of federal punitive policy. Conflicting figures produced by seventeen departments using fifty-four different data sets had compromised the federal government's ability to create effective programs. For instance, by surveying victims, the LEAA found little, if any, increase in property crimes in 1975, while the FBI reported that such crimes increased nearly 10 percent that year. The only inference that crime statistics made clear was that intensified police patrol and technological advances had failed to impact urban violence and crime. From the perspective of Carter's domestic policy staff, the criminal justice data available to them was virtually useless. Indeed, Carter deliberately avoided discussing the crime rate at all in his public statements on the issue. All of the administration's consultants confirmed to the White House that "we simply do not know why the rate seems to be declining. It may suddenly go up." If measuring the crime rate posed the "single biggest issue in the American criminal justice system today," as law enforcement consultants told White House officials, then the Office of Justice Assistance, Research, and Statistics could preserve old partnerships with states and private organizations and at the same time offer a more sensible strategy for national law enforcement that improved the research and statistical capabilities of the federal government.[13]

On a ninety-degree day in early July 1978, Carter formally began remaking the War on Crime from the White House Rose Garden when he announced his Justice System Improvement Act and sent it to Congress. The Democratic majority in both chambers of Congress rejected most of Carter's domestic policy proposals, but the president found a receptive congressional audience for the idea that it was time to "phase down the LEAA program." The Justice System Improvement Act that would divide and dissolve much of the LEAA passed in December 1979. The legislation invested directly in local programs, moving closer to Carter's desired target and cutting out the states as middlemen. The administration assured states that their share of law enforcement block grants would remain constant, but the Office of Justice Assistance would also devise new formula grants that took into account crime rates, local criminal justice expenditures, and tax bases in determining how to direct available federal funds. Using population and crime data to ascertain the needs of a given community, Carter hoped that the formula approach would foster a more effective and equitable funding structure. The Justice System Improvement Act's formula grants would reduce the amount of federal criminal justice funds used for hardware, salary increases, and construction, and instead direct that money toward research, local empowerment, and community participation. Local governments confronting high crime rates "will be given greater discretion to select projects and programs particularly suited to their own crime reduction and criminal justice needs," Carter told Congress, and national law enforcement programs would remain focused on urban centers.[14]

The legislation gave state and local governments a three-year window during which they could receive federal crime control grants via the LEAA; thereafter, they were expected to operate their respective law enforcement programs independently. As Assistant Attorney General Benjamin Civiletti told the press, "The scheme is to get more money to the counties, major cities and high crime areas with less red tape, less overhead, less bog-down in both money and time than through the prior grant process." The act reduced the planning requirements the Safe Streets Act had tied to federal funding so that states would no longer need to submit a criminal justice plan the size of a telephone book every year. And cities like Los Angeles, Chicago, Atlanta, and Newark now provided the federal government with one grant application a year for all criminal justice programs instead of forty separate proposals.[15]

The Justice System Improvement Act was not the only example, under Carter, of at once pulling back from some investments in law enforcement while making new ones aimed more specifically at America's cities. Even as Carter cut off LEAA funding for police hardware programs, he sent Congress the policy that would bring his Urban Initiatives Anti-Crime program to fruition. As a housing hardware program framed as an urban revitalization initiative, the Public Housing Security Demonstration Act of 1978 targeted the nation's most troubled housing projects that resembled Pruitt-Igoe in the years leading up to its demolition: the Jeffries Homes and Douglass Projects in Detroit, Lafayette Courts in Baltimore, the Robert Taylor Homes in Chicago, and Larchmont Gardens in Miami, among thirty-nine others. Residents of these large housing projects—each had more than 1,200 units—faced some of the worst living conditions in the country. The federal government decided that they required a crime control package to be improved and secured.[16]

DEFENSIBLE SPACE

As a visible manifestation of both socioeconomic and crime problems, public housing projects offered Carter a viable testing site for punitive urban policy. The Federal Housing Authority handled 2 million units inhabited by 3.4 million Americans when Carter took office. The administration was particularly concerned about 152 "problem projects" scattered throughout the nation. These were large family projects in "problem neighborhoods of distressed cities" where citizens of color—the large majority of them children under the age of eighteen—constituted 63 percent of all residents and where drug abuse, property theft, and violence seemed to be more pressing issues than unemployment or inflation. These sites were "breeding grounds for crime, vandalism, delinquency and despair," in Secretary of Housing and Urban Development Patricia Harris's description. In an attempt to address the distinct set of issues that low-income residents confronted in housing projects and their surrounding areas, Carter announced his Urban Initiatives Anti-Crime program in July 1978, the same month he proposed to dissolve the LEAA. The program would serve as the central component of his national urban policy.[17]

When Congress passed the Public Housing Security Demonstration Act of 1978 in late October, it set the legislative mandate for the president's Urban Initiatives Anti-Crime program. Linking crime prevention with urban redevelopment, the policy sought to address the needs of the majority of public housing tenants, who had, in the words of Carter officials, "low income levels, high unemployment rates, high percentages of people receiving Aid for Dependent Children, high percentages of female-headed single parent households, and high percentages of youth." The administration hoped that by the end of March 1980, with $41 million at its disposal from a range of federal agencies and with local governments and organizations contributing $8 million more, the

Public Housing Security Demonstration Act could make public housing "more attractive and less crime-ridden."[18] As the first major law enforcement assignment given to HUD, the Public Housing Security Demonstration Act made residential security the agency's main concern in the 1970s.

The legislative expression of Carter's Urban Initiatives Anti-Crime program, the Public Housing Security Act renewed federal partnerships with local governments. It resembled the programs of the Kennedy and Johnson administrations, when the national government intervened at the local level directly in an attempt to improve troubled low-income communities with carefully planned, comprehensive social welfare and punitive interventions. With HUD acting as the lead agency and under the direction of Lynn Curtis, the Urban Initiatives Anti-Crime program focused primarily on improving safety and security for public housing residents by promoting physical rehabilitation, management assistance, law enforcement measures, and partnerships with city governments. At the same time, the program brought together officials from thirteen separate federal agencies, a new federal nonprofit organization called ACTION (the Agency for Voluntary Service), local criminal justice and law enforcement employees, community leaders, security directors, tenants, and municipal authorities. With a shrinking congressional allocation, the LEAA committed nearly half a million dollars for a program supporting victims and witnesses. The Department of Labor handled the youth employment dimension of the program, allocating $8 million toward public conservation and improvement projects that offered employment to "at-risk" youth living in federally assisted housing. The administration believed its interagency, community-based approach offered a "model of partnership and cooperation for the 1980s" that restored the type of federalism that made the New Deal and the Great Society successful.[19]

On the surface, the Urban Initiatives Anti-Crime Program represented an important shift away from traditional approaches to crime control, which had focused on local police forces, prisons, and court systems. As HUD planners explained in the program's First Annual Report to Congress, the Public Housing Security Act was meant to "cover causes as well as symptoms, inner human motivations and environmental factors, community and criminal justice perspectives, prevention and control, 'law and order' and social reform, and structural as well as incremental change."[20] By embracing Carter's Urban Initiatives Anti-Crime Program and the Public Housing Security Act, federal policy-makers intended to keep residents safer and to ease the task of monitoring high crime areas. Yet by establishing stronger partnerships between social and law enforcement institutions and devoting the majority of funds to surveillance and security needs, the policy vastly enhanced the scope and power of punitive authorities in the most deteriorated and segregated public housing sites in the country.

Carter was not the first to connect public housing conditions with crime control issues. The security measures at the heart of the Carter administration's Urban Initiatives Anti-Crime Program were inspired by architectural plans that had been commissioned under Nixon and Ford, with the aim of creating what planners and policymakers called "defensible space." The concept envisioned a direct correlation between poor building design, families on public assistance, and crime. It was articulated by New York City architect Oscar Newman, first in his 1972 book *Defensible Space* and then in public housing guidelines he de-signed throughout the 1970s. *Defensible Space*, backed by more than $150,000 in grants from the LEAA and HUD, investigated the failures of Pruitt-Igoe and jump-started a new approach to crime control. Noting that doubling patrol forces in and around housing projects "had no measurable effect on the reduction of crime," Newman proposed a solution that involved replacing high-rise projects with smaller enclaves of defensible space in which physical hardware, rather than police pa-trol, would provide a type of omniscient surveillance that increased the risk of apprehension and therefore acted as a powerful deterrent against criminal behavior.[21] Premised on the assumption that the design of housing projects encouraged residents to resort to crime, the plan to craft defensible space promised to enhance surveillance and improve safety.

By treating the physical arrangement and social organization of housing projects as the root cause of their problems, Newman's research created a vital new battleground for the War on Crime. Newman rea-soned that the design of high-rises, a "peculiar mixture of large concentrations of low-income families located in high crime areas, in building forms that make inhabitants particularly vulnerable to criminal activity," perpetuated crime. In Newman's view, when the criminogenic forces of housing project architecture combined with residents' own cultural pathologies, the units tended to either "reinforce or counteract social weakness." The attempt by urban developers to combine retired, older Americans in housing projects with young families had "backfired and fostered criminal tendencies among the low-income young," who, according to Newman, were left largely unsupervised by their single mothers, and engaged in rampant theft and vandalism. Rather than risk apprehension by venturing outside public housing developments, it was easier for these youths to commit such acts inside buildings and among their neighbors.[22]

In March 1973, shortly after Newman shared the findings of his research with the Department of Justice, the LEAA invested $2 million into a major new defensible space program that relied on architects to design buildings, public schools, street patterns, and public transportation systems to foster "the elimination of physical conditions that encourage crimes of opportunity." Outside of housing projects, these programs focused on "target hardening" techniques such as street lighting and gated walkways. A precursor to James Q. Wilson and George Kelling's broken windows theory in the 1980s, which posited that the presence of a broken window invited further vandalism, for Ford aide Malcolm Barr and other White House officials, the plan to build defensible space entailed "an approach to facilitate physical and social integration," bringing law enforcement institutions, security equipment, and officers into every elevator, walkway, and courtyard of public housing developments. The construction of new barriers, walls, and gates in areas of segregated poverty cultivated a carceral climate that increasingly mirrored the techniques used in penal institutions themselves.[23]

Seeking to foster defensible space in targeted areas, the Nixon and Ford administrations increased patrol in public housing and expanded law enforcement's authority in urban social programs. In Atlanta, the LEAA awarded nearly half a million dollars to add fifteen patrolmen to the federally funded housing project there and to operate two storefront police offices to hasten police response time. In Pittsburgh, the defensible space program brought together the local police department, the Housing Authority, the State Criminal Justice Planning Commission, and the Tenant's Organization. Supported largely by the LEAA, the Housing Authority operated a special housing security force composed of fifty guards patrolling ten high-rise apartment buildings and eighteen community service officers to function as liaisons between residents and police in late 1973. The service officer position offered tenants a new prospect for steady employment (the positions each paid $8,000 a year), but the program was not primarily a jobs initiative; the "number one priority" of the force was to prevent vandalism and destruction of property. While the security force dissolved after a year of operation, and with it the jobs it had provided residents, the closed-circuit televisions that the Housing Authority installed in every housing project in Pittsburgh remained.[24] Grassroots participation in surveillance and patrol programs typically lasted only through the process of implementation.

The defensible space measures of the early and mid-1970s also brought the private sector into public housing and its expanding carceral network. The LEAA's largest single competitive private contract went to Westinghouse Corporation of Baltimore in the spring of 1974 to "reduce crime in homes, schools, business and transportation through environmental design" at a cost of $2 million. Charles Work, a deputy administrator for the agency, described the contract as crucial to the larger aim of the LEAA to redesign crime out of America's cities. "In many communities the environment is custom-made for crime," he said. "Streets are often poorly lighted and deserted, doors and windows can be easily entered, and bus and subway stops offer natural lurking places for the criminal." With some of the highest rates of reported crime and violence in the nation, Westinghouse would create a "model environmental design" for defensible space in Baltimore's schools, transportation systems, commercial centers, and homes.[25]

Working with the Westinghouse planners, HUD, and the LEAA, the Baltimore Housing Authority began to remodel the high-rise housing projects at Lafayette Courts, making them heavily guarded and secure in order to realize the defensible space concept. By the mid-1970s, a private security guard monitored the entrances of the housing project from behind a bullet-proof booth. Twenty-four hours a day, seven days a week, guards were present to check identification as each resident entered the Lafayette Courts project. An audio monitoring system allowed the guard to listen to all conversations and activities that took place inside the project's elevators, and he or she could watch residents enter and exit the grounds on several television monitors inside the booth. Such measures in Baltimore, Pittsburgh, Atlanta, and elsewhere made it easier for private security guards and local law enforcement authorities to patrol troublesome neighborhoods and watch residents. But by the late 1970s, it became clear that the defensible space had failed to improve the violent circumstances that characterized many urban communities. Rather than scrapping the unsuccessful plan entirely, federal policymakers decided that the earlier security measures had not gone far enough.[26]

THE NEW DOMESTIC SECURITY

Although the Carter administration's attention to social conditions seemed like the return of liberal approaches to domestic social programs, his urban policies instead mainly built on the defensible space concept and other legacies of his Republican predecessors. In order to address what Carter officials described as an "interrelated cause-effect web of poverty, institutional racism, relative deprivation, limited employment opportunity, poor education, inadequate housing, broken homes, and reduced family function," the administration moved defensible space and other housing security efforts initiated by the Nixon and Ford administrations to the forefront of its Urban Initiatives Anti-Crime Program.[27] In the process, Carter's policies reinforced the collaborations between law enforcement, housing, and private-sector institutions that Baltimore and other cities had forged earlier in the decade.

For the first round of funding from HUD, the administration selected thirty-nine test sites from a pool of nearly 200 applications submitted by housing authorities across the country, with the hope that the hybrid social program could be applied nationwide based on the test sites' experience. In housing projects, as the black planner and criminologist Victor Rouse suggested to HUD secretary Harris, "hardware" and "software" approaches needed to be combined for an effective residential security system. The idea was to use hardware grants for security measures with software grants for community-based programs that directly engaged residents and grassroots organizations.[28] Funds would be "co-targeted" among HUD, the Departments of Labor and Health, Education, and Welfare, and what remained of the LEAA.

Seeking to expand upon and make more "innovative" its previous defensible space program in the Lafayette Courts project, the Baltimore Housing Authority began working on its Urban Anti-Crime grant application as soon as the Public Housing Security Demonstration Act passed in October 1978. In addition to the high-rises in which Lafayette Courts tenants lived, the local housing authority sought to address the severe crime problems in the low-rises and townhomes of the nearby Flag House Courts. Both housing projects were almost exclusively African American, and most of the residents were under the age of eighteen. Of those residents under age eighteen, 80 percent lived in a single-parent household. Within the projects as a whole, 80 to 90 percent of families received public assistance.[29] Living in extreme segregation and poverty, the residents of Lafayette Courts and the Flag House Courts represented the primary group whom federal policymakers and local authorities sought to reach with new national crime control strategies.

The Baltimore planners thought installing an automatic access control system would be a cost-effective way to increase security without having to pay for additional manpower. In order to enable police and security guards to move about the high-rises outside the confines of the guard booths that had been established mid-decade, HUD funding made possible the installation of magnetic card readers at the door of each entrance that only registered residents with access cards could open. Urban Anti-Crime program director Lynn Curtis recognized that the electronic identification system would "dehumanize the already disadvantaged public housing residents," but did not use his influence to reject the proposal. Instead, Curtis trimmed the budget for the installation of the system submitted by the Baltimore Housing Authority planners from $600,000 to half a million dollars as a compromise. After all, the security measure met the basic criteria for the Urban

Anti-Crime program under the terms of the Public Housing Security Act, which aimed, first and foremost, to increase surveillance and patrol methods "to whatever point diminishing returns set in."[30]

Although the Carter administration's urban policies leaned heavily toward electronic monitoring systems and other hardware measures, officials believed that for security programs to successfully function, some planned activities must emerge from the people who lived in the housing project themselves. Past experience taught program officials that "receiving 'help' from outsiders often perpetuates the sense of impotence and powerlessness that is a cause as well as a consequence of poverty," as HUD planners explained. Including a degree of input from tenants would be a means of "enabling the poor to take charge of their own lives, on helping them gain a feeling of competence and worth, a sense of being somebody who matters"—but not without strong oversight from federal and local officials. As such, software programs focusing on the management of public housing projects to improve "the exterior personalization of buildings to facilitate tenant social interaction and stake," as well as tenant involvement and youth employment, were to receive roughly half of the funds allocated by the Public Housing Security Demonstration Act of 1978. This stipulation opened new funding possibilities for social organizations that had frequently been denied federal assistance during the War on Crime.[31]

Even as the act demonstrated a commitment to citizen-based initiatives and grassroots representation, under the terms of the program, community groups could not operate their plans without approval from the city or the federal government. The Public Housing Security Act required all neighborhood groups to include delegates from the mayor's office and local police, court, and corrections officials in their decision-making. Now law enforcement and criminal justice institutions could involve themselves in virtually any community-based effort. Empowering HUD to direct a law enforcement program marked an attempt on the part of the Carter administration to steer federal crime control priorities away from continued investment in local police forces, but HUD went on to support local housing authorities in creating special forces of their own and making law enforcement authorities an integral aspect of every part of the Urban Anti-Crime program.

Residents of Chicago's Robert Taylor Homes quickly discovered the Carter administration's limited view of community participation in low-income urban neighborhoods when they called for their own "War on Crime." In February 1978, five months before Carter announced his Urban Anti-Crime program, the Afro-American Patrolman's League and tenant organizations united to form the League to Improve the Community. The league demanded that HUD fund unarmed resident patrols to keep tenants safe, since public crime control programs and private security guards seemed incapable of providing the tenants safety. At the time the Chicago police estimated that roughly 10 percent of the city's rapes, murders, and assaults occurred in the massive complex, which consisted of twenty-eight high-rises housing 20,000 tenants.[32] The league's "War on Crime" resembled the approach of the juvenile delinquency programs federal policymakers developed during the Kennedy and Johnson administrations. As envisioned by the league, tenant patrols would address the problem of youth crime and gangs with education, counseling, and job training measures, rather than with police patrol, security guards, and hardware.

Months after HUD rejected the proposal by the League to Improve the Community, the Public Housing Security Act measures were approved and the national agency implemented a more punitive version. Aware that young people disproportionately committed crime in and around housing projects and that young people in the nation's "problem projects" also suffered from an unemployment rate of 60 percent and above, the 1978 act mandated that public housing authorities share resources with the Department of Labor to train and place youth in crime-fighting and security positions. The idea was that by paying young residents to install hardware, landscape, help in maintaining and repairing buildings, and work in drug treatment and senior citizen programs, they could gain valuable skills and training in the field of crime prevention. This experience would eventually benefit the youth in the larger labor market, where law enforcement and criminal justice careers offered good job security. One housing authority used its demonstration grant to train youth in security hardware and to establish a small business to offer continued employment to program participants. At another housing project, a local community college worked with young residents to provide vocational training and partnered with unions to establish apprenticeship programs. Some of the youth who participated in the federal housing project security programs even received college credit for their community service contributions.[33]

The emphasis on grassroots involvement was in part a measure of necessity. The League to Improve the Community's demands echoed similar concerns among community organizations and resident advisory councils elsewhere about the planned influx of armed police officers and private security guards patrolling the hallways and corridors of housing projects. Aware that residents would be unreceptive to such measures, policymakers and planners created trained tenant patrols to join officers in deterring crime and vandalism. Urban police forces were undermanned and overtaxed anyway, and the tenant patrols promised to solve the twin problems of lack of adequate surveillance and lack of community involvement and participation in law enforcement. White House officials argued that their "people-oriented" approach could "have a greater, more cost-effective impact on crime prevention for the dollar" than would a full, top-down imposition. And residents would welcome tenant patrols as an alternative to the further encroachment of law enforcement officials and private security officers in their neighborhoods.[34]

Working together, law enforcement authorities, security guards, residents, and youth would enhance security at the housing project test sites using "team policing" techniques. Police officers and residents alike underwent special training. The Anti-Crime program stressed the need for "sensitivity workshops" for the police who patrolled the housing projects, so that officers would understand "social dynamics" in the dwellings and work more closely with management to contain crime. Housing authority officials also carefully screened the residents they employed for the patrol program, requiring them to submit to at least six weeks of training conducted by local law enforcement authorities. In Baltimore's Lafayette Courts and other housing projects that received funding from the Public Housing Security Act, the teams helped organize "floor watch" programs and intervened in moments of family crisis.[35] Mostly the tenant security forces and local police officers sat side-by-side in guard booths, rode the elevators together, and walked the hallways in pairs in order to maintain a consistent and omnipresent level of patrol.

To improve general communication between police departments and residents, new community centers inside housing projects served as police precinct substations and a base for the patrol teams. These units mirrored the police department outposts that the LEAA began implementing in housing projects and storefronts in the late 1960s, but the Urban Anti-Crime program introduced new security technologies into the centers' general operation to foster defensible space. In Baltimore, the Tenant Activity Center was established in a vacant building between Lafayette Courts and the Flag House Courts. It included a computer that connected to the electronic card access system, so that authorities could monitor residents as they entered and exited the premises. The center also provided a desk for the tenant and police patrols and provided radio equipment to keep the patrol teams connected to the staff at the center. So as not to operate solely as a crime control institution, welfare workers and volunteer ministers offered various social services to residents at the centers.[36]

Even though many White House officials shared the belief of Carter's domestic policy advisor David Rubenstein that "jobs for kids in this program are just as important as sensitively trained police in housing projects," their insights were not reflected in the way federal policymakers and housing authorities allocated funding for the Urban Anti-Crime program. In New Orleans, for example, the St. Thomas housing project received $1.2 million from Public Housing Security Act funds. Half went to physical security and modernization, $53,000 to community development, and $260,000 to programs that employed youth in the security field. A four-bedroom apartment in the St. Thomas project was converted into the Anti-Crime Program Center, where the resident council acting as the program advisory board met, and where the youths who were responsible for installing security hardware and working on improving the general facilities to create defensible space picked up their modest paychecks. In Detroit, the Jeffries Homes and the Douglass projects spent $1.3 million on physical security hardware; roughly half a million for youth employment opportunities that involved installing light fixtures, fences, and a new lobby control system; and just

$50,000 to fund the forty-person youth security patrol and pay the salary of the new Safety and Security Coordinator.[37]

The conditions of the Robert Taylor Homes in Chicago warranted the largest grant from the Department of Housing and Urban Development under the Public Housing Security Demonstration Act. In the summer of 1979, the Carter administration allocated $3.4 million to provide additional surveillance and security measures for the project, matched by an additional $2 million from the city of Chicago. Nearly $3 million of the investment went to hardware, half a million dollars for youth employment to install security measures and make repairs, and a quarter of a million dollars for tenant organizations. Even though the tenants who organized the League to Improve the Community had wanted to fund community programs in the Taylor Homes, the local housing authority decided instead to focus the program on the reconstruction of lobbies, the use of fences to secure courtyards, the installation of vandal-proof mailboxes, the creation of security outpost offices, and surveillance technologies in elevators. Tenants were hired as building security managers to monitor the lobbies and establish block watches and patrols while young residents worked as receptionists and security aides. The city supplemented these community-based patrols with a thirty-man police force to monitor tenants.[38] Using the "vertical policing" technique, which had been developed by the LEAA in the early 1970s, many of these officers simply rode up and down the elevators all day.

The federal "revitalization" programs implemented in rural towns and suburban communities during the Carter administration contrasted sharply with the measures policymakers introduced in the Robert Taylor Homes and other "problem projects" in low-income urban areas. In the same year when the last traces of Pruitt-Igoe disappeared from the St. Louis skyline, the National Association of Towns and Townships and the American Association of Small Cities opened up office headquarters in Washington.[39] These organizations, representing largely working and middle-class white constituencies who also suffered from inflation, economic stagnation, and budget shortages, lobbied successfully for a share of federal resources. Under Carter, the Department of Health, Education, and Welfare and the Department of Labor formulated an interagency agreement to build 300 rural health clinics and to train 500 local residents to staff them. Carter also offered $2.5 billion in water and sewer grants to small communities, supplementing improvements with job training programs for 1,750 rural Americans who participated in public works measures—a far broader employment program than the training in surveillance and security technologies that a smaller number of urban youth received. Fostering defensible space was the federal government's primary objective in segregated black urban communities, whereas in segregated white communities in smaller suburban and desolate areas, social welfare provisions and grassroots involvement proved to be more than a symbolic gesture.

Over time, law enforcement institutions and techniques infiltrated public housing developments and the lives of their residents as a result of the Urban Anti-Crime program. Living in a gated environment guarded by patrols in uniform, plainclothes guards, and resident security aides, tenants now interacted with law enforcement officers upon leaving and entering their own apartments on a daily basis, having to show identification and use several sets of keys to enter their own homes in some housing projects. The Department of Housing and Urban Development used the bulk of the $41 million budget granted by the Public Housing Security Demonstration Act to secure lobbies with electronic surveillance, to improve doors and locks with metal bars, and to augment public housing patrol forces by paying the salaries of law enforcement officials.[40]

By training low-income urban teenagers for careers in the law enforcement and security industries, Carter's punitive urban policy addressed high unemployment problems while attuning youth to crime control needs in their own communities. But, in a more insidious way, a measure framed as a means of empowerment—or a path out of poverty—was in fact enclosing these youth further inside the law enforcement apparatus and the carceral state. Installing security cameras in the playgrounds, lobbies, and corridors of their communities ultimately made young residents complicit, to a degree, in the general surveillance and social control of themselves and their families. The various surveillance practices that federal policymakers supported created new opportunities for apprehension that continued to filter already marginalized

Americans into the criminal justice system. Meanwhile, recreational facilities, health care services, and basic infrastructure continued to deteriorate. When planners surveyed residents in Baltimore's Lafayette Courts and the Flag House Courts asking whether or not the magnetic card strip readers, the team policing approach to patrol, and the defensible space measures had improved conditions in the projects, tenants in high- and low-rises alike agreed that their circumstances had worsened. Moreover, by 1982, after three years of the program, officials could not determine whether the Urban Anti-Crime program had a measurable impact on crime. The ultimate outcome of nearly all the programs national policymakers launched during the previous two decades of the crime war had similarly failed to reduce the problem in a meaningful way.[41]

URBAN FIRE

The long-term impact of the federal government's decision to manage urban problems by divesting from the War on Poverty and expanding the War on Crime was evident not only in the dynamite that demolished Pruitt-Igoe's fifty-seven acres but also in the flames that literally consumed the nation's cities from within. If large-scale urban civil disorder was a relic of the 1960s, the American cities that constituted the battlegrounds of the crime war continued to burn during the 1970s. In the South Bronx, vacant lots and the ashes of apartment buildings destroyed by fire were so prevalent that the landscape seemed to have been a literal battlefield. "The overall effect of driving through areas of the central and south Bronx is that of driving through Berlin shortly after the second World War," a researcher reported to Ford's domestic affairs advisor Jim Cannon in 1975. "Shell after shell of empty burned out buildings greets the eye, relieved here and there with empty lots, which are left after the buildings themselves have been completely demolished. An occasional packing case in which people are actually living punctuates this dreary landscape." While the South Bronx may have represented a more extreme case of the impact of poverty, abandonment, and fire, other neighborhoods in New York were burning, too—in Brownsville, Bushwick, and Bedford-Stuyvesant in Brooklyn; and in Harlem and the

Lower East Side in Manhattan. Businesses set some of the fires, reasoning that the prospect of collecting insurance money offered more promise than maintaining a business in an area of extreme poverty. Despairing residents, however, set most of the fires themselves, seeking thrills, relocation, and metal to sell.[42]

Astute observers of urban social trends saw the conflagration coming. As early as 1970, Daniel Patrick Moynihan mentioned the fire-setting phenomenon to President Nixon. For Moynihan, arson in "slum neighborhoods, primarily black," was linked to the "certain types of personalities which slums produce," and it paralleled general crime problems. *"Fires are in fact a 'leading indicator' of social pathology* for a neighborhood," Moynihan wrote Nixon. "They come first. Crime, and the rest, follows." Shortly after Moynihan penned his memo on the subject, the incidence of urban fires sharply rose and the federal government contracted with private firms to investigate the trend. With a $90,000 grant from the LEAA, the Aerospace Corporation's Arson Investigation Study determined that the property losses from arson amounted to $1.2 billion in 1974, compared with only $325 million in 1964. Almost immediately after the Aerospace Corporation report and the release of data sets from the National Fire Protection Association confirming its conclusions, the Senate Permanent Subcommittee on Investigations called a series of hearings to begin planning a federal fight against what was fast becoming a "nationwide epidemic."[43]

Fire characterized the urban landscape for the remainder of the decade. In declining cities, the Department of Justice declared in 1979 that arson had reached "near-plague proportions." In that year alone, police departments across the United States reported 13,000 deliberately set or suspicious fires, and estimated that young people set about a quarter of these fires, accounting for more than half of all arson cases in some jurisdictions. Urban fire setting had become the nation's fastest-growing major crime. Even as the LEAA under Jimmy Carter closed down offices, discharged employees, and prepared to cut off its law enforcement assistance to states, the Department of Justice made an "Arson Control Strategy" a top priority, and the LEAA launched a $4 million anti-arson program in 1979.[44] The effort to contain the urban firestorm was the agency's final battle.

Amid the rubble and abandoned buildings on Boston Road and Charlotte Avenue in the South Bronx, President Jimmy Carter takes a moment to speak to the press during his hour-long visit to the blighted area in October 1977. *Photograph by Dan Farrell. New York Daily News Archive, Getty Images*

In drawing Nixon's attention to urban fire setting in 1970, Moynihan argued that crime constituted a precondition for subsequent riots—which tended to be characterized by mass fire setting. "Fires in the black slums peak in July and August," Moynihan wrote. "The urban riots of 1964–1968 could be thought of as epidemic conditions of an endemic situation." And while the federal government did not confront any major incidents of urban civil disorder in the 1970s, that lull ended early in the new decade. The eruption of Miami's Liberty City housing project in May 1980 reopened familiar debates about pathology, poverty, crime, and decay that had inspired the launch of the War on Crime during the Johnson administration. While the urban uprisings of the mid-1960s seemed to call for a federal response in the form of the LEAA, the riot in Liberty City and the enduring marginalization of low-income black Americans seemed to fully justify the termination of the agency and the full integration of urban and crime control policy.[45]

The disorder in Liberty City began after an all-white jury acquitted four Miami police officers charged with the brutal death of black insurance agent, former Marine, and beloved Liberty City resident Arthur McDuffie during a routine traffic stop. Miami had an official black unemployment rate of 23 percent—some estimates placed it as high as 50 percent—and frequent drug raids and high levels of patrol made police brutality rampant. African American and West Indian residents turned their outrage into physical violence immediately after the McDuffie verdict on May 8, 1980. In an attempt to provide a constructive outlet for the community, black moderate political leaders called a silent vigil. The 5,000 residents who arrived to protest in front of the Miami Police Department courthouse were anything but silent, however, chanting "We want justice!" The militant turn of the vigil quickly spiraled out of control. Although Liberty City (nicknamed "Germ City" by its young residents for its high incidence of drug abuse and crime) bore the brunt of the damage from the riot, eruptions occurred in neighboring black communities of Brownsville, Overtown, and Coconut Grove.[46]

Unlike the more contained urban civil disorder in the 1960s, the Liberty City riot spread to white communities nearby and was extremely violent. While black-owned businesses were largely unaffected, the participants torched factories, clothing stores, and supermarkets along Northwest 54th Street—the central commercial district of the neighborhood—leaving most of its businesses virtually empty or completely destroyed. Bands of both black and white citizens hunted for residents to shoot, and some even mutilated and burned civilians. It took 3,600 National Guardsmen and the local police department four days and 800 arrests to halt the uprising.[47]

From the South Bronx to Liberty City, the fires in the epicenters of the War on Crime represented a material expression of the long-term impact of the punitive transformation of domestic policy, with Carter's presidency serving as a critical turning point. During the campaign and in the early years of his administration, Carter promised to restore confidence in the federal government and foreign affairs by stressing equity and human rights. He played up combating poverty in developing nations, reviving urban centers, preventing the spread of nuclear weapons, and solving international ruptures through diplomatic negotiation. His election gave many Americans hope that their quality of life would improve. And as a Southern Democrat committed to antidiscrimination and integration, and who recruited Patricia Harris to serve as the first African American woman in a cabinet position, Carter was a symbol of racial progress. But he was a Democrat of a different sort than Kennedy and Johnson. Uninterested in actively developing policies that would generate opportunities for poor and marginalized citizens, Carter emphasized instead "traditional" American values and the "common good." He abandoned the Keynesian policy of spending to combat the recession and turned instead to high interest rates and tax cuts. He combated the combined impact of unemployment and double-digit inflation by promoting economic restructuring based on a service economy, causing white unemployment rates to drop and black ones to rise. And he began to scale back from social welfare programs almost immediately on taking office.[48]

The Carter administration's response to the Liberty City uprising epitomized the larger shortcomings of his domestic urban policies. Roughly a month after order was restored, Carter attended a meeting with local leaders. His administration had continued to make broad cuts to domestic programs, and Carter informed the audience that he could not provide any new programs or federal investment for the devastated area but would "meet the community half-way" in any plans they devised to rebuild the riot-torn neighborhoods of the city. As the *Miami Times* reported, "The audience was almost speechless." When Carter left the conference hall, destined for Air Force One, black youth and Liberty City residents threw bottles and bricks at the president and his entourage.[49] In the end, most of the federal grant money Carter managed to provide benefited business owners, many of whom followed the lead of the retailers Sears, JC Penney, and Grand Way Supermarket: they left the riot area after the incident and never came back.[50]

To many of Carter's constituents, his laissez-faire attitude toward the Liberty City crisis was yet another example of the ways in which his policies—from deregulation to welfare retrenchment—had betrayed, rather than advanced, the progressive social changes of the postwar period. In hindsight, Carter's largely symbolic hour-long visit to the arson-riddled South Bronx in October 1977 was indicative of his failed promises and policy regressions. "When we saw the sadness in Jimmy Carter's face when he came to the Bronx," wrote the editors of New York City's African American daily the *Amsterdam News* in November 1979, "we believed him when he told us that he was going to see to it that something would be done. . . . We looked forward to real training and real jobs." Growing disenchantment among former supporters of the president, in the pages of the *Amsterdam News*, in the living rooms of recently laid-off citizens, and on Capitol Hill compelled Senator Edward Kennedy to challenge Carter in the 1980 Democratic primary. "We are instructed that the New Deal is old hat and that our best hope is no deal at all," Kennedy said of Carter, charging that the president had "left behind the best traditions of the Democratic Party."[51] Kennedy had a point: the Carter administration synthesized the approaches of his liberal and conservative predecessors and laid the groundwork for the Cold War and crime war policies of the Reagan administration.

In effect, Carter positioned Reagan to continue the drive toward privatization, the unprecedented growth of the military-industrial complex, and the rise of mass incarceration.[52] Rather than a sharp pivot away from the New Frontier and the Great Society as Kennedy and others implied in their critiques of Carter, Reagan's policies were more the outgrowth of a process that liberals themselves had developed within a broad bipartisan political consensus, involving the merger of social welfare and law enforcement programs and the deep commitment to crime control as a viable response to socioeconomic inequality and institutional racism.

Although Carter charged HUD with easing police-community tensions, empowering residents, and fostering greater safety, his federal law enforcement and security measures ended up doing something else entirely in Baltimore, Chicago, Miami, and other targeted cities. Carter's punitive urban policy fortified the projects and installed security equipment in such a way that made tenants more fearful and less safe. For example, when residents in Liberty City erupted in the spring of 1980, the Dade County Housing Authorities had just begun to put to use the $739,606 grant HUD had allocated to the city's Urban Anti-Crime program for Larchmont Gardens—a project in the riot area. A year after the uprising, in the summer of 1981, tenants in Larchmont Gardens became increasingly concerned about defensible space measures in the housing project. Residents wanted HUD to address much-needed plumbing repairs and rodent control, rather than the fences and the high-intensity outdoor lighting fixtures that federal policymakers hoped would improve security. And they regarded the tenant patrols as "little more than sophisticated baby sitting services," according to the Police Foundation's evaluation of the Larchmont Gardens program. Activities such as installing security screens, sweeping the lobbies, and answering phones in the housing project's police mini-station may have kept "at risk" youth occupied, but the work "provided little substance." As in Baltimore's Lafayette Courts and Chicago's Robert Taylor Homes, conditions at the Liberty City site continued to deteriorate despite the implementation of the Public Housing Security Act, and crime dramatically increased.[53] Supervision and omnipresent surveillance, however, had been successfully imposed.

In the context of widening inequality, frequent fire setting, and crime, prospects for low-income Americans living in Larchmont Gardens and other isolated and segregated communities seemed grim. "The fact is, that in many urban areas, there is no governance," Patricia Harris told the Urban League in 1977. "No one is meeting the needs of people who live there." The case of Pruitt-Igoe made clear to Harris and other HUD officials that the concentration of crime in federally funded public housing led residents to abandon their homes as quickly as possible, yet the Carter administration's Urban Anti-Crime program did little to address the problems Harris herself had identified. The guarding and gating of housing projects only perpetuated criminogenic dynamics and prompted residents to leave if they had the means to do so. Illicit and informal economies took over the units they left behind, and the presence of drug dealers and drug users produced more crime and vandalism in turn.[54] Narcotics trafficking and organized crime flourished in these deserted spaces, producing escalating violence that continued to drive residents out of public housing, either by moving truck or by hearse. Many of these facilities, like Pruitt-Igoe, were eventually deemed irredeemable and demolished as residents who lived in and around these dwellings faced another type of large-scale removal. As high-rise housing projects and the homes they once offered disappeared from the urban landscape during the Reagan era and beyond, young black women and men from urban areas continued to be funneled into the ever-expanding national prison system. After nearly two decades, federal policymakers' investment in the War on Crime had set the stage for the era of mass incarceration.

9

FROM THE WAR ON CRIME TO THE WAR ON DRUGS

When Ronald Reagan took office in 1981, he inherited the largest law enforcement system in the world, one that had been in development since the mid-1960s. In two decades, a bipartisan political consensus had modernized and expanded the carceral state, disinvesting from social welfare measures while escalating crime control and penal programs in response to the threat of collective violence. Reagan's "War on Drugs" marked the culmination of this long mobilization—a fight against crime that seemed to produce only more crime. Yet his national policies also marked a turning point with respect to the contours of poverty and institutionalized racism in America. The Reagan administration exacerbated the tendency within federal crime control programs to reinforce crime in the low-income African American communities that had been the main targets for punitive intervention, and as a result, the nation witnessed an explosion of urban violence and drug abuse.

Over the course of his political career, Reagan redefined notions of governmental accountability by refusing to enact policy that attempted to address unemployment, failing school systems, blighted housing conditions, and other historical inequalities. He was influenced by conservative think tanks such as the Heritage Foundation and the American Enterprise Institute that had emerged in the early 1970s in response to the social changes of the 1960s. As a base for neoconservative thinkers, many of whom—like Reagan—had once participated in left-wing movements and supported liberal causes, these institutions produced policy recommendations that came to echo earlier arguments against the War on Poverty, theorizing that domestic policies in the 1960s led to a decline in morality and defiance of traditional authority. New political opportunities opened for these conservative interests during the Carter administration, as Americans grew increasingly anxious about the decline of the U.S. economy and the crisis in American cities. Inflation made Republican tax principles, cuts in government social spending to encourage private investment, and reduced government regulation appealing to new sections of the white electorate.[1]

Reagan embraced the neoconservative policy platform during the 1980 presidential campaign and beyond, premising his domestic programs on the idea that the Great Society had contributed to the breakdown of familial, education, and religious institutions. Edward Banfield, Charles Murray, and other figures influenced the strategies federal policymakers developed for the War on Crime during the 1970s and provided the intellectual backbone of the "Reagan revolution" in the 1980s. These thinkers argued that "liberal language" had birthed the so-called underclass by preventing policymakers and the public from recognizing welfare as the source of poverty and the free market as its solvent. Charging that welfare encouraged dependency, laziness, and single motherhood, and that social programs were thus more harmful than helpful, Reagan acted upon the tradition that viewed community pathology as the root cause of crime. "Only our deep moral values and strong institutions can hold back that jungle and restrain the darker impulses of human nature," Reagan told the International Association of Chiefs of Police in the fall of 1981. His War on Drugs proceeded to support a whole new level of surveillance and law enforcement penetration into the urban "jungle" in order to preserve domestic tranquility for "traditional" Americans.[2] Reagan magnified the war at home by making the ongoing battle against urban street crime the foremost domestic concern of his White House.

Although the Reagan administration built upon the strategies its predecessors pursued for the War on Crime, including the militarization of local police forces, the criminalization of social programs, and mass incarceration, his administration made unique and important contributions in each of these areas. Reagan implemented some of the most draconian legislative proposals of Richard Nixon and Gerald Ford regarding domestic surveillance, the criminal code, and mandatory minimum sentences. He fought the War on Drugs by increasing the scale of the raids, stings, and tactical police units that had characterized the urban landscape from the Nixon administration onward. But he intensified such operations by creating new partnerships between domestic law enforcement and defense agencies.

Jimmy Carter had already begun to phase out the Law Enforcement Assistance Administration (LEAA), and the Reagan administration further centralized the national crime control program. Reagan and many other federal policymakers considered the LEAA among the long list of wasteful and inefficient national social programs. "Massive federal expenditures of the Great Society sort and not spending much time defining the problem is dead," Deputy Attorney General Stanley Morris declared when the Department of Justice shut down the LEAA in 1982.[3] The LEAA had already established the scaffolding of the modern carceral complex at the state level, and federal crime control programs remained extremely active in many American cities. With even stronger oversight over punitive urban social programs in the absence of the LEAA, national policymakers continued to actively shape law enforcement by working with local officials directly. This facilitated the ongoing merger of social services and crime control measures and stepped up the criminalization of welfare recipients and public housing tenants.

Meanwhile, the Reagan administration took policymakers' shared set of assumptions about race and crime and ran with them. Reagan led Congress in criminalizing drug users, especially African American drug users, by concentrating and stiffening penalties for the possession of the crystalline rock form of cocaine, known as "crack," rather than the crystallized methamphetamine that White House officials recognized was as much of a problem among low-income white Americans. The pathological understanding of black poverty and crime shared by the bipartisan consensus promoted racial profiling, prison overcrowding, and new discourses about "black youth gangs" during the 1980s that heightened the racial disparities within the American criminal justice system. When alarming numbers of African American men and women entered penal institutions as a result of the strategies that federal policymakers supported, the Supreme Court made it virtually impossible to challenge racial bias in the American law enforcement and criminal justice systems, most notably in the 1987 *McCleskey v. Kemp* ruling.

The inherent racism within the criminal justice system was difficult to ignore by the mid-1980s, however. During the War on Poverty, black Americans constituted roughly one third of the prison population. The War on Crime and the War on Drugs inflated their numbers to over half of those incarcerated in the American prison system, which expanded fivefold from 1965 to 1988. At just under 30 percent of the national population combined, two thirds of these inmates today are African American and Latino.[4] This staggering fact stemmed from the punitive transformation of domestic policy that was already in place, a socioeconomic and policy climate that Reagan stepped into and made even more destructive from the perspective of low-income urban Americans who were the policy's primary targets.

ARMING THE TROOPS

Democratic members of the pro-crime consensus worked alongside the Reagan administration to bring about a new level of militaristic policing in segregated urban neighborhoods and at the nation's borders, treating the War on Drugs as any other war. "Crime is a national defense problem," said Senator Joe Biden in 1982. "You're in as much jeopardy in the streets as you are from a Soviet missile." Oklahoma's congressman Glenn English further explained: "We in the Democratic Party realize that the war on drugs has to be fought like World War II—a complete and thorough effort, one dedicated to victory at any cost." Democrats went on to support Reagan's crime control legislation overwhelmingly, as they had supported such legislation since the Johnson administration. Senators Edward Kennedy and Biden introduced various bills that eventually led Congress to pass, by a 406–16 vote in the Democratic majority House, the Comprehensive Crime Control Act of 1984. The legislation marked the official beginning of the War on Drugs.[5]

Framing the federal crime control program as a drug control measure fostered new connections between the military and the Department of Justice, a partnership the Reagan administration had forged in the years leading up to the passage of the 1984 legislation. Immediately after Reagan's inauguration, White House officials set out to revise the Posse Comitatus Act of 1878, which prohibited military involvement in domestic crime control. Reagan's Military Cooperation with Civilian Law Enforcement Agencies Act passed at the end of his first year in office. It permitted defense agencies to provide local police forces access to weapons, intelligence, research, and military bases to improve drug interdiction efforts. Following the administration's lead, when Congress reauthorized the Department of Defense (DOD) in 1982, it expanded the Military Cooperation Act's definition of "indirect military involvement" to include the exchange of information, equipment, facilities, and manpower. The new authorization allowed the Navy to offer vessels to the Coast Guard and air surveillance assistance to local law enforcement, the Air Force to give information on sea and air traffic to police, and the Army to lend aircraft and helicopters to customs and the Drug Enforcement Agency (DEA).[6] Defense agencies would now share responsibilities with local law enforcement by land, air, and sea.

The extension of military power into domestic law enforcement primarily functioned to seal off the United States from "undesirable influences" within the rest of the Western Hemisphere. The LEAA had sponsored special equipment and training programs for local police officers administered by military forces following urban unrest in the 1960s, but the transnational scope of the War on Drugs required even closer collaborations between local authorities and the Army, the Navy, the Marines, and the Central Intelligence Agency (CIA). Building from the partnerships established by the Military Cooperation Act, Reagan directed Vice President George H. W. Bush to implement the border control dimension of the administration's law enforcement program. Early in 1982, Bush called the South Florida Task Force to coordinate all law enforcement and defense activities in the Miami area. A year later, Reagan expanded the program as the National Narcotics Border Interdiction System. Under Bush's direction, the interdiction system coordinated federal, state, and local law enforcement and defense resources in an international antidrug effort targeting Mexico and the Caribbean.[7]

With the militaristic turn in domestic law enforcement already underway and patrol at the nation's borders established, the administration led Congress in renewing the War on Drugs. Hailed by Reagan's attorney general William French Smith as "the most far-reaching and substantial reform of the criminal justice system in our history," the Comprehensive Crime Control Act of 1984 offered the first significant revision of the federal criminal code since the beginning of the century. In addition to reinstating the federal death penalty and obliterating the federal parole system, the legislation imposed many of the punitive strategies that Congress rejected during the Nixon and Ford administrations. Policymakers had questioned the constitutionality of the pretrial detention provisions that the DC Crime Control Act of 1970 contained. Fourteen years later, they introduced this practice in states and locales far outside the District and its African American majority, authorizing judges to indefinitely hold defendants deemed potential "dangers to the community" when setting bail via the Comprehensive Crime Control Act. The legislation also included the Armed Career Criminal Act, a combination of the two major crime control programs the Ford administration created. This section of the 1984 act required a mandatory minimum of five years in prison for any person who used a firearm in connection with a violent crime and a sentence of fifteen years to life for a third strike. As a result of these provisions combined, the average prison sentence increased 33 percent, from forty-six months in 1980 to sixty-one months in 1986.[8]

By implementing the most draconian elements of Nixon and Ford's discretionary programs on a national scale, the 1984 act transformed American policing. The legislation's forfeiture provisions permitted local law enforcement to seize as much as 90 percent of cash and property from accused drug dealers, which brought the federal government, local police departments, and civilian whistle blowers lucrative returns from the assets of drug dealers and other criminals. Nixon's Comprehensive Drug Abuse Prevention and Control Act of 1970 included a civil forfeiture clause, but the 1984 amendments allowed police departments to keep the majority of proceeds for themselves, leading to substantial budgetary increases in local law enforcement.

If state and local governments initially resisted the massive imposition on limited local resources to fight a war that eluded serious and violent crime, the promise of huge cash grants obtained through drug forfeitures subdued these views among many officials. After the legislation passed, gross receipts of all seizures increased from $100 million to over $1 billion within three years. Sharing the federal forfeiture surplus with state and local governments would advance the entire system and improve state-level investigations. As Vice President Bush said, "We can use the criminals' own property to help finance law enforcement." The LEAA was no longer needed.[9]

Much like the stings that the Ford administration supported a decade earlier, these forfeiture practices not only strongly resembled entrapment but made mass arrests possible. The small-scale stings of the earlier period led to the apprehension of hundreds of Americans. During the War on Drugs, the forfeiture practices led to the arrests of thousands more. Whereas 250 suspects were detained in Washington, DC's "Operation Got Ya Again" in 1976, in 1988 Miami police arrested 5,000 suspects in a single sting. Even if a suspect was released and acquitted on all charges, his or her property was still subject to forfeiture. Low-income citizens unable to secure adequate legal representation lost income, assets, and material goods that could never be recovered.[10]

Forfeiture seizures also created new ways for officers to engage in white-collar criminal activity. It is impossible to determine the extent to which "skimming from the top," or reporting only a portion, of confiscated property occurred (and continues to occur) among law enforcement authorities. But stories of those officers caught in the act have come to light. One of the most famous cases involved former Federal Bureau of Intelligence (FBI) undercover agent Dan Mitrione Jr., who stole more than ninety pounds of cocaine and accepted $850,000 in bribes and payoffs. The practice had grown so pervasive that police departments began conducting internal investigations and dismissing "bad apples" from forces in the early 1990s, such as the "Operation Big Spender" investigation the Los Angeles County Sheriff's Office conducted to weed out money scheming and corruption from within, ultimately convicting nineteen deputies.[11]

Federal policymakers recognized that states needed additional support to handle new prisoners, many of them arrested on drug charges, serving longer terms in already-overcrowded facilities. The 1984 legislation established a national clearinghouse at the Department of Justice to assist states in expanding penal institutions with block grants. During the Ford and Carter presidencies and Reagan's first term, the prison population at the state level ballooned from 204,000 inmates to 400,000. The cost of each new bed, ranging from $30,000 to $90,000, posed a strain on state governments, and federal policymakers needed to address that cost to accommodate for the increasingly punitive sentencing guidelines they implemented. Beyond the clearinghouse, federal policymakers looked to private industry to assume some of the responsibility for the expanding carceral state, spurring the launch of prisons for profit. Coinciding with the Comprehensive Crime Control Act, in 1984 the Corrections Corporation of America opened the nation's first private prison facility in Texas. It was the beginning of a new plane of American penality.[12] With parole eviscerated, new sentencing practices in place, local police forces profiting from federal forfeiture provisions, and public and private prison construction underway, by the end of Reagan's first term, the national government's two-decades-long War on Crime had been reborn as the War on Drugs.

PUNITIVE URBAN POLICY

The drug war loomed heavily over segregated urban neighborhoods that were already confronting extreme surveillance and poverty. With federal social programs focused on arresting drug users and dealers and patrolling the nation's borders, the Reagan administration proceeded to eliminate half a million families from the welfare rolls, 1 million Americans from food stamps, and 2.6 million children from school lunch programs. "In the inner cities today, families, as we've always thought of them, are not even being formed," Reagan said in a 1986 radio address to the nation. "We're in danger of creating a permanent culture of poverty as inescapable as any chain or bond; a second and separate America, an America of lost dreams and stunted lives." Like his intellectual and political forebears, Reagan believed block grants were the best way to address the "culture of poverty." He reinvigorated the New Federalism that had steered domestic spending during the Nixon administration by introducing nine new block grant programs in his 1982 budget. Earlier forms of block grants had increased federal spending on social programs, however, and particularly in the law enforcement realm. Reagan's version *reduced* the amount of funding the national government granted to the states for general purposes and resulted in less federal accountability and oversight. Congress enthusiastically supported this policy, consolidating fifty-seven programs and terminating sixty-two more to reduce spending on social programs by 12 percent from previous levels via the Omnibus Reconciliation Act of 1981. Since Reagan's block grant program failed to take inflation into account, the legislation created an even greater loss of public assistance for American families in need. As a result, the number of Americans living below the poverty line drastically increased on Reagan's watch, from about 26 million in 1979 to 33 million in 1988. Homelessness, too, emerged as a major new national problem.[13]

By casting his retrenchment from domestic programs as part of his larger commitment to preserving traditional American values in the face of outside influences—be they social welfare provisions or the "underclass" itself—Reagan believed he had effectively ushered in a "renewal of our fundamental beliefs and values as a nation."[14] Ironically, although he gained popularity by pledging to fight big government, Reagan's revival of the fight against the USSR's "evil empire" sponsored the largest military buildup in the history of the United States. As the administration continued to cut federal spending on domestic programs, seeking instead private solutions to socioeconomic inequality, it wasted billions of dollars on a "Star Wars" space-based system to intercept enemy missiles under the Strategic Defense Initiative. The decision to invest in aerospace, defense, and local law enforcement at the direct expense of the most isolated and marginalized Americans exacerbated the many inequalities already in place.

With poverty and unemployment at an all-time high in the context of Reagan's Cold War, the emergence of crack in the streets and public housing projects of "high crime" urban neighborhoods was a tragic expression of the cumulative impact of twenty years of disinvestment, neglect, and overpolicing. Crack use became visible to policymakers and the public in the same year that the Comprehensive Crime Control Act of 1984 passed, when income inequality had returned to higher levels than the nation experienced before World War II. Despite the merger of defense and local law enforcement agencies and the ongoing drug war battles at the nation's borders, the administration had not succeeded in curtailing the international trade and production of narcotics. Instead, military involvement seemed to stimulate this economy. Cocaine imports increased by 50 percent between 1982 and 1984, when sixty-three tons of cocaine entered the United States despite the efforts of Vice President Bush's Interdiction System, and the price of the drug fell accordingly. As a result, cocaine became more available and more affordable in the United States.[15]

In blighted urban landscapes undergoing plant closures, deteriorated and abandoned buildings made ideal spaces for crack dealers, who set up twenty-four-hour centers for consumption, sales, and distribution. The problem was concentrated in housing projects especially, where, nearly a decade prior, Carter had launched his multimillion-dollar defensible space design for public housing. One resident of New York's Winbrook complex described living conditions in the housing project where drug sales flourished: "At night, when people are trying to rest, hallways are being used for smoking crack, stairwells are being slept in, elevators are being mutilated with people using them for personal bathrooms. . . . There are brand new doors that have been put on that have been taken off." Officials estimated that 97,000 young people under the age of sixteen used crack heavily in New York state, the majority of whom lived in public housing. Federal policymakers ignored the socioeconomic milieu that gave rise to crack abuse, viewing it instead as the root cause of violence in the inner city, the decay of housing projects, and the rise of urban gangs employing highly sophisticated weapons.[16]

Continuing the policy path Nixon, Ford, and Carter pursued during the 1970s, Reagan responded to the devastating impact of unemployment and urban divestment as it materialized in crack abuse by attacking social welfare programs and replacing them with punitive ones that targeted racially marginalized Americans. The Anti–Drug Abuse Act of 1986, or the "Drug Free America Act," as Reagan called it, doubled the already unprecedented level of funding Congress allocated to domestic crime and drug control programs during the president's first term and tripled drug enforcement resources so that national expenditures on criminal justice reached a record high of nearly $3.5 billion. Reagan placed the issue of narcotics treatment and education at the center of his "national crusade against drugs" when he spoke to the American public, and Nancy Reagan's "Just Say No" campaign had left its mark on public school curriculums. The title of the legislation itself implied its programs would emphasize treatment and rehabilitation. But in practice, and in the tradition of federal law enforcement programs since the Johnson administration, the $900 million allocated by Congress for drug abuse programs during Reagan's presidency went mostly for the purchase of helicopters, airplanes, and intelligence-gathering facilities.[17]

Complementing the new scale of investment into the militarization of American police, Congress included mandatory minimum sentences for "offenses involving one hundred grams of heroin, five hundred grams of cocaine or five grams of cocaine freebase known as crack," among twenty-nine other mandatory minimum sentences stipulated by the Anti–Drug Abuse Act of 1986. As drug-related arrests surged, the disproportionate number of black Americans who abused crack rather than powdered cocaine rendered the law virtual "apartheid sentencing." With the War on Drugs in full swing and focused on the problem in segregated urban areas, in 1986 *Time Magazine* anointed the crack phenomenon the "issue of the year" and *Newsweek* called it "an authentic national crisis."[18]

Yet the massive amount of political and public support Reagan's drug crusade received was not based upon an actual shift in drug use. Instead, the perception of drug addiction as a major domestic problem arose from extensive news coverage of "crackheads" that evoked long-held associations between black Americans and crime and rationalized the racial discrepancies within the American criminal justice system. Although Reagan pledged to aim his drug crusade at major kingpins, in practice and due in large part to the structures already in place, the War on Drugs led to the mass incarceration of black and Latino men, who constituted as much as 90 percent of new inmates for drug offenses in many states. And despite the fact that white citizens account for roughly 70 percent of all monthly drug users and 65 percent of drug abuse arrests, and that white high school seniors reported a significantly higher rate of drug use than their African American counterparts between 1979 and 2000, black citizens remain two-thirds of prisoners serving time for drug possession.[19]

Federal policymakers imposed the War on Drugs as a local priority by tying federal grants to drug-related arrests and offering patrol officers training in narcotics investigations to enhance their ability make those arrests. Discretionary law enforcement assistance had been measured by arrest rates during the era of the War on Crime, and most of this funding went to urban areas. Beginning in the 1980s, police departments across the United States received special drug control grants. In the predominately white rural area of Jackson Country, Wisconsin, for example, local law enforcement quadrupled their federal subsidy by quadrupling the number of drug-related apprehensions.[20]

Even though federal policymakers had dissolved the LEAA earlier in the decade, crime control programs continued in its image with an extraordinary scale of funds at their disposal. Federal policymakers increased FBI funding more than fourfold (from $86 million in 1981 to $181 million in 1991), generously expanded the DEA (from a budget of $86 million to more than $100 million), enlarged antidrug allocation for the DOD (from $33 million to more than $100 million), and increased the U.S. Bureau of Prisons by 30 percent.[21] With even greater discretion and less congressional oversight in the absence of the LEAA, the FBI, the DEA, and the DOD would together serve as the grantmaking arm of the national law enforcement program.

The demise of the LEAA did not end crime control planning at the federal level, but instead allowed the Reagan administration to form crime control boards and committees as an alternative to major bureaucratic institutions. In 1987, Reagan convened a National Drug Policy Board by executive order. Chaired by Attorney General Ed Meese, who was the former White House counselor during Reagan's first term, the board brought together the secretaries of Defense, State, Housing and Urban Development, Labor, and Education; the CIA director; the national security advisor; and other relevant cabinet officials and consultants to coordinate all activities concerning public safety needs. The consolidation of control over local law enforcement policy at the national level meant that the small group of men on the policy board made critical decisions from their leather armchairs in the meeting rooms of the White House that would play out in the lives of millions of Americans, low-income black and Latino Americans in particular.[22]

To implement the Reagan administration's strategies nationwide and coordinate the activities of criminal justice, law enforcement, and military officials at all levels of government, White House officials created Drug Policy Boards, chaired by U.S. attorneys, in every judicial district. In a marked retreat from the federal government's approach to social policy in the 1960s, the board was prohibited from awarding "restrictive categorical grants" or "attaching conditions to Federal grants that are unrelated to the purpose of the grants; detracting from the administration's zero tolerance policy; and establishing highly prescriptive and burdensome requirements."[23] Although this approach allowed state and local governments to design their own drug control programs, the board had the power to closely evaluate these programs to ensure they followed the general objectives of the War on Drugs and the policing strategies federal policymakers believed would fight that war effectively.

As the federal body responsible for designing and overseeing national punitive programs, the Drug Policy Board carried forth some of the Reagan administration's most controversial directives with respect to crime control and drug enforcement, developing the policies that would go on to inform the Omnibus Anti–Drug Abuse Act of 1988. "I join the Chairman in emphasizing that we cannot tolerate criminals who violate our borders, terrorize our communities, or poison our citizens," Reagan announced when he received the board's first annual report from Meese to great media fanfare in June 1988. "Likewise, we cannot tolerate drug users who provide the illegal market for the drugs or who benefit from the taxpayers' generosity through Federal grants, contracts, or loans." The board recommended greater accountability for these drug users by encouraging drug testing programs in public and private workplaces and making federal student loans "conditional upon a college's adopting an effective anti-drug program," and withdrawing federal student aid from those convicted of drug offenses.[24] The 1988 legislation went on to require mandatory drug testing for all federal employees and forbid drug users federal grants or assistance. Following the board's suggestions, the programs of the War on Drugs would shape every facet of American life within their reach.

Carter had rendered all urban policy as punitive policy, and the Drug Policy Board addressed social welfare programs accordingly. Indeed, as it evolved during the Reagan administration, antidrug policy forged even stronger linkages between social welfare and crime control programs, expanding general surveillance and the carceral state in the process. The Anti–Drug Abuse Act of 1988 institutionalized the recommendations of the Drug Policy Board by requiring that public housing projects remain drug free, and included provisions to terminate the lease of public housing tenants who abused narcotics. Previous programs that increased patrol and surveillance in public housing areas, from the "defensible space" initiatives of the Nixon and Ford administrations to Carter's Urban Anti-Crime program, criminalized racially marginalized communities. Now, under the terms of the 1988 policy, any tenant who engaged in illegal activity in the vicinity of a public housing site could be evicted, and any person convicted of a drug offense would be permanently eliminated from all federal benefits.

Rhetorically, the Reagan administration fought its domestic social war to "crack down on the drug users—from the kid on the street to the beautiful people in Beverly Hills," as Bush promised in Connecticut early in his presidential bid. But the terms of the 1988 act concentrated resources on the former "high-risk" user. Given the reported extent of adolescent drug abuse, the Office of Juvenile Justice and Delinquency Prevention (one of the remaining vestiges of the national law enforcement program during the Nixon and Ford years) worked so that the federal government would "specifically designate 'high risk youth' as a primary target group" in its Anti–Drug Abuse Act. The cabinet-level Drug Policy Board also shared the Department of Justice's priority, seeking to foster "the commitment of resources targeted at high-risk youth (defined as children from low-income households, runaways, drop-outs, products of dysfunctional families, and juveniles in the criminal justice system) through joint public-private job opportunities and educational assistance programs." For the Reagan administration and Congress, the drug trade and drug traffickers placed America "under siege," and the president believed the legislation and its focus on "high-risk youth" gave law enforcement officials "just the weapons they need to fight an effective war."[25]

Reagan comfortably signed the Anti–Drug Abuse Act of 1988 ten days after his vice president won the presidential election, knowing that the direction of federal law enforcement programs would carry forth his legacy. During his presidential campaign, which had placed a critique of prison furlough programs and the image of black convicts front and center, Bush looked toward innovative new ways to expand the nation's carceral institutions while cutting the cost of imprisonment. Worried about the severe problem of prison overcrowding, Bush endorsed lease-purchase arrangements, whereby private firms built correctional facilities and leased them back to the federal government in the long term. "This approach would enable us to bring new institutions into operation much more quickly and would allow the government involved to spread out its acquisition costs over 20 or 30 years," Bush wrote hopefully in a memorandum. To house new offenders entering correctional institutions without further straining state resources, the Anti–Drug Abuse Act proposed using civil property seized in forfeitures to fund prison construction.[26] With reported rates of crime decreasing amid Bush's expansion and privatization plans, the explosion in prison populations during the 1990s did not reflect actual crime. Mass incarceration and the justice disparities that supported it reflected legal changes, crime control investments, and punitive strategies at all levels of government. If the national law enforcement program did not survive from its own logic during the War on Crime, by the time Bush took office, the carceral state had become undeniably self-perpetuating.

REMAKING BLACK CRIMINALITY

African American youth remained the foremost target of national law enforcement strategies during the Reagan administration, just as they had been ever since Johnson called the War on Crime in 1965. But Reagan intensified the coordinated assault on black youth gangs during the War on Drugs. Kennedy's antidelinquency measures included gang outreach programs, the Juvenile Justice and Delinquency Prevention Act of 1974 moved to institutionalize gang members and potential gang members, and the impetus behind Ford's Career Criminal and Concentrated Urban Law Enforcement programs was the intent to remove gang members from their communities. All of these attempts to fight gang violence only worsened the problem. In the era of the War on Drugs, gang members operated sophisticated crime networks and carried Uzis, Mac-10 machine guns, and semiautomatic rifles. The days of Molotov cocktails, fist fights, and Saturday Night Specials were of the previous period.[27]

Federal officials and law enforcement authorities understood the gang problem not as the consequence of failing urban public schools, unemployment, poverty, and the frequent encounters with police officers that came with those conditions, but as the result of permissive legal sanctions. "Young gang members arrested by law enforcement, if convicted, receive light sentences—especially for first offenses," the California Attorney General's Office concluded. "These factors make it difficult for young people to say no to becoming a gang member."[28] The solution lay in creating even more opportunities for law enforcement authorities to arrest gang members and sentencing guidelines that would ensure long stays in prison as a deterrent tactic.

Following the passage of Reagan's Anti–Drug Abuse Act and in line with this deterrent theory, in late 1988 the California state legislature targeted African American and Chicano residents with a series of penal code revisions. Gang violence in Los Angeles had proliferated in a policy climate of punitiveness and austerity: the number of reported gang homicides increased 87 percent between 1986 and 1987, averaging the loss of two lives a day.[29] California's Street Terrorism and Enforcement Prevention (STEP) Act of 1988 made participation in a street gang a criminal offense. Under the terms of this new criminal sanction, anyone who "willfully promoted or assisted" in any criminal activity with any gang member could be sent to state prison. Complementing the STEP provision, the legislature doubled the mandatory minimum sentence for those convicted of the sale or transportation of drugs to 100 days in the county jail. And, in an attempt to cut down on gang members who "tagged" public structures with graffiti, state representatives made it a crime to sell a spray paint container under six ounces to a minor and attached a penalty of $1,000, six months in jail, or both.[30]

With the STEP provision and penal reforms in place, police forces were expected to identify and arrest as many gang members as possible throughout the state. In Los Angeles the police department's Community Resources Against Street Hoodlums (CRASH) force delivered on this expectation by perfecting the art of mass arrests. Police Chief Daryl Gates formed the unit just as the national juvenile justice system was getting off the ground in the mid-1970s to fight the rising problem of gang violence in South and East Los Angeles and "return the streets to the citizens," in the words of CRASH lieutenant Bruce Hagerty. The series of police sweeps the force conducted reached their height in the spring of 1988, when 1,000 officers swept through South Central in a caravan of patrol cars on a Friday night and made another round of sweeps the next day. More than 1,400 predominately black residents faced arrest for traffic citations, parking fines, curfew violations, outstanding warrants, "gang-related behaviors," and drunk driving in the largest mass arrest in the city since the Watts uprising of 1965. In order to avoid further straining the county jails, the officers booked suspects in mobile units across the street from Memorial Coliseum.[31]

Mass arrests ensured that young residents in targeted communities would be in constant contact with crime control and penal institutions. The police classified more than half of the suspects as gang members but filed charges against only thirty-two of the residents. The sweep merely established and extended criminal justice records for the other 1,421 detainees. Law enforcement authorities claimed that Operation Hammer had substantially reduced the gang problem, and mass arrests on random weekends persisted in South Central and spread to San Fernando Valley, although subsequent sweeps involved a smaller force of 100 to 200 officers. The last major episode in Operation Hammer occurred one August weekend in 1989, when the CRASH force arrested 352 suspects in South Central after a fifty-six-year-old woman was injured during a drive-by shooting.[32]

Los Angeles Police Department officers representing the Community Resources Against Street Hoodlums (CRASH) unit bring arrested residents to headquarters after a routine antigang sweep in June 1988. *Photograph by Jean-Marc Giboux/Liaison. Hulton Archive, Getty Images*

As support for Operation Hammer waned in the face of critique and controversy, the Los Angeles Police Department quickly revived the concept of "defensible space" that emerged during the Nixon administration and that Carter implemented widely in his urban policy programs. Law enforcement authorities erected roadblocks, sawhorses, and concrete barriers in black "high-crime" neighborhoods in an attempt to monitor and restrict the everyday activities of residents. Working directly with William Bennett, Reagan's former secretary of education and President Bush's director of the Office of Drug Control Policy, the Los Angeles Police Department initiated the most substantial defensible space program in 1990, called "Operation Cul de Sac." The city hoped to prevent gang members from selling drugs by putting up permanent barricades to create an "artificial community." The resulting carceral environment blocked off streets from nonresidents and provided officers the means to easily occupy a neighborhood should circumstances require additional security. The department erected barricades in a dozen neighborhoods, the largest of which stood across the street from Jefferson High School in South Central's apex.[33]

The Cul de Sac measure effectively enhanced the ongoing criminalization of urban space and urban residents. As the *Los Angeles Sentinel* observed, the measure "automatically associates all teen-age youth in the barricaded zone with [criminal] activity." The heightened presence of patrol meant that officers could tell residents relaxing on their porches to go inside their homes. The roadblocks meant that residents were more likely to get pulled over and arrested by stationed officers if they aroused any suspicion, and they prevented emergency vehicles from entering the area in the event of a serious injury. The general level of surveillance "defensible space" fostered in this form meant that if residents planned a gathering, they ran the risk of having it broken up by the police. "This just allows the police to do whatever they want here. We have to answer their questions and submit to the harassment whether or not we are in a gang. It is all legal," an African American youth living in the barricaded area remarked of the living environment the program created. Local law enforcement authorities claimed that Operation Cul de Sac had brought drive-bys down by 86 percent, and the police department and the federal government moved to make permanent barriers in Miami, Phoenix, Washington, DC, Chicago, and other communities where drug transactions were frequently reported, regardless of how residents in those communities responded to such intrusions.[34]

When historic numbers of racially marginalized citizens came under penal supervision in the mid-1980s as a result of Operation Cul de Sac, state-level initiatives like STEP, and the strategies developed by the Drug Policy Board, the Supreme Court made it impossible to challenge the inherent racism in American crime control practices. During the Reagan administration, the Court emerged as "a loyal foot soldier in the Executive's fight against crime," as Justice John Paul Stevens noted. Indeed, in the punitive policy milieu of the 1980s, the Supreme Court not only compromised the Fourth Amendment by upholding the constitutionality of a number of unreasonable searches and seizures, but it defended racial bias in the law enforcement and criminal justice systems.[35]

The Supreme Court's ruling in 1987's *McCleskey v. Kemp* declared targeted racial profiling acceptable for the sake of public safety. Sentenced to the death penalty for killing a white Atlanta police officer, Warren McCleskey appealed on the grounds that the all-white jury administered the verdict in a racially discriminatory manner. The Court upheld McCleskey's sentence. "If we accepted McCleskey's claim that racial bias has impermissibly tainted the capital sentencing decision," the majority opinion stated, "we could soon be faced with similar claims as to other types of penalty." The alarming statistics McCleskey's lawyers produced on racial discrepancies in Georgia sentencing failed to persuade the Court. "In order to successfully challenge racial bias in the criminal justice process, offenders would need to prove that discretion had been abused or that law enforcement enacted or maintained a statute because of an anticipated racially discriminatory effect." Discrimination was simply a regrettable but inevitable consequence of the everyday functioning of the criminal justice and law enforcement systems, the Court reasoned. Racial profiling in all aspects of the criminal justice system seemingly responded to realities on the ground, and thus enabled authorities to effectively enforce the law and promote public safety.[36]

In the era of "multiculturalism," when many Americans believed that civil rights gains had solved historical inequality, the Supreme Court tacitly endorsed the assumptions about race and crime that had undergirded law enforcement practices immediately following Emancipation and that had become national policy at the height of the civil rights movement. Courts immediately used the *McCleskey* precedent to absolve the system from charges of racial discrimination in crack sentencing laws. And in upholding principles of broad police discretion, the ruling made local law enforcement comfortable to engage in rampant racial profiling. Following the precedent set by the *McCleskey* ruling, the Supreme Court went on to uphold the practice of turning a routine traffic stop into an opportunity to conduct a drug search in 1991's *Florida v. Bostick* and 1996's *Ohio v. Robinette*. The Court ruled that the reason police stopped motorists was insignificant as long as an actual traffic violation occurred. Federal officials began actively encouraging local law enforcement to manipulate consent from reluctant drivers, known as a "pretext" stop, as a strategy to fight the drug war from the outset.

In 1984, the DEA launched "Operation Pipeline" to provide officers training in using pretext stops effectively. The program flourished after the Supreme Court endorsed the practice, training 25,000 officers in forty-eight states over a fifteen-year period.[37]

With the racism in police discretion nearly impossible to challenge or prove, law enforcement authorities became comfortable to overtly encourage racial profiling as a strategy to prevent future crime and apprehend suspects. A confidential handbook distributed by the California Attorney General's Office entitled "Crips & Bloods Street Gangs" from 1988 provides a rare window into the systemic dimensions of racism within police departments. With input from Department of Justice officials, "Crips & Bloods Street Gangs" provided law enforcement officers strategies to identify, arrest, and "deal with" members of the Crips and Bloods—"the most notorious black street gangs in California."[38] Gang violence had certainly surged since Crips, Bloods, and other organized youth groups formed in the late 1960s and early 1970s, and in many ways law enforcement authorities embraced the type of profiling the California Attorney General's Office promoted as their only available means to promote public safety. But in doing so, law enforcement authorities justified a type of police discretion that associated virtually all African American men in California and elsewhere, as well as their romantic partners and their families, as potential gang members or criminals.

The "typical profile characteristics" of Crip and Blood members met only two basic criteria for the California attorney general: they were black men between the ages of thirteen and forty years old. More specifically, they tended to have "very egocentric personalities," shown by an individual member's "womanizing" and tendency to "[brag] about his very successful business dealings." Beyond sporting red or blue clothing and accessories to signify their group affiliation, gang members wore "heavy gold chains, national sports team shirts, brand name jogging suits, British Knights tennis shoes, and pagers." However, since the Crips and Bloods had become attuned to the fact that law enforcement authorities profiled them in this manner, members "began to turn in their designer jogging suits for a more neutral look to fit in with society."[39] Thus, regardless of whether he dressed in the brands and colors associated with gang activity, any African American man could be a suspected gang member.

The California Attorney General's Office warned that at airports, in another attempt to "throw off law enforcement authorities," gang members "have not been dressing in gang attire." Any African American traveler could then "fit the profile" of a gang member. This profiling included his traveling companions. The Attorney General's Office advised:

> If a gang member uses airline transportation, he is normally accompanied by a female. The gang member is usually black and the woman is often white. If law enforcement officials stop a gang member for questioning, many times they will not suspect that the white female is with him. The female is typically used to carry the cocaine and the money. This tactic has been used to deceive law enforcement officials nationwide.

Evoking the language and ideas that grounded Jim Crow–era legal sanctions against miscegenation, the California Attorney General's Office gave authorities license to stop and question any black man traveling with a white woman—a profiling that coincided with a marked rise in interracial marriages in the United States. In addition to inviting law enforcement to stop, interrogate, and search black men and white women who appeared to be romantically involved, the attorney general's instructions rendered African American families suspect, whether they traveled by plane or by car. "It is common to see two adult gang members and a juvenile gang member riding together," California Department of Justice officials wrote. Any father with another adult and his child outside of the home then fit the description of a criminal.[40]

Finally, the California Attorney General's Office flagged African Americans who responded willingly and calmly to police interrogations as potential gang members. During routine traffic stop situations, the California Department of Justice advised officers to check to see if the driver or occupants had placed their hands out of the window, or on the dashboard or windshield. "Because many gang members have frequent encounters with law enforcement in the Los Angeles area," the authors recognized, "gang members typically react this way."[41] Given the extensive and all-too-often aggressive policing of black neighborhoods, experience may have taught residents that cooperating with police would prevent the encounter from escalating into violence. For law enforcement authorities, this action signaled that seemingly law abiding citizens were likely to be, in fact, criminals. The rendering of black citizens as suspect, regardless of their class status, had characterized American policing since Emancipation. Now, under the shield of statistical "truth" that grounded widespread assumptions about race and criminality and the Supreme Court's refusal to accept criminal justice racism as fact, members of law enforcement had the license to exercise their discretion to stop, question, harass, and detain any and every person whom they suspected of being a gang member, as they saw fit.

Under the broad terms of the "Crips & Bloods" handbook and other profiling measures state and federal officials developed to suppress criminal activity, CRASH units often resorted to strategies that exacerbated community warfare. Just as the FBI's Counter-Intelligence Program (COINTELPRO) exploited ideological rifts among black radicals in the late 1960s and early 1970s, CRASH teams provoked disputes between rival gangs. The officers encouraged Crip sets to walk on the street openly armed so members could be easily arrested. They used incarceration as a threat to reap information in exchange for law enforcement favors. And they resorted to driving members to enemy neighborhoods and yelling "Crip" to create an opportunity for a street battle.[42] The War on Crime and crime itself had always mutually reinforced one another, and now the relationship between the paramilitary urban gangs and the antigang police forces had emerged as mutually reinforcing.

Much like the way in which Detroiters responded to the surveillance and violent consequences of the Stop the Robberies, Enjoy Safe Streets (STRESS) force in 1972, black residents and mainstream civil rights organizations spoke out against the devastating impact of CRASH patrol and the antidrug sweeps. Community members recognized what the California Attorney General's Office made clear in its 1988 handbook: that such programs promoted racist law enforcement practices by encouraging officers to act on the assumption that all black men in low-income neighborhoods in Los Angeles fit the "gang profile." Because most of the residents who were rounded up, assaulted, and arrested during Operation Hammer and similar campaigns never served prison or jail time, the program seemed to have little point other than meeting arrest quotas and making future convictions more likely by establishing criminal records. "Those youngsters know you can't put them all in jail," Charles Norman, the director of Los Angeles's Community Youth Gang Services remarked of the sweeps. "And when they go in the jail, they come back a little meaner and a lot tougher, and the problem just gets worse."[43] Regardless of whether programs like Operation Hammer effectively contained the problem of violence in segregated urban communities—an issue that only spread in the decade after gangs and drugs emerged as major national issues—mass arrests ensured that young residents in targeted communities would be in constant contact with crime control and penal institutions. And that they would most likely serve long sentences in prison.

If the Los Angeles CRASH force came to resemble a gang in itself, elsewhere police officers assumed the role of drug dealers—mirroring the mobsters that local police and federal agents played in the Ford-era stings. In Southeast Florida, where Vice President Bush's interdiction system battled drug traffickers, the sheriff's offices in Broward and Polk Counties manufactured and distributed their own crack supply. On the seventh floor of the county courthouse, the Broward Sheriff's Office used 2.2 pounds of powered cocaine obtained via seizure to produce $20,000 worth of street-value crack. Within two months, the department made some 2,300 arrests by dealing its own drug. In Polk County, the Sheriff's Office manufactured eleven ounces of crack to compensate for the insufficient supply it obtained during seizures and arrest sweeps. Responding to charges of entrapment, Polk County spokesman Con Dougherty concluded, "These are people who went out on the streets to buy crack. They're addicts."[44] A number of cases had been dismissed due to the possession of bogus crack, and law enforcement theory held that if police departments themselves made the drug, district attorneys could better prosecute users.

Although the Cleveland Police Department did not produce its own crack, it encouraged undercover drug dealers to operate in black neighborhoods. Recalling the controversial tactical police units and fencing decoys launched during the Nixon and Ford era, undercover operations in Cleveland and elsewhere partially funded by crime control grants were key to sustaining and creating criminal networks. One informant testified before a federal grand jury that he made more than half a million dollars in drug sales and returned all of the money to the Cleveland Police Department, which funneled the cash into a larger sting operation.[45] Encouraged by the lofty "zero tolerance" goals of Reagan's drug war, urban law enforcement agencies resorted to extreme measures to achieve results. No matter if this involved producing and distributing drugs to fight a war on drugs. The purpose was to identify and eventually confine African American drug users and criminals by any means necessary.

The citizens of Los Angeles confronted the largest incident of urban civil disorder in the twentieth century in April 1992, when residents burned, cleaned out businesses, and attacked civilians in the punitive milieu that had developed since the Watts uprising in 1965. Imagine if public institutions responded to the request for jobs, recreational facilities, and improved schools and housing that twenty local gang leaders demanded when they met with the Los Angeles County Board of Supervisors back in 1974—just after Congress passed the Juvenile Justice and Delinquency Prevention Act.[46] Thereafter, the majority of federal grants for low-income youth focused on juvenile detention facilities, security hardware, and social programs staffed by police officers rather than the vocational and educational opportunities the leaders of the Crips and Bloods wanted. The federal government's resistance to these types of socioeconomic solutions between 1965 and 1992 informs the question of the purpose the national crime control program and the mass incarceration it spawned might have ultimately served.

What is remarkable about the Youth Service Bureaus, the STRESS unit, and the criminal enterprises the federal government supported like Operation Sting, the Career Criminal Program, and the CRASH squad, among many other programs, is that their lack of success and the violence and crime they advanced seemed fundamentally irrelevant to national, state, and local policymakers in their relentless drive to police urban space and eventually entire populations of young men of color inside prison walls. State-sanctioned violence is often seen as a response to crime, but in the case of the federal government and the urban police forces that it modernized, it should be understood as preemptive. By acting on *potential* crime in the various patrol and surveillance programs that received widespread implementation in designated urban areas, and by manufacturing crime in order to fight crime in decoy and sting operations, the strategies policymakers adopted for the national law enforcement program unleashed self-perpetuating forces that converged in the mass incarceration of American citizens. Stemming from the continuous expansion of the carceral state, these forces continue to compromise the democratic values of equality and liberty, and the principle of freedom and justice for all.

EPILOGUE

Reckoning with the War on Crime

The punitive transformation of domestic policy in the late twentieth-century United States followed a historical pattern. In the shadow of Emancipation, national policymakers stopped at the extension of formal equality, and instead, new criminal laws and penal systems emerged in the form of Black Codes and convict leasing. The systematic criminalization and incarceration of newly freed people and their descendants shaped local and state law enforcement practices from the beginnings of Reconstruction in 1865 until the start of the War on Crime in 1965. After the dismantling of Jim Crow, as militarized police forces and a criminal justice apparatus capable of sustaining a new threshold of prisoners took hold, the developments of the earlier period matured into a markedly different approach to social control and state authority.

Merging equal opportunity and crime control programs within the Great Society satisfied federal policymakers' desire to expose poor Americans to dominant values while suppressing the groups of "antisocial" and "alienated" black youth that officials blamed for incidents of collective violence in the second half of the 1960s. National priorities increasingly shifted from fighting black youth poverty to fighting black youth crime for the remainder of the decade as policymakers introduced new patrol and surveillance measures in targeted urban communities. In the absence of programs that provided a concrete means to access decent shelter, education, and employment, poverty and crime increased during the ensuing fifteen years of the national law enforcement program. That the crime control strategies federal policymakers developed proved to have the opposite impact in the cities and neighborhoods that they placed under siege is one of the most disturbing ironies in the history of American domestic policy.

By the time Ronald Reagan took office in 1981, African Americans had become vulnerable on two fronts: a struggle against one another and a struggle with the institutions and policies that federal policymakers developed to fight the War on Crime. Together, the strategies at the core of the national law enforcement program—preemptive patrols that aimed to catch robberies in progress, sting operations that created underground economies, juvenile delinquency policy that criminalized generations of black youth while decriminalizing their white counterparts, firearms sanctions that brought federal law enforcement authorities to the streets, Career Criminal court units that created an expedited criminal justice system for gang members, and security programs that made housing projects resemble detention centers—hastened the trend toward internal violence and incarceration. The process of implementing these measures eventually gave rise to a historically distinct carceral network composed of punitive and social welfare institutions, with statistical discourses of black criminality and pathological understandings of poverty serving as its intellectual foundation.

In effect, the federal government's long mobilization of the War on Crime promoted a particular type of social control, one that signals that the targeted arrest of racially marginalized Americans and the subsequent creation of new industries to support this regime of control are among the central characteristics of domestic policy in the late twentieth century. The decisions that policymakers and officials, acting in closed circles or as part of a larger coalition, made at the highest levels had immeasurable consequences for low-income Americans and the nation, however unintended some of these choices may have been at different times and in different political moments. Ultimately, however, the bipartisan consensus of policymakers fixated on the policing of urban space and eventually removing generations of young men and women of color from their communities to live inside prisons. We can excuse the set of actions and choices these historical actors made as a product of their time or as merely an electoral tactic, but by doing so, we will continue to avoid confronting legacies of enslavement that still prevent the nation from fully realizing the promise of its founding principles.

Until recently, the devastating outcomes of the War on Crime have gone relatively unnoticed. For many Americans, it appeared as though discrimination ended with the civil rights movement and the United States had moved beyond race-based systems of exploitation. Alongside the tremendous growth of American law enforcement over the last fifty years, a formidable black middle class surfaced and African Americans assumed positions of power with greater visibility—from the rise of black mayors in the 1970s to displays of black wealth for popular consumption to the presidency of Barack Obama. These achievements promoted discourses of cultural pathology and "personal responsibility" even further, making it seem as though the systematic incarceration of entire groups of racially marginalized Americans reflected the natural order of things.

Political representation and the fact that some black Americans have amassed substantial wealth and capital do not mean that historical racism and inequality has ended. African Americans grew more affluent after 1965, but by the end of the twentieth century, the net financial assets of the highest fifth of black households were $7,448—only $448 above that of the lowest fifth of white American households.[1] And the black middle class has always been concentrated in the public sphere and social services, where mobility is tied to the extent of state spending on domestic programs.

In celebrating the racial inclusion championed by African American activists and their allies in classrooms across the nation during Black History Month every year, the fact that many of the critical reforms of the postwar period have been negated by national crime control priorities remains unrecognized. For instance, nine years after the passage of the Voting Rights Act, at the dawn of the mass incarceration era, the Supreme Court ruled it constitutional to deny convicted felons the right to vote. States have consistently removed convicts from voter rolls ever since the Court's 1974 *Richardson v. Ramirez* decision. Today nearly 6 million American citizens, most of whom have already served their sentences, are deprived of the franchise. As a result of racial disparities in American policing and criminal justice practices, an estimated one out of every thirteen African Americans will not vote in the 2016 election due to a prior conviction. Because of this felon disenfranchisement and the set of punitive policies behind it, a key civil rights gain of the 1960s has come undone. To make an already questionable situation worse, the U.S. census mainly counts people who are incarcerated in state and federal prisons as residents of the county where they are serving time, and census counts in turn determine representation. Although rural areas are home to the minority of the U.S. population, they are home to the majority of prisons. In other words, urban Americans (who tend to favor Democrats) lost representation because of how felon disenfranchisement works, and rural districts (that tend to favor Republicans) gained extra representation because of how the prison system works. Meanwhile, as mobility remains stagnant, public schools and many urban neighborhoods are more segregated today than they were before the civil rights movement.[2]

We must revisit the principles of community representation and grassroots empowerment that guided the early development of the Great Society in order to begin moving toward a more equitable and just nation. The Johnson administration included grassroots representatives and organizations in the administration of social welfare programs, but this policy directive proved to be fleeting. Promising initiatives that had been designed by grassroots organizations and that received federal funding directly during the first year of the War on Poverty were increasingly required to include public officials and municipal authorities in top-level positions following the Watts uprising in August 1965. Before community action programs were given a chance to work on a wider level and for entire communities rather than individuals, federal policymakers decided to defund them and switch course. Police forces took on a more prominent role in urban life and in social services in low-income neighborhoods. One can only imagine what the United States might look like today had the bipartisan political consensus mobilized behind the principle of "maximum feasible participation" that steered the War on Poverty's community action programs with the same level and length of commitment as they gave to the War on Crime.

Out of their sense that society was becoming unraveled in the context of civil rights and antiwar protests, federal policymakers held African Americans accountable for the turmoil and instability and took the wrong policy turn, opting to deploy militarized police forces in urban neighborhoods and to build more prisons instead of seeking to resolve the problems that caused the unrest in the first place. Once the Nixon administration moved to terminate the Office of Economic Opportunity and increasingly partnered its activities with the Law Enforcement Assistance Administration (LEAA), community involvement in federal social programs was largely relegated to the law enforcement realm. Even within the crime control apparatus, only about 2 percent of the grants the LEAA awarded to urban police departments went to tenant patrols and other community-based programs.[3] The White House and the Justice Department were far more interested in supporting measures that stimulated omnipresent patrol, defensible space, and new law enforcement technologies in low-income neighborhoods while fusing police, corrections, and antidelinquency initiatives with social welfare programs.

Put bluntly, due to its own shared set of assumptions about race and its unwillingness to disrupt the racial hierarchies that have defined the social, political, and economic relations of the United States historically, the bipartisan consensus that launched the punitive intervention did not believe that African Americans were capable of governing themselves. Nixon expressed this sentiment overtly to his chief of staff H. R. Haldeman. "There has never in history been an adequate black nation," the president said, "and they are the only race of which this is true."[4] In a less conspicuous form, Jimmy Carter stressed grassroots participation as a critical component of his administration's punitive urban program. Yet authorities refused to fund citizen groups such as the League to Improve the Community in Chicago's Robert Taylor Homes, which advocated strategies that were very much in line with the stated commitments of the administration but sought to implement those strategies without oversight from police and public housing authorities. When Reagan took office, the rhetoric of community involvement vanished from the domestic policy arena, never to return. Stemming from the punitive shift in urban social programs during the previous decade, over the course of the 1980s, law enforcement officers came to provide the primary (and in some areas the *only*) public social services to residents.

As the first line of contact between government authorities and the public, police officers assume various duties depending on the groups of citizens they are charged with protecting. Throughout the twentieth century and into the twenty-first, police patrols in white and middle-class communities are expected to guard property from outsiders. In segregated low-income urban communities, on the other hand, their task is to search for suspects and remove offenders and potential offenders from the streets. Disproportionate numbers of African Americans received criminal records and prison sentences as a result of the differential approaches to public safety that policymakers enshrined in crime control legislation.

By introducing greater numbers of mostly white police officers in the nation's most isolated urban areas, federal policymakers polarized both residents and law enforcement authorities. Only 4 percent of sworn police officers who fought the War on Crime during the second half of the 1960s and through the 1970s were of African American descent, a low figure given the overrepresentation of black Americans both in national arrest rates and inside the prison system. James Baldwin observed the impact of this dynamic as early as 1961. "The only way to police a ghetto is to be oppressive," Baldwin wrote in *Nobody Knows My Name*. For black residents, police officers represented "the force of the white world and that world's criminal profit and ease, to keep the black man corralled up here, in its place . . . like an occupying soldier in a bitterly hostile country." Baldwin went on to observe that the police officer faced "daily and nightly, the people who would gladly see him dead, and he knows it."[5] With suspicion on both sides, the problem, as Baldwin identified it, lay not in the individual policeman but in the systemic forces that supported questionable and sometimes deadly policing practices. The response of outside forces on the segregated urban beat and the response of residents to the presence of those forces were the outcomes of both historical developments and socioeconomic circumstance. Yet the officer had few alternatives but to act in the manner in which she or he had been conditioned and trained.

More than a half century after Baldwin's insights, aggressive policing practices and mass incarceration have become the foremost civil rights issue of our time. Instead of being criminalized, low-income citizens must be empowered to change their own circumstances and must be fully integrated in public institutions at all levels. Crime control *is* a local matter. Residents in communities should be responsible for keeping their own communities safe. Various national reforms such as police body cams merely continue the use of taxpayer dollars to fund new equipment for police forces, a process that began with the Law Enforcement Assistance Act of 1965. The militarization of American police and the overpolicing of black neighborhoods is a policy path that has consistently proven highly unsuccessful as a crime reduction strategy and fuels mass incarceration and the racial disparities within the nation's enormous carceral complex. Now is the time to try new strategies—from residency requirements for police to civilian review boards to autonomous grassroots social programs to job *creation* measures for the "at-risk" groups that policymakers originally labeled "potentially delinquent" outside of the service economy—that will enable us to confront finally the entrenched systemic inequalities and civil liberties violations that exist within the criminal justice system as well as the persistence of inequality in the United States.

In August 2014, during the series of demonstrations in Ferguson, Missouri, images of law enforcement authorities drawing M-4 carbine rifles and dropping tear gas bombs on protesters and civilians alike shocked much of the American public. Ferguson looked like a war zone, prompting new discussions about the nation's punitive domestic policy priorities among the general public, scholars, and policymakers. Outrage over the deaths of unarmed African American citizens and the general lack of police accountability for those killed in the year after the death of Michael Brown and the Ferguson outbreak alone—including Ezell Ford, Dante Parker, Akai Gurley, Tamir Rice, Laquan McDonald, Natasha McKenna, Tony Robinson, Anthony Hill, Meagan Hockaday, Mya Hall, Walter Scott, Freddie Gray, Alexia Christian, Icarus Randolph, Sandra Bland, Sam Dubose, and Christian Taylor—has set a new climate for social movements and federal action. The conditions of the police encounters that ended in the loss of each of their lives, and the lives of thousands of other innocent citizens that will never be known, would not have existed and could have been avoided entirely had federal policymakers decided to respond in a different way to the civil rights movement and the enlightened protest of the 1960s.

Questions of intent, or the degree to which federal policymakers foresaw the consequences of the choices they made with respect to urban social programs in black communities, are only relevant to a certain extent. The issue is to uncover the series of decisions that made contemporary mass incarceration possible in order to discover our own actual history. The domestic policies at the center of this book shaped the lives of black women and men, their families, and their communities. These policies will shape life prospects for black children, and their children's children, even if the American criminal justice system is transformed once again. Ending the War on Drugs will not resolve the nation's policing and prison problems. Even if all the citizens serving time for drug convictions were released, the United States would still be home to the largest penal system in the world. And as long as law enforcement remains at the forefront of domestic urban policy and remains focused on young urban citizens of color, the regressive impulses of the last half-century will continue to erode American democracy. Barring fundamental redistributive changes at the national level, the cycle of racial marginalization, socioeconomic isolation, and imprisonment is ever more likely to repeat itself.

NOTES

ACKNOWLEDGMENTS

INDEX

NOTES

INTRODUCTION: ORIGINS OF MASS INCARCERATION

1. Lyndon Johnson, "Statement of the President on Establishing the President's Commission on Law Enforcement and the Administration of Justice," *Public Papers of Presidents of the United States: Lyndon B. Johnson*, 1965 (Washington, DC: U.S. Government Printing Office, 1966), 382.

2. Johnson's War on Crime remains largely absent from histories of his administration, the War on Poverty, and the Great Society. Julian E. Zelizer's *The Fierce Urgency of Now: Lyndon Johnson, Congress, and the Battle for the Great Society* (New York: Penguin Press, 2015) is indicative. Urban historians, too, have been late to recognize the consequences of the punitive social programs in the long and short terms. Heather Thompson unearthed new directions for the field in her groundbreaking 2010 article from the *Journal of American History*. In calling for historians to "think critically about mass incarceration and begin to consider the reverberations of this never-before-seen phenomenon," Thompson makes a profound case for why the rapid expansion of the American carceral state needs to be at the center of work that considers the rise of conservatism, the decline of the labor movement, and urban inequality within U.S. history in general and the postwar period in particular. Heather Thompson, "Why Mass Incarceration Matters: Rethinking Crisis, Decline, and Transformation in Postwar American History," *Journal of American History* 97, no. 3 (December 2010): 703–758, 705. I borrow this definition of mass incarceration from David Garland, *The Culture of Control:*

Crime and Social Order in Contemporary Society (Chicago: University of Chicago Press, 2002), 5–6. Lawrence D. Bobo and Victor Thompson have suggested we refer to mass incarceration as "racialized mass incarceration," given the undeniable racial disparities within the nation's prison system and the historical criminalization of African Americans. See Bobo and Thompson, "Racialized Mass Incarceration: Poverty, Prejudice, and Punishment," in *Doing Race: 21 Essays for the 21st Century*, ed. Hazel R. Markus and Paula Moya (New York: W. W. Norton, 2010): 322–355, 327.

3. Although the LEAA has been largely overlooked by scholars, some of the most extensive treatments of the agency in the existing literature include Thomas E. Cronin, Tamia Z. Cronin, and Michael E. Millakovich, *U.S. v. Crime in the Streets* (Bloomington: Indiana University Press, 1981); Malcolm Feeley and Austin Sarat, *The Policy Dilemma: Federal Crime Policy and the Law Enforcement Assistance Administration, 1968–1978* (Minneapolis: University of Minnesota Press, 1980); Barry Mahoney, *The Politics of the Safe Streets Act, 1965–1973: A Case Study in Evolving Federalism and the National Legislative Process* (PhD diss., Columbia University, 1976); Christian Parenti, *Lockdown America: Police and Prisons in the Age of Crisis* (London: Verso Press, 1999); Vesla Mae Weaver, "Frontlash: Race and the Politics of Punishment" (PhD diss., Harvard University, 2007); "$236-Million Allocated by U.S. to Help the States Fight Crime," *New York Times*, January 19, 1970, 28; Martin Weil, "U.S. Fund Aids War on Crime," *Washington Post*, January 19, 1970, A1; "Crime Fighters' Funds to Rise $310 Million in Year; War on Poverty to Become a Secondary Engagement," *Wall Street Journal*, February 3, 1970; Fred P. Graham, "Crime," *New York Times*, February 3, 1970, 23. See Beth Lynch, *Dollars and Sense of Justice: A Study of the Law Enforcement Assistance Administration as It Relates to the Defense of the Criminal Justice System* (Washington, DC: National Legal Aid and Defender Association, 1973); Weaver, "Race and Politics," 115; General Briefing of the LEAA, U.S. Department of Justice, April 1977, folder 10, LEAA [3], box 25, Annie Gutierrez Files, 1-21-1987, Jimmy Carter Presidential Library; Memorandum to Donald T. Regan from Charles Hobbs and Richard L. Williams, subj.: "The Anti-Drug Abuse Budget," MacDonald Files, Anti-Drug Abuse Budget, 1987–, Working Papers OA 16316, Ronald Reagan Presidential Library.

4. On the evolution of the American carceral state from the early republic to the twentieth century, see Marie Gottschalk, *The Prison and the Gallows: The Politics of Mass Incarceration in America* (Cambridge: Cambridge University Press, 2006); and Rebecca McLennan, *The Crisis of Imprisonment: Protest, Politics, and the Making of the American Penal State, 1776–1941* (New York: Cambridge University Press, 2008). More recently, Gottschalk's *Caught:*

The Prison State and the Lockdown of American Politics (Princeton, NJ: Princeton University Press, 2014) enhances our view of the ways in which the carceral state extends beyond prisons themselves to the probation and parole systems, reentry programs, and immigration detention centers. Works that consider the criminalization of African Americans and the rise of American prisons in the eighteenth and nineteenth centuries include Douglas A. Blackmon, *Slavery by Another Name: The Re-Enslavement of Black Americans from the Civil War to World War II* (New York: Anchor, 2009); Mary Ellen Curtin, *Black Prisoners and Their World: Alabama, 1865–1900* (Charlottesville: University of Virginia Press, 2000); Kali Gross, *Colored Amazons: Crime, Violence, and Black Women in the City of Brotherly Love: 1880–1910* (Raleigh: Duke University Press, 2006); Talitha LeFlouria, *Chained in Silence: Black Women and Convict Labor in the New South* (Chapel Hill: University of North Carolina Press, 2015); Alex Lichtenstein, *Twice the Work of Free Labor: The Political Economy of Convict Labor in the New South* (New York: Verso, 1996); David M. Oshinsky: *"Worse than Slavery": Parchman Farm and the Ordeal of Jim Crow Justice* (New York: Free Press, 1997); David Rothman, *The Discovery of the Asylum: Social Order and Disorder in the New Republic* (New York: Transaction, 1971).

5. I borrow this conception from Matthew Lassiter, who articulates the bipartisan dimensions of many domestic policies in the post-World War II U.S. through the framework of consensus. See Lassiter, "Political History beyond the Red-Blue Divide," *Journal of American History* 98 (December 2011): 760–764.

6. Katherine Beckett, *Making Crime Pay: Law and Order in Contemporary American Politics* (New York: Oxford University Press, 1997); Jonathan Simon, *Governing through Crime: How the War on Crime Transformed American Democracy and Created a Culture of Fear* (New York: Oxford University Press, 2009); Weaver, "Frontlash: Race and the Development of Punitive Crime Policy," *Studies in American Political Development* 21 (Fall 2007): 230–265; and Weaver, "Race and Politics"; Bruce Western, *Punishment and Inequality in America* (New York: Russell Sage Foundation, 2006) also ground their discussions of mass incarceration in the national politics of crime control in the 1960s. Naomi Murakawa's important recent study on federal punitive policies pushes us back to the Truman administration and emphasizes the role of congressional representatives in Murakawa, *The First Civil Right: How Liberals Built Prison America* (New York: Oxford University Press, 2014).

7. Exact figures for the number of people incarcerated in the United States in 1865 are not available. By averaging the number of incarcerated people as recorded by the U.S. Census Bureau of 1860 (at 19,086) and 1870 (at 32,901), we

can assume the total prison population was around 25,994 individuals. Margaret Werner Cahalan, U.S. Department of Justice, Bureau of Justice Statistics, "Historical Corrections Statistics in the United States, 1850–1984," (Washington, DC: U.S. Government Printing Office, December 1986), 28. Not including jails, the exact numbers of Americans imprisoned in federal and state facilities were 210,895 in 1965; 240,593 in 1975; 502,507 in 1985; roughly 1 million in 1995; and 1.4 million in 2005. The incarceration rate itself has swelled from 108 per 100,000 Americans in 1965 to the 698 per 100,000 that it is today. This remarkable incarceration rate is second only to Seychelles. U.S. Department of Justice, "Prisoners 1925–1981," *Bureau of Justice Statistics Bulletin* (Washington, DC: U.S. Government Printing Office, December 1982), 2; Jeremy Travis, Bruce Western, and Steve Redburn, eds. *The Growth of Incarceration in the United States: Exploring Causes and Consequences* (Washington, DC: National Academies Press, 2014), 2; Bobo and Thompson, "Racialized Mass Incarceration," 326; U.S. Department of Justice, "Prisoners in 1994," *Bureau of Justice Statistics Bulletin* (Washington, DC: U.S. Government Printing Office, August 1995); 2; U.S. Department of Justice, "Prisoners in 2005," *Bureau of Justice Statistics Bulletin* (Washington, DC: U.S. Government Printing Office, November 2006), 2; U.S. Department of Justice, "Prisoners in 2013," *Bureau of Justice Statistics Bulletin* (Washington, DC: U.S. Government Printing Office, November 2014), 2.

8. Within prisons for adult men, black Americans constitute 37 percent of those incarcerated, followed by white Americans at 32 percent, and Latino Americans at 22 percent. E. Ann Carson, "Prisoners in 2013," *Bureau of Justice Statistics Bulletin*, U.S. Department of Justice (Washington, DC: U.S. Government Printing Office, September 2014), 1, available at http://www.bjs.gov/content/pub/pdf/p13.pdf.

9. More than half of young black men in major urban centers are currently in prison or jail, and across the nation black men are 6.5 times more likely than white men and 2.5 times more likely than Latino men to be living behind bars. Bruce Western, *Punishment and Inequality in America* (New York: Russell Sage Foundation, 2006), 31, 195; see Michelle Alexander, *The New Jim Crow: Mass Incarceration in the Age of Colorblindness* (New York: New Press, 2011), 16; Heather C. West, William J. Sabol, and Sarah J. Greenman, "Prisoners in 2009," *Bureau of Justice Statistics Bulletin*, U.S. Department of Justice (Washington, DC: U.S. Government Printing Office, rev. October 27, 2011).

10. Although the FBI began gathering statistics in 1930, its Uniform Crime Report did not provide national figures until 1958, and even then these rates disproportionately reflected the statistics compiled by urban police departments. The growth of the national statistics apparatus gave rise to the field of

criminology and has produced a massive literature on crime rates. While social scientists agree that crime rose in the 1970s, it had declined by the early 1980s, and then went up again at the end of the decade with the War on Drugs in full swing. Although crime began to decline during the Clinton administration, when the prison population exploded, the best research on this issue has yet to reveal a direct relationship between crime trends and incarceration. Punitive practices, too, tend to have no direct relationship to actual conditions. Between 1975 and 1989, for instance, the average prison time for violent offenses tripled, even though violent crime levels remained constant. Strom Thurmond quoted in Senate Subcommittee on Criminal Laws and Procedures, Committee on the Judiciary, *Controlling Crime Through More Effective Law Enforcement: Hearing before the Subcommittee on Criminal Laws and Procedures*, 90th Cong., 1st sess., March 7, 1967, 47; Fred J. Cook, "There's Always a Crime Wave—How Bad Is This One?," *New York Times*, October 6, 1968, SM38; Milton Eisenhower et al., *To Establish Justice: To Insure Domestic Tranquility: Final Report on the National Commission on the Causes and Prevention of Violence* (Washington, DC: U.S. Government Printing Office, 1969).

11. During the House Judiciary subcommittee hearings considering Johnson's Safe Streets Act in March 1968, Elliot H. Lumbard, former chair of the New York State Crime Commission, testified that the FBI Uniform Crime Report "should not collect or be a statistical tool. It has a stake to a certain degree in the system." Another witness put it simply: "Is crime going up or is crime going down? We do not honestly know." Lumbard quoted in Carl Bernstein, "FBI Jealousy Hinted in Gap in Crime Statistics," *Washington Post*, March 10, 1968, B4; Milton Eisenhower et al., *To Establish Justice: To Insure Domestic Tranquility: Final Report on the National Commission on the Causes and Prevention of Violence* (Washington, DC: U.S. Government Printing Office, 1969). On the relationship between incarceration and crime, see Travis, Western, and Redburn, eds., *The Growth of Incarceration in the United States*, chap. 5. See also Angela Davis, *Are Prisons Obsolete?* (New York: Seven Stories Press, 2003), 92; Gottschalk, *Prison and the Gallows*, 25; Murakawa, *First Civil Right*; Weaver, "Race and Crime Policy," 258, 260–261; Western, *Punishment and Inequality*; Bureau of Justice Statistics, "Bridging Gaps in Police Crime Data," September 1999, available at: http://www.bjs.gov/content/pub/pdf/bgpcd.pdf; Daniel Bell offered a nuanced critique of crime statistics five years before Johnson declared the "War on Crime" in "The Myth of Crime Waves: The Actual Decline of Crime in the United States," in *The End of Ideology: On the Exhaustion of Political Ideas in the Fifties*, rev. ed. (Cambridge, MA: Harvard University Press, 2000), 151–174.

12. See especially Michael W. Flamm, *Law and Order: Street Crime, Civil Unrest, and the Crisis of Liberalism in the 1960s* (New York: Columbia University Press,

2005); Thomas and Mary Edsall, *Chain Reaction: The Impact of Race, Rights, and Taxes on American Politics* (New York, 1991). Notable treatments focusing on the rise of the conservative right include Lisa McGirr, *Suburban Warriors: The Origins of the New American Right* (Princeton, NJ: 2002); Kevin Kruse, *White Flight: Atlanta and the Making of Modern Conservatism* (Princeton, NJ: Princeton University Press, 2007); Matthew D. Lassiter, *The Silent Majority: Suburban Politics in the Sunbelt South* (Princeton, NJ: Princeton University Press, 2007); Jill Quadagno, *The Color of Welfare: How Racism Undermined the War on Poverty* (New York: Oxford University Press, 1994).

13. The politics of crime control figures prominently in the literature on the carceral state. A sampling includes Beckett, *Making Crime Pay*; Katherine Beckett, "Setting the Public Agenda: 'Street Crime' and Drug Use in American Politics," *Social Problems* 41 (1994): 425–447; James D. Calder, "Presidents and Crime Control: Kennedy, Johnson and Nixon and the Influences of Ideology," *Presidential Studies Quarterly* 12, no. 4 (1982): 574–589; Dillon Davey, *The Politics of Prison Expansion: Winning Elections by Waging War on Crime* (Westport, CT: Praeger, 1998); Flamm, *Law and Order*; Gottschalk, *Prison and the Gallows*; Gottschalk, *Caught*; John Hagan, *Who Are the Criminals?: The Politics of Crime Policy from the Age of Roosevelt to the Age of Reagan* (Princeton, NJ: Princeton University Press, 2012); Nancy Marion, *A History of Federal Crime Control Initiatives, 1960–1993* (Westport, CT: Praeger, 1994); Lisa Lynn Miller, *The Perils of Federalism: Race, Poverty, and the Politics of Crime Control* (New York: Oxford University Press, 2010); Stuart Scheingold, *The Politics of Law and Order: Street Crime and Public Policy* (New York: Longman, 1984). Placing race at the center of her analysis, Vesla Weaver breaks from the dominant view and describes the rise of federal crime control policies as a "frontlash" to the upheaval of the Second Reconstruction. See Weaver, "Race and Crime Policy," and Weaver, "Race and Politics."

14. The body of work on state-level factors in contributing to mass incarceration is extensive. Some of the best studies include Ruth Wilson Gilmore, *Golden Gulag: Prisons, Surplus, Crisis, and Opposition in Globalizing California* (Berkeley, CA: University of California Press, 2007); Julilly Kohler-Hausmann, "'The Attila the Hun Law': New York's Rockefeller Drug Laws and the Making of the Punitive State," *Journal of Social History* 44 (2010): 71–95; Alex Lichtenstein, "Flocatex and the Fiscal Limits of Mass Incarceration: Toward a New Political Economy of the Postwar Carceral State," *Journal of American History* 102 (June 2015): 113–125; Mona Lynch, *Sunbelt Justice: Arizona and the Transformation of American Punishment* (Stanford, CA: Stanford Law Books, 2010); Joshua Page, *The Toughest Beast: Politics, Punishment, and the Prison Officers Union in California* (New York: Oxford University Press, 2011); Robert

Perkinson, *Texas Tough: The Rise of America's Prison Empire* (New York: Picador, 2010); Heather Schoenfeld, "The Politics of Prison Growth: From Chain Gangs to Work Release Centers and Supermax Prisons, Florida, 1955–2000" (PhD diss., Northwestern University, 2009). The Sentencing Project has also conducted a number of studies examining the role of the states. See especially Ryan S. King, Marc Mauer, and Tracy Huling, "Big Prisons, Small Towns: Prison Economics in Rural America" (Washington, DC: The Sentencing Project, February 2003), available at http://www.sentencingproject.org/doc/inc_bigprisons.pdf.

15. Work on the black activists and organizations that mobilized in support of punitive programs includes James Forman, "Racial Critiques of Mass Incarceration: Beyond the New Jim Crow," *NYU Law Review* 87, no. 1 (2012): 101–146; Michael Javen Fortner, *Black Silent Majority: The Rockefeller Drug Laws and the Politics of Punishment* (Cambridge, MA: Harvard University Press, 2015); and Fortner, "The Carceral State and the Crucible of Black Politics: An Urban History of the Rockefeller Drug Laws," *Studies in American Political Development* 27, no. 1 (2013): 14–35. In her review of *Black Silent Majority*, Donna Murch provides a powerful critique of the view that African Americans ultimately precipitated the rise of the carceral state by calling for intensive policing, stricter sentencing laws, and the imprisonment of drug users. See "Who's to Blame for Mass Incarceration?," *Boston Review*, October 16, 2015, available at http://bostonreview.net/books-ideas/donna-murch-michael-javen-fortner-black-silent-majority.

16. A number of studies have shown that white Americans are overwhelmingly more punitive and have higher levels of confidence in the law enforcement and criminal justice systems than their African American counterparts. According to a recent survey conducted by the Pew Research Center, roughly 70 percent of African Americans as compared to 37 percent of whites feel that black citizens are treated unfairly by police and the courts. Pew Research Center, "King's Dream Remains an Elusive Goal; Many Americans See Racial Disparities," (Washington, DC: Pew Research Center, 2013), 7–8, available at http://www.pewsocialtrends.org/files/2013/08/final_full_report_racial_disparities.pdf; see also The Sentencing Project, "Race and Punishment: Racial Perceptions of Crime and Support for Punitive Policies," (Washington, DC: The Sentencing Project, 2014), available at http://sentencingproject.org/doc/publications/rd_Race_and_Punishment.pdf; Frank Newport, "Gallup Review: Black and White Attitudes Towards the Police," August 20, 2014, available at http://www.gallup.com/poll/175088/gallup-review-black-white-attitudes-toward-police.aspx.

17. Michelle Alexander, *The New Jim Crow: Mass Incarceration in the Age of Colorblindness* (New York: The New Press, 2010). On urban policing and its

development, see Christopher Lowen Agee, *The Streets of San Francisco: Policing and the Creation of a Cosmopolitan Liberal Politics, 1950–1972* (Chicago: University of Chicago Press, 2014); Radley Balko, *The Rise of the Warrior Cop: The Militarization of America's Police Forces* (New York: Public Affairs, 2014); Robert M. Fogelson, *Big City Police: An Urban Institute Study* (Cambridge, MA: Harvard University Press, 1977); Marisol LeBron, "Violent Arrest: Punitive Governance and Neocolonial Crisis in Contemporary Puerto Rico" (PhD diss., New York University, 2014); Christian Parenti, *Lockdown America: Police and Prisons in the Age of Crisis* (New York: Verso, 2000). A sampling of the vast literature on race and American criminal justice includes Lawrence D. Bobo and Victor Thompson, "Unfair by Design: The War on Drugs, Race, and the Legitimacy of the Criminal Justice System," *Social Research* 73, no. 2 (2006): 445–472; Angela Davis, "Race and Criminalization: Black Americans and the Punishment Industry," in *The Angela Y. Davis Reader*, ed. Joy James (New York: Blackwell, 1998), 61–73; Gilmore, *Golden Gulag*; Mark Mauer, *Race to Incarcerate* (New York: New Press, 1999); Glenn Loury, ed., *Race, Incarceration and American Values* (Cambridge, MA: MIT Press, 2008); Jerome G. Miller, *Search and Destroy: African-American Males in the Criminal Justice System* (Cambridge: Cambridge University Press, 1996); Dora Marie Provine, *Unequal under Law: Race in the War on Drugs* (Chicago: University of Chicago Press, 2007); Dorothy Roberts, "Constructing a Criminal Justice System Free of Racial Bias: An Abolitionist Framework," *Columbia Human Rights Law Review* 39 (2007): 272; Robert J. Sampson and William Julius Wilson, "Toward a Theory of Race, Crime, and Urban Inequality," in *Crime and Inequality*, ed. John Hagan and Ruth Peterson (Palo Alto, CA: Stanford University Press, 1995), 37–54; Michael Tonry, *Malign Neglect: Race, Crime, and Punishment in America* (New York: Oxford University Press, 1995); Weaver, "Race and Crime Policy;" Bruce Western and Becky Petit, "Incarceration and Social Inequality," *Daedalus* 139, no. 3 (2010).

18. For comprehensive accounts of the War on Drugs before the 1980s, see David T. Courtwright, *Forces of Habit: Drugs and the Making of the Modern World* (Cambridge, MA: Harvard University Press, 2001); Kathleen Frydl, *The Drug Wars in America, 1940–1973* (New York: Cambridge University Press, 2013); David F. Musto, *The American Disease: Origins of Narcotic Control* (New Haven, CT: Yale University Press, 1973; rev. ed., 1987). For examinations that focus on the control of specific narcotic substances, see Paul Gootenberg, *Andean Cocaine: The Making of a Global Drug* (Chapel Hill: University of North Carolina Press, 2009); Lisa McGirr, *The War on Alcohol: Prohibition and the Rise of the American State* (New York: W. W. Norton, 2015); Joseph F. Spillane, *Cocaine: From Medical Marvel to Modern Menace in the United States, 1884–1920* (Baltimore, MD: Johns Hopkins University Press, 2000). Matthew Las-

siter's recent and forthcoming work explores the uncharted dimensions of the War on Drugs beyond urban centers. See "Impossible Criminals: The Suburban Imperatives of America's War on Drugs," *Journal of American History* 102 (June 2015): 126–140.

19. Isabel Wilkerson provides a gripping account of the mass movement of African Americans between World War I and Vietnam, urging us to view the millions who fled the mob violence and sharecropping regimes of the southern states as refugees in Wilkerson, *The Warmth of Other Suns: The Epic Story of America's Great Migration* (New York: Vintage, 2011). For a comprehensive account of the development of the black freedom movement at midcentury and beyond, see Robin D. G. Kelley, *Race Rebels: Culture, Politics and the Black Working Class* (New York: Free Press, 1996); Manning Marable, *Race, Reform, Rebellion: The Second Reconstruction and Beyond in Black America*, 3rd ed. (Jackson: University of Mississippi Press, 2007); and Nikhil Pal Singh, *Black Is a Country: Race and the Unfinished Struggle for Democracy* (Cambridge, MA: Harvard University Press, 2005).

20. On the exclusion of African Americans from the New Deal, see Steve Fraser and Gary Gerstle, eds., *The Rise and Fall of the New Deal Order* (Princeton, NJ: Princeton University Press, 1989); Linda Gordon, *Pitied but Not Entitled: Single Mothers and the History of Welfare, 1890–1935* (New York: Free Press, 1994); Ira Katznelson, *When Affirmative Action Was White: An Untold History of Racial Inequality in Twentieth-Century America* (New York: W. W. Norton, 2005); George Lipsitz, *The Possessive Investment in Whiteness: How White People Profit from Identity Politics* (Philadelphia: Temple University Press, 1998); Harvard Sitkoff, *A New Deal for Blacks: The Emergence of Civil Rights as a National Issue, Volume 1: The Depression Decade* (New York: Oxford University Press, 1978). As Mason Williams has shown, prior to the federal intervention in the 1960s, urban coalitions had worked to implement various social reforms. See *City of Ambition: FDR, LaGuardia, and the Making of Modern New York* (New York: W. W. Norton, 2014). On the Economic Opportunity Act and the War on Poverty from a federal viewpoint, see Marisa Chappell, *The War on Welfare: Family, Poverty, and Politics in Modern America* (Philadelphia: University of Pennsylvania Press, 2009); Michael L. Gillette, *Launching the War on Poverty: An Oral History* (New York: Oxford University Press, 2010); Michael B. Katz, *The Undeserving Poor: From the War on Poverty to the War on Welfare* (New York, 1990); James T. Patterson, *America's Struggle against Poverty, 1900–1994* (Cambridge, MA: Harvard University Press, 1994); Michael B. Katz, ed., *The "Underclass Debate:" Views from History* (Princeton, NJ: Princeton University Press, 1992); Jennifer Mittelstadt, *From Welfare to Workfare: The Unintended Consequences of Liberal*

Reform, 1945–1965 (Chapel Hill: University of North Carolina Press, 2005); Quadagno, *The Color of Welfare*. For grassroots perspectives on the War on Poverty, see Premilla Nadasen, *Welfare Warriors: The Welfare Rights Movement in the United States* (New York: Routledge, 2004); Annelise Orleck, *Storming Caesar's Palace: How Black Mothers Fought Their Own War on Poverty* (New York: Beacon, 2006); Annelise Orleck and Lisa Gayle Hazirjan, eds., *The War on Poverty: A New Grassroots History* (Athens: University of Georgia Press, 2011); Rhonda Williams, *The Politics of Public Housing: Black Women's Struggles against Urban Inequality* (New York: Oxford University Press, 2005).

21. Others have also pointed out the limitations of liberal support for racial equality in the 1960s and the ways in which social welfare programs were inseparable from social control desires, with the effect of preserving the racial hierarchies that have plagued the country historically. See Francis T. Cullen and Cheryl Leo Jonson, "Rehabilitation and Treatment Programs," in *Crime and Public Policy*, ed. James Q. Wilson and Joan Petersilia (New York: Oxford University Press, 2011); David Theo Goldberg, *The Racial State* (Malden, MA: Blackwell, 2002); Charles Mills, "Liberalism and the Racial State," in *State of White Supremacy: Racism, Governance, and the United States*, ed. Moon-Kie Jung, Joao H. Costa Vargas, and Eduardo Bonilla-Silva (Palo Alto, CA: Stanford University Press, 2011), 27–46; Mical Raz, *What's Wrong with the Poor? Psychiatry, Race, and the War on Poverty* (Chapel Hill: University of North Carolina Press, 2013); Daryl Scott, *Contempt and Pity: Social Policy and the Image of the Damaged Black Psyche* (Chapel Hill: University of North Carolina Press, 1997); Robert Self, *All in the Family: The Realignment of American Democracy since the 1960s* (New York: Hill and Wang, 2012).

22. See Murakawa, *First Civil Right*; Naomi Murakawa, "The Origins of the Carceral Crisis: Racial Order as 'Law and Order' in Postwar American Politics," in *Race and American Political Development*, ed. Joseph Lowndes, Julie Novkov, and Dorian T. Warren (New York: Routledge, 2008), 234–255; and Weaver, "Race and Crime Policy," and Weaver, "Race and Politics," for further discussion on the criminalization of civil rights activists and urban civil disorder. On the direct relationship between punitive policies and "social threat" see Bruce Western, Meredith Kleykamp, and Jake Rosenfeld, "Crime, Punishment, and American Inequality," in *Social Inequality*, ed. Katherine Neckerman (New York: Russell Sage, 2004), 782–785. A few scholars have considered the ways in which uprisings in the 1960s shaped subsequent urban living conditions and policy at the federal, state, and local levels. See Sidney Fine, *Violence in the Model City: The Cavanaugh Administration, Race Relations, and the Detroit Riot of 1967* (East Lansing: Michigan State University Press, 2007); Robert M. Fogelson, *Violence as Protest: A Study of Riots and*

Ghettos (Garden City, NY: Doubleday, 1971); Gerald Horne, *Fire This Time: The Watts Uprising and the 1960s* (New York: Da Capo, 1997); Michael B. Katz, *Why Don't American Cities Burn?* (Philadelphia: University of Pennsylvania Press, 2011); Kevin Mumford, *Newark: A History of Race, Rights, and Riots in America* (New York: NYU Press, 2008).

23. The specific targeting of black men between the ages of fifteen and twenty-four for national law enforcement programs runs through the memoranda and internal reports examined in this book. Within the Johnson administration, Nicholas deB. Katzenbach et al., *The Challenge of Crime in a Free Society: A Report by the President's Commission on Law Enforcement and Administration of Justice* (Washington, DC: U.S. Government Printing Office, 1967), 5, 35, 44; and Otto Kerner et al., *Report of the National Advisory Commission on Civil Disorders* (New York: Bantam Books, 1968) contain the most clearly articulated public expressions of this agenda.

24. Johnson's merger of welfare and crime control functions was not entirely unique. The two systems had worked in tandem since the birth of the American republic, sharing similar goals and attitudes about poor people and treating socioeconomically isolated and racially marginalized Americans as a criminal class. Beginning in the nineteenth century, social welfare programs imposed varying degrees of supervision on targeted immigrant and poor communities with reformatories, settlement houses, orphanages, training schools, and community chests. In order to advocate on behalf of the urban European ethnic groups of immigrants they sought to rehabilitate, social welfare reformers often embraced scientific racism and aggressive policing strategies. A number of scholars have demonstrated the ways in which reformers have used punitive measures, often focused on low-income youth, in order to achieve their social welfare and rehabilitative goals. See Miroslava Chávez-García, *States of Delinquency: Race and Science in the Making of California's Juvenile Justice System* (Berkeley: University of California Press, 2012); Julilly Kohler-Hausmann, "Guns and Butter: The Welfare State, the Carceral State, and the Politics of Exclusion in the Postwar United States," *Journal of American History* 102 (June 2015): 87–99; Khalil Gibran Muhammad, *The Condemnation of Blackness: Race, Crime, and the Making of Modern Urban America* (Cambridge, MA: Harvard University Press, 2010); Anthony M. Platt, "Saving and Controlling Delinquent Youth: A Critique," *Issues in Criminology* 5, no 1 (Winter 1970): 1–25; Anthony M. Platt, *The Child Savers: The Invention of Delinquency* (New Brunswick, NJ: Rutgers University Press, 2009); Geoff Ward, *The Black Child Savers: Racial Democracy and Juvenile Justice* (Chicago: University of Chicago Press, 2012); and Michael Willrich, *City of Courts: Socializing Justice in Progressive Era Chicago* (New York: Cambridge University Press, 2003).

25. Although the Partnership for Health Act of 1966 was the first legislation to include block grant provision, this law consolidated health care programs to award $23 million to states directly. The Omnibus Safe Streets and Crime Control Act of 1968 was the first major instance of block grant funding, with an allocation of $300 million in federal funding to the states.

26. Many others have similarly directed our attention to the bipartisan dimensions of crime control policy in their considerations of mass incarceration. They emphasize the crucial role of Democrats, including Edward Kennedy, Joe Biden, Al Gore, and Charles Rangel, who co-partnered with the Reagan administration in the drug war era. At the executive level, much attention has been given to Bill Clinton's 1994 Crime Bill, a policy on which he reflected during a speech at the 106th Convention of the NAACP in July 2015: "I signed a bill that made the problem worse, and I want to admit it." See Michelle Alexander, *The New Jim Crow: Mass Incarceration in the Age of Colorblindness* (New York, 2011); Gottschalk, *Caught*; Murakawa, *First Civil Rights*; Simon, *Governing through Crime*; Weaver, "Race and Crime Policy," and Weaver, "Race and Politics." On more recent bipartisan partnerships, see David Dagan and Steven M. Teles, "The Conservative War on Prisons," *Washington Monthly*, November–December 2012, 25–31; Newt Gingrich and Pat Nolan, "Prison Reform: A Smart Way for States to Save Money and Lives," *Washington Post*, January 7, 2011; Kara Gotsch, "Bipartisan Justice: Fixing America's Punitive and Penal System Has Politicians Crossing Party Lines," *American Prospect*, December 6, 2010, A22. Video of Clinton's address to the NAACP can be found at http://www.naacp.org/news/entry/president-bill-clinton-speech-at-naacp-106th -convention.

27. Garland, *Culture of Control*; Garland, *Punishment and Welfare: A History of Penal Strategies* (Surrey, UK: Ashgate, 1987); Michel Foucault, *Discipline and Punish: The Birth of the Prison* (New York, 1977); Kohler-Hausmann, "Guns and Butter"; Loïc Wacquant, *Punishing the Poor: The Neoliberal Government of Social Insecurity* (Raleigh: Duke University Press, 2009) similarly understand the carceral state as a network of programs strongly tied to the welfare state. The political scientist Joe Soss has also written extensively on the criminalization of welfare and its ties to the carceral state in the late twentieth century. See especially Soss, "The New Politics of Inequality: A Policy-Centered Perspective," with Jacob S. Hacker and Suzanne Mettler in *Remaking America: Democracy and Public Policy in an Age of Inequality*, ed. Joe Soss, Jacob S. Hacker, and Suzanne Mettler (New York: Russell Sage Foundation, 2007), 3–24; Joe Soss, Richard C. Fording, and Sanford F. Schram, *Disciplining the Poor: Neoliberal Paternalism and the Persistent Power of Race* (Chicago: University of Chicago Press, 2011), as well as a number of Soss's coauthored arti-

cles. See also Marie Gottschalk, "Democracy and the Carceral State in America," *Annals of the American Academy of Political and Social Science* 651 (January 2014): 288–295; Bernard Harcourt, *Against Prediction: Punishing and Policing in an Actuarial Age* (Chicago: University of Chicago Press, 2007); William J. Novak, "Police Power and the Hidden Transformation of the American State," in *Police and the Liberal State*, ed. Markus D. Dubber and Mariana Valverde (Stanford, CA: Stanford Law Books, 2008); Carla Shedd, "Countering the Carceral Continuum: The Legacy of Mass Incarceration," *Criminology and Public Policy* 10, no. 3 (2011): 865–871; Thompson, "Why Mass Incarceration Matters," 706.

28. Juvenile Delinquency Prevention and Control Act of 1968, Pub L. No. 90-445, 82 stat. 462 (1968); House Committee on Education and Labor, *Juvenile Delinquency Prevention Act of 1967: Hearings before the Subcommittee on Education*, 90th Cong., 1st sess., May 10, 1967, 301 (Statement of Attorney General Ramsey Clark).

29. In *The Condemnation of Blackness*, Muhammad powerfully demonstrates the ways in which white social scientists such as Nathaniel Southgate Shaler and Frederick Hoffman relied on new statistics on black crime in the post-Emancipation era to produce, in Shaler's words, "a new understanding of black people's true racial capacity" (33). Hoffman's *Race Traits and Tendencies of the American Negro* (New York: Macmillan Co., 1896) remained the standing authority on race and crime until the Depression. In contrast to Hoffman's view that cultural and behavioral traits made black Americans particularly susceptible to crime and criminal activity, W.E.B. Du Bois emphasized the socioeconomic factors that shaped African American crime patterns and questioned statistical measures of crime rates in the *The Philadelphia Negro: A Social Study* (Philadelphia: University of Pennsylvania Press, 1899). Policymakers in the North did not legally target black Americans as explicitly as their southern counterparts, but various infractions on the books against "suspicious characters," disorderly conduct, keeping and visiting disorderly houses, drunkenness, and violations of city ordinances made possible new forms of everyday surveillance and punishment in the lives of African Americans in the Northeast, Midwest, and West. See also Jeffrey S. Adler, "Less Crime, More Punishment: Violence, Race, and Criminal Justice in Early Twentieth-Century America," *Journal of American History* 102 (June 2015): 34–46.

30. For discussions on the influence of eugencis in the development of criminal justice policies, see Muhammad, *The Condemnation of Blackness*; Chávez-García, *States of Delinquency*; Amy LaPan and Tony Platt, " 'To Stem the Tide of Degeneracy': The Eugenic Impulse in Social Work," in *Mental Disorders in*

the Social Environment: Critical Perspectives, ed. Stuart A. Kirk (New York: Columbia University Press, 2005), 139–164; and Steven Selden, *Inheriting Shame: The Story of Eugenics and Racism in America* (New York: Teachers College Press, 1999).

31. Richard A. Cloward and Lloyd E. Ohlin, *Delinquency and Opportunity: A Theory of Delinquent Gangs* (1960; repr., Florence, KY: Routledge, 2000). My view of the role of social scientists in shaping domestic policy during this period has been deeply informed by Alice O'Connor, *Poverty Knowledge: Social Science, Social Policy, and the Poor in Twentieth-Century U.S. History* (Princeton, NJ: Princeton University Press, 2001). See also Lawrence Bobo, "Inequalities That Endure? Racial Ideology, American Politics, and the Peculiar Role of the Social Sciences," in *The Changing Terrain of Race and Ethnicity,* ed. Maria Krysan and Amanda E. Lewis (New York: Russell Sage Foundation, 2004); Michael Tonry and David A. Green, "Criminology and Public Policy," in *The Criminological Foundations of Penal Policy: Essays in Honor of Roger Hood,* ed. Lucia Zedner and Andrew Ashworth (Oxford: Oxford University Press, 2003); William Stuntz, "The Pathological Politics of Criminal Law," *Michigan Law Review* 100, no. 3 (2001): 505–600; Ta-Nehisi Coates, "Black Pathology and the Closing of the Progressive Mind," *Atlantic,* March 21, 2014.

32. The literature on Moynihan and the impact of *The Negro Family: A Case for National Action* (Washington, DC: Office of Policy Planning and Research, U.S. Department of Labor, March 1965) is extensive. See Daniel Geary, *Beyond Civil Rights: The Moynihan Report and Its Legacy* (Philadelphia: University of Pennsylvania Press, 2015); Katznelson, *When Affirmative Action Was White;* James T. Patterson, *Freedom Is Not Enough: The Moynihan Report and America's Struggle over Black Family Life from LBJ to Obama* (New York: Basic Books, 2010); Lee Rainwater and William L. Yancy, *The Moynihan Report and the Politics of Controversy* (Cambridge, MA: MIT Press, 1967); Kerner et al., *Report of the National Advisory Commission,* 21, 392; Katzenbach et al., *Challenge of Crime,* 57; James Yuenger "Commission Sought and Got Facts on Urban Riots: Kerner," *Chicago Tribune,* March 1, 1968, 1.

33. Only 500,000 crimes were reported in suburbs, and 170,000 in rural areas. Katzenbach et al., *Challenge of Crime,* 5.

34. Western compared incarceration rates from African American men born between 1945 and 1950 and from those born between 1965 and 1969. The generation born in the postwar period without a high school degree had a less than one in five chance of going to prison or jail by the age of thirty, whereas 60 percent of the group born after 1965, with a similar level of educational attainment, were at risk for incarceration. Western, *Punishment and Inequality,* 31, 195. This "mass incarceration generation" is more likely to spend at least part of their lives behind bars than to serve in the military or receive

some form of government benefits. Employment prospects, which drastically declined after 1970, exacerbated this generational trend. As sociologist William Julius Wilson has shown, for every 100 black women aged twenty to twenty-four, there were nearly seventy employed black men, but by the early 1980s "there were fewer than 50 such men for every 100 women." See William Julius Wilson, *The Truly Disadvantaged: The Inner City, the Underclass, and Public Policy* (Chicago: University of Chicago Press, 1990); William Julius Wilson, *When Work Disappears: The New World of the Urban Poor* (New York: Vintage, 1997); and Wilson's larger body of work. Devah Pager has further deepened our understanding of the contours of African American inequality, revealing that even black men without a prior criminal record have as much difficulty (if not more) securing employment than formerly incarcerated white men, in *Marked: Race, Crime, and Finding Work in an Era of Mass Incarceration* (Chicago: University of Chicago Press, 2007).

35. James Q. Wilson, "Crime in the Streets," *Public Interest* 5, (1966): 32.

36. November 2, 1970, memorandum to Bud Krogh from Geoff Shepard, folder "OA #5505 Part VII St. Louis Police Programs," box 76, Egil "Bud" Krogh Collection, Richard Nixon Presidential Library (hereafter, RNPL); March 17, 1970, memorandum to Krogh from Charles Rogovin, folder "Proposals- LEAA Trip," box 26, Krogh Collection, RNPL.

37. November 2, 1970, memorandum to Bud Krogh from Geoff Shepard.

38. Ibid.; Marvin Wolfgang, Robert M. Figlio, and Thorsten Sellin, *Delinquency in a Birth Cohort* (Chicago: University of Chicago Press, 1972), 22; Marvin E. Wolfgang, University of Pennsylvania, "Youth and Violence," HEW Report, 1970. See Robert Martinson, "What Works?—Questions and Answers about Prison Reform," *Public Interest* 35 (1974): 22–54, 27, 50, 49; Robert Martinson, "The Paradox of Prison Reform—I: The 'Dangerous Myth,'" *New Republic*, April 1, 1972, 23–25, 25; Robert Martinson, "The Paradox of Prison Reform—II: Can Corrections Correct?," *New Republic*, April 8, 1972, 13–15; Robert Martinson, "The Paradox of Prison Reform—III: The Meaning of Attica," *New Republic*, April 15, 1972, 17–18; Robert Martinson, "The Paradox of Prison Reform—IV: Planning for Public Safety,'" *New Republic*, April 29, 1972, 21–23; Charles Murray and Louis A. Cox, *Beyond Probation: Juvenile Corrections and the Chronic Delinquent* (New York: Sage, 1979); James Q. Wilson, "'What Works?' Revisited: New Findings on Criminal Rehabilitation," *Public Interest* 61 (1980): 3–18.

39. Gwynne Pierson, "Institutional Racism and Crime Clearance," in *Black Perspectives on Crime and the Criminal Justice System*, ed. Robert L. Woodson (Boston: G. K. Hall, 1977), 110.

40. The federal government's focus on young African American men was also due, in part, to the fact that Latino crime patterns were importantly absent from the FBI Uniform Crime Report, since the bureau decided not to measure Latino arrest

rates. For a brief period, between 1980 and 1987, the FBI began to collect crime data by ethnicity in an attempt to fill in that statistical void. Before that window and until as recently as 2014, the majority of available statistics tabulated arrest data by race, with categories for white, black, Asian or Pacific Islander, and American Indian or Alaska Native. As such, Latinos largely vanished from American crime data, especially during the period at the center of this study. The available research that accounted for Latino crime and arrest rates has been incorporated as much as possible into the analysis presented in this book. Works that have helped bridge the existing statistical gaps by enhancing our view of the criminalization and policing of Latino and Chicano Americans include Rodolfo F. Acuna, *Occupied America: A History of Chicanos*, 8th ed. (New York: Pearson, 2014); Juanita Diaz-Cotto, *Chicana Lives and Criminal Justice: Voices from El Barrio* (Austin: University of Texas Press, 2006); Edward J. Escobar, *Race, Police, and the Making of a Political Identity: Mexican Americans and the Los Angeles Police Department, 1900–1945* (Berkeley: University of California Press, 1999); Kelly Lytle Hernandez, *Migra! A History of the U.S. Border Patrol* (Berkeley: University of California Press, 2010); Suzanne Oboler, ed., *Behind Bars: Latino/as and Prison in the United States* (New York: Palgrave Macmillan, 2009); and Victor M. Rios, *Punished: Policing the Lives of Black and Latino Boys* (New York: New York University Press, 2011). Some of the best analysis of Latino crime and incarceration rates can be found in Michael Tonry and Matthew Melewski, "The Malign Effects of Drug and Crime Control on Black Americans," in *Crime and Justice: A Review of Research*, ed. Michael Tonry, vol. 37 (Chicago: University of Chicago Press, 2008); Jeremy Travis, Bruce Western, and Steve Redburn, eds., *The Growth of Incarceration in the United States: Exploring Causes and Consequences* (Washington, DC: National Academies Press, 2014), 61–64. On white-collar crime, see Max Schanzenbach and Michael L. Yager, "Prison Time, Fines, and Federal White-Collar Criminals: The Anatomy of a Racial Disparity," *Journal of Criminal Law and Criminology* 96 (Winter 2006): 757–794.

41. Victor M. Rios has astutely described the transformation of urban social institutions, particularly those serving low-income young people, as a "youth control complex" in Rios, *Punished,* and Victor M. Rios, "The Hyper-Criminalization of Black and Latino Male Youth in the Era of Mass Incarceration," *Souls: A Critical Journal of Black Politics, Culture, and Society* 8, no. 2 (2006): 40–54. See also Alice Goffman's discussion on the impact of policing and supervision in low-income black urban Americans in Goffman, "On the Run: Wanted Men in the Philadelphia Ghetto," *American Sociological Review* 74 (June 2009): 339–357; Tommie Shelby, "Liberalism, Self-Respect, and Troubling Cultural Patterns in Ghettos," in *The Cultural Matrix: Understanding Black Youth*, ed. Orlando Patterson with Ethan Fosse (Cambridge, MA: Harvard University Press, 2015), 498–532.

42. April 16, 1971, memorandum for Ehrlichman from Krogh, subj.: "Domestic Policy Issues—1971–1972," box 14, Krogh Collection, RNPL.

1. THE WAR ON BLACK POVERTY

1. Lyndon Johnson, "Special Message to Congress on Law Enforcement and the Administration of Justice," March 8, 1965, American Presidency Project, http://www.presidency.ucsb.edu/ws/?pid=26800; "Statement of the President on Establishing the President's Commission on Law Enforcement and the Administration of Justice," *Public Papers of Presidents of the United States: Lyndon B. Johnson*, 1965 (Washington, DC: U.S. Government Printing Office, 1966), 382; "President Forms Panel to Study Crime Problems," *New York Times*, July 27, 1965, 1.

2. John F. Kennedy, "Remarks Recorded for the Ceremony at the Lincoln Memorial Commemorating the Centennial of the Emancipation Proclamation," September 22, 1962, President's Office Files, Speech Files, John F. Kennedy Presidential Library (hereafter, JFKPL); John F. Kennedy, "Civil Rights Message to the Nation" (1963), in *The Kennedy Years and the Negro*, ed. Doris E. Saunders (Chicago: Johnson Publishing Company, 1964), 112.

3. *Message from the President Relative to Civil Rights*, 88th Cong., 1st sess., H. Doc. 124, serial 12567 (June 19, 1963), 7; ibid.; Sanford Kravitz and Ferne K. Kolodner, "Community Action: Where Has It Been? Where Will It Go?," *Annals of the American Academy of Political and Social Science* 385 (September 1969), 30–40, 32; "Negro Unemployment Scored by AFL-CIO," *Chicago Defender*, May 18, 1963, 1.

4. Robert W. Fairlie and William A. Sundstrom, "The Racial Unemployment Gap in Long-Run Perspective," *American Economic* Review 2, no. 87 (May 1997): 306–310, 307; *Message from the President Relative to Civil Rights*, 88th Cong., 1st sess., H. Doc. 124, serial 12567 (June 19, 1963), 7; Kravitz and Kolodner, "Community Action," 30–40, 32.

5. New York, Los Angeles, Chicago, Philadelphia, Detroit, San Francisco–Oakland, Boston, Pittsburgh, St. Louis, Washington, Cleveland, and Baltimore had the highest concentrations of African Americans throughout most of the twentieth century. Robert W. Fairlie and William A. Sundstrom, "The Racial Unemployment Gap in Long-Run Perspective," *American Economic Review* 2, no. 87 (May 1997): 306–310, 307; *Message from the President Relative to Civil Rights*, 88th Cong., 1st sess., H. Doc. 124, serial 12567 (June 19, 1963), 7; Kravitz and Kolodner, "Community Action," 30–40, 32; George Bain, "Black Sore of New York," *Globe and Mail*, October 16, 1963, 7.

6. James B. Conant, "Idle Youth in City Slums Are Social Dynamite," *Washington Post*, June 11, 1961, E3; Conant also quoted in Josephine Ripley,

"Negro—and Teen Crime," *Christian Science Monitor*, May 29, 1961, 5; Ralph McGill, "Social Dynamite," *Hartford Courant*, October 27, 1961, 18; Goldberg quoted in Ripley, "Negro—and Teen Crime," 5.

7. *Message from the President Relative to Civil Rights*; Kennedy, "Remarks Recorded."

8. Kennedy quoted in Kravitz and Kolodner, "Community Action," 33; Youth Offenses and Control Act of 1961, Pub. L. No. 87-274, 75 Stat. 572 (1961).

9. "The National Juvenile Delinquency Picture," *Personnel and Guidance Journal* 38 (1959): 278.

10. John F. Kennedy, "Special Message to Congress on the Nation's Youth," February 14, 1963, American Presidency Project, http://www.presidency.ucsb.edu /ws/?pid=9561. See Bill Bush, *Who Gets a Childhood?: Race and Juvenile Justice in Twentieth-Century Texas* (Athens: University of Georgia Press, 2010); Michael W. Flamm, *Law and Order: Street Crime, Civil Unrest, and the Crisis of Liberalism in the 1960s* (New York: Columbia University Press, 2005), 15; Donna Murch, *Living for the City: Migration, Education, and the Rise of the Black Panther Party in Oakland, California* (Chapel Hill: University of North Carolina Press, 2010), 59–60. See also Megan Stubbendeck, "'This Wrong Is Being Done to My People': Street Gangs, Historical Agency, and Crime Politics in Postwar America" (PhD diss., University of Virginia, 2013); Kravitz and Kolodner, "Community Action," 30–40, 33; "The National Juvenile Delinquency Picture," *Personnel and Guidance Journal* 38 (1959): 278; September 14, 1965, memorandum from James Symington to Bill Moyers, folder "President's Committee on Juvenile Delinquency and Youth Crime," FG 731 (June 10, 1964–), box 403, Lyndon Baines Johnson Presidential Library (hereafter, LBJPL); Kravitz and Kolodner, "Community Action," 33.

11. Jay R. Williams and Martin Gold, "From Delinquent Behavior to Official Delinquency," *Social Problems* 20, no. 2 (Autumn, 1972): 209–229; Heidi Matiyow Rosenberg, "Federal Policy toward Delinquent Youth: Legislative and Programmatic Milestones from Kennedy to Ford, 1960–1976," (PhD diss., University of Michigan, 2008), 94; Daniel Patrick Moynihan, *Maximum Feasible Misunderstanding: Community Action in the War on Poverty* (New York: Free Press, 1969), 14.

12. Richard A. Cloward and Lloyd E. Ohlin, *Delinquency and Opportunity: A Theory of Delinquent Gangs* (1960; repr., Florence, KY.: Routledge, 2000); Flamm, *Law and Order,* Chapter chap. 1; Robert H. Terte, "Slums and Suburbs Provide: Deprived Need Specialists 'Total' Attack Begun to De-Fuse 'Social Dynamite' in Slums," *New York Times*, April 9, 1963, pg. 33.

13. Terte, "Slums and Suburbs Provide"; Frank Tannenbaum, *Crime and the Community* (New York: Columbia University Press, 1938), 16–20 (quotation

from pg. 20); "50 Young Hoodlums Seized in Battle," *Chicago Daily Tribune*, June 4, 1961, pg. 30.

14. Cloward and Ohlin, *Delinquency and Opportunity*, 211.

15. See Alice O'Connor, *Poverty Knowledge: Social Science, Social Policy, and the Poor in Twentieth-Century U.S. History* (Princeton, NJ: Princeton University Press, 2001);. May 31, 1962, "Report to the President Transmitted by President's Committee on Juvenile Delinquency and Youth Crime," folder " PCJD-OJD Background Materials, Key Internal Developments 1962," box 4, Knapp Papers, JFKPL.

16. February 7, 1969, interview with Francis Frances Fox Piven, folder "Notes: Misc," box 7, Richardson White Papers, Box 7, JFKPL; November 27, 1961, "Causation of Delinquency," an address given by David L. Hackett, Executive Director, PCJDYC before the Institute on Juvenile Delinquency, South Western Legal Foundation Dallas, Texas, November 27, 1961, folder 11/61, box 2, Richardson White Jr. Papers (Office of Juvenile Delinquency 1961–1968), JFKPL.

17. Senate Committee on Labor and Public Welfare, *Extension of the Juvenile Delinquency Act: Hearings before the Subcommittee on Employment and Manpower*, 88th Cong., 1st sess. (August 8–9, 13, and 15–16, 1963), 20, 23 (Statement of Celebrezze); August 5, 1963, letter, "New Steps to Secure Extension of the Juvenile Delinquency Act," from David L. Hackett to the Attorney General, folder "PCJD-OJD Background Materials, Key Internal Developments 1962," box 4, Knapp Papers, JFKPL; "Delinquents Are People: Progress Report of the Federal Anti-Delinquency Program," prepared by the Office of Juvenile Delinquency and Youth Development, Department of Health, Education, and Welfare, in cooperation with the PCJDYC April 1965," folder " 'Delinquents Are People' 4/65," box 2, Knapp Papers Published Background Materials, Histories, JFKPL; May 31, 1963, memorandum to the Attorney General from David L. Hackett, Executive Director, subj.: "OMAT and the Federal Delinquency Program," folder "Hackett: Memorandum and Notes (2)," box 7, Richardson White Jr. Papers (subject file), JFKPL.

18. May 31, 1963, memorandum to the Attorney General from David L. Hackett,. Executive Director, subj.: "OMAT and the Federal Delinquency Program," folder, "Hackett: Memorandum and Notes (2)," box 7, Richardson White Jr. Papers (subject file), Box 7, JFKPL; see also William Finnegan, "New Haven," chap. 1 in *Cold New World: Growing Up in a Harder Country* (New York: Modern Library, 1999), 1–92.

19. "Delinquents Are People;" March 24, 1966, letter to Symington from Robert Johnson, folder, "Robert Jonson, Untitled Monograph, Section I, 1966," box 3, Knapp Files Published Background Materials Histories, JFKPL; "Counter-Attack on Delinquency: The Program of the Federal Government to Stimulate

Communities to Develop Rational Answers to a Growing Crisis," prepared by the President's Committee on Juvenile Delinquency and Youth Crime: The Attorney General, Chairman, The Secretary of HEW, The Secretary of Labor, folder, "Counter Attack on Delinquency 6/64," box 2, Knapp Files Published Background Materials Histories, JFKPL.

20. Kennedy, *Message from the President Relative to Civil Rights.* Announcing a one-year, $800,000 federal grant that the committee had awarded to a massive "human renewal" program in New Haven, Kennedy explained the rationale for his administration's wide-ranging antidelinquency program. "These people find themselves in strange, alien surroundings. Many have the added problem of racial discrimination . . . they are surrounded by crime, illiteracy, illegitimacy, and human despair." Kennedy cited overcrowded schools, substandard housing, and unemployment as the factors most directly responsible for this environment, and concluded: "Finding no work and little hope, too many of them turn to juvenile crime to obtain the material goods they think society has denied them. Others turn to drink and narcotics addiction. And soon the cycle repeats itself, as this dispossessed generation bears children little better equipped than their parents to cope with urban life." November 27, 1961, "Causation of Delinquency" an address given by David L. Hackett, Executive Director, PCJDYC before the Institute on Juvenile Delinquency, South Western Legal Foundation Dallas, Texas, November 27, 1961, folder, "11/61," box 2, Richardson White Jr. Papers (Office of Juvenile Delinquency 1961–1968), JFKPL; September 14, 1965, memorandum from Symington to Moyers; undated press release (likely October 18, 1963), President's Office Files, Departments and Agencies, Committee on Juvenile Delinquency and Youth Crime, JFKPL, available at: http://www.jfklibrary.org/Asset-Viewer/Archives/JFKPOF-093-007.aspx.

21. "Counter-Attack on Delinquency."

22. The total costs for Mobilization for Youth in its first three years amounted to $12 million: $6.3 million from the president's committee, $4.2 million from New York City, and $2 million from the Ford Foundation. Bernard Gavzer, "Uncle Sam 'Slumming' in Lower East Side," *Hartford Courant*, July 29, 1962, 24A2.

23. February 21, 1969, interview with Lloyd Ohlin and Leonard Cottrell, folder "Notes: Misc," box 7, Richardson White Papers, JFKPL; Ohlin quoted in O'Connor, *Poverty Knowledge*, 127; Matiyow Rosenberg, "Federal Policy," 81; William Rice, "Progress Cited by President's Delinquency Unit," *Washington Post*, August 16, 1963, B6.

24. David Miller, "Boys Seek a Clubhouse Deal with City," *New York Herald Tribune*, March 10, 1960, 3; David Miller, "Things Get Going for the Boys," *New York Herald Tribune*, August 19, 1961, 1.

25. Fassier quoted in Miller, "Boys Seek a Clubhouse Deal"; Joseph P. Fried, "News of Realty: Center for Boys," *New York Times*, May 11, 1967, 77.

26. John F. Kennedy, "Special Message to the Congress on the Peace Corps," March 1, 1961, American Presidency Project, available at http://www.presidency .ucsb.edu/ws/?pid=8515; "Counter-Attack on Delinquency"; Kennedy, "Special Message to the Congress on the Nation's Youth."

27. "Delinquents Are People," emphasis in original; Marylyn Bibb, "Gang-Related Services of Mobilization for Youth," in *Juvenile Gangs in Context: Theory, Research, and Action*, ed. Malcolm W. Klein (Englewood Cliffs, NJ: Prentice-Hall, 1967), 181–182; "An Agency Statement Regarding the General Objectives of Mobilization for Youth," adopted June 1963, folder "1/63–9/63," box 5, Knapp Papers (PCJD-OJD Background Materials, Key Internal Developments), JFKPL.

28. Gavzer, "Uncle Sam 'Slumming'"; "Precedents for Success," *Washington Post*, October 31, 1964, 24A2; "Counter-Attack on Delinquency"; "Delinquents Are People"; May 31, 1962, Remarks of the President to the President's Committee on Juvenile Delinquency and Youth Crime, folder "Remarks on Report of PCJDYC," box 38, President's Office Files, Speech Files, John F. Kennedy Library, digital identifier JFKPOF-038-033; Bibb, "Gang-Related Services," 179.

29. Rice, "Progress Cited," B6.

30. See Matiyow Rosenberg, "Federal Policy," 88; Abraham Tannenbaum, "Mobilization for Youth in New York City," in *Developing Programs for the Educationally Disadvantaged*, ed. Harry Passow (New York: Teacher's College Press, 1968); "Delinquents Are People"; G. K. Hodenfield, "Dropout Solution: Train the Tots," *Atlanta Journal-Constitution*, October 23, 1964, 6; Rice, "Progress Cited," B6.

31. On the disciplinary functions of social welfare programs, see especially Michel Foucault, *Discipline and Punish: The Birth of the Prison* (New York, 1977), pt. 4; Daryl Scott, *Contempt and Pity: Social Policy and the Image of the Damaged Black Psyche, 1880–1996* (Chapel Hill: University of North Carolina Press, 1997); Anthony M. Platt, "Saving and Controlling Delinquent Youth: A Critique," *Issues in Criminology* 5, no 1. (Winter 1970): 1–25; Platt, *The Child Savers: The Invention of Delinquency* (New Brunswick, NJ: Rutgers University Press, 2009); Geoff Ward, *The Black Child Savers: Racial Democracy and Juvenile Justice* (Chicago: University of Chicago Press, 2012); "Delinquents Are People"; Bibb, "Gang-Related Services," 181–182; "Counter-Attack on Delinquency," 33, 39.

32. Hackett quoted in Moynihan, *Maximum Feasible Misunderstanding*, 71; "Delinquents Are People"; Bibb, "Gang-Related Services," 181–182.

33. "Counter-Attack on Delinquency"; June 14, 1962, memorandum from W. C. Lawrence to Dr. Lloyd Ohlin, subj.: "Youth Project St. Louis, Missouri," folder

"Project Field Reports 6/11/62–6/15/62," box 5, Knapp Papers (PCJD-OJD Background Materials, Key Internal Developments), JFKPL.

34. June 14, 1962, memorandum from Lawrence to Ohlin.

35. "Minutes of the Demonstration Projects Review Panel Meeting February 13–15, 1964," 20–21, folder "PCJD-OJD Background Materials Technical Review Panel, Meeting Minutes 2/64," box 7, Knapp Papers, JFKPL.

36. Ibid.; "Delinquents Are People."

37. January 30, 1969, Interview with Boone, folder "Notes: Misc," box 7, Richardson White Papers, JFKPL.

38. Heller quoted in O'Connor, *Poverty Knowledge*, 156.

39. Lyndon B. Johnson, State of the Union Address, January 8, 1964, American Presidency Project, available at http://www.presidency.ucsb.edu/ws/?pid=26787.

40. Congress allocated a total of $962.5 million for the War on Poverty, dedicating $340 million for Community Action Programs alone. Economic Opportunity Act of 1964; John F. Kennedy, Establishment of Peace Corps, March 1, 1961, The Miller Center, available at http://millercenter.org/president/speeches/detail /3366; Economic Opportunity Act of 1964; Sar A. Levitan, "The Community Action Program: A Strategy to Fight Poverty," *Annals of the American Academy of Political and Social Science* 385 Evaluating the War on Poverty (1969): 63–75; O'Connor, *Poverty Knowledge*, 169.

41. Kennedy in House Committee, *Economic Opportunity Act of 1964*, 312.

42. "Delinquents Are People"; O'Connor, *Poverty Knowledge*, 170.

43. Quoted in Stephen M. David, "Leadership of the Poor in Poverty Programs," *Proceedings of the Academy of Political Science* 29, Urban Riots: Violence and Social Change (1968): 86–100, 93, 91; Noel A. Cazenave, *Impossible Democracy: The Unlikely Success of the War on Poverty Community Action Programs* (Albany: State University of New York Press, 2007).

44. O'Connor, *Poverty Knowledge*, 171.

45. Walsh quoted in Susan Abrams Beck, "The Limits of Presidential Activism: Lyndon Johnson and the Implementation of the Community Action Program," *Presidential Studies Quarterly* 17, Bicentennial Considerations and the Eisenhower and L. B. Johnson Presidencies (1987): 541–557, 546; O'Connor, *Poverty Knowledge*, 171.

46. House Committee, *Economic Opportunity Act of 1964*, 305; Richard K. Fenn, "The Community Action Program: An American Gospel?," *Science and Society* 33 (1969): 209–222, 209.

47. June 21, 1964 Report on "Juvenile Delinquency," folder "Juvenile Delinquency," box 40, Office Files of Bill Moyers, LBJPL.

48. "Report of the President's Task Force of the Los Angeles Riots"; Governor's Commission to Investigate the Los Angeles Riots, *Violence in the City: An*

End or a Beginning? (December 1965), available at http://www.usc.edu/libraries /archives/cityinstress/mccone/contents.html.

49. "Text of Johnson Statement on Harlem Riots," *Los Angeles Times*, July 22, 1964, 17; Johnson quoted in Douglas Kiker, "Johnson Vows to Halt Street Violence Anywhere in the Nation," *Boston Globe*, August 13, 1964, 6.

50. Johnson, "Special Message to Congress on Law Enforcement and the Administration of Justice."

51. President's Task Force on Manpower Conservation, "One-Third of a Nation: A Report on Young Men Found Unqualified for Military Service," January 1, 1964 (Washington, DC: U.S. Government Printing Office), 20–22, 3–5.

52. Gunnar Myrdal, *An American Dilemma: The Negro Problem in Modern Democracy* (New York: Harper and Row, 1944), 929.

53. Moynihan quoted in Lee Rainwater and William L. Yancy, *The Moynihan Report and the Politics of Controversy* (Cambridge, MA: MIT Press, 1967), 24.

54. According to James T. Patterson, on March 15 the Department of Labor printed one hundred copies, "99 of which went into a safe." James T. Patterson, *Freedom Is Not Enough: The Moynihan Report and America's Struggle over Black Family Life from LBJ to Obama* (New York: Basic Books, 2010), 42; Daniel Patrick Moynihan, *The Negro Family: A Case for National Action* (Washington, DC: Office of Policy Planning and Research, U.S. Department of Labor, March 1965), 47, 137. See also Ta-Nehisi Coates, "The Black Family in the Age of Mass Incarceration," *Atlantic Monthly*, October 2015, available at http://www.theatlantic.com/magazine/archive/2015/10/the-black-family-in -the-age-of-mass-incarceration/403246/.

55. This view synthesized three decades of scholarship on the "Negro Problem," particularly by the sociologists E. Franklin Frazier and Nathan Glazer. Moynihan drew heavily on the work of psychologist Kenneth Clark, who placed a perceived "tangle of pathology" in black urban communities at the center of his explanation for the breakdown in black family structure in *Dark Ghetto* (New York: Harper and Row, 1965). Though less influential on Moynihan himself, Oscar Lewis explained poverty in Mexico City in his 1961 book *The Children of Sanchez: Autobiography of a Mexican Family* (New York: Random House) through a "culture of poverty" lens, and many Americans were familiar with Michael Harrington's argument in *The Other America* (New York: Macmillan, 1962), published three years before the release of *The Negro Family*. *The Other America* depicted economic discrepancies in the United States through the idea that poor people were culturally trapped in their status. See Moynihan, *Negro Family*, 9, 35, 41; Rainwater and Yancey, *Moynihan Report*, 26–27, 76; Moynihan quoted in Patterson, *Freedom Is Not Enough*, 43.

56. Lyndon Johnson, "Commencement Address at Howard University: To Fulfill These Rights," June 4, 1965, *Public Papers of the Presidents of the United States: Lyndon B. Johnson, 1965* (Washington, DC: U.S. Government Printing Office, 1966), vol. 2, entry 301, 635–640; See also chap. 1, "Doctor of Laws," in Ira Katznelson, *When Affirmative Action was White: An Untold History of Racial Inequality in Twentieth-Century America* (New York: W. W. Norton, 2005), 1–24; Patterson, *Preface*.

57. Senate Committee, *Law Enforcement Assistance Act*, 34. Scheuer and Kennedy were not the only liberals involved in steering the Law Enforcement Assistance Act through Congress. Edwin E. Willis of Louisiana, the southern Democrat judged so liberal by his constituency that the more conservative Patrick Caffery defeated him after ten terms in Congress in the 1968 Democratic primary, chaired the House Committee on the Judiciary's hearings on the legislation. A special subcommittee oversaw the hearings, and included the moderate Republican John Lindsay of New York, Democrat James Corman of Los Angeles, and Roy McVicker of Colorado. On the Senate side, Birch Bayh of Indiana and moderate Republican Jacob Javits of New York joined Kennedy on the Senate Committee on the Judiciary, which oversaw its own set of hearings and reported the bill. House Committee on the Judiciary, *Law Enforcement Assistance Act: House Hearings before Subcommitte No. 3 Committee on the Judiciary*, 89th Cong., 1st sess. (May 20, 1965), 15 (Statement of James Scheuer); ibid., 34 (Statement of Edward Kennedy).

58. House Committee on the Judiciary, *Law Enforcement Assistance Act: House Hearings before Subcommittee No. 3 Committee on the Judiciary*, 89th Cong., 1st sess. (May 20, 1965), 12 (Statement of Congressman James H. Scheuer).

59. Terms emerged at different times and in different political and social climates to describe the areas where racial and ethnic minorities lived in concentration, neighborhoods where residents were largely deprived of access to adequate food, sanitation facilities, health care, education, and other basic public services. In the 1960s and 1970s, "disadvantaged area," "inner-city," and "ghetto" came into political and academic use to describe these places, with "slum" remaining the default term throughout most of the twentieth century. All of these expressions embodied the cultural and behavioral assumptions policymakers and much of the American public had about racially marginalized citizens. Describing the black urban neighborhoods at the center of this study as what they were—areas of segregated poverty—is an attempt to avoid reproducing the racism and the pathological connotations intrinsic to the terms policymakers, public figures, and scholars used to describe these spaces and the people who lived within them.

60. Johnson, "Commencement Address at Howard University."

2. LAW AND ORDER IN THE GREAT SOCIETY

1. House Committee on Education and Labor, *Antipoverty Program in New York City and Los Angeles: House Hearing before the Committee on Education and Labor*, 89th Cong., 1st sess. (August 7, 1967), 115 (Statement of Alfred F. Cannon).

2. Gerald Horne, *Fire This Time: The Watts Uprising and the 1960s* (1995; repr., Cambridge, MA: Da Capo, 1997), 3.

3. August 19, 1965, Letter from Hruska to Katzenbach in Senate Judiciary Committee, *Report on the Law Enforcement Assistance Act of 1965*, 89th Cong., S. Rep. No. 672 (1965), 4.

4. House Committee, *Antipoverty Program*, 109 (Statement of Reverend H. H. Brookins); September 17, 1965, "Report of the President's Task Force on the Los Angeles Riots, August 11–15, 1965" (Revised Master), 6, folder "Califano: Los Angeles Riots, Ramsey Clark Report," box 47, Office Files of Joseph A. Califano, Lyndon Baines Johnson Presidential Library (hereafter, LBJPL).

5. "Report of the President's Task Force on the Los Angeles Riots," June 16, 1967, memorandum for President from Califano, 2, folder "Watts," box 58, Califano Files, LBJPL; Ralph McGill, "A White Ghetto Poverty Enigma," *Atlanta Constitution*, April 5, 1966, 1.

6. Horne, *Fire This Time*, Introduction; Governor's Commission to Investigate the Los Angeles Riots, *Violence in the City: An End or a Beginning?* (December 1965), available at http://www.usc.edu/libraries/archives/cityinstress/mccone/contents.html.

7. Some of the participants sent buildings and entire blocks into flame and smoke, but most of the so-called rioters simply seized the opportunity to obtain consumer goods that would have been otherwise unattainable. A woman dragged a couch through the streets but stopped at every intersection, waiting for a green light. A married couple in their sixties carried a couch to their home, periodically stopping on the sidewalk to rest along the way. A young mother and her children took a kitchen set but realized they neglected to take enough chairs for everyone to eat at the table. When the family went back out to retrieve the missing seat, each member was arrested. And when twelve-year-old Leo Kidd and his younger brother Randy went to buy Alka-Seltzer for their aunt and the boys decided to help themselves to food and refreshments— as everyone around them was doing—both children faced looting charges. See Bayard Rustin, "The 'Watts Manifesto' and the McCone Report," *Commentary Magazine*, March 1, 1966, 29–35; Ron Arias, "Rage and Reason in Watts," *People Magazine*, August 13, 1990; Brookins in "Watts: Riot or Revolt?," *CBS Reports*, Columbia Broadcasting System Television Network (December 7, 1965).

8. As Horne reminds us: "The Watts uprising was no mindless riot but rather a conscious, though inchoate, insurrection." Horne, *Fire This Time*, 3; David O. Sears and John B. McConahay, *The Politics of Violence: The New Urban Blacks and the Watts Riot* (Boston: Houghton Mifflin, 1973), 13.

9. Yorty quoted in *Crips and Bloods: Made in America*, directed by Stacy Peralta (The Gang Documentary, Balance Vector Productions, Verso Entertainment, 2008); Horne, *Fire This Time*, 3.

10. Brown quoted in Art Berman, "Some Coast Violence Goes on as Governor Says 'Worst Is Over'," *Washington Post*, August 17, 1965, A1; Parker quoted in Otto Kerner et al., *Report of the National Advisory Commission on Civil Disorders* (New York: Bantam Books, 1968), 14; June 16, 1967 memorandum for President from Califano; "Riot Suits for $4,330,000 Name City as Defendant," *Los Angeles Sentinel*, June 23, 1966, A1.

11. All of the areas placed under curfew were at least 55 percent black. In the Watts district and other neighborhoods inside the central city, African Americans amounted to some 85 percent of the population. "Report of the President's Task Force of the Los Angeles Riots"; Governor's Commission to Investigate the Los Angeles Riots, *Violence in the City*.

12. The NAACP Legal Defense Fund stepped in, filing a suit on behalf of more than 4,000 residents who claimed they had no legal representation when they were arraigned for charges brought about during the Watts riot. Of those arraigned, 1,232 had no previous arrest record, and 1,164 had received minor citations before. The Supreme Court refused to hear the case. "Judge Says Riot Trials Stripped City of Police," *Los Angeles Times*, July 8, 1966, sf9; Rustin, "Watts Manifesto"; "80 Percent of Watts Rioters Jailed," *Baltimore Afro-American*, December 18, 1965, 17; Berman, "Some Coast Violence."

13. Charles Hillinger, "Burning Buildings Symbolize Spirit of Hate Underlying Violent Rioting," *Los Angeles Times*, August 14, 1965, 2; 75; Wallace Turner, "Discontent and Hate Viewed as Factors in Coast Violence," *New York Times*, August 15, 1965, 1; quoted in Horne, *Fire This Time*, 36.

14. "Report of the President's Task Force on the Los Angeles Riots," 22–23. Johnson's friend and Crime Commission appointee Leon Jaworski implicated civil rights laws in the rising crime rate by asking the National Conference of Bar Presidents: "If a civil rights leader . . . disobeys a law or court decree because it offends his moral beliefs of what is right . . . [and is] excused from obeying the law on such grounds, why shouldn't members of the crime syndicate be granted similar exemption from obeying the law?" Believing that the actions of civil rights protesters would encourage widespread lawlessness and criminality, Jaworski warned: "A moral callousness of the preservation of what we now consider to be right and decent, reminiscent of the days of the fall of the Roman

empire, may well follow." I am also appropriating the language of Arizona senator Paul Fannin here, who believed federal social programs left residents "aimless, demoralized," and with no other option but to engage in violent activity "in an environment which breeds crime and criminals." See Senate Committee, *Controlling Crime*, 898; Jaworski quoted in Robert Wiedrich, "Growing Disrespect for Laws Called Threat to Our Nation," *Chicago Tribune*, February 17, 1968, W18; Parker quoted in "Watts: Riot or Revolt?"; Evelle Younger, "Bill of Rights" in n.d. memorandum from Pollner to Mitchell, "Re: Anticipated Criminal Activity Facing New Administration and Proposed Action to Combat Same," box 24, Martin Anderson Collection, Richard Nixon Presidential Library (hereafter, RNPL); ibid., 23.

15. Jacob Javits quoted in Gareth Davies, *From Opportunity to Entitlement: The Transformation and Decline of Great Society Liberalism* (Lawrence: University Press of Kansas, 1999), 107; see also Chapter 4, "Watts and Its Aftermath: The Rise of Income Strategy," in Davies; Lee Rainwater and William L. Yancey, *The Moynihan Report and the Politics of Controversy* (Cambridge, MA: MIT Press, 1967), chap. 5; James D. Calder, "Presidents and Crime Control: Kennedy, Johnson and Nixon and the Influences of Ideology," *Presidential Studies Quarterly* 12, no. 4 (1982): 580; Lyndon B. Johnson, *National Strategy against Crime: A Proposed Three-Stage Strategy against Crime*, 89th Cong., 2nd sess., H. Doc 407, serial 12724-3 (March 9, 1966), 1209; John A. Averill, "Hit Poverty and Crime Will Fall, Johnson Says," *Los Angeles Times*, October 16, 1966, 3.

16. Michael W. Flamm, *Law and Order: Street Crime, Civil Unrest, and the Crisis of Liberalism in the 1960s* (New York: Columbia University Press, 2005), chap. 3; Vesla Mae Weaver, "Frontlash: Race and the Development of Punitive Crime Policy," *Studies in American Political Development* 21 (Fall 2007): 230–265.

17. See chap. 8 in Alice O'Connor, *Poverty Knowledge: Social Science, Social Policy, and the Poor in Twentieth-Century U.S. History* (Princeton, NJ: Princeton University Press, 2001), 196–210.

18. "Behind the Riots: Family Life Breakdown in Negro Slums Sows Seeds of Race Violence; Husbandless Homes Spawn Young Hoodlums, Impede Reforms, Sociologists Say; Racing a Booming Birth Rate," *Wall Street Journal*, August 16, 1965, 1; "Hot Summer," *New York Times*, August 15, 1965, E1.

19. "Behind the Riots." CBS News went on to feature Moynihan in a special report on the unrest that aired in December 1965, less than four months after the disorder. See "Watts: Riot or Revolt?" In the wake of the uprisings in Newark and Detroit in July 1967, Moynihan also provided extensive commentary in NBC News' own special report. See *NBC Special Reports*, National Broadcasting Company Television Network (September 15, 1967).

20. Brimmer in Draft Presidential Statement for Release with the Final Report to the Task Force on the Los Angeles Riots, folder "Los Angeles Riots: Ramsey Clark Report," box 47, Califano Files, LBJPL; "Report of the President's Task Force on the Los Angeles Riots," 3; September 17, 1965, "Report of the President's Task Force on the Los Angeles Riots, August 11–15, 1965" (Revised Master), folder "Califano: Los Angeles Riots, Ramsey Clark Report," box 47, Office Files of Joseph A. Califano, 1, LBJPL; Robert Thompson, "Johnson Orders $29 Million Watts Rehabilitation Work: First Phase to Focus on 45 Projects," *Los Angeles Times*, September 3, 1965, 3. Thomas McDermott, the vice president of the Police Chiefs Association of Southeastern Pennsylvania, submitted an article to the Senate entitled "Gangs in the Streets" from the *Philadelphia Evening Bulletin* which concluded in the summer of 1966: "Those who . . . seek to understand and try to help correct the housing and other conditions which stir unrest cannot help but be both repelled and discouraged by the activity of roaming groups of hoodlums interested only in violence for the sake of violence." By clinging to the idea that a marginal group of troubled slum "riff raff" engaged in rioting, politicians backing law enforcement measures could "strip from these outbreaks any legitimacy as a form of social or economic protest," as a Philadelphia police captain testified. See Senate Committee, *Controlling Crime*, 1133; ibid.; Robert Bauman, "The Black Power and Chicano Movements in the Poverty Wars in Los Angeles," *Journal of Urban History* 33, no. 2 (January 2007): 277–295.

21. "Concerns of the Office of Juvenile Delinquency and Youth Development" attached to November 10, 1965, memorandum from Bernard Russell Director to James Vorenberg, box 94, Records of the President's Commission on Law Enforcement and the Administration of Justice: Series 6: Task Force on Juvenile Delinquency, LBJPL.

22. October 1, 1965, "President's Committee on Juvenile Delinquency Briefing Booklet," xiv–cont., box 104, Office Files of Bill Moyers, LBJPL.

23. Ibid.

24. George H. Esser Jr., "Widening the Horizons of the Culturally Deprived," *ALA Bulletin* 60, Federal Library Legislation, Programs, and Services (1966): 175–178.

25. Stephen M. David, "Leadership of the Poor in Poverty Programs," *Proceedings of the Academy of Political Science* 29, Urban Riots: Violence and Social Change (1968): 92–93. Schultze quoted in O'Connor, *Poverty Knowledge*, 172.

26. Milton Eisenhower et al., *To Establish Justice: To Insure Domestic Tranquility: Final Report on the National Commission on the Causes and Prevention of Violence* (Washington, DC: U.S. Government Printing Office, 1969), xiv, 19.

27. "Controlling Crime through More Effective Law Enforcement Hearings," 44 (Statement of William A. Johnson, Superintendent of Police, Grand Rapids, MI and President, Michigan Association of Chiefs of Police); White House

Press Release, "Text of the Remarks by the President at the Conference of State Committees on Criminal Administration," October 15, 1966, folder "Crime Message #1," LBSSA Files, LBJPL; John A. Averill, "Hit Poverty and Crime Will Fall, Johnson Says," *Los Angeles Times*, October 16, 1966, 3.

28. Additional grants came from other executive departments, such as the Department of Health, Education, and Welfare, which sponsored much of the commission's research on juvenile delinquency. Louis Dombrowski, "Urge 'Revolution' in Approach to Crime in U.S.," *Chicago Tribune*, February 19, 1967, 28.

29. These members were joined by attorney and member of the Pennsylvania Pardon Board Genevieve Blatt; Boston district attorney Garrett Byrne; and attorneys Ross L. Malone, Lewis Franklin Powell, Robert Gerald Storey, and William Pierce Rogers, as well as former New York City mayor Robert F. Wagner; July 28, 1966, Letter from Sam Yorty to the President, folder 27, "FG 273 President's Commission on Law Enforcement and the Administration of Justice," box 40, LBJ Confidential Files, LBJPL; Max Freedman, "National Crime Commission's Strategy Has at Least One Flaw," *Los Angeles Times*, August 5, 1965, A5.

30. December 3, 1966, memorandum from James Vorenberg to Joseph A. Califano, 7, folder 1, "1966–67 Task Force on Crime," box 1, Legislative Background Files Safe Streets Act of 1968, LBJPL; "Law Institute Suggests Code of Police Arrest Procedures," *Hartford Courant*, March 6, 1966; John P. Mackenzie "'Frisk' Plan Snarls Law Institute," *Washington Post*, May 18, 1966, A2.

31. Johnson Asks Crime Panel for Answers," *Chicago Tribune*, September 9, 1965, D23.

32. Transcript of September 8, 1965, Meeting, 30–31, folder "Transcripts of Commission Meetings 9/8/65–11/11–12-66," 1 of 3, box 55, Records of the President's Commission on Law Enforcement and the Administration of Justice (hereafter, RPCLEAJ), Series 2, Executive Director James Vorenberg's Files, LBJPL.

33. Lyndon Johnson, *National Strategy against Crime: A Proposed Three-Stage Strategy Against Crime*, 89th Cong., 2nd sess., H. Doc 407, serial 12724-3 (March 9, 1966), 8; Monroe W. Karmin, "Combating Crime," *Wall Street Journal*, December 28, 1966; Nicholas deB. Katzenbach et al., *The Challenge of Crime in a Free Society: A Report by the President's Commission on Law Enforcement and Administration of Justice* (Washington, DC: U.S. Government Printing Office, 1967), 123.

34. February 24, 1966, memorandum from Bruce J. Terris to James Vorenberg, subj.: "The Members of the Commission and Poverty," box 214, RPCLEAJ, Series 12, Task Force on Assessment, LBJPL; Katzenbach in January 12, 1966, "The President's Commission on Law Enforcement and the Administration of Justice," folder "FG 763 PCLEAJ (Citizens Adv. Com) 8/19/65," box 409, Field Group 763, February 21, 1961, LBJPL.

35. Judge Parsons offered up some of his experiences in federal court where he rarely encountered "slum youth." Contrary to the Crime Commission's general and final assessment, Parsons found juvenile delinquency to be a far greater problem "among the middle class and upper middle class people." Transcript of December 29, 1966, Meeting, folder "Transcripts of Commission Meetings 1/11/–12-66, 12/28–30-66, 1/21–22/67 3 of 3," box 57, RPCLEAJ, Series 2 Executive Director James Vorenberg's Files, LBJPL; Vorenberg and Parsons in November 12, 1966, Official Report of the Proceedings before the US DOJ in the Matter of the PCLEAJ, 403–404, folder "Transcripts of Commission Meetings 9/8/65–11/11–12/66 2 of 3," box 55, RPCLEAJ Series 2, LBJPL.

36. Hoover in Transcript of September 8, 1965, Meeting, 16; Katzenbach et al., *Challenge of Crime*, 60, 63.

37. "Remarks by the President at the Conference of State Committees on Criminal Administration."

38. By 1965, the FBI National Academy had trained 4,500 officers at all levels. The Department of Health, Education, and Welfare also provided vocational training for police, and the Treasury Department's Bureau of Narcotics Training Schools gave instruction to narcotics enforcement officials. *Crime, Its Prevalence, and Measures of Prevention. Message from the President of the United States Relative to Comments on Crime, Its Prevalence, and Measures of Prevention,* 89th Cong., 1st sess., H. Doc. 103, serial 12677-3 (March 8, 1965), 4; "Law Enforcement Assistance Expenditures," folder "Administrative History DOJ," box 3, Administrative Histories, vol. 4, pt. 5 and 5a, Department of Justice, LBJPL; House Committee on the Judiciary, *Law Enforcement Assistance: Hearing before Subcommittee No. 3 of the Committee on the Judiciary,* 89th Cong., 1st sess. (May 20, 1965), 19–21 (Statement of Nicholas deB. Katzenbach, Attorney General).

39. Senate Committee on the Judiciary, *Law Enforcement Assistance Act: Senate Hearings before a Subcommittee of the Committee on the Judiciary,* 89th Cong., 1st sess. (July 23, 1965), 37 (Statement of Beverly Briley, Chairman of the League of Cities Law Enforcement Committee and Mayor of Nashville).

40. Ibid., 32 (Statement of Katzenbach).

41. Senate Committee on the Judiciary, *Law Enforcement Assistance Act of 1965: Hearing before the Senate Committee on the Judiciary,* 89th Cong., 1st sess. (July 22, 1965), 4, 6 (Statement of Katzenbach); Gomberg quoted in "Plea for Federal Role in Crime Drive Hailed," *Hartford Courant,* March 11, 1966, 4.

42. "Law Enforcement Assistance Expenditures."

43. "Granting Activity 1965–1966," folder "Volume IV, LEA Part V, LEA—Narrative History" [1 of 2], box 3, 42 LBJAHDOJ vol. 4, pt. 5 and Va., LBJPL; July 28, 1966, Letter from Katzenbach to President from AG, folder "Volume IV, LEA Part V,

LEA—Documentary Supplement" [2 of 2], box 3, 52 LBJAHDOJ vol. 4, pt. 5 and Va., LBJPL; "War on Crime Theory: Make 'Em Look Silly," *Hartford Courant*, March 15, 1966, 11B.

44. According to the FBI Uniform Crime Report that year, Los Angeles had the highest crime rate in the nation, seen as a result of a severe lack of policemen on the city's most troubled streets. "Project Sky Knight: A Demonstration in Aerial Surveillance and Crime Control," box 26, Egil Krogh Collection, RNPL; "Administrative History of the DOJ," folder "Administrative History of the DOJ," box 3, LBJAHDOJ vol. 4, pt. 5 and Va., LBJPL.

45. "Project Sky Knight: A Demonstration in Aerial Surveillance and Crime Control."

46. Senate Committee on the Judiciary, *Law Enforcement Assistance Act of 1965: Hearing before the Senate Committee on the Judiciary*, 89th Cong., 1st sess. (July 30, 1965), 67 (Statement of Congressman James H. Scheuer); ibid., 8 (Statement of Katzenbach); "Granting Activity 1965–1966."

47. Leonard Downie Jr., "Police Explain 'Dick Tracy' Radio Plans," *Washington Post*, March 12, 1966, B2; Alfred E. Lewis, "LBJ Names City Crime Commission," *Washington Post*, July 17, 1965, A1.

48. Alfred E. Lewis, "Police Training Planned at All Levels with Goal of 'Model' City Departments," *Washington Post*, June 28, 1966, A1; Letter from Katzenbach to President.

49. In the summer of 1968, 800 youth from South Central also went camping with LAPD officers at Camp Radford in the San Bernardino Mountains. This was part of an "effort to combat the anti-police attitudes learned in the inner city." "Los Angeles Community Relations Program," November 1968, folder "LAPD, Youth Service," box 26, Krogh Files, RNPL. In "Los Angeles Police Department Community Relations Program—Youth Services Material"; News Clipping, "SRO Grant Contains No Surprise Curbs," *Tucson Arizona Citizen*, August 2, 1966, in folder "Manpower Development and Training Act-Police Programs," box 232, Crime Commission Records Task Force on Police Files, LBJPL; Brochure, "Portable Playstreets: An Answer to the Long Hot Summers," folder "Cabinet Meeting 8/2/67" [3 of 4], Cabinet Papers, LBJPL.

50. "Text of the Remarks by the President at the Conference of State Committees on Criminal Administration."

51. "President's Committee on Juvenile Delinquency and Youth Crime Briefing Booklet."

52. Both the Economic Opportunity Act and the Secondary Education Act of 1965 amounted to ten times that of the programs instituted under the Law Enforcement Assistance Act. And the Johnson administration created a new cabinet-level agency that fall with the enactment of the Housing and Urban

Development Act, which received an initial $7.5 billion allocation from Congress. *Housing and Urban Development Act of 1965*, Pub. L. No. 89-117, 79 Stat. 451 (1965); Economic Opportunity Act of 1964, 1967. "Crime, LEAA, The Law Enforcement Assistance Administration." Issue Brief no. IB77024, Library of Congress Research Service, November 29, 1979; Senate Subcommittee on State, Justice, Commerce, and the Judiciary, *Hearings on Appropriations FY 81, Part 2*, 96th Congress, 2nd sess. (1980).

3. THE PREEMPTIVE STRIKE

1. Lyndon Johnson, "Annual Message to Congress on the State of the Union," 1967, *Public Papers of the Presidents of the United States: Lyndon B. Johnson, 1968–69*, vol. 1, entry 14, pp. 25–33 (Washington, DC: Government Printing Office, 1970); Remarks by the President for Cabinet Meeting Wednesday, April 19 1967, folder "Cabinet Meetings," box 58, Personal Papers of Ramsey Clark, Lyndon Baines Johnson Presidential Library (hereafter, LBJPL); 10-15-66 White House Press Release, Office of the White House Press Secretary, "Text of the Remarks by the President at the Conference of State Committees on Criminal Administration," folder "1967 Crime Message #1," box 3, Legislative Background Files SSA 1968, LBJPL; Nicholas deB. Katzenbach et al., *The Challenge of Crime in a Free Society: A Report by the President's Commission on Law Enforcement and Administration of Justice* (Washington, DC: U.S. Government Printing Office, 1967), 6.

2. Economic Opportunity Act of 1966, Pub.L. No. 89-794, 95 Stat. 519 (1966); see also *Examination of the War on Poverty*, Staff and Consultant Reports, Prepared for the Sub-Committee on Employment, Manpower, and Poverty of the Committee on Labor and Public Welfare, U.S. Senate, vol. 3, September 1967, 797–798, quoted in Richard K. Fenn, "The Community Action Program: An American Gospel?" *Science and Society* 33, no. 2 (Spring 1969): 209–222, 216.

3. N/T, N/D Document p. 16, folder 1, "1966–67 Task Force on Crime," box 1, Legislative Background Files SSA 1968, LBJPL; November 30, 1967, memorandum from Willard Wirtz to Joseph Califano, "A Summary of the Department of Labor's Efforts Related to the Recommendations Made by the President's Commission on Law Enforcement and the Administration of Justice," p. 2, folder "1967 Crime Message Follow Up 3 of 3," box 4, Legislative Background Files SSA 1968, LBJPL.

4. Juvenile Delinquency Prevention and Control Act of 1968, Pub. L. No. 90-445, 82 Stat. 462 (1968). The phrase "in danger of becoming delinquent" appears in the first paragraph of sec. 2 of the legislation.

5. Katzenbach et al., *Challenge of Crime*, vi.

6. Ibid., 6. The acknowledgment of structural racism often was used as a device to frame arguments for the expansion of American law enforcement. As North Carolina senator Sam Ervin stressed, "a nationwide war on crime is as imperative as our continuing war on poverty and unemployment." Senator Edward Kennedy echoed Ervin's sentiment by noting, "It has become increasingly recognized that criminal behavior is intertwined with social forces—that many who transgress the law have themselves been transgressed—by their home life, by their environment, by their lack of opportunity." *The Law Enforcement Assistance Act of 1965 Hearings*, July 22, 1965, 4, 33.

7. Richard B. Stolley, "A Crisis Worse than Anyone Imagined: Report," *Life* magazine, February 24, 1967, 24; Katzenbach et al., *Challenge of Crime*, 6, 59.

8. Katzenbach et al., *Challenge of Crime*, 95.

9. This language is from a Los Angeles Police Department Community Relations Program report. Police officers in the city came to interact with some 8,000 students a week. The report stated, "Police and school officials agree that this program, presented in an atmosphere of learning, is invaluable in creating a sense of concern for orderly behavior and responsibility for the maintenance of law and order." The program involved the distribution of pamphlets from police officers to primary and secondary schoolchildren. This would "provide students with an appreciation of the role of the police and their own responsibilities as good citizens." In 1968, more than 210,000 students from grade 1 through grade 12 were exposed to this program. "Los Angeles Police Department Community Relations Program," November 1968, box 26, Egil Krogh Collection, Richard Nixon Presidential Library (hereafter, RNPL); Katzenbach et al., *Challenge of Crime*, 100.

10. Katzenbach et al., *Challenge of Crime*, 99, 98.

11. The statistics proved for commission members that urban centers, and urban centers alone, created the conditions that bred crime. "Burglary, robbery, and serious assaults occur in areas characterized by low income, physical deterioration, dependency, racial and ethnic concentrations, broken homes, working mothers, low levels of education and vocational skill, high unemployment, high proportions of single males, overcrowded and substandard housing, high rates of tuberculosis and infant mortality, low rates of home ownership or single family dwellings, mixed land use, and high population density," the Crime Commission claimed. Ibid., 35, 59; August 18, 1966, "Meeting on Crime-Justice"; October 15, 1966, White House Press Release.

12. January 30, 1967, memorandum from Joe Califano to the President, folder "1967 Crime Message #1," box 3, Legislative Background Files SSA 1968, LBJPL; Tom Lambert, "Johnson, 3 Senators Praise Crime Report," *Los Angeles Times*, February 19, 1967, 8; Berry quoted in David Canfield, "Crime Study Reaction

Good; Report Is Called Most Complete Study Ever," *Chicago Tribune*, February 20, 1967, C11; William F. Buckley Jr., "Conservative Doesn't Feel Society Owes the Criminal," *Los Angeles Times*, January 30, 1967. The response that worried Johnson officials the most came from Americans of Italian descent. Organizations like the Sons of Italy wrote to the administration outraged over the report's depiction of the Costra Nostra organized crime group as exclusively Italian (see Katzenbach et al., *Challenge of Crime*, 192). May 10, 1967, memorandum from Califano to the President, folder "FG 763 PCLWAJ (Citizens Adv. Com) 2/24/67–5/19/67," box 409, EX FG 763, LBJPL.

13. December 3, 1966, memorandum from Vorenberg to Califano. November 24, 1966, Telegram from Ramsey Clark to the President "Re: Implementation of National Crime Commission Report," folder "FG 135 DOJ (1967)," box 28, LBJ Confidential File FB 120 (1966), LBJPL.

14. Monroe W. Karmin, "Combating Crime," *Wall Street Journal*, December 28, 1966; Katzenbach et al., *Challenge of Crime*, 123; November 16, 1967, memorandum from HUD Secretary Robert C. Weaver to Califano, folder "1967 Crime Message Follow Up 3 of 3," box 4, Legislative Background Files SSA 1968, LBJPL; "Report on Action Taken by Department of Health, Education, and Welfare Related to Recommendations of the President's Commission on Law Enforcement and the Administration of Justice," attached to memorandum received March 28, 1968, from HEW Secretary Wilbur J. Cohen to Joseph Califano, folder "1967 Crime Message Follow Up 3 of 3," box 4, Legislative Background Files SSA 1968, LBJPL.

15. November 27, 1967, memorandum from Califano to Warren Christopher, folder "1967 Crime Message Follow Up 3 of 3," box 4, Legislative Background Files SSA 1968, LBJPL; Memorandum from Cohen to Califano.

16. Katzenbach et al., "Challenge of Crime," 16.

17. For the most thorough account of the Detroit Rebellion, see Sidney Fine, *Violence in the Model City: The Detroit Riot, Race Relations, and the Detroit Riot of 1967* (East Lansing: Michigan State University Press, 2007). See also Dan Georgakas and Mavin Surkin, *Detroit: I Do Mind Dying* (1975; repr., Cambridge, MA: South End Press, 1998); Heather Ann Thompson, *Whose Detroit: Politics, Labor, and Race in a Modern American City* (Ithaca, NY: Cornell University Press, 2004); Minutes of 8/2/67 Cabinet Meeting, folder "Cabinet Meeting 8/2/67 [4 of 4]," box 9, Cabinet Papers, LBJPL.

18. July 24, 1967, memorandum from Ben Wattenberg to the President, folder "7/24/67 Remarks to the Nation After Authorizing the Use of Federal Troops in Detroit," box 243, Statements of LBJ July 6, 1967–July 29, 1967, LBJPL; Fine, *Violence in the Model City*; "Events of the Early Morning of July 24th (as taken from the wires)," folder "Detroit Chronology July 23–31 (2)," box 58, Office Files

of Joseph A Califano, LBJP; July 24, 1967, Telegram from Governor George Romney to Attorney General Ramsey Clark, folder "1967 Riot Misc. Reports," box 345, George Romney Gubernatorial Papers, University of Michigan Bentley Historical Library.

19. July 24, 1967, Remarks to the Nation after Authorizing the Use of Federal Troops in Detroit, folder "7/24/67 Remarks to the Nation after Authorizing the Use of Federal Troops in Detroit," box 243, Statements of LBJ July 6, 1967–July 29, 1967, LBJPL. Johnson went on to state: "We seek peace based on one man's respect for another man and upon mutual respect for the law. We seek a public order that is built on steady progress in meeting the needs of all of our people." "Excerpts from President Lyndon B. Johnson's Address to the Nation on Civil Disorders, July 27, 1967" in Otto Kerner et al., *Report of the National Advisory Commission on Civil Disorders* (New York: Bantam Books, 1968), 538–540, 323. Unlike the dominant perception of the Watts uprising, the average participant in Detroit's unrest had a more diverse background. A federal research study revealed that most of the participants were in their twenties and thirties, only about a quarter were under twenty, and an additional quarter were over age thirty-five. Perhaps more significantly, four out of five of the participants had jobs and were employed at the time of the rebellion—even if the majority reported had been out of work at some time in the year leading up to it. The residents over age twenty-five were generally more educated than black Americans of the same age group. August 8, 1967, memorandum from Williard Wirtz to the President, folder "Detroit Chronology July 23–31 (1)," box 58, Office Files of Califano, LBJPL.

20. Minutes of August 2, 1967, Cabinet Meeting, folder "Cabinet Meeting 8/2/67 [4 of 4]," box 9, Cabinet Papers, LBJPL; Ron Porambo, *No Cause for Indictment: An Autopsy of Newark* (New York: Holt, Rinehart and Winston, 1971); Kerner et al., *Report of the National Advisory Commission* (1968). See also Tom Hayden, *Rebellion in Newark: Official Violence and Ghetto Response* (New York: Vintage Books, 1967); Kevin Mumford, *Newark: A History of Race, Rights, and Riots* (New York: New York University Press, 2007).

21. Minutes of August 2, 1967, Cabinet Meeting; Guardsmen quoted in Gene Roberts, "Troops Battle Detroit Snipers, Firing Machine Guns From Tanks," *New York Times*, July 26, 1967, 1. Martin quoted in "The Newark Tragedy: A Week Long Inquiry," *Washington Post*, July 24, 1967, A1; Homer Bigart, "Newark Riot Deaths at 21 as Negro Sniping Widens," *New York Times*, July 16, 1967, 1.

22. Beyond indiscriminate violence, state and local law enforcement authorities also joined in the looting and general destruction during the disorders. Black participants tended to spare those businesses identified as black-owned, but white Newark police officers took it upon themselves to shoot the windows of

the stores with "Soul Brother" tags. According to testimony before the Governor's Commission on the Newark riot, state troopers broke into a dry cleaners and smashed windows, threw clothes from racks, and emptied the cash register. These cases may have been exceptional, but in the end many police departments profited from the loot, selling televisions, sofas, guns, and liquor at auction. Minutes of August 2, 1967, Cabinet Meeting; Porambo, *No Cause for Indictment*; Kerner et al., *Report of the National Advisory Commission* (1968); Guardsmen quoted in Roberts, "Troops Battle Detroit Snipers"; Officer quoted in "The Newark Tragedy"; Wayne Thomis, "Detroit Holocaust: Why Wheels Stopped in Motor City," *Chicago Tribune*, July 28, 1967, 4. See Mumford, *Newark*, 125; Russell Sackett, "In a Grim City, a Secret Meeting with the Snipers," *Life* magazine, July 28, 1967, 27; "New Jersey Panel Assesses Police of Racial Prejudice during Newark Riot," *Wall Street Journal*, February 12, 1968, 8; Jerry M. Flint, "National Guard Leaving Detroit," *New York Times*, July 29, 1967, 1.

23. This administration and Johnson's Crime Commission relied instead on FBI studies concluding that "matters of police brutalities, for the most part, have little merit," based on the 3 percent conviction rate of accused officers. Transcript of December 28, 1966 Meeting, 708, folder "Transcripts of Commission Meetings 1/11/–12-66, 12/28-30-66 , 1/21–22/67 3 of 3," box 57, Records of the President's Committee on Law Enforcement and the Administration of Justice, Series 2, LBJPL. Transcript of September 8, 1965, Meeting, 107.

24. Furr quoted in Dale Wittner, "Billy Furr, Caught in the Act of Looting Beer," *Life* magazine, July 28, 1967, 21–22 (dialect in article); August 8, 1967, memorandum from Wirtz to the President.

25. Remarks of the President before the IACP; Minutes of August 2, 1967, Cabinet Meeting; Ward Churchill and Jim Vander Wall, *The COINTELPRO Papers: Documents from the FBI's Secret War against Dissent* (New York: South End Press, 1990), 92.

26. Minutes of August 2, 1967, Cabinet Meeting. For the most thorough discussion of Stokely Carmichael and his role in the Black Power Movement, see Peniel Joseph, *Stokely: A Life* (New York: Basic Books, 2014), especially Chapter 12, "The World Stage: London, Cuba, and Vietnam, July 13-September 5, 1967;" Carmichael quoted in "Sniping," *Washington Post*, July 28, 1967, A16.

27. Minutes of August 2, 1967, Cabinet Meeting.

28. Letter from President Johnson to Honorable Mike Mansfield, U.S. Senate, Washington, DC, folder "1967 Crime Message Follow Up 2 of 3," box 4, Legislative Background Files SSA 1968, LBJPL; "E. Large City Special Grants," folder "OLEP (Gen 1969)," Records of the Law Enforcement Assistance Administration, National Archives, College Park, Maryland.

29. Fulwood and Murphy, quoted in "2d Neighborhood Center Opened by D.C. Police," *Washington Post*, September 7, 1968, B2.

30. "Los Angeles Police Department Community Relations Program Report," November 1968, folder "LAPD Youth Services," box 26, Krogh Files, RNPL.

31. When federal policymakers, law enforcement, and criminal justice officials used the term "delinquency" or "delinquent," they often took the concept as a given, without clearly defined parameters. A Juvenile Delinquency report from 1967 defined delinquents as "children who get into trouble with the law," but on the whole delinquency was defined spatially, endemic to "slum areas, where delinquency is highest," as Johnson officials put it. The definition used in the text comes from the January 11, 1967, Letter to Arthur Rossett from Charles Schinitsky, Attorney in Charge, The Legal Aid Society, Family Court Branch, folder "Correspondence Re Task Force Report," box 93, RPCLEAJ Series 6: Task Force on Juvenile Delinquency, LBJPL. See also July 21, 1964, Report on "Juvenile Delinquency," folder "Juvenile Delinquency," box 40, Office Files of Bill Moyers, LBJPL; N/T, N/D Document p. 12, Legislative Background, SSA 1968; Symington quoted in Cliff Sessions, "Poor Moms, Dads Can Be Replaced," *Chicago Defender*, October 26, 1965, 11; Lyndon Johnson, "Special Message to the Congress Recommending a 12-Point Program for America's Children and Youth," February 8, 1967, American Presidency Project, available at http://www.presidency.ucsb.edu/ws/?pid=28438; Wirtz in Minutes of 8/2/67 Cabinet Meeting; June 16, 1967, memorandum from Califano to the President, pg. 3, folder "Watts," box 58, Office Files of Califano, LBJPL.

32. November 29, 1966, memorandum from Hugh M. Durhan, Criminal Division to James C. Gaither, White House Liaison Officer for Task Force on Law Enforcement and Administration of Justice, 27, folder 2, "1966–67 Task Force on Crime II," box 1, Legislative Background Files SSA 1968, LBJPL.

33. Symington quoted in Sessions, "Poor Moms, Dads Can Be Replaced"; *Chicago Defender*, October 26, 1965, 11; Lyndon Johnson, "Special Message to the Congress Recommending a 12-Point Program for America's Children and Youth"; Jaworski and Parsons in Transcript of September 21, 1966, Crime Commission Meeting, 25, 46, folder "Transcripts of Commission Meetings 6/27–29/66, 9/20–21/66 1 of 3," box 56, RPCJEAJ Series 2, LBJPL.

34. Roughly two thirds of the bureaus were located in black urban areas. The theoretical seeds of the Youth Service Bureaus came from President Kennedy's Committee on Juvenile Delinquency and Youth Crime, which included staff and leadership that went on to serve on the Crime Commission in addition to Symington. Although the President's Committee had disbanded, its ideas found new energy during the Johnson administration in the Crime Commission's recommendations. Johnson, "Special Message to the Congress Recommending a 12-Point Program"; U.S. Department of Health, Education, and Welfare, Social and Rehabilitative Service, Youth Development and Delinquency Prevention Administration *Youth Service Bureaus and*

Delinquency Prevention (Washington, DC: U.S. Government Printing Office, 1973), 3; California Youth Authority, *National Study of Youth Service Bureaus*, 45–47; Sessions, "Poor Moms, Dads"; California Youth Authority, *National Study of Youth Service Bureaus; Final Report to the Youth Development and Delinquency Prevention Administration* (Washington, DC: Youth Development and Delinquency Prevention Administration, 1973), 45–47.

35. Johnson, "Special Message to the Congress Recommending a 12-Point Program."

36. Johnson's Crime Commission noted of the bureau design, "It is essential that acceptance of the bureau's services be voluntary; otherwise the dangers and disadvantages of coercive power would merely be transferred from the juvenile court to it." Katzenbach et al., *Challenge of Crime*, 83.

37. Ibid., 20.

38. Juvenile Delinquency Prevention and Control Act of 1968.

39. U.S. Department of Health, Education, and Welfare, Social and Rehabilitative Service, Youth Development and Delinquency Prevention Administration *Youth Service Bureaus and Delinquency Prevention* (Washington, DC: U.S. Government Printing Office, 1973). Excerpts from "Juvenile Delinquency and Youth Crime," Task Force Report to the President's Commission on Law Enforcement and Administration of Justice, 1967, 396–399, app. B, 44–45. California Youth Authority, *National Study of Youth Service Bureaus*, 66.

40. "Introduction" in Robert L. Woodson, ed., *Youth Crime and Urban Policy: A View from the Inner City* (Washington, DC: American Enterprise Institute for Public Policy Research, 1981), 6; California Youth Authority, *National Study of Youth Service Bureaus*, 159–160.

41. California Youth Authority, *National Study of Youth Service Bureaus*, 86.

42. Ibid., 183–184, 175–176, vii.

43. The California Youth Authority offered both commissions an early example of such a program. With money from Kennedy's Juvenile Delinquency programs and state funds, in 1961, the Youth Authority started testing community treatment alternatives by bringing juvenile offenders into community centers for counseling and therapy. Ibid., 175–176.

44. Officials in the Department of Health, Education, and Welfare were concerned about the underlying pathological assessments and the punitive emphasis of the Youth Service Bureaus, which relied "heavily on the relationship between low family economic status and delinquency and, concomitantly, giving short shrift to the issues of middle-class and suburban delinquency." While individual, social, and family pathologies were "clearly a major concern," the administration's view of the issue overlooked "the importance of fundamental changes in structure and expansion of efforts" in public institutions. House Committee on Education and Labor, *Juvenile Delinquency and*

Prevention Act of 1967 Hearings before the General Subcommittee on Education, 90th Cong., 1st sess. (May 10, 1967), 328 (Statement of Executive Director James Vorenberg, President's Commission on Law Enforcement and the Administration of Justice); January 3, 1967, letter from Lisle C. Carter Jr., Assistant Secretary Individual and Family Services, HEW, to Jim Vorenberg, folder "Correspondence Re: Task Force Report," box 93, RPCLEA Series 6, LBJPL.

45. Although data on juvenile incarceration rates before 1990 are inconsistent, the rate of incarceration was 241 per 100,000 youth in 1975; by 1979, it had reached a rate of 251 per 100,000 youth; and by 1983, it had soared to 290 per 100,000 youth (peaking in 1995 at a rate of 381 per 100,000 youth). See Bradford Smith, "Children in Custody: 20-Year Trends in Juvenile Detention, Correctional, and Shelter Facilities," *Crime and Delinquency* 44 (1998): 526–543; Annie E. Casey Foundation, "Reducing Youth Incarceration in the United States," February 2013, available at http://www.aecf.org/m/resourcedoc/AECF -DataSnapshotYouthIncarceration-2013.pdf. On the racial disparities within the American criminal justice system, see Michelle Alexander, *The New Jim Crow: Mass Incarceration in the Age of Colorblindness* (New York: New Press, 2011), 16; Heather C. West, William J. Sabol, and Sarah J. Greenman, "Prisoners in 2009," *Bureau of Justice Statistics Bulletin*, rev. October 27, 2011, U.S. Department of Justice; Bruce Western, *Punishment and Inequality in America* (New York: Russell Sage Foundation, 2006); Katzenbach et al., *Challenge of Crime*, 59.

46. To underscore the importance of the commission's work, Johnson warned: "The Civil Peace has been shattered in a number of cities. The American people are deeply disturbed. They are baffled and dismayed by the wholesale looting and violence that has occurred both in small towns and great metropolitan centers." Johnson, "Remarks upon Signing the Order Establishing the National Advisory Commission on Civil Disorders, American Presidency Project, available at http://www.presidency.ucsb.edu/ws/index.php?pid=28369; and "Appendix B: Remarks of the President upon Issuing an Executive Order Establishing a National Advisory Commission on Civil Disorders, July 29, 1967," Kerner et al., *Report of the National Advisory Commission* (1968), 536. Roy Reed, "President Calls for Free Inquiry on Nation's Riots," *New York Times*, July 30, 1967, 1; "Appendix J: A Statement on Methodology," Kerner et al., *Report of the National Advisory Commission* (1968), 574; October 1, 1968, memorandum from Califano for the President from Joe Califano, folder "FG 763 PCLEAJ (Citizens Adv. Comt.) 1/1/68," box 409, EX FG 763 2/21/61, LBJPL.

47. Kerner et al., *Report of the National Advisory Commission* (1968), 1. Anthony Platt provides an excellent analysis of the politics of these various presidential task forces. See Anthony Platt, *The Politics of Riot Commissions, 1917–1970: A Collection of Reports and Critical Essays* (New York: Collier Books, 1971).

48. Hugh Davis Graham, "On Riots and Riot Commissions: Civil Disorder in the 1960s," *Public Historian* 2, no. 4 (1980): 7–27, 19.

49. Kerner et al., *Report of the National Advisory Commission* (1968), 223, 218, 224, 222.

50. Ibid., 219 (emphasis in original).

51. Ibid; Kerner et al., *Report of the National Advisory Commission on Civil Disorders* (Washington, DC: U.S. Government and Printing Office, 1967), 160, 162, 159; Kerner et al., (1968), 319.

52. Kerner et al., (1967), 158, 165, 167; Kerner et al., *Report of the National Advisory Commission* (1968) 319.

53. Kerner et al., *Report of the National Advisory Commission* (1968) 304, 307; Katzenbach et al., *Challenge of Crime*, 95. Moreover, paraphrasing the Crime Commission, Kerner Commission members suggested that if police departments remained "lily-white," "a feeling may develop that the community is not being policed to maintain civil peace but to maintain the status quo." Kerner et al., (1968), 315. Black police officers would not only increase the stability of black families, according to members, but also make residents more comfortable with new levels of law enforcement personnel in their everyday lives.

54. Kerner et al., (1967), 167.

55. Ibid., 168.

56. Kerner et al., (1967), 158; Kerner et al., (1968), 300.

57. Kerner et al., (1967), 21, 392; Katzenbach et al., *Challenge of Crime*, 57; James Yuenger "Commission Sought and Got Facts on Urban Riots: Kerner," *Chicago Tribune*, March 1, 1968, 1.

58. The cabinet largely blamed the outbreak on delinquency problems. "School truancy can be very dangerous," Clark commented at a cabinet meeting on April 3. "There have been as many as 17,000 truants from Negro schools on that day in Memphis." Minutes of April 3, 1968, Cabinet Meeting, folder "Cabinet Meeting 4/3/68 [1 of 4]," box 13, Cabinet Papers, LBJPL; March 29, 1968, Remarks of the President before the Philadelphia Police Athletic League, folder "3-29-68 Remarks of the President before the Philadelphia Police Athletic League," box 270, Statements of LBJ July 6, 1967–July 29, 1967, LBJPL.

59. Shriver Quoted in Gareth Davies, *From Opportunity to Entitlement: The Transformation and Decline of Great Society Liberalism* (Lawrence: University Press of Kansas, 1999), 191.

60. Robert Wiedrich, "Growing Disrespect for Laws Called Threat to Our Nation," *Chicago Tribune*, February 17, 1968, W18.

4. THE WAR ON BLACK CRIME

1. Richard Nixon, "Toward Freedom from Fear" (Nixon for President Committee, 1968).
2. For the best discussion of block grants and partisanship as they relate to the politics of crime control and race, see Vesla Mae Weaver, "Frontlash: Race and the Development of Punitive Crime Policy," *Studies in American Political Development* 21 (Fall 2007): 230–265; Martha J. Bailey and Nicolas J. Duquette, "How Johnson Fought the War on Poverty: The Economics and Politics of Funding at the Office of Economic Opportunity," *Journal of Economic History* 74, no. 2 (June 2014): 351–388.
3. Phillips quoted in Gareth Davies, *From Opportunity to Entitlement: The Transformation and Decline of Great Society Liberalism* (Lawrence: University Press of Kansas, 1999), 217.
4. July 13, 1970, memorandum for Bud Krogh, *no author,* "Review of 'Brainstorming Session' Outlining Administration Responses and Initiatives towards the Crime Problem for the Next Year (Santarelli, Kallen, Persce-Drug Issue Not Discussed)," box 25, Egil Krogh Files, Richard Nixon Presidential Library (hereafter, RNPL); Peter Stuart, "Revolt in Law Enforcement?" *Christian Science Monitor,* April 21, 1970, 2.
5. Michelle Alexander provides an excellent discussion of criminal justice discretion in Chapter 3, "The Color of Justice," in *The New Jim Crow: Mass Incarceration in the Age of Colorblindness* (New York: New Press, 2011), 97–139; See also James Vorenberg, "Narrowing the Discretion of Criminal Justice Officials," *Duke Law Journal* 4 (September 1976): 661–697.
6. Nixon, "Toward Freedom from Fear"; Vesla Mae Weaver, "Frontlash: Race and the Politics of Punishment" (PhD diss., Harvard University, 2007), 54.
7. Although black voters secured Agnew's victory in the 1966 Maryland gubernatorial race, he lost much of this initial support after he attributed the cause of the 1968 Baltimore riot to the shortcomings of black leaders in the community. Nixon, "Toward Freedom from Fear"; "Complete Text of the 1968 Republican Platform," *Congressional Quarterly Almanac* 24 (1968): 987–994.
8. Thomas E. Cronin, Tamia Z. Cronin, and Michael E. Millakovich, *U.S. v. Crime in the Streets* (Bloomington: Indiana University Press, 1981), 60–61; Elliott Currie and James Q. Wilson, "The Politics of Crime: The American Experience," in *The Politics of Crime Control,* ed. Kevin Stenson and David Cowell (London: Sage Publications, 1991), 33–61, 34; James D. Calder, "Presidents and Crime Control: Kennedy, Johnson and Nixon and the Influences of Ideology," *Presidential Studies Quarterly* 12, no. 4 (1982): 574–589; Nixon, "Toward Freedom from Fear"; Mitchell quoted in Nancy Marion, *A History*

of Federal Crime Control Initiatives, 1960–1993 (New York: Praeger, 1994), 70; "Complete Text of the 1968 Republican Platform"; Mitchell quoted in Ronald J. Ostrow, "Richardson to Shift Focus at Justice Department," *Los Angeles Times*, June 17, 1973, H1.

9. Dean quoted in Cronin et al., *U.S. v. Crime in the Streets*, 76. See John Dean, *Blind Ambition* (New York: Pocket Books, 1970), 389–390.

10. Muskie quoted in "U.S. Can't Put a Wall around Negro," *Chicago Tribune*, September 16, 1968, 5. See also Weaver, "Race and Politics," 84. Popular vote totals are based on "Congressional Quarterly's Guide to U.S. Elections," 4th Ed. (2001). On the 1968 election, see Rick Perlstein, *Nixonland: The Rise of a President and the Fracturing of America* (New York: Scribner, 2008); Warren F. Kimball, "The Election of 1968," *Diplomatic History* 28, no. 4: 513–528.

11. The council included former LAPD police chief Thomas Reddin, Professor Walter Murray (who served as special consultant to the Watts Area Re-Development and Rehabilitation Project), and a number of U.S. attorneys, district attorneys, and members and former presidents of the International Association of Chiefs of Police, the National Law Enforcement Association, and the American Bar Association. Richard Nixon's Advisory Council on Crime and Delinquency—Recommendations. Attached to December 20, 1968, letter from Martin Pollner to Martin Anderson, folder "Crime 3 of 3," box 24, Martin Anderson Files, RNPL; undated policy brief for President-Elect Nixon, "Improving State and Local Law Enforcement and Criminal Justice," box 24, John Dean Collection, RNPL.

12. H. R. Haldeman, *The Haldeman Diaries: Inside the Nixon White House* (New York: G. P. Putnam and Sons, 1994), 66. This particular diary entry received much attention from the national news media and scholars, but it is worth repeating.

13. August 1, 1970, memorandum from Egil Krogh to the president in "Law Enforcement Assistance Administration Denver Trip by President Monday August 3, 1970," box 47, Egil Krogh Files, RNPL; May 8, 1970, "Draft Remarks for President Before the Regional Meeting of State Planning Agencies of Region VII of the LEAA Phoenix, AZ," folder "Proposals—President's LEAA Trip (1970)," box 26, Krogh Files, RNPL; May 1, 1970, memorandum from Skoler to Rogovin, Velde, and Coster, subj.: "Policy Statements—LEAA Technical Assistance Responsibilities," folder "OLEA (Gen) 1970," box 37, Records of the Law Enforcement Assistance Administration (hereafter, RLEAA), National Archives II; May 1, 1970, memorandum from Skoler to Rogovin, Vede, and Coster, subj.: "Policy Statements—LEAA Technical Assistance Responsibilities," folder "OLEA (Gen) 1970," box 37, RLEAA.

14. California, Connecticut, Delaware, Florida, Georgia, Illinois, Iowa, Kentucky, Maryland, Massachusetts, Michigan, Minnesota, Mississippi, Missouri, New

Jersey, New Mexico, New York, North Dakota, Ohio, Pennsylvania, Rhode Island, Utah, Washington, West Virginia, and Wisconsin all had state criminal justice planning agencies underway before Nixon took office. Omnibus Crime Control and Safe Streets Act of 1968, Pub. L. No. 90-351, 82 Stat. 197 (1968).

15. August 2, 1970, presentation by Richard W. Velde, for President's Meeting in Denver, folder "LEAA Trip—August," box 21, Krogh Files, RNPL; August 1, 1970, memorandum from Krogh to the President; Professor quoted in Paul Houston, "Safe Streets: Is U.S. Money Helping Win War on Crime?" *Los Angeles Times*, April 4, 1971, F1.

16. June 23, 1969, address by Charles H. Rogovin before the National Association of Attorneys General at the College of the Virgin Island Charlotte Amalie, St. Thomas, Virgin Islands, box 25, Krogh Files, RNPL; friend quoted in Deirdre Carmody, "He Loves Cops: Charles Howard Rogovin," *New York Times*, July 23, 1970, 16; Charles Rogovin, "The Genesis of the Law Enforcement Assistance Administration: A Personal Account," *Columbia Human Rights Law Review* 5 (1973): 9–26.

17. Edith Flynn, "Report on the Task Force on Corrections," 4th National Symposium on Law Enforcement Science and Technology May 1–3, 1972, Washington, DC, box 19, RLEAA.

18. On the relationship between the LEAA and the HUD, see "Housing Authority Sets Up Own 72-Man Security Force," *New Pittsburgh Courier*, January 29, 1972, 1; "U.S. Crime Probe Gets HUD Funds," *Chicago Daily Defender*, September 15, 1970, 15. On the LEAA and the CIA and the army, see Stuart Schrader, "American Streets, Foreign Territory: How Counterinsurgent Police Waged the War on Crime" (PhD diss., New York University, 2015); Paul G. Edwards, "Area Police Confirm CIA Aid," *Washington Post*, February 7, 1973, D1; Thomas Lippman, "D.C. Police Now Free of White House," *Washington Post*, June 22, 1975, 1; Three CIA consultants received a $166,000 grant from the LEAA to help the department reorganize its intelligence files. Ibid.; David Burnham, "C.I.A. Will Curb Training It Provides Police Forces," *New York Times*, March 6, 1973, 29. Legal issues concerning the CIA's relationship with local police departments have recently resurfaced, and the agency launched an internal investigation in the fall of 2011 to determine whether its work with the New York Police Department after the September 11 attack violated laws prohibiting intelligence-gathering at home. See Mark Mazzetti, "C.I.A. Examining Legality of Work with Police Dept.," *New York Times*, September 13, 2011, A31. On the LEAA and Law Enforcement Education Programs, see August 2, 1970, presentation by Richard W. Velde, for President's Meeting in Denver, folder "LEAA Trip—August," box 21, Krogh Files, RBPL; Weaver, "Race and Crime Policy," 257; "ECSU Law Enforcement Program Set," *New Journal and Guide*, August 30, 1969, B13. On the LEAA and public relations programs

promoting the crime issue, see Jim Carmody, "A Series in the Name of Justice," *Washington Post*, October 11, 1974, B8; John C. Waugh, "Mitchell Hints Plan for 'Massive Citizen War on Crime,'" *Christian Science Monitor*, February 12, 1969, 4; "California to Get New Law Grant," *New York Times*, August 27, 1974, 30.

19. Planning did not originate with the Nixon administration, as Johnson appointed more commissions and task forces than any other president. But with respect to crime control, White House officials and state bureaucrats steered the course of the law enforcement revolution. The top LEAA administrators viewed planning as "the process of consciously exercising rational control over the development of the physical environment and of certain aspects of the social environment, in light of a common scheme of values, goals, and assumptions." If insufficient planning created mismanagement of the War on Poverty, policymakers hoped that by carefully developing programs, encouraging experimentation, and supporting academic research, the War on Crime would prove far more "successful." "Planning Assistance: Problems and Implications" LEAA box 37 OLEP (Gen) 1970, RLEAA; Cronin et al., *U.S. v. Crime in the Streets*, 79.

20. N.d. memorandum from Pollner to Mitchell, "Re: Anticipated Criminal Activity Facing New Administration and Proposed Action to Combat Same," Anderson Files, box 24, RNPL.

21. Paul W. Valentine, "Police Auditors Criticized," *Washington Post*, October 26 1972, A1. Elsewhere, the New York City firm Touche Ross and Company received $2.1 million from the city of Detroit and $1 million for law enforcement consulting services in other cities. The International Association of Chiefs of Police gave enthusiastic testimony in congressional hearings as soon as the federal government began to take an interest in crime control in the mid-1960s, and the association quickly evolved into a lucrative law enforcement consulting institution. The LEAA found the group to have highly questionable practices, but awarded it multimillion-dollar grants to cover its hefty consulting fees. "Police Lose Funds for Helicopters," *Washington Post*, January 22, 1972, A3; Glen Elsasser, "Vast Waste of Funds Charged," *Chicago Tribune*, April 7, 1972, 3.

22. Glen Elsasser, "U.S. Finds Alabama Misused Funds for Fight on Crime," *Chicago Tribune*, April 30, 1972, 5; Kenneth Reich, "U.S. Refuses to Hold Back Alabama Funds," *Los Angeles Times*, February 20, 1971, A7.

23. Both Rogovin and Ruth remained on as private consultants for the agency, however, until Ruth stepped in to serve as special prosecutor during the Watergate investigation with former Crime Commission member James Vorenberg. John Herbers, "Senators Seek to Divert Anticrime Funds to Cities," *New York Times*, November 22, 1969, 38; Peter Stuart, "Revolt in Law Enforcement?" *Chris-*

tian Science Monitor, April 21, 1970, 2; Paul G. Edwards, "Deputy Ruth Says Job Was Depressing," *Washington Post*, October 13, 1974, A16.

24. Patricia Sullivan, "Jerris Leonard: Justice Department Official," *Washington Post*, August 3, 2006, B6; Fred P. Graham, "Head of I.T.T. Denies Link of Suits and Aid to G.O.P," *New York Times*, March 16, 1972, 1. On the murder of Fred Hampton, see Jeffrey Haas, *The Assassination of Fred Hampton: How the FBI and the Chicago Police Murdered a Black Panther* (Chicago: Chicago Review Press, 2011); Rod Bush, *We Are Not What We Seem: Black Nationalism and the Class Struggle in the American Century*, rev. ed. (New York: New York University Press, 2000); Ward Churchill and Jim Vander Wall, *Agents of Repression: The FBI's Secret Wars against the Black Panther Party and the American Indian Movement* (New York: South End Press, 2001). On the Kent State killings, see William W. Scranton et al., *Report of the President's Commission on Campus Unrest* (Washington, DC: U.S. Government Printing Office, 1970); I. F. Stone, *The Killings at Kent State: How Murder Went Unpunished* (New York: Vintage Books, 2nd printing, 1971) Dean J. Kotlowski, *Nixon's Civil Rights: Politics, Principle, and Policy* (Cambridge, MA: Harvard University Press, 2002).

25. Leonard doubled the size of the LEAA's auditing staff to supervise grant expenditures and the flow of federal funds. To support projects that Leonard determined had the potential to "revolutionize criminal justice," he established another bureaucratic layer to the national law enforcement apparatus by creating regional offices that gave final approval for anticrime plans. March 31, 1971, memorandum from Trubow to Jerris Leonard, subj.: "Fund Flow and Expenditure Problems," folder "OLEP (Gen) 1971," box 38, RLEAA; Robert Smith, "U.S. Crime Agency Is Decentralized" *New York Times*, May 19, 1971, 28; Walter R. Gordon, "Problems Sinking Law Agency," *Baltimore Sun*, March 29, 1971, A1.

26. John Herbers, "Senators Seek"; March 13, 1970, memorandum from Norval C. Jesperson to Skoler, subj.: "Policy: Role of LEAA in Operation Settings," folder "OLEP (Gen) 1970," box 37, RLEAA; Kenneth Reich, "U.S. Funds Misused in Florida, Audit Charges," *Los Angeles Times*, June 10, 1971, 28.

27. A separate bathroom was customary practice for "an executive level three grade earning $40,000 a year," a $2,000 raise over Rogovin's salary at the agency. "Lush and Plush," *Washington Post*, October 13, 1972, B10; Cronin et al., *U.S. v. Crime in the Streets*, 92–93.

28. "Arkansas Studies Crime Funds' Use," *New York Times*, January 2, 1972, 63; Kotz and Woodward, "U.S. Adrift in Crime Fight"; "The Nation," *Los Angeles Times*, July 29, 1971, 2.

29. "Sarasin Hits Monagan Record," *Hartford Courant*, August 29, 1972, 11; Sullivan, "Jerris Leonard."

30. "Planning Assistance: Problems and Implications"; undated letter to Speaker of the House from the Attorney General (likely January 28, 1970), Egil Krogh Collection, box 21, RNPL.

31. Mayors of Flint, Kalamazoo, Urbana, and Madison, among other cities, signed the petition, and Democrats from the Midwest, the Northeast, and the Sun Belt all cosponsored Harke's amendment, including Senators Alan Bible (Nevada), Howard Cannon (Nevada), Ralph Yarborough (Texas), Joseph Tydings (Maryland), and Birch Bayh (Illinois). John Herbers, "Senators Seek to Divert Anticrime Funds to Cities," *New York Times*, November 22, 1969, 38; The National Institute of Law Enforcement and Criminal Justice gave Maryland a grant in excess of $1 million, the bulk of which went to other federal agencies and nearly half of which went to the Army. One such collaboration involved a $175,000 grant to the Army to develop a homemade-bomb neutralizer. The Army contributed a mere $30,000 to the project for domestic crime control, but received seven of the eight neutralizers, with the final device going to the Department of Justice. The project was designed to counter what Ralph Miller, the chief of munitions support at the U.S. Army Explosion Ordinance Center, called "the radical threat" by injecting a chemical into a package containing a homemade bomb. Kotz and Woodward, "U.S. Adrift in Crime Fight."

32. "Planning Assistance: Problems and Implications," folder "OLEP (Gen) 1970," box 37, RLEAA; undated memorandum, "How Do We Accomplish Mobilization of All Our Human Resources for an All-Out War on Crime?" folder (n.d. 68–70, " 'Crime' 3 of 3," box 24, Anderson Files, RNPL; March 20, 1970, memorandum from Huston to Krogh, folder "Internal Security," box 14, Krogh Files, RNPL.

33. May 10, 1969, "Program Announcement: Special Grants for Crime Control Projects in Largest Cities," DOJ, LEAA; LEAA, folder "OJEP (Gen) 1969," box 37, RLEAA; "E. Large City Special Grants," n.d., folder "OLEP (Gen) 1969," box 37, RLEAA; December 14, 1970, memorandum, subj.: "Discretionary Funds Program for FY 1971," from Velde and Coster to Attorney General, folder "OLEP (Gen) 1971," box 38, RLEAA.

34. "City Asks U.S. Approval of 6 Anticrime Projects," *Washington Post*, June 7, 1969, B4; "President Pledges War on D.C. Crime," *Washington Post*, January 28, 1969, A1.

35. "The Breakdown in law and order may be attributed to wrong-headed public policies," the House wrote in its Committee Report of the DC Bill (submitted by South Carolina's John McMillan), implicitly condemning Great Society programs, which seemingly operated under "the notion that sympathy should be shown to bad men" who demonstrated an "innate hostility toward, and

defiance of, the police," resulting in a "failure on the part of many citizens to discharge their civic responsibilities" that demanded a set of punitive strategies. "D.C. Crime," in *CQ Almanac 1967*, 23rd ed. (Washington, DC: Congressional Quarterly, 1968), "Statement of the President upon Signing the District of Columbia Crime Bill," December 27, 1967, American Presidency Project, available at http://www.presidency.ucsb.edu/ws/?pid=28644. The work of James Forman Jr. and Lauren Pearlman provides comprehensive accounts of the politics of crime control in DC. See James Forman Jr., "Racial Critiques of Mass Incarceration: Beyond the New Jim Crow," *NYU Law Review* 87, no. 1 (2012): 101–146; Lauren Pearlman, *Democracy's Capital: Local Protest, National Politics, and the Struggle for Civil Rights in Washington, D.C.* (Chapel Hill: University of North Carolina Press, forthcoming).

36. "Remarks of the Attorney General: End-of-the-Year Briefing to RN" (December 1969), box 17, Krogh Files, RNPL; Richard Nixon, State of the Union Address, January 22, 1970, American Presidency Project, available at http://www.presidency.ucsb.edu/ws/?pid=2921; Lyndon Johnson, "Statement of the President upon Signing the District of Columbia Crime Bill," December 27, 1967, American Presidency Project, available at http://www.presidency.ucsb.edu/ws/?pid=28644; Cronin et al., *U.S. v. Crime in the Streets*, 94–95; June 19, 1970, memorandum from John Dean to Egil Krogh, "Administration Position on Various Crime Bills," folder "John Dean—Responses to Crime Bill 1970–71," box 23, Krogh Files, RNPL; "City Asks U.S. Approval of 6 Anticrime Projects," *Washington Post*, June 7, 1969, B4; "President Pledges War on D.C. Crime," *Washington Post*, January 28, 1969, A1.

37. The "narcotics addict" category received special attention from members of Nixon's domestic council, who labored to turn drug abuse into a criminal issue. As Nixon's chief crime control strategist Bud Krogh asserted: "Probably no more predictable person exists than the addict who must raise money to feed his habit. . . . Only when the addict appears to have 'graduated' to crimes of violence can he be subjected to pretrial detention." June 19, 1970, memorandum from Dean to Krogh. District of Columbia Court Reorganization Act of 1970, Pub. L. 91-358, 84 Stat. 473 (1970); Herbert L. Packer, "A Special Supplement: Nixon's Crime Program and What It Means," *New York Review of Books*, October 22, 1970; "City Asks U.S. Approval of 6 Anticrime Projects," *Washington Post*, June 7, 1969, B4; "T.R.B. Comments: Home-Grown Police State," *Boston Globe*, August 10, 1969, A6.

38. On the rise and long-term impact of these sentencing measures, within the federal system and beyond, see Alfred Blumstein, Jacqueline Cohen, Susan E. Martin, and Michael H. Tonry, eds., *Research on Sentencing: The Search for Reform*, vol. 1 (Washington, DC: National Academies Press, 1983); Marc

Mauer, *Race to Incarcerate* (New York: New Press, 2006); Charles J. Ogletree Jr. and Austin Sarat, eds., *Life without Parole: America's New Death Penalty* (New York: New York University Press, 2012); Franklin Zimring, "Sentencing Reform in the United States: Some Sobering Lessons from the 1970s," *Northern Illinois University Law Review* 2 (1981): 1–18; Fauntroy quoted in Terrance Wills, "Policeman against Citizen: 'The Law of the Jungle: No-Knock Bill Stirs Heat from Senate to Pulpit," *Globe and Mail*, May 18, 1970, 3; District of Columbia Court Reorganization Act of 1970; Philip Warden, "Crime Bill Seen as U.S. Model," *Chicago Tribune*, July 24, 1970, 5; June 19, 1970, memorandum from Dean to Krogh; Packer, "Special Supplement"; "T.R.B. Comments."

39. Wills, "Policeman against Citizen"; "6 Seized in Yonkers in a Numbers Raid," *New York Times*, February 18, 1970, 35; Heather Thompson, "Why Mass Incarceration Matters: Rethinking, Decline, and Transformation in Postwar American History," *Journal of American History* 97 (2010): 703–758; Julilly Kohler-Hausmann, " 'The Attila the Hun Law': New York's Rockefeller Drug Laws and the Making of the Punitive State," *Journal of Social History* 44 (2010): 71–95; Jeffrey Fagan and Martin Guggenheim, "Preventive Detention and the Judicial Prediction of Dangerousness for Juveniles: A Natural Experiment," *Journal of Criminal Law and Criminology* 86 (1996): 415–448; Adam Klein and Benjamin Wittes, "Preventive Detention in American Theory and Practice," *Harvard National Security Journal* 2 (2011): 85–191.

40. "E. Large City Special Grants," n.d., folder "OLEP (Gen) 1969," box 37, RLEAA; December 14, 1970, memorandum from Velde to Coster, subj.: "Discretionary Funds Program for FY 1971," folder "OLEP (Gen) 1971," box 38, RLEAA.

41. The decision to focus on street crime and burglary in these smaller cities reflected the sense that robbery occurred more frequently than any other violent crime. N.d. memorandum from Leonard to Ehrlichman, 1971, "High Impact Program" attached to October 5, 1972, memorandum for Bud Krogh from Geoff Shepard, "LEAA High Impact City Program," Krogh Files, RNPL.

42. Danziger quoted in Cronin et al., *U.S. v. Crime in the Streets*, 97.

43. Eleanor Chelimsky, *High Impact Anti-Crime Program: National Level Evaluation Final Report*, vol. 2 (Washington, DC: Department of Justice, National Institute of Law Enforcement and Criminal Justice, Law Enforcement Assistance Administration, 1976), 101; Author interview with Ann Goetchus and Carol Kaplan, November 2, 2011. Initially, Atlanta did not make the short list of cities eligible for funds, but Mayor Sam Massell presented a strong appeal to the Justice Department by demonstrating how closely his law enforcement measures aligned with the larger objectives of the War on Crime. F. C. Jordan Jr., The Mitre Corporation, "National Impact Program

Evaluation: A History of the Cleveland Impact Program" (Washington, DC: U.S. Department of Justice, Law Enforcement Assistance Administration, 1975), xiii; Leonard to Ehrlichman, 1971, "High Impact Program."

44. N.d. memorandum from Leonard to Ehrlichman, 1971, "High Impact Program"; Chelimsky, *High Impact Anti-Crime Program*, 190–191; Jack Anderson and Les Whitten, "Crime War Lags in Targeted Cities," *Washington Post*, November 29, 1975, B10. High Impact efforts included police training and tuition incentives, salary increases, and increase in administrative staff. High Impact funds in Atlanta went toward improving police training and education by introducing tuition incentives and psychological testing as a modernization program. To professionalize the force, the federal grants supported a 22 percent increase in patrolmen's salaries and enabled the Atlanta police chief to hire an administrative assistant and redesign report forms to ease the completion process for policemen. Baltimore also used High Impact funds to focus on police desk work, and employed civilians in order to free officers for street patrol at a cost of nearly half a million dollars. "First Installment," *Baltimore Sun*, October 27, 1972, A11.

45. Jordan, "National Impact Program Evaluation," 50, 60; Chelimsky, *High Impact Anti-Crime Program*, 293.

46. National Security Center Report quoted in Mitchell C. Lynch, "Federal Law Enforcement Aid," *Wall Street Journal*, July 7, 1976, 14; Jack Anderson and Les Whitten, "Crime War Lags"; Chelimsky, *High Impact Anti-Crime Program*, chap. 10, Summary; ibid.

47. This was the second and only time the prison population dropped. Between 1940 and 1950, state and federal prison authorities decarcerated by 7,543 inmates before restoring previous levels in the 1950s. Justice Policy Institute Analysis of U.S. Department of Justice Data, "The Punishing Decade: Prison and Jail Estimates at the New Millennium," May 2000, Justice Policy Institute, available at http://www.justicepolicy.org/images/upload/00-05_rep_punish ingdecade_ac.pdf. The federal government had established a tepid approach to the national prison system until the Nixon administration. Before the 1890s, persons convicted on federal charges were confined in state prisons. The federal government created a law enforcement apparatus of its own in the 1920s, via Prohibition and the rise of the FBI in 1924. Under Hoover's control, as the federal government began investigating crimes previously restricted to local agencies, the three federal prisons operating out of the Department of Justice evolved into the Bureau of Prisons in 1939. Construction on a new federal prison system began, and by the end of the 1940s, thirteen new correctional facilities opened. On the rise of the Department of Justice and the Bureau of Prisons, see Rebecca McLennan, *The Crisis of Imprisonment: Protest,*

Politics, and the Making of the American Penal State, 1776–1941 (New York: Cambridge University Press, 2008); Lisa McGirr, *The War on Alcohol: Prohibition and the Rise of the American State* (New York: W. W. Norton, 2015); see also Margaret Werner Cahalan, "Historical Corrections Statistics in the United States, 1850–1984," U.S. Department of Justice, Bureau of Justice Statistics (Washington, DC: U.S. Government Printing Office, 1986), 69.

48. November 13, 1969, memorandum for Attorney General Mitchell from Nixon, folder "Corrections 1 of 3 1970–71," box 11, Krogh Files, RNPL.

49. June 2, 1969, letter from John Mitchell to John Ehrlichman, box 46, Clapp Files, RNPL; December 30, 1972, address by Richard W. Velde, before the American Association for the Advancement of Science, box 19, RLEAA; William G. Nagel, "An American Archipelago: The United States Bureau of Prisons," presented at the luncheon general session, National Institute for Crime and Delinquency; Statler-Hilton Hotel, Boston, June 25, 1974, folder 14, box 78, Noel Sterrett— Issues Office Files, Jimmy Carter Presidential Library (hereafter, JCPL).

50. House Committee on the Judiciary, *Prison Construction Plans and Policy: Hearings before the Subcommittee on Courts, Civil Liberties, and the Administration of Justice*, 94th Cong., 2nd sess. (July 30, 1975), 103 (Statement of Carlson). The Bureau of Prisons director cited Norval Morris, *The Future of Imprisonment* (Chicago: University of Chicago Press, 1974) and James Q. Wilson, *Thinking about Crime* (New York: Basic Books, 1975) to argue against rehabilitative programs in his testimony.

51. Carlson, in House Committee on the Judiciary, *Prison Construction Plans and Policy*, 112.

52. Carlson, ibid., 466.

53. Fogel, ibid., 77; Carlson, ibid., 101–101; September 17, 1971, memorandum from Egil Krogh to John Ehrlichman re: Corrections, folder "Corrections 1 of 3 1970–71," box 11, Krogh Collection, RNPL.

54. Carlson, House Committee on the Judiciary, *Prison Construction Plans and Policy*. The commission estimated that the average daily population in corrections would balloon from 1.3 million in 1965 to some 1.8 million by the mid-1970s. Nicholas deB. Katzenbach et al., *The Challenge of Crime in a Free Society: A Report by the President's Commission on Law Enforcement and Administration of Justice* (Washington, DC: U.S. Government Printing Office, 1967), 160; Otto Kerner et al., *Report of the National Advisory Commission on Civil Disorders* (New York: Bantam Books, 1968), 392; National Advisory Commission on Criminal Justice Standards and Goals, *Task Force Report on Corrections* (Washington, DC: U.S. Government Printing Office, 1973).

55. September 17, 1971, memorandum from Egil Krogh to John Ehrlichman Re: Corrections, folder "Corrections 1 of 3 1970–71," box 11, Krogh Collection,

RNPL. The average sentence in 1945 was 16.5 months; by 1965 it had jumped to nearly three years, and by 1975 incarcerated Americans served an average of just under four years. December 30, 1972, address by Velde; February 8, 1978, open letter to Attorney General Griffin Bell from Milton G. Rector, President of National Council on Crime and Delinquency, folder 16, box 11, Gutierrez Files, JCPL; "Functions of the National Clearinghouse for Correctional Programming and Architecture," box 38, Office of Criminal Justice Administration 1972, RLEAA; "Long Range Master Plan"; William G. Nagel, "On Behalf of a Moratorium on Prison Construction," *Crime and Delinquency* 23: 154 (1977): 154–171; Cahalan, "Historical Corrections Statistics in the United States, 1850–1984," 72.

56. The data on the number of Latino inmates in the federal and state prison system remain incomplete. The Bureau of Justice Statistics, which itself formed in 1980 and has since set the standard for correctional counts, did not consistently account for Latino prisoners until the early 1990s. Most of the statistics available from prior to this period use the categories of black, white, and "other races" to reflect racial compositions. Since Latino inmates represented more than the 1 percent to 3 percent of those attributed to the latter category, we can assume they were counted as either black or white. N.d. memorandum from Pollner to Mitchell "Re: Anticipated Criminal Activity Facing New Administration and Proposed Action to Combat Same," 39, Anderson Files, box 24, RNPL. December 6, 1971, address by AG Mitchell, "New Doors, Not Old Walls," at the National Conference on Corrections, Williamsburg, VA, 1971, Krogh Files, box 15, RNPL.

57. Key discussions of the prisoners' rights movement in the 1960s and 1970s can be found in Dan Berger, *Captive Nation: Black Prison Organizing in the Civil Rights Era* (Chapel Hill: University of North Carolina Press, 2014); Robert Chase, "We Are Not Slaves: Rethinking the Rise of Carceral States through the Lens of the Prisoners Rights Movement," *Journal of American History* 102 (June 2015): 73–86; and Robert Chase and Norwood Andrews, eds., *Sunbelt Prisons and Carceral States: Incarceration, Immigration Detention/Deportation, and Resistance* (Chapel Hill: University of North Carolina Press, forthcoming); Garrett Felber, "Those Who Know Don't Say: The Nation of Islam and the Forgotten Politics of the Civil Rights Era" (PhD diss., University of Michigan, 2016); and Heather Thompson, *Blood in the Water: The Attica Uprising of 1971 and Its Legacy* (New York: Pantheon, 2016). For narrative accounts of the prison uprisings during this period, see Charles E. Silberman, *Criminal Violence, Criminal Justice* (New York: Vintage, 1978); Bert Useem and Peter Kimball, *States of Siege: U.S. Prison Riots, 1971–1986* (New York: Oxford University Press, 1989). Carlson in "Prison Construction Plans and Policy" Hearings,

107; memorandum from Pollner to Mitchell, "Re: Anticipated"; November 13, 1969, "Statement by the President," box 30, Anderson Files, RNPL.

58. Lawrence Meyer, "Prison Plans to Skirt Rehabilitation," in Appendix to "Prison Construction Plans and Policy" Hearings, 296–304, 298.

59. Quoted in Bob Kuttner, "Virginia Prison Tests Behavior Modification," *Washington Post*, August 1, 1974, B1.

60. Meyer, 297, "Prison Construction Plans and Policy" Hearings, 300.

61. Mitchell, "New Doors, Not Old Walls."

62. Doyle quoted in opening remarks of Chairman Robert W. Kastenmeier in "Prison Construction Plans and Policy" Hearings, 2; Policy Statement, Board of Directors, National Council on Crime and Delinquency, "The Nondangerous Offender Should Not Be Imprisoned," in "Prison Construction Plans and Policy" Hearings, Appendix: 380–384. Liberal criminologists in the 1970s joined the growing chorus challenging the construction of new prisons. See Erik Olin Wright, ed., *The Politics of Punishment* (New York: Harper and Row, 1973); Alvin J. Bronstein, "Reform without Change: The Future of Prisoners' Rights," *Civil Liberties Review* 4, no. 3 (September–October 1977); Andrew Von Hirsch, *Doing Justice: The Choice of Punishments: Report of the Committee for the Study of Incarceration* (New York: Hill and Wang, 1976); Twentieth Century Fund, *Fair and Certain Punishment: Report of the Twentieth Century Fund Task Force on Criminal Sentencing* (New York: McGraw-Hill, 1976).

63. Omnibus Crime Control and Safe Streets Act of 1970, Pub. L. 91-644, 84 Stat. 1880 (1971); December 30, 1972, Address by Velde; "Prison Construction Plans and Policy" Hearings, 301.

64. April 20, 1970, memorandum to Krogh from Velde, folder "Prisoner Rehabilitation," box 18, Krogh Files, RNPL. Law Enforcement Assistance Administration, U.S. Department of Justice, *Sage Streets: The LEAA Program at Work* (Washington, DC: U.S. Government Printing Office, 1971); Weaver, "Race and Crime Policy," 248; December 30, 1972, address by Velde; n.d. memorandum from Dave Miller to Bud Krogh, subj.: "LEAA Region 6: Meetings with Ed La-Pedis and Staff," February 18, 1970, box 25, Krogh Files, RNPL; Cronin et al., *U.S. v. Crime in the Streets*, 87; September 17, 1971, memorandum from Egil Krogh to John Ehrlichman Re: Corrections, folder "Corrections 1 of 3 1970–71," box 11, Krogh Collection, RNPL.

65. Fogel in "Prison Construction Plans and Policy" Hearings, 77; "Magnitude of the Wave of Jail and Prison Construction in the United States during the 1970s," National Moratorium on Prison Construction, January 1977, folder 1, box 11, Gutierrez Files, JCPL. "Strategies for Controlling Crime: A Position Paper," prepared by the Administration of Justice Division, National Urban

League, March 1978, folder 8, box 12, Gutierrez Files, JCPL; Nagel, "On Behalf of a Moratorium," 162.

66. Nagel, "On Behalf of a Moratorium," 159.

67. Nagel, "An American Archipelago," as appendix to "Prison Construction Plans and Policy" Hearings, 399, "Magnitude of the Wave."

68. There has yet to be established any direct correlation between incarceration and crime, as leading sociologists have consistently demonstrated in recent years. See especially Bruce Western, James Austin, and Tony Fabelo, "The Diminishing Returns of Increased Incarceration: A Blueprint to Improve Public Safety and Reduce Costs" (Washington, DC: JFA Institute, 2004); Robert H. Defina and Thomas M. Arvanites, "The Weak Effect of Imprisonment on Crime: 1971–1998," *Social Science Quarterly* 53 (2002): 407–420; Jenni Gainsborough and Marc Mauer, "Diminishing Returns: Crime and Incarceration in the 1990s (Washington, DC: The Sentencing Project, 2000); Dan Kahan, "Social Influence, Social Meaning, and Deterrence," *Virginia Law Review* 83 (1997): 349–395; Ryan S. King, Marc Mauer, and Malcolm C. Young, "Incarceration and Crime: A Complex Relationship (Washington, DC: The Sentencing Project, 2005); James P. Lynch and William J. Sabol, "Assessing the Effects of Mass Incarceration on Informal Social Control in Communities," *Criminology and Public Policy* 3 (2004): 267–294. Nagel, "On Behalf of a Moratorium," 159.

69. The Congressional Research Service argued that unemployment rates "could describe 82% of the year-to-year variation in new admissions to prisons." "Prison Population and Costs—Illustrative Projections to 1980," Library of Congress Congressional Research Service," in Appendix to "Prison Construction Plans and Policy" Hearings, 430–469, 435; Hearings, 8.

70. "Magnitude of the Wave."

71. "Prison Construction Plans and Policy" Hearings, 297, 301.

72. Richard Nixon, "Annual Address of the State of the Union Delivered to a Joint Session of the Congress, 1971," American Presidency Project, available at http://www.presidency.ucsb.edu/ws/?pid=3110.

73. Nixon also transferred many programs administered by the OEO to other federal departments. In one of his most controversial appointments, Nixon positioned Howard Phillips to succeed Donald Rumsfeld as director of the OEO and ordered Phillips to withhold community action funds in anticipation of the agency's dissolution. However, a federal district court forced the unconfirmed Phillips to resign and ruled that the president could not withhold funds that had been allocated by Congress. Even though the court ruling kept the agency alive, Ford officially closed the office in 1975 and replaced it with the Civil Services Administration. Bill Hazlett, "Concern over Crime Causing Widening Crack in Fiscal Dam," *Los Angeles Times*, April 3, 1973, E1; "The

Fading of the New Federalism," *Washington Post*, August 13, 1973, A22; Lou Cannon and David S. Broder, "Nixon's 'New Federalism' Struggles to Prove Itself," *Washington Post*, June 17, 1973, A1.

5. THE BATTLEGROUNDS OF THE CRIME WAR

1. January 16, 1970, memorandum from Daniel Patrick Moynihan to the President, folder "Black Vote (72)," box 10, Egil Krogh Files, Richard Nixon Presidential Library (hereafter, RNPL).

2. Edward C. Banfield, "Why Government Cannot Solve the Urban Problem," *Daedalus* 97 (1968): 1231–1241, 1232; Joel Lieske, "Book Review: *The Unheavenly City*," *American Journal of Sociology* 80 (1974): 765–767, 765; Richard Bernstein, "E. C. Banfield, Maverick on Urban Policy Issues, Dies," *New York Times*, October 8, 1999, C21; Edward C. Banfield, *The Unheavenly City* (Boston: Little Brown, 1970) and *The Unheavenly City Revisited* (1974; repr. Prospect Heights, IL: Waveland Press), 281.

3. George F. Will, "A Gold Medal Thinker," *Washington Post*, March 3, 2012, A17.

4. Wilson's doctoral thesis argued that while the constraints of municipal government limited black political leaders from accomplishing many of their objectives, formal political participation was necessary to build a black middle class. See James Q. Wilson, "Negro Leaders in Chicago" (PhD diss., University of Chicago, 1959); James Q. Wilson, *Negro Politics: The Search for Leadership* (New York: Free Press, 1960); Edward C. Banfield and James Q. Wilson, *City Politics* (New York: Vintage, 1963), 333, 348; Banfield quoted in Megan French-Marcelin, "Community Underdevelopment: Federal Aid and the Rise of Privitization in New Orleans" (PhD diss., Columbia University, 2014), 40–41.

5. James Q. Wilson, *Varieties of Police Behavior* (Cambridge, MA: Harvard University Press, 1968), 299, 16 (emphasis in original), 3.

6. The Executive Directors of the International Association of the Chiefs of Police, the Vera Institute, and the International Sheriffs' Association all sat on the board of the Police Foundation in 1970. Anne Hebald, "Foundation to Upgrade Police Units," *Washington Post*, September 15, 1970, C2.

7. The New York City Police Department was modeled after the Metropolitan Police Service in London, instituted in 1829. Patrick V. Murphy, "The Development of Urban Police," *Current History* 70 (1976): 245–248.

8. Murphy quoted in David Burnham, "Neighborhood Police," *New York Times*, December 31, 1970, 7; Douglas Robinson, "Murphy Plans Innovations for Police," *New York Times*, September 18, 1970, 1; Rudy Johnson, "Murphy to Set up Area 'Police Chiefs,'" *New York Times*, November 16, 1970, 14.

9. Atlanta also had a "decoy squad" which led to the death of seven people; "Solution to Crime Is Police Professionalism—Murphy," *Atlanta Daily World*, May 3, 1974, 1.

10. Murphy quoted in Robinson, "Murphy Plans Innovations"; C. Gerald Fraser, "Police to Expand Two-Man Plainclothes Patrols," *New York Times*, March 4, 1971, 39.

11. Murphy quoted in Fraser, "Police to Expand"; Joyce quoted in Lawrence Van Gelder, "New Crime Patrol Walks in Shadows," *New York Times*, November 13, 1970, 38; "Police Kill Man in Queens Holdup," *New York Times*, November 19, 1970, 37.

12. Officer quoted in Eric Pace, "Street Crime Cut by Disguise Artists," *New York Times*, September 3, 1972, 24.

13. Fraser, "Police to Expand"; Robert D. McFadden, "'Defensive' Police Shots Kill a Girl, 16," *New York Times*, January 28, 1973.

14. Pace, "Street Crime Cut"; Murphy quoted in "Solution to Crime Is Police"; Robinson, "Murphy Plans Innovations."

15. Law Enforcement Assistance Administration, 3rd Annual Report of the Law Enforcement Assistance Administration Fiscal Year 1971 (Washington, DC: U.S. Government Printing Office, 1972), 172–173; Austin McCoy, "Left City Politics: Progressive Responses to Economic Crisis in the Midwest, 1967–1987" (PhD diss., University of Michigan, 2016).

16. Nichols refused to disclose specific numbers or information about the unit because he believed exposure would lessen the program's "psychological impact" by depriving it of "the major effect, which is a deterrent effect." House Select Committee on Crime, *Street Crime in America: The Police Response: Hearings before the House Select Committee on Crime*, 93rd Cong., 1st sess. (April 12, 1967), 385 (Statement of John F. Nichols); Kathleen Schultz and Ann Bruetsch, *Detroit under STRESS* (Detroit: From the Ground Up Organization, 1973), Labadie Special Collections, University of Michigan; Frances Ward, "Crime in the Streets: Detroit Solution Provokes Controversy," *Los Angeles Times*, January 22, 1973, A1. See Heather Ann Thompson, *Whose Detroit?: Politics, Labor, and Race in a Modern American City* (Ithaca, NY: Cornell University Press, 2001), chaps. 4 and 6, for a discussion of STRESS and the social movement to abolish it. *Street Crime in America Hearings*, 382, 385, 408 (Statement of Nichols); Ibid., 392 (Statement of James Bannon); Ward, "Crime in the Streets"; *Street Crime in America Hearings*, 392 (Statement of James Bannon).

17. "Detroit (Mich) Police Department Analysis of STRESS, Submitted by John F. Nichols, Commissioner," in *Street Crime in America Hearings*, 418.

18. Thompson explores these cases in greater detail in *Whose Detroit?*; see chap. 6; "Detroit (Mich) Police Department Analysis of STRESS," 418; Michael Graham, "How the City of Detroit Tries to Make Its Streets Safe," *Chicago*

Tribune, December 26, 1971, A8; Ward, "Crime in the Streets"; "Detroit (Mich) Police Department Analysis"; *Street Crime in America Hearings*, 394, 387 (Statements of John P. Ricci and Nichols); Ibid., 392 (Statement of Bannon).

19. Robert L. Pisor, "Detroit Policeman Is Charged with Murder in 6th Killing," *Washington Post*, March 23, 1973, A3; Peterson quoted in Michael Graham, "How the City of Detroit Tries to Make Its Streets Safe," *Chicago Tribune*, December 26, 1971, A8.

20. "Detroit Policemen Accused in Slaying," *New York Times*, March 23, 1973, 34; "Officer with Busy Gun Held in Killing," *New Journal and Guide*, March 31, 1973, 1.

21. *Street Crime in America Hearings*, 387 (Statement of Nichols); Jenkins quoted in Agis Salpukas, "Black Police Ask Detroit End Unit," *New York Times*, March 11, 1972, 14; Henderson quoted in Thompson, *Whose Detroit?*, 99; Agis Salpukas, "3 Detroit Policemen Charged in Shooting," *New York Times*, March 25, 1972, 62.

22. Agis Salpukas, "Detroit Altering Decoy Operation," *New York Times*, March 18, 1972, 28; Ward, "Crime in the Streets"; "Detroit Police Mistake Deputies for Gamblers," *Globe and Mail*, March 10, 1972, 3; Agis Salpukas, "A Cops 'n' Cops Story," *New York Times*, March 12, 1972, E2.

23. *Street Crime in America Hearings*, 390–391 (Statements of Nichols and Bannon).

24. Jerry M. Flint, "Detroit Manhunt Stirs Controversy," *New York Times*, January 8, 1973, 26; "Another STRESS Cop Dies, 1 Critical," *Chicago Daily Defender*, December 28, 1972, 5; Nichols quoted in "Police Angered by STRESS Killing," *Baltimore Afro-American*, January 6, 1973, 1; Brown quoted in Thompson, *Whose Detroit?*, 147.

25. *Street Crime in America Hearings*, 404 (Statement of Ronald Martin); Flint, "Detroit Manhunt Stirs"; William Richards, "Police Search Tactics Enrage Blacks in Detroit," *Washington Post*, January 12, 1973, A3; Pastor Leroy Cannon quoting officers in "Angry Crowd Protests Manhunt," *Baltimore Afro-American*, January 20, 1974, 3.

26. Richards, "Police Search Tactics Enrage."

27. Petition quoted in Ward, "Crime in the Streets"; "Detroit Police Chief Defends STRESS Unit," *Baltimore Afro-American*, April 28, 1973, 3.

28. *Street Crime in America Hearings*, 386, 410 (Statement of Nichols); ibid.

29. Letter to *Detroit News* quoted in Thompson, *Whose Detroit?*, 100; Letter to Nichols quoted in "Detroit (Mich) Police Department Analysis of STRESS, submitted by John F. Nichols, Commissioner," 421; *Street Crime in America Hearings*, 386 (Statement of Nichols).

30. Bannon quoted in Ward, "Crime in the Streets"; William K. Stevens, "Tactics of an Elite Police Unit Election Issue in Detroit," *New York Times*, June 11, 1973, 30.

31. Stevens quoted in Stevens, "Tactics of an Elite"; Flint, "Detroit Manhunt Stirs"; Ward, "Crime in the Streets."

32. Spokesman quoted in Len Lear, "Anti-Crime Team (ACT) Lowers Crime Rates in North and West Phila.," *Philadelphia Tribune*, July 7, 1973, 1; "U.S. to Probe Police 'Breach,'" *Baltimore Sun*, August 7, 1974, C22; *Street Crime in America Hearings*, 387; "Mayor Young Kills STRESS in Detroit," *Baltimore Afro-American*, March 16, 1974, 3; Lear, "Anti-Crime Team."

33. "Mayor Young Kills STRESS"; "Detroit's STRESS Unit Abolished by Mayor Young," *Philadelphia Tribune*, March 19, 1974, 5.

34. Reginald Stuart, "Detroit Recalling Police in Wave of Youth Crime," *New York Times*, August 17, 1976, 1; James Campbell, "Detroit Street Crime Up: Mayor Imposes Curfew to Curb Teen Crime," *Baltimore Afro-American*, July 9, 1983, 1.

35. *Street Crime in America Hearings*, 404 (Statement of Congressman Sam Steiger).

36. Johnson officials rejected Edward M. Kennedy's proposal for a "West Point" academy for police officers for this reason in 1968. January 5, 1968, memorandum from Joe Califano to the President, folder "1968 Follow Up," box 2, Legislative Background Files Safe Streets Act of 1968, Lyndon Baines Johnson Presidential Library.

37. "The Federal Role in Crime Prevention," Republican Committee on Planning and Research—Task Force on Crime, box 24, Martin Anderson Files, RNPL.

38. June 15, 1971, Policy Statement, folder "Special Action Office for Drug Abuse Prevention," box 31, Egil Krogh Files, RNPL.

39. Ambrose had previously supervised the Secret Service and the Bureaus of Narcotics and Customs at the Treasury Department in the late 1950s, and the anti-narcotics trafficking measures he instituted at the borders rendered him an apt man for the job. Christian Parenti, *Lockdown America: Police and Prisons in the Age of Crisis* (New York: Verso, 2000), 13; Radley Balko, *Rise of the Warrior Cop: The Militarization of America's Police Forces* (New York: Public Affairs, 2013), 105; June 15, 1971, Policy Statement; Robert M. Smiths, "New Drug Agency to Fight Pushers on Lower Levels," *New York Times* January 19, 1972, 1; Ambrose quoted in Andrew H. Malcolm, "Violent Drug Raids against the Innocent Found Widespread," *New York Times*, June 25, 1973, 1.

40. Senate Select Committee, *Final Report of the Select Committee to Study Governmental Operations with Respect to Intelligence Activities: Supplementary Staff Reports on Intelligence Activities and the Rights of Americans, Book 3*, 94th Cong., 2nd sess., S. Rep. No. 94-755 (April 23, 1976), 5; memorandum from G. C. Moore to W. C. Sullivan, February 29, 1968, quoted in *Final Report of the Select Committee to Study Governmental Operations with Respect to Intelligence Activities*, 3–4.

41. Initially, COINTELPRO-BLACK HATE directed its efforts at Martin Luther King's Southern Christian Leadership Conference, the Student Nonviolent

Coordinating Committee, the Nation of Islam, and the Revolutionary Action Movement; December 15, 1969, memorandum from San Diego Field Office to FBI Headquarters, in *Final Report of the Select Committee*, 221–222; Balko, *Rise of the Warrior Cop*, 76. See also Roy Wilkins and Ramsey Clark, *Search and Destroy: A Report by the Commission on Inquiry into the Black Panthers and Police* (Washington, DC: Metropolitan Applied Research Center, 1973) for a detailed discussion of COINTELPRO activities leading to the murder of Hampton and Clark.

42. December 1, 1969, memorandum, Los Angeles Field Office to FBI Headquarters, in *Final Report of the Select Committee*, 222; Hoover quoted in Huey P. Newton, "War against the Panthers: A Study of Repression in America" (PhD diss., University of California, Santa Cruz, 1980), 108–109; Hoover quoted in Elaine Brown, *A Taste of Power: A Black Woman's Story* (New York: Anchor Books, 1993), 211.

43. Parenti, *Lockdown America*, 22; Balko, *Rise of the Warrior Cop*, 79, 132; Dial Torgerson, "Police Seize Panther Fortress in 4-Hour Gunfight, Arrest 13," *Los Angeles Times*, December 9, 1969, 1.

44. Parenti, *Lockdown America*, 12.

45. Nixon quoted in James Markham "President Calls for 'Total War' on U.S. Addiction," *New York Times*, March 21, 1972, 1; Malcolm, "Violent Drug Raids," 1; Balko, *Rise of the Warrior Cop*, 121, 119.

46. "Police Drug Task Force Activated," *Los Angeles Sentinel*, October 5, 1972, C15; Quotes in Malcolm, "Violent Drug Raids."

47. G. R. Newman, "Sting Operations," Community Oriented Policy Services, *Problem Oriented Guide for Police Response Guides Series*, U.S. Department of Justice No. 6, 2007, 1.

48. Klose and Shaffer, "New Chapter."

49. The warehouse was located at 2254 25th Place, NE. Ruth Jenkins, "The Sting II: 'Got Ya Again' Police Trick Gets 'Fencers,'" *Baltimore Afro-American*, July 17, 1976, 15; Ben A. Franklin, "Police 'Part' Is a Trap for 60 Thieves," *New York Times*, March 8, 1976, 18; Ron Shaffer, "Business Was Brisk: 'The Italian Connection' Worked Well for Police Fences," *Washington Post*, March 2, 1976, A1.

50. Ron Shaffer and Alfred E. Lewis, "Police Fencing Ring Works after Couple of False Starts," *Washington Post*, March 2, 1976, B1. "Bonano" quoted in Rufus King, "Looking for the Lost Mafia," *Harpers*, January 1, 1977, 68.

51. "Detective quoted in Ben A. Franklin, "Police 'Part' Is a Trap"; "Larocca" quoted in "D.C. Police Stage Dragnet," *Human Events*, March 13, 1976, 5; Klose and Shaffer, "New Chapter"; Sally Quinn, "Mustard, Tabasco, Easy on the Hamburger: A Touch of Tabasco with a Sting," *Washington Post*, March 5, 1976, B1.

52. Klose and Shaffer, "New Chapter"; Quinn, "Mustard, Tabasco, Easy on the Hamburger."

53. "Corleone" quoted in Ron Shaffer, "'Bless You, My Son,' 'Don' Told Suspects," *Washington Post*, March 5, 1976, C1; "D.C. Police Stage Dragnet"; Quinn, "Mustard, Tabasco, Easy on the Hamburger"; Klose and Shaffer, "New Chapter."

54. Lill quoted in Shaffer, "Business Was Brisk"; Sanford Ungar, "Tempting the Criminal," *Washington Post*, December 26, 1976, 79; Jenkins, "Sting II."

55. Silbert quoted in Klose and Shaffer, "New Chapter"; Jenkins, "Sting II"; Velde quoted in Klose and Shaffer, "New Chapter."

56. Kevin Klose and Ron Shaffer, *Surprise! Surprise!: How the Lawmen Conned the Thieves* (New York: Viking, 1977); Klose and Shaffer, "New Chapter in Crime War," *Washington Post*, July 8, 1976, A1; Velde quoted in Ungar, "Tempting the Criminal"; Jeff Prugh, "Police 'Fences' Buy 1.5 Million in Stolen Goods," *Los Angeles Times*, October 6, 1976, A7; "Federal Funds Used Break up Fencing Operation," *Christian Science Monitor*, October 21, 1976, 14.

57. Sandy Banisky, "'Bear Trap II' Snares 47 in Stolen-Goods Ruse," *Baltimore Sun*, November 27, 1979, A1; "'Sting' Operation Thrives in Eight Months with Aid of Thieves, Burglars," *New Journal and Guide*, August 11, 1978, 11; "100 Seized, More Arrests Expected in 'Operation Sting' in Nashville," *New York Times*, November 10, 1977, 33.

58. "'Sting' Operation Thrives."

59. "Crime Control and Law Enforcement: Political Position for 1970 Elections," n.d., box 25, Krogh Files, RNPL.

60. *Final Report of the Select Committee*, 188; Balko, *Rise of the Warrior Cop*, 100.

6. JUVENILE INJUSTICE

1. The original name for the CRASH unit was TRASH (for "Total Resources Against Street Hoodlums). Sanchez quoted in Barry P. Grier, "'Death Envelope' Sparks TRASH Program," *Los Angeles Sentinel*, December 6, 1973, A3; Nancy Boyarsky, "Justice and the 10 O'Clock Curfew," *Los Angeles Times*, January 26, 1975, E1; Committee on Education and Labor, *Hearings before the Subcommittee on Equal Opportunities on Juvenile Justice and Delinquency Prevention and Runaway Youth*, 93rd Cong., 2nd sess. (March 29, April 21, May 1, 2, 8, and 21, 1974), 22 (Statement of Los Angeles Police Chief Ed Davis).

2. Boyarsky, "Justice and the 10 O'Clock Curfew."

3. Ibid.

4. A special amendment to the 1974 act strengthened the influence of the federal government and private consultants at all levels of the prison system. The legislation created a National Institute of Corrections, which brought together an advisory board from the spectrum of federal law enforcement and criminal justice agencies and private-sector groups to set priorities within carceral institutions and award contracts to firms to implement those priorities. Designed

to operate as a small consultant group appointed by the attorney general and removed from public accountability in the Bureau of Prisons, the institute served as an information clearinghouse and trained law enforcement and social service personnel. In order to equip penal authorities with stronger tools to manage unprecedented numbers of inmates, the institute supported research on a range of pressing issues, including correctional security, classification systems, and gang control programs. Along with the Office of Juvenile Delinquency Prevention also created by the 1974 Act, the National Institute of Corrections has endured as a legacy of the punitive reforms of this period. "Juvenile Delinquency," *CQ Almanac*, 30th ed., 1974, 278–282, available at http://library.cqpress.com/cqalmanac/cqal74-1224674.

5. Juvenile Justice and Delinquency Prevention Act of 1974, Pub. L. No. 93-415, 88 Stat. 1109 (1974), 9–10. This amounts to roughly $850 million in today's dollars. Beth Lynch, *Dollars and Sense of Justice*; "The Justice Department's Fight against Youth Crime: A Review of the Office of Juvenile Justice and Delinquency Prevention of the Law Enforcement Assistance Administration," prepared by Robert W. Woodson, Consultant to the House Subcommittee on Crime, House Subcommittee on Crime of the Committee on the Judiciary, 95th Cong., 2nd sess. (December 1978), 3; Senate Committee on the Judiciary, *Ford Administration Stifles Juvenile Justice Program: Hearing before the Subcommittee to Investigate Juvenile Delinquency*, 94th Cong., 1st sess. (April 29, 1975), 95.

6. "The Justice Department's Fight against Youth Crime," 3; Joseph G. Weis and John Sederstrom, "The Prevention of Serious Delinquency: What to Do?" (Washington, DC: U.S. Department of Justice, Office of Juvenile Justice and Delinquency Prevention, National Institute for Juvenile Justice and Delinquency Prevention, 1982), 2. The terms "hard core delinquent" and "acting out youth" are from "Rural Programs," prepared for the Office of Juvenile Justice and Delinquency Prevention, Law Enforcement Assistance Administration, Department of Justice, May 1979, 9. Health, Education, and Welfare funded 90 percent of the cost for special programs and facilities for runaways. Steven Nicholas, Associate Director of Focus Runaway House in Las Vegas in House Committee on Education and Labor, *Juvenile Delinquency Prevention and Runaway Youth Hearings before the Subcommittee on Equal Opportunities*, 93rd Cong., 2nd sess., held in Los Angeles, March 29; Washington, DC, April 21, May 1, 2, 8, and 21, 1974, 272.

7. Matthew Lassiter has powerfully demonstrated the ways in which state institutions and politicians successfully "insulated most white youth from the carceral state" by positioning white youth, suburban middle-class white youth in particular, as "innocent victims" who must be shielded from criminal laws.

See "Impossible Criminals: The Suburban Imperatives of America's War on Drugs," *Journal of American History* 102 (June 2015): 126–140.

8. Juvenile Justice and Delinquency Prevention Act of 1974.

9. The Department of Labor defined "disadvantaged" as "those on public assistance and those whose family income levels are below the poverty guidelines established under criteria issued by the Office of Management and Budget." April 8, 1976, "Summer Youth Employment Programs Fact Sheet," Gerald Ford Presidential Library (hereafter, GFPL), Richard Parsons Collection, box 17, "Summer Jobs for Urban Youth"; ibid.; National Advisory Commission on Criminal Justice Standards and Goals, "Report of the Task Force of Juvenile Justice and Delinquency Prevention" (Washington, DC: U.S. Government Printing Office, 1976), 23.

10. In 1974, juveniles accounted for one third of all felony arrests nationwide and almost 50 percent of arrests in cities. Moreover, police departments with at least seventy-five officers were required to establish a juvenile investigation unit as part of the state-level criminal justice planning agency. National Advisory Commission on Criminal Justice Standards and Goals, "Report of the Task Force of Juvenile Justice and Delinquency Prevention" (Washington, DC: U.S. Government Printing Office, 1976), 1; Federal Bureau of Investigation, *Uniform Crime Reports, 1974* (Washington, DC: U.S. Government Printing Office, 1975); Larry Carson, "An Ever Costlier Battle against Juvenile Crime," *Baltimore Sun*, September 14, 1975, K2; Senate Committee on the Judiciary, *Ford Administration Stifles Juvenile Justice Program*, 2; Menlo Park Police Chief Victor I. Cizanckas quoted in Bill Hazlett, "Police Urged to Place More Emphasis on 'People Problems,'" *Los Angeles Times*, October 11, 1973, OC1; Paul A. Strasburg, "Recent National Trends in Serious Juvenile Crime," in *Violent Juvenile Offenders: An Anthology*, ed. Robert A. Mathias et al. (San Francisco: National Council on Crime and Delinquency, 1984), 9.

11. May 15, 1975, memorandum to Jonathan Rose, Douglas Marvin, Jack Fuller from Malcolm Barr, Director Office of Public Relations, subj.: "Draft Papers for Consideration in Preparation of the Presidential Crime Message," GFPL, Parsons Collection, box 3, "Crime Message of 6-19-75—Action Memoranda May 1–8 1975"; National Advisory Commission on Criminal Justice Standards and Goals, "Report of the Task Force on Juvenile Justice and Delinquency Prevention" (Washington, DC: U.S. Government Printing Office, 1976), 4.

12. As measured by the FBI's crime index, large cities witnessed a 12 percent crime increase in 1974, while suburban and rural areas reported a 20 percent crime increase that year. Federal Bureau of Investigation, *Uniform Crime Reports, 1974* (Washington, DC: U.S. Government Printing Office, 1975), sec. 2, "Crime and the Offender."

13. Marvin Wolfgang, Robert M. Figlio, and Thorsten Sellin, *Delinquency in a Birth Cohort* (Chicago: University of Chicago Press, 1972), 22; Marvin E. Wolfgang, University of Pennsylvania, "Youth and Violence," HEW Report (Washington, DC: U.S. Government Printing Office, 1970).

14. In addition to the work of Moynihan and James Q. Wilson, other influential works that saw delinquency and black crime in this fatalistic view and that strongly influenced national policymakers and officials included Walter Miller, *Violence by Youth Gangs and Youth Groups as a Crime Problem in Major American Cities* (Washington, DC: U.S. Department of Justice, Office of Juvenile Justice and Delinquency Prevention, 1975) and Wolfgang et al., *Delinquency in a Birth Cohort.* The RAND Corporation in California and the National Institute of Law Enforcement and Criminal Justice also contributed a number of influential reports on black juvenile delinquency and violence. For a historical perspective on this problem, see "Fortress California," chap. 2 in Donna Murch, *Living for the City: Migration, Education, and the Rise of the Black Panther Party in Oakland, California* (Chapel Hill: University of North Carolina Press, 2010); Marvin E. Wolfgang, "Seriousness of Crime and a Policy of Juvenile Justice," in *Delinquency, Crime, and Society,* ed. James F. Short (Chicago: University of Chicago Press, 1976), 273; Senate Committee on the Judiciary, *Implementation of the Juvenile Justice and Delinquency Prevention Act of 1974 Hearings before the Subcommittee on Juvenile Delinquency,* 95th Cong., 1st sess. (September 27, 1977), 12 (Statement of Charles Work); Wolfgang, "Seriousness of Crime," 22.

15. Wolfgang, "Seriousness of Crime."

16. Juvenile Justice and Delinquency Prevention Act of 1974.

17. Charles Work in March 29, 1974, Hearings.

18. Wolfgang, "Seriousness of Crime"; Bayh in Senate Committee on the Judiciary, *Ford Administration Stifles Juvenile Justice Program,* 117; *Implementation of the Juvenile Justice and Delinquency Prevention Act Hearings*; House Committee on Education and Labor, *Juvenile Delinquency Prevention and Runaway Youth Hearings before the Subcommittee on Equal Opportunities,* 93rd Cong., 2nd sess., held in Los Angeles, March 29; Washington, DC, April 21, May 1, 2, 8, and 21, 1974.

19. "Juvenile Justice and Delinquency Prevention and Runaway Youth," 99 (Statement of Kirtkpatrick).

20. "Message to Congress: Johnson on Children and Youth," in *Congressional Quarterly Almanac 1967,* 23rd ed., 20-54-A–20-58-A (Washington, DC: Congressional Quarterly, 1968).

21. "Juvenile Delinquency."

22. By serving on the House Select Committee, Chisholm hoped to "protect the most powerless and helpless in this entire situation, the juveniles who have

been just cast aside at the bottom of everybody's priorities because they are not a real power group in the sense of the word to be reckoned with in our country in terms of money and grants." In Hearings before the Subcommittee on Equal Opportunities of the Committee on Education and Labor, House of Representatives, 93rd Cong., 2nd sess., on HR 6265 and HR 9298, held in Los Angeles, March 29, and Washington, DC, April 21, May 1, 2, 8, and 21, 1974, 434; Steiger quoted ibid.

23. On July 1, an overwhelming majority (329 to 20) approved the bill. Albert H. Quie, the Republican from Minnesota, argued that "juvenile justice and delinquency prevention programs are not separate entities and should not be treated separately," and introduced an amendment that shifted responsibility to the LEAA from HEW. The House rejected the transfer, with only 114 Republicans and thirty Democrats supporting the measure. "Juvenile Delinquency," *Congressional Quarterly Almanac 1974* (Washington, DC: Congressional Quarterly, 1975), 278–282.

24. *Implementation of the JJDPA Hearings*, September 28, 1977, 68, 69 (Statement of Robin S.); ibid., 70, 71 (Statement of Jeff M.).

25. *Implementation of the JJDPA Hearings*, 69 (Statement of Robin S.); Senate Committee on the Judiciary, *Ford Administration Stifles Juvenile Justice Program*, 27 (Statement of Bayh in Exhibit No. 3).

26. Daniel D. Smith, Associate Director, National Center for Juvenile Justice, "A Summary of Reported Data Concerning Young People and the Juvenile Justice System, 1975–1977," app. in Senate Committee on the Judiciary, *Hearings before the Senate Committee on the Judiciary on the Reauthorization of the Juvenile Delinquency and Prevention Act of 1974*, 96th Cong., 2nd sess., March 28, 1980, 454.

27. Ibid., 455; "Street Girls of the 70s," *The Nation*, April 20, 1974, 486–488.

28. Juvenile Delinquency and Prevention Act of 1974, 27; *Hearings before the Senate Committee on the Judiciary on the Reauthorization of the JJDPA*, 248; March 7, 1978, Oversight Hearing on the Runaway Youth Act 59, 77–79.

29. Even in areas with significant black populations, private and nonprofit organizations tended to focus on white youth, Boston's Bridge, Inc. program (short for "Bridge over Trouble Waters) was established in 1970 to help "wandering" or homeless children. By 1978, the organization and its streetwork team served some 21,458 youth with medical and dental services and counseling. But in a city with a 22 percent black population, only 11 percent of the youth who benefited from Bridge, Inc.'s rehabilitative and preventive services were black. Marget B. Saltonstall, The Bridge, Inc., "Greater Boston Street Youth: Their Characteristics, Incidence, and Needs," app. in March 28, 1980, Hearings, 499–501; judge quoted in Arnold Binder, "Putting the Rod

Back in Parental Hands: 'Diversion' Programs Take Old-New Approach to Disciplining Errant Youth," *Los Angeles Times*, July 21, 1976, E7.

30. Kenneth quoted in "Runaways Tell Senate Panel of Ordeal in Adult Jails," *Miami Herald*, September 12, 1973; U.S. General Accounting Office, "Federally Supported Centers Provide Needed Services for Runaways and Homeless Youths" (Washington, DC: U.S. Government Printing Office, September 26, 1983), March 28, 1980, Hearings, 185.

31. The National Statistical Survey on Runaway Youth found that Latino youth had the highest incidence of running away, at a rate of 4.6 percent, with black youth following closely behind at a rate of 3.2 percent, and white youth the lowest at a rate of 2.9 percent. National Statistical Survey on Runaway Youth Part 1, prepared under contract for HEW (Princeton, NJ: Opinion Research Corporation, March 7, 1978); Oversight Hearing on the Runaway Youth Act, 276; "Rural Programs," prepared for the Office of Juvenile Justice and Delinquency Prevention (Law Enforcement Assistance Administration, Department of Justice, May 1979), 9.

32. Carol Osmon, "Mini-bikes Help 'Rescue' Juvenile Offenders," *Christian Science Monitor*, February 25, 1976, 19; April 29, 1975, Hearings, 73; Senate Committee on the Judiciary, *Ford Administration Stifles Juvenile Justice Program*, 73.

33. "Children in Custody: Advance Report on the 1977 Census of Private Juvenile Facilities," U.S. Department of Justice, Law Enforcement Assistance Administration, National Criminal Justice Information and Statistics Service; Smith, "Summary of Reported Data," 455.

34. The Nixon administration attempted to completely phase out the Office of Economic Opportunity in 1973 and severely cut its funding. Governor Ronald Reagan of California led other states in slashing the budget for social programs, trimming $80 million from social welfare and environmental programs in the state. On the basis of "reduced caseload projections," public assistance programs were hit the hardest, with a $16 million reduction, in addition to cutting the Head Start program in half, giving the preschool program for low-income youth enough funds to continue its operations for an additional six months while state planners developed "stronger" regulations for participation. Bill Robertson, "Public Aid Programs Are Hardest Hit by Budget Slash," *Los Angeles Sentinel*, July 5, 1973, A4.

35. May 15, 1975, memorandum to Jonathan Rose, Douglas Marvin, Jack Fuller from Malcolm Barr, Director Office of Public Relations, subj.: "Draft Papers for Consideration in Preparation of the Presidential Crime Message," GFPL, Parsons Collection Box 3, "Crime Message of 6-19-75—Action Memoranda May 1–8 1975."

36. David Rosenzweig, "Black Principal Describes School as 'Ft. Crenshaw'; Terror Makes Learning Impossible, Supervisors Told; Crackdown Urged Principals

Call for Help on Violence in Schools," *Los Angeles Times*, December 19, 1972, 3A; John, Kendall, "A Ghetto Is Slow to Die," *Los Angeles Times (1886–Current File)*, 1975, B1; Thompson quoted in Jack V. Fox, "Atmosphere of Fear Was So Thick You Could Cut It," *Los Angeles Sentinel*, January 25, 1973, A9; Davis in "Juvenile Justice and Delinquency and Runaway Youth Hearings," 18, 21 (Statement of Davis).

37. "Violence—Growing Blot that Hurts U.S. Schools," *Christian Science Monitor*, August 26, 1976, 13.

38. On the policing of urban public schools, see Thompson, "Why Mass Incarceration Matters: Rethinking Crisis, Decline, and Transformation in Postwar American History," *The Journal of American History*, Vol. 97, No.3 December 2010: 703–58, 710–11. The legacy of these early school disciplinary programs and surveillance measures has endured in what some have termed the "School-to-Prison Pipeline," whereby the "zero tolerance policies," special anti-truancy forces, and other school disciplinary and patrol practices have funneled disturbing numbers of low-income youth out of schools and into juvenile detention and prisons in recent decades. See Aaron Kupchick, *Homeroom Security: School Discipline in an Age of Fear* (New York: New York University Press, 2010); Monique Morris, "Race, Gender, and the School-to-Prison Pipeline: Expanding Our Discussion to Include Black Girls," African American Policy Forum, New York, 2012; American Civil Liberties Union, "Locating the School-to-Prison Pipeline," available at https://www.aclu.org/files/images/asset_upload_file966 _35553.pdf; April 29, 1975, Hearings, 105 (Statement of Bayh); National Institute of Education, U.S. Department of Health, Education, and Welfare, "Violent Schools—Safe Schools: The Safe School Study Report to Congress" (Washington, DC: U.S. Government Printing Office, 1978), 2.

39. Principal quoted in Gene Weingarten, "East Bronx Story—Return of the Street Gangs," *New York Magazine*, March 27, 1972; Iver Peterson "Student Violence and Teacher Militance Are Plaguing the Nation's Schools," *New York Times*, October 14, 1974, 25.

40. As a former New York City public school teacher, Congresswoman Shirley Chisholm made her colleagues aware of the connections between youth crime and school disciplinary measures. "When school systems are not able to cope with the uniqueness and specific needs of black children," Chisholm explained as she opened the Subcommittee on Equal Opportunity's hearings on juvenile delinquency, "we find the development of discipline problems." House Committee on Education and Labor, *Hearings before the Subcommittee on Equal Opportunities on Juvenile Justice Delinquency Prevention and Runaway Youth*, 93rd Cong., 2nd sess. (May 21, 1974), 455, 472 (Statements of Chisholm and Leon Hall, Director, Southern Regional Council).

41. March 29, 1974, Hearings (Statement of Kenneth E. Kirkpatrick).

42. National Advisory Commission on Criminal Justice Standards and Goals, "Report of the Task Force of Juvenile Justice and Delinquency Prevention" (Washington, DC: U.S. Government Printing Office, 1976), 789.

43. "Justice Department's Fight against Youth Crime," 3.

44. Ibid.

45. Quoted in Maurice Carroll, "Carey Urges Harsher Law against Juvenile Violence," *New York Times*, December 10, 1975, 1. On the Willie Bosket Case, see Simon I. Singer, Jeffrey Fagan, and Akiva Liberman, "The Reproduction of Juvenile Justice: A Case Study of New York's Juvenile Offender Law," in *The Changing Borders of Juvenile Justice: Transfer of Adolescents to the Criminal Court*, ed. Jeffrey Fagan and Franklin E. Zimring (Chicago: University of Chicago Press, 2000), 353–377.

46. Brooks in *Black Perspectives on Crime and the Criminal Justice System*, ed. Robert L. Woodson (Boston: G. K. Hall, 1977), 156; Sister Fattah, ibid., 158; Jerome G. Miller, "The Issue of Violent Juvenile Crime," in *Violent Juvenile Offenders: An Anthology*, ed. Robert A. Mathias et al. (San Francisco: National Council on Crime and Delinquency, 1984) 381–382; excerpted from the statement of Jerome G. Miller, July 9, 1981, at the hearing before the Subcommittee on Juvenile Justice of the Committee on the Judiciary, U.S. Senate, 97th Cong., 1st sess., on "The Problem of Juvenile Crime" (Washington, DC: U.S. Government Printing Office, 1981), 175–182.

47. Robert Martinson, "What Works?—Questions and Answers about Prison Reform," *Public Interest* 35 (1974): 22–54, 27, 50, 49; Robert Martinson, "The Paradox of Prison Reform—I: The 'Dangerous Myth,'" *New Republic*, April 1, 1972, 23–25, 25; Robert Martinson, "The Paradox of Prison Reform—II: Can Corrections Correct?," *New Republic*, April 8, 1972, 13–15; Robert Martinson, "The Paradox of Prison Reform—III: The Meaning of Attica," *New Republic*, April 15, 1972, 17–18; Robert Martinson, "The Paradox of Prison Reform—IV: Planning for Public Safety,'" *New Republic*, April 29, 1972, 21–23; Selwyn Raab, "Study Finds Recidivism Rate of Convicts Lower than Expected," *New York Times*, November 7, 1976, 60; Jerome G. Miller, "Rehabilitating Criminals: Is It True That Nothing Works?," available at http://www.prisonpolicy.org/scans/rehab.html; *Mistretta v. United States*, 488 U.S. 361 (1989).

48. Most notably, the criminologist Elliot Currie exposed the flaws in Murray and Cox's argument. Charles Murray and Louis A. Cox, *Beyond Probation: Juvenile Corrections and the Chronic Delinquent* (New York: Sage Publications, 1979); James Q. Wilson, "'What Works?' Revisited: New Findings on Criminal Rehabilitation," *Public Interest* 61 (1980): 3–18, 13, 17; Jerome G.

Miller, *Search and Destroy: African-American Males in the Criminal Justice System* (Cambridge: Cambridge University Press, 1996), 123–124.

49. Office of Juvenile Justice and Delinquency Prevention, "Project New Pride" (July 1979), available at https://www.ncjrs.gov/pdffiles1/Digitization/59017NCJRS.pdf; Ward Morehouse III, "Child Crime: Community-Based Programs Can Make a Difference," *Christian Science Monitor*, June 20, 1978, 14; "Denver Project to Aid Delinquents Is Hailed," *New York Times*, December 12, 1977, 28; Janice Joseph, *Black Youths, Delinquency, and Juvenile Justice* (New York: Praeger, 1995), 141.

50. Thomas S. James and Jeanne M. Granville, "Practical Issues in Vocational Education for Serious Juvenile Offenders," in *Violent Juvenile Offenders: An Anthology*, ed. Robert A. Mathias et al. (San Francisco: National Council on Crime and Delinquency, 1984), 338, 340–341; "Denver Project to Aid Delinquents," 28.

51. James and Granville, "Practical Issues in Vocational Education," 338, 345; "LEAA Reports on Crime Projects; Denver Succeeds, Cincinnati Fails," *Afro-American*, December 31, 1977, 16.

52. Saxbe quoted in Ronald J. Ostrow, "Criminal Rehabilitation 'a Myth,' Saxbe Says," *Los Angeles Times*, October 1, 1974, A4; National Advisory Commission on Criminal Justice Standards and Goals, "Report of the Task Force of Juvenile Justice and Delinquency Prevention" (Washington, DC: U.S. Government Printing Office, 1976), 13.

53. May 5, 1975, memorandum to Jonathan Rose et al.

54. Ibid.; Senate Committee on the Judiciary, *Part II Career Criminals: Hearing before the Subcommittee on Criminal Laws and Procedures*, 95th Cong., 2nd sess., September 27, 1978, 12.

55. On the targeted removal of low-income urban residents, the material impact of this process, and the growth of American penal populations, see Todd Clear, *Imprisoning Communities: How Mass Incarceration Makes Disadvantaged Neighborhoods Worse* (Oxford: Oxford University Press, 2009) and Amy E. Lerman and Vesla Weaver, *Arresting Citizenship: The Democratic Consequences of American Crime Control* (Chicago: University of Chicago Press, 2014); May 15, 1975, memorandum to Jonathan Rose et al.; Senate Committee on the Judiciary, *Part II, Career Criminals: Hearing before the Subcommittee on Criminal Laws and Procedures*, 95th Cong., 2nd sess. (September 27, 1978), 12; Anthony M. Platt, "Saving and Controlling Delinquent Youth: A Critique," *Issues in Criminology* 5, no. 1 (Winter 1970): 1–25, 3.

7. URBAN REMOVAL

1. Reading Copies of Presidential Speeches and Statements, folder "September 24, 1974 International Association of Chiefs of Police," box 1, Gerald Ford Presidential Library (hereafter, GFPL); June 17, 1975, memorandum for Jim Connor from Dick Cheney, folder "Crime Message (2)," box 9, James E. Connor Files, GFPL.

2. "Elements of a Program," April 11, 1975, attachment to memorandum from Parsons to Cannon, subj.: "Crime Program," Parsons Files, box 4, "Crime Message of 6/19/1975—Background materials, Feb 15–May 14 1975," GFPL; Remarks of the President at the Yale Sesquicentennial Convocation Dinner, Yale Law School, Parsons Collection, box 4, "Crime Message of 6-19-75—Background materials, Feb 15–May 14 1975, "GFPL.

3. After chatting with his former professor Myers McDougal, who interviewed the future president before he was admitted to Yale Law, Ford started his address just before 10:00 p.m. May 15, 1975, memorandum to Jonathan Rose, Douglas Marvin, Jack Fuller from Malcolm Barr, Director, Office of Public Relations, subj.: "Draft Papers for Consideration in Preparation of the Presidential Crime Message," Parsons Collection, box 3, "Crime Message of 6-19-75—Action Memoranda May 1–8 1975," GFPL; April 25, 1975, Remarks of the President at the Yale Sesquicentennial Convocation Dinner.

4. Federal policymakers relied heavily upon the work of James Q. Wilson to justify their attack on repeat offenders. The May 15 memorandum read: "As it is clear that most crimes are committed by repeaters (J. Q. Wilson) there will be a reduction in the crime rate simply through incapacitation." April 25, 1975, Remarks of the President at the Yale Sesquicentennial Convocation Dinner, May 15, 1975; memorandum to Jonathan Rose et al.

5. James Naughton, "Ford Safe as Guard Seizes a Gun Woman Pointed at Him on Cast; Follower of Manson Is Charged," *New York Times*, September 6, 1975, 49.

6. May 15, 1975, memorandum to Jonathan Rose, Douglas Marvin, Jack Fuller from Malcolm Barr, Director, Office of Public Relations, subj.: "Draft Papers for Consideration in Preparation of the Presidential Crime Message," Parsons Collection, box 3, "Crime Message of 6-19-75—Action Memoranda May 1–8 1975," GFPL.

7. Edward M. Kennedy, "Punishing the Offenders," *New York Times*, December 6, 1975, 29.

8. Excerpts of Remarks by Governor Ronald Reagan: Citizens Committee for Law Enforcement Needs, Los Angeles, August 1, 1973, OA 190 Research Files: Legal Affairs, Law and Order RR Statements (3/3), Ronald Reagan Gubernatorial Files, Ronald Reagan Presidential Library (hereafter, RRPL).

9. Work in Hearings before the Subcommittee on Criminal Laws and Proce- dures of the Committee on the Judiciary, U.S. Senate, 95th Cong., 2nd sess. on S.28 and S.3216, pt. 2, Career Criminals (September 27, 1978), 7.

10. Ibid.; "Elements of a Program"; "Some Random Notes on Crime and Correc- tions/ Sykes Memo," folder "Crime and Criminal Justice [4]," box 33, Issues Office-Bleicher, 1976 Campaign Files, Jimmy Carter Presidential Library (hereafter, JCPL); Curtis in May 17, 1978, Hearings, 14; "Magnitude of the Wave of Jail and Prison Construction in the United States during the 1970s," National Moratorium on Prison Construction, January 1977, folder 1, box 11, Gutierrez Files, JCPL; "Jimmy Carter on Prisons," sent as a memorandum to Sam Bleicher. Re: Paper on Prisons, folder "Crime and Criminal Justice [4], box 33—Issues Office Bleicher, 1976 Campaign Files, JCPL"; February 8, 1978, Open Letter to Attorney General Griffin Bell from Milton G. Rector, President of National Council on Crime and Delinquency, folder 16, box 11, Gutierrez Files, JCPL; Justice Policy Institute, "The Punishing Decade: Prison and Jail Estimates at the Millennium" (Washington, DC: Justice Policy Institute, May 2000).

11. Joseph G. Weis and John Sederstrom, "The Prevention of Serious Delin- quency: What to Do?" (Washington, DC: U.S. Department of Justice, Office of Juvenile Justice and Delinquency Prevention, National Institute for Juvenile Justice and Delinquency Prevention, 1982), 18.

12. "Elements of a Program."

13. Saxbe quoted in "Prosecute More Felons," *Chicago Defender*, October 7, 1974, 4; and quoted in Joel Weisman, "Saxbe Sees Prospect of U.S. Police," *Washington Post*, August 28, 1974, A1.

14. "Prisons Urged for 15% of Young Felons," *Los Angeles Times*, August 21, 1975, 2.

15. Ford Speech before the International Association of Chiefs of Police, Wash- ington Hilton Hotel, Washington, DC, Tuesday, September 24, 1974. Reading Copies of Presidential Speeches and Statements, 1974–1977, older "September 24, 1974 IACP," box 1, GFPL; "Picture Painted of a Criminal," *Los Angeles Times*, September 28, 1976, A1; Nicholas von Hoffman, "Throwing Money at Crime: The Multibillion-Dollar Nightstick," *Washington Post*, Oc- tober 8, 1976, B3; quoted in Judith Cummings, "Funds to End Youth-Gang Violence Termed Misspent," *New York Times*, October 29, 1976, 92.

16. Senate Committee of the Judiciary, *Hearings before the Subcommittee on Criminal Laws and Procedures on S. 28 and S. 3216 Part II Career Criminals*, 95th Cong., 2nd sess. (September 27, 1978), 33 (Statement of Earl Silbert).

17. Ibid. (Statement of Carol S. Vance, DA of Harris County, Texas).

18. George C. Smith, Chairman, *National District Attorneys Association—Career Criminal Committee Report for Year 1977* in Joint Economic Committee,

Hearing before the Subcommittee on Economic Growth and Stabilization on Urban Crime Policy, 95th Cong., 2nd sess. (May 17, 1978).

19. James J. Kilpatrick, "Rehabilitation Be Hanged: Lock Career Criminal Up," *Baltimore Sun*, November 21, 1976, K5.

20. September 27, 1978, Hearings, 63 (Statement of James F. Kelley, Prosecuting Attorney for the 19th Judicial Circuit, Indianapolis).

21. Mahoney quoted in "Urban Crime Policy: Hearing before the Subcommittee on Economic Growth and Stabilization," 95th Cong., 2nd sess. (May 17, 1978), 32 (Statement of George C. Smith, Prosecuting Attny., Columbus, chairman of National CC committee, National District Attnys. Assoc).

22. "New Crime Game," *Afro-American*, October 5, 1974, 4; "$37 Million for Juvenile Crime but Minority Groups Ignored," *Baltimore Afro-American*, December 30, 1978, 8.

23. May 17, 1978, Hearings, 26 (Statement of Smith); James J. Kilpatrick, "Rehabilitation Be Hanged: Lock Career Criminal Up," *Baltimore Sun*, November 21, 1976, K5; September 27, 1978, Hearings (Statement of William A. Hamilton, President, Institute for Law and Social Research); Peter W. Greenwood, "Career Criminal Prosecution: Potential Objectives," *Journal of Criminal Law and Criminology* 71, no. 85 (1980): 85–88; National Institute of Justice, "National Directory of Career Criminal Programs" (Rockville, MD: National Criminal Justice Reference Service, 1980).

24. Silbert in September 27, 1978, Hearings, 29.

25. In Mathias testimony, May 17, 1978, Hearings, 48.

26. September 27, 1978, Hearings, 29 (Statement of Silbert); May 17, 1978, Hearings, 48 (Statement of Mathias), 2 (Statement of Smith).

27. African Americans in Watts and Compton between the ages of sixteen and nineteen had a 62 percent rate of unemployment; Davis in March 29, 1974, Hearings, 25–26; Rosenzweig, "Black Principal Describes School as 'Ft. Crenshaw'"; Yusuf Jah and Sister Shah'Keyah, *Uprising: Crips and Bloods Tell the Story of America's Youth in the Crossfire* (New York: Touchstone Books, 1997), 26; quoted in Joseph B. Treaster, "Violence of Youth Gangs Is Found at a New High," *New York Times*, May 1, 1976, 42.

28. May 15, 1975, memorandum to Jonathan Rose et al.

29. Walter B. Miller, *Violence by Youth Gangs and Youth Groups as a Crime Problem in Major American Cities* (Washington, DC: U.S. Government Printing Office, 1975), 44.

30. A 1973 study conducted by the Bureau of Alcohol, Tobacco, and Firearms traced the source of half of the firearms used in New York City to South Carolina, Georgia, Florida, and Virginia. For sociological considerations of the use of criminal law to contain the threat marginalized groups posed to state

power, see Georg Rusche, "Labor Market and Penal Sanction," *Crime and Social Justice* 10 (Fall–Winter, 1978): 2–8 (orig. 1933); Richard Quinney, *Criminal Justice in America: A Critical Understanding* (Boston: Little, Brown, 1974); Steven Spitzer, "Toward a Marxian Theory of Deviance," *Social Problems* 22 (1975): 638–651; Bruce Western, *Punishment and Inequality in America* (New York: Russell Sage Foundation, 2006), 55; National Advisory Commission on Criminal Justice Standards and Goals, "Report of the Task Force of Juvenile Justice and Delinquency Prevention" (Washington, DC: U.S. Government Printing Office, 1976), 152; William Claiborne, "N.Y. Guns Traced to South," *Washington Post*, December 18, 1973, A3.

31. House Committee on Appropriations, *Hearings before the Subcommittees of the Committee on Appropriations—Supplemental Appropriations of FY 1976*, 94th Cong., 1st sess., pt. 2 (Tuesday, October 21, 1975), 691. Here, the United States was unique. Unlike most of Western Europe and Asia, licensing and registration were required to possess a handgun, and a number of European, Asian, and African countries prohibited handgun possession altogether.

32. Ibid; "Introduction of S. 2186 (Ford gun control bill) by Senator Fong," July 26, 1975 (extract from the Congressional record) and "S. 2186, a bill to ban the importation, manufacture, sale, and transfer of Saturday Night Specials, to improve the effectiveness of the Gun Control Act of 1968, to ban possession, shipment, transportation, and receipt of all firearms by felons, and for other purposes," 94th Cong., 1st sess. Included in Senate Judiciary Committee, *Hearings before the Subcommittee to Investigate Juvenile Delinquency*, 94th Cong., 1st sess. (April 23, July 22, October 26, 1975), 985–1021.

33. "Memorandum on the Problem of the Criminal Use of Handguns," March 26, 1975. Included in April 23, July 22, October 26, 1975 Hearings, 616–707, 12.

34. October 21, 1975 Hearings, 616 (Statement of Rex Davis); "Gun Control Unit Faces Shakeup," *Washington Post*, December 1, 1976, C25.

35. Juan Williams and Alfred Lewis, "1,100 Illegal Guns Seized in Raids," *Washington Post*, November 19, 1976, C2; Bureau of Alcohol, Tobacco, and Firearms, "Significant Criminal Enforcement Project," supplemental material in October 21, 1975, Hearings, 654–655.

36. "Gun Control Unit Faces Shakeup."

37. Joan Petersilia and Peter W. Greenwood, "Mandatory Prison Sentences: Their Project Effects on Crime and Prison Population" (Santa Monica, CA: RAND Corporation, October 1977). Petersilia worked as a research associate at RAND, while Greenwood served as the director of RAND's Criminal Justice program and coauthored work on Criminal Careers and Habitual Felons. Both James Q. Wilson and Daniel Glaser reviewed drafts of the article. In September 27, 1978, Hearings, 411.

38. See Robert L. Woodson, ed., *Black Perspectives on Crime and the Criminal Justice System* (Boston: G. K. Hall, 1977), for further critique of Miller's methodology.

39. Miller quoted in "Gun-Toting Teen Gangs Called Threat to Schools," *Chicago Tribune*, May 1, 1976, 6; and quoted in Joseph B. Treaster, "Violence of Youth Gangs Is Found at a New High," *New York Times*, May 1, 1976, 42; Claudia Luther, "L.A. Called One of 3 Cities with Youth Gang Crisis," *Los Angeles Times*, November 20, 1975, C1.

40. Miller estimated there were as many as 2,700 gangs with 81,500 members in the six largest cities in the United States, figures he said were conservative. The greatest concentrations appeared to be in "New York, with 315 gangs, 8,000 verified members and another 20,000 alleged members." Los Angeles and Philadelphia had "the highest proportion of gang members . . . six out of every 100 male youths in those cities were associated with a gang or a group . . . most of the victims continue to be members of gangs"; Miller quoted in Cummings, "Funds to End"; and quoted in Treaster, "Violence of Youth Gangs"; and Clayton Jones, "Target: Youth Gang Violence," *Christian Science Monitor*, June 22, 1976, 3.

41. "Gun-Toting Teen Gangs"; Harry Kelly, "Teen Criminals Deserve Adult Penalties: Ford," *Chicago Tribune*, September 28, 1976, 6; George Skelton, "Ford Proposes Adult Punishment for Juveniles Who Commit Vicious Crimes," *Los Angeles Times*, September 28, 1976, B5.

42. Wilson in Woodson, *Black Perspectives*, 51; "The Justice Department's Fight against Youth Crime: A Review of the Office of Juvenile Justice and Delinquency Prevention of the Law Enforcement Assistance Administration," prepared by Robert W. Woodson, Consultant to the House Subcommittee on Crime. House Subcommittee on Crime of the Committee on the Judiciary, 95th Cong., 2nd sess. (December 1978).

43. December 7, 1973, Policy/Position Paper, subj.: "Crime, Crimes of Violence," (3A 2a) Governor's Office—Cabinet Office Files, RRPL.

44. Gerald Ford, *Special Message to Congress on Crime*, June 19, 1975, American Presidency Project, available at http://www.presidency.ucsb.edu/ws/?pid =5007; "Elements of a Program"; December 7, 1973, Policy/Position Paper.

45. "Excerpts of Remarks by Governor Ronald Reagan California Sheriff's Association, Palo Alto, June 12, 1974," Governor's Office 181- RF- H and W- Drug Abuses (2/2), RRPL.

46. Statement by Charles Johnson, Special Narcotics Prosecutor in New York, in Woodson, *Black Perspectives*, 162.

47. National Advisory Commission on Criminal Justice Standards and Goals, "Report of the Task Force of Juvenile Justice and Delinquency Prevention" (Wash-

ington, DC: U.S. Government Printing Office, 1976), fig. 6: Total Population of U.S. State and Federal Prisons, 1962–1976, 12; "Some Random Notes on Crime and Corrections/ Sykes Memo," folder "Crime and Criminal Justice [4]," box 33, Issues Office-Bleicher, 1976 Campaign Files, JCPL; Curtis in May 17, 1978, Hearings, 14; "Magnitude of the Wave of Jail and Prison Construction in the United States During the 1970s"; box 11, "Jimmy Carter on Prisons"; February 8, 1978, open letter to Attorney General Griffin Bell; Justice Policy Institute, "The Punishing Decade: Prison and Jail Estimates at the Millennium" (Washington, DC: Justice Policy Institute, May 2000).

48. Eric G. Woodbury, "Prison Overcrowding and Rhodes v. Chapman: Double-Celling by What Standard?," *Boston College Law Review* 23, no. 3 (May 1, 1982), 713–760; Malcolm M. Feely and Edward L. Rubin, *Judicial Policy Making and the Modern State: How the Courts Reformed America's Prisons* (New York: Cambridge University Press 2000).

49. *Rhodes v. Chapman*, 452 U.S. 344 (1981).

50. September 27, 1978, Hearings, 87, 89 (Statement of Lloyd Bentsen).

51. African Americans have experienced higher rates of victimization for all crimes since at least 1973, and for homicides since 1976. By 1985, the possibility of becoming a homicide victim was 1 in 21 for black males and 1 in 131 for white males. James Allen Fox and Marianne W. Zawitz, *Homicide Trends in the United States* (U.S. Bureau of Justice Statistics, 2007), available at http://www .bjs.gov/index.cfm?ty=pbdetail&iid=966; Marshall DeBerry and Anita Timrots, *Criminal Victimization in the United States, 1983* (National Crime Victimization Survey, Bureau of Justice Statistics, 1985), available at http://www .bjs.gov/index.cfm?ty=pbdetail&iid=3503; Bill Boyarsky, "Carter, in Detroit, Scores Ford on Crime, Then Offers 16-Point Plan to Reduce It," *Los Angeles Times*, October 16, 1976, A23.

8. CRIME CONTROL AS URBAN POLICY

1. Eugene Meehan, *The Quality of Federal Policymaking: Programmed Failure in Public Housing* (Columbia: University of Missouri Press, 1979), 71; Katharine G. Bristol, "The Pruitt-Igoe Myth," *Journal of Architectural Education* 44, no. 3 (May 1991): 163–171; Simon Winchester, "They've Come a Long Way in St. Louis," *The Guardian*, May 15, 1974, 16; Stanley Ziemba, "Faced with a 'Cabrini,' St. Louis Tore It Down," *Chicago Tribune*, April 26, 1981, B10.

2. "The Urban Crisis," n.d.; 1976 Presidential Campaign-Issues Office—Noel Sterrett; folder "Memoranda (Nodak)," box 88, Jimmy Carter Presidential Library (hereafter, JCPL); March 31, 1980, "Urban Initiatives Anti-Crime Program First Annual Report to Congress in Response to the Public Housing

Demonstration Act of 1978 and as Part of the President's National Urban Policy," Administration—Staff Offices, Ethnic Affairs, folder "Anti-Crime Program [Lynn A. Curtis]," box 1, JCPL; Jimmy Carter radio interview with Bill Moyers on the 1976 campaign, Public Broadcasting Systems, May 6, 1976; quoted in Thomas E. Cronin, Tamia Z. Cronin, and Michael E. Millakovich, *U.S. v. Crime in the Streets* (Bloomington: Indiana University Press, 1981), 120.

3. Thirteen percent of black Americans were unemployed at the end of 1976. Moreover, by 1977, the typical woman prisoner in the United States was black and under the age of thirty, according to a $289,025 study by the LEAA and the California Youth Authority. The agencies interviewed some 3,000 women in fifteen state prisons and forty-two local jails for the project. "Strategies for Controlling Crime: A Position Paper," Prepared by the Administration of Justice Division, National Urban League, March 1978, folder 8, box 12, Gutierrez Files, JCPL; "LEAA Study Shows: High Numbers of Women Prisoners Are Young Blacks," *Philadelphia Tribune*, August 13, 1977, 4; "Typical State Inmate Called Black, 26, Dropout," *Baltimore Sun*, May 1, 1977, B2.

4. Jimmy Carter, "National Urban Policy Message to the Congress," March 27, 1978. American Presidency Project, available at http://www.presidency.ucsb.edu/ws/?pid=30567.

5. Ibid.

6. Curtis in May 17, 1978, Hearings before the Subcommittee on Economic Growth and Stabilization of the Joint Economic Committee, 95th Cong., 1st sess., 7, 14.

7. April 4, 1978, memorandum from Curtis to Gregg Gutierrez, folder 8, box 25, JCPL; press release, LEAA/ACTION Launch Urban Crime Prevention Program, December 2, 1980, folder 7, "Community Anti-Crime Legislation," box 3, White Files, JCPL; "More LEAA Funds Sought," *Baltimore Sun*, May 23, 1978, A9.

8. In 1965, the nation spent $4.6 billion on criminal justice; by 1977, the figure had reached $23 billion, or roughly $17 billion in constant 1965 dollars. Spending at the state and local levels followed the federal government's example and grew 87 percent from 1971 to 1976. Federal government spending more than doubled (101.6 percent), state government spending was up by 94.1 percent, and the local government increase was 81.6 percent. January 4, 1978, memorandum to Annie Gutierrez from Bill Albers, subj.: "LEAA/NIJ Proposal," folder 8, box 25, Gutierrez Files, JCPL; "US DOJ LEAA News Release 2-2-78," folder 11, "Crime Statistics," box 12, Gutierrez Files, JCPL; see also "Expenditure and Employment Data for the Criminal Justice System," 1976; General Briefing of the LEAA, Department of Justice April 1977, folder 10, "LEAA [3]," box 25, Gutierrez Files, JCPL; July 19, 1976, letter to Arnold

Sagalyn, Coordinator, Task Force on Crime and Criminal Justice from Daniel Glaser, Professor, 1976 Campaign Issues Office-Sam Bleicher, folder "Law Enforcement—Arnold Sagalyn," box 26, JCPL; September 18, 1976, letter to Governor Carter from Sam Bleicher Thru Stu Eizenstat Re: Re-authorization of the LEAA, folder "Law Enforcement," box 36, JCPL; "The Future Role of the Law Enforcement Assistance Administration: A Draft NCSCJPA Policy Statement—Revised January 31, 1977," folder 12, box 25, Gutierrez Files, JCPL.

9. The LEAA's budget exceeded even the FBI's $513 million allocation by nearly a quarter of a billion dollars. July 10, 1978, letter to Congress from Office of the White House Press Secretary, folder 1, box 25, Neustadt Files, JCPL; September 18, 1976, letter to Governor Carter from Sam Bleicher; John M. Goshko, "LEAA's Fate Weighed at Justice Dept.," *Washington Post*, April 9, 1977, A1; March 28, 1977, memorandum for Peter Flaherty, Deputy Attorney General from Bill Albers, subj.: "LEAA Recommendations," folder 10, box 25, Gutierrez Files, JCPL; "In the Nation," *Baltimore Sun*, June 21, 1977, A9; John M. Goshko, "LEAA's Fate Weighed at Justice Dept.," *Washington Post*, April 9, 1977, A1; July 19, 1976, letter to Arnold Sagalyn; September 18, 1976, Letter to Governor Carter from Sam Bleicher; Boyarsky, "Carter, in Detroit."

10. November 2, 1977, memorandum for Attorney General from Vice President, subj.: "Crime Message," folder 4, box 164, Eizenstat Files, JCPL. Carter sent the request to the attorney general in a September 16, 1977, memorandum for his cabinet officials. "Crime Program," folder 2, box 164, Eizenstat Collection, JCPL; Roger Twigg, "Pomerleau Faults LEAA Study Release," *Baltimore Sun*, April 17, 1977, B8; "A Good Concept Gone Awry," *Los Angeles Times*, July 28, 1977, D6.

11. The complainants included the Police Legal Office Program, a Farm Equipment and Theft Program, a Multi-Agency Narcotic Unit Manual, a Labor Relations Training Program, a National Law Enforcement Equipment Information Center, an Organized Crime Bulletin, and the Uniform Crime Report Validation Program. Document, n.t., n.d., folder 6, "National Minority Advisory Council on Criminal Justice," box 17, White Files, JCPL; "Consensus Statement Resulting from Criminal Justice Leaders' Meeting," December 20, 1977, Columbia, Maryland, folder 8, box 25, Gutierrez Files, JCPL; January 27, 1978, letter to the President from Noel C. Bufe, Chairman, National Conference of State Criminal Justice Planning Administrators, folder 8, box 25, Gutierrez Files, JCPL.

12. July 10, 1978, letter to Congress from Office of the White House Press Secretary, folder 1, box 25, Neustadt Files, JCPL; February 25, 1978, memorandum for Stu Eizenstat from Annie M. Guiterrez, subj.: "President's Response to Bourne Memo on Crime Rate," folder 1, "Civil Rights-Court Reform-Crime

Issues," box 164, Eizenstat Files, JCPL; "Bell Updates Crime Data Unit," *Chicago Tribune*, August 22, 1977, 7.

13. January 4, 1978, memorandum to Annie Gutierrez from Bill Albers, subj.: "LEAA/NIJ Proposal," folder 8, box 25, Gutierrez Files, JCPL; Margaret Gentry, "LEAA Study Challenges '74–'75 FBI Crime Data," *Washington Post*, May 25, 1977, A5; December 31, 1977, memorandum to Annie Gutierrez, Domestic Policy Staff, from Bill Albers, Consultant to ACTION, subj.: "The Crime Rate," folder 8, box 25, Gutierrez Files, JCPL; February 25, 1978, memorandum for Stu Eizenstat; January 4, 1978, memorandum to Annie Gutierrez.

14. The Senate voted to eliminate the agency 67 to 8. "Senate Votes to Permit Wider Local Choices in Spending LEAA Funds," *Baltimore Sun*, May 22, 1979, A8; "The Future Role of the Law Enforcement Assistance Administration"; January 25, 1978, letter to LEAA Officials from George L. Hanbury, City Manager City of Virginia Beach, folder 8, "LEAA [1]," box 25, Gutierrez Files, JCPL; July 10, 1978, letter to Congress from Office of the White House Press Secretary, folder 1, Neustadt Files, box 25, JCPL; August 3, 1977, letter from James M. H. Gregg, Assistant Administrator Office of Planning and Management to Honorable William F. Hyland, AG State of New Jersey Trenton, NJ, folder 8, "LEAA [1]," box 25, Gutierrez Files, JCPL; "Attorney General to Delay Filling Top LEAA Posts," *Washington Post*, March 3, 1978, C6; Thomas B. Edsall, "Lawmen Link LEAA to Chaos in Plans," *Baltimore Sun*, May 2, 1978, D3. June 20,1977, DOJ Press Release, folder 10, "LEAA [3]," box 25, Gutierrez Files JCPL; "Good Concept Gone Awry," D6; July 10, 1978, letter to Congress from Office of the White House Press Secretary.

15. July 10, 1978, letter to Congress from Office of the White House Press Secretary.

16. June 20, 1977, Department of Justice Press Release, folder 10, "LEAA [3]," box 25, Gutierrez Files, JCPL; "Good Concept Gone Awry," D6; July 10, 1978, letter to Congress from Office of the White House Press Secretary.

17. On July 19, 1978, Carter announced his intention to make public housing a major part of his national urban policy. July 10, 1978, letter to Congress from Office of the White House Press Secretary; Patricia Harris speaking in July 10, 1978, "Remarks of the President upon Announcement of LEAA Reorganization," folder 1, box 25, Neustadt Files, JCPL; "Urban Initiatives Anti-Crime Program First Annual Report to Congress," 2; Langley Carlton Keyes, *Strategies and Saints: Fighting Drugs in Subsidized Housing* (Washington, DC: Urban Institute Press, 1992) 28.

18. The Public Housing Security Act of 1978 was included under Title II of the Housing and Community Development Act of 1978. "Urban Initiatives Anti-Crime Program"; July 1,1980, letter to Stephen R. Aiello, Special Assis-

tant to the President for Ethnic Affairs, from Lynn A. Curtis, Director, Urban Initiatives Anti-Crime Program, Ethnic Affairs-Aiello, folder "Urban Anti-Crime Initiatives [Meeting] Shoreham Hotel 7-15-80," box 10, JCPL; July 10, 1978, letter to Congress from Office of the White House Press Secretary; September 27, 1979, press release, "HUD Announces Finalists in Urban Initiatives Anti-Crime Program," HUD News, Washington, DC, folder 7, "Community Anti-Crime Legislation [1]," box 3, White Files, JCPL; March 31, 1980, "Urban Initiatives Anti-Crime Program First Annual Report to Congress."

19. July 1, 1980, letter to Stephen R. Aiello; "Urban Initiatives Anti-Crime Program First Annual Report to Congress."

20. "Urban Initiatives Anti-Crime Program First Annual Report to Congress," i.

21. While the housing projects were originally conceived under "a vision of the new contemporary man no longer tied to his own individual hearth and garden," Newman argued that by the early 1970s, the effect of this environment was to "produce crime, fear, and decay instead of freedom." Newman found that in New York City, a massive high-rise project and a modest six-story unit across the street from one another and virtually identical in size, population density, and social demographics experienced markedly different levels of violence: the high-rise had a 56 percent higher crime rate than the project across the street. Oscar Newman, *Design Guidelines for Creating Defensible Space* (Washington, DC: National Institute of Law Enforcement and Criminal Justice, Law Enforcement Assistance Administration, Department of Justice, 1976), 18, 35; "Architects Scored on Housing Projects," *New York Times*, July 19, 1976, 31; "Crime Fight Study Turns to New Field," *Los Angeles Times*, March 22, 1973, L12.

22. "Crime Fight Study Turns to New Field"; Newman, *Design Guidelines for Creating Defensible Space*, 17, 23; "'Utopian' Projects Fail by Design," *Washington Post*, July 24, 1976, D1; Newman quoted in "Aged Mixed with Young Blamed for Project Crime," *Chicago Tribune*, July 19, 1976, 5.

23. In his history of the development and decline of public housing from the 1930s to the present, Lawrence J. Vale describes the incorporation of architectural design and urban planning into public policy as "design politics." See *Purging the Poorest: Public Housing and the Design of Twice Cleared Communities* (Chicago: University of Chicago Press, 2013). "Crime Fight Study Turns to New Field"; Newman, *Design Guidelines for Creating Defensible Space*, 17, 23; "'Utopian' Projects Fail by Design," D1; Newman quoted in "Aged Mixed with Young Blamed," 5; May 15, 1975, memorandum to Jonathan Rose, Douglas Marvin, Jack Fuller from Malcolm Barr, Director Office of Public Relations, subj.: "Draft Papers for Consideration in Preparation of the Presidential Crime Message," Parsons Collection, box 3, "Crime Message of 6-19-75—Action Memoranda May 1–8 1975," Gerald Ford Presidential Library (hereafter, GFPL); see James Q.

Wilson and George L. Kelling, 'Broken Windows: The Police and Neighborhood Safety," *Atlantic Monthly*, March 1982, available at www.theatlantic.com/politics/crime/windows.htm.

24. "Aged Mixed with Young Blamed," 5; "$450,000 Grant to Boost Policing of Low Income Areas," *Atlanta Daily World*, June 25, 1974, 1; "Housing Force in Operation"; "Revised Housing Authority Security Force OKed," *New Pittsburgh Courier*, December 29, 1973, 29.

25. Work quoted in "LEAA Puts $2 Million for New Anti-Crime Plans," *Baltimore Afro-American*, May 25, 1974, 5; Police Foundation, "Evaluation of the Urban Initiatives Anti-Crime Program: Baltimore, MD Case Study" (John F. Kennedy School of Government for U.S. Department of Housing and Urban Development, Office of Policy Development and Research, 1984).

26. Tense relations between the security guards and tenants led the Housing Authority to modify the program to allow resident security aides to sit with the guard in the booth. The aides were screened by the Housing Authority and received six months of classes and six months of on-the-job training. Meanwhile, the Housing Authority created Security Coordinator and Security Operations Supervisor positions to advise both the contractual guard companies and the Baltimore City Police Department. "Evaluation of the Urban Initiatives Anti-Crime Program: Baltimore, MD," 7, 8.

27. March 31, 1980, "Urban Initiatives Anti-Crime Program First Annual Report to Congress," 8.

28. March 31, 1980, "Urban Initiatives Anti-Crime Program First Annual Report to Congress"; April 4, 1978, "Coordination of Anti-Crime Programming Between LEAA and HUD," memorandum from Lynn A. Curtis to James M. H. Gregg, folder 8, "LEAA [1]," box 25, Gutierrez Files, JCPL; April 4, 1978, memorandum from Curtis to Gregg.

29. "Evaluation of the Urban Initiatives Anti-Crime Program: Baltimore, MD," 14, 25.

30. In the event that an uninvited guest should attempt to enter the housing project, a "man trap" feature was installed into the entrances, which now included two sets of doors that closed automatically after a matter of seconds (the system was shortly altered after it was installed after residents were frequently caught between the two doors). Ibid., 10, 14, 25.

31. In New York City, where no tenant patrols existed in 1968, by the time the Carter administration introduced its public housing program, there existed 156 such patrols in 251 housing projects throughout the city. In the Johnson Housing Project in Harlem, twenty teenagers formed a special group in the larger 300-person volunteer tenant patrol. They alerted the adults when they observed crime, such as burglary, in their hallways and on the streets sur-

rounding the project. "Urban Initiatives Anti-Crime Program First Annual Report to Congress"; Ward Morehouse III, "FOCUS: Tenants Mount Crime Vigils," *Christian Science Monitor*, March 23, 1978, 2.

32. "Summary: ACTION-LEAA Anti-Crime Proposal," May 8, 1978, folder 8, box 3, White Files, JCPL; December 29, 1978, "LEAA/ACTION Memorandum of Agreement for the Urban Crime Prevention Program," folder 7, box 3, White Files, JCPL; Clarence Page, "Taylor Homes Residents Declare War on Crime," *Chicago Tribune*, February 13, 1978, C14; Edith Herman, "A 'Forgotten' Story of Pain in the Inner City," *Chicago Tribune*, July 15, 1979, M3.

33. "Urban Initiatives Anti-Crime Program First Annual Report to Congress"; U.S. Department of Justice, LEAA Grant Manager's memorandum, Project Summary, Jack Watson—Cabinet Secretary Stephen Page, folder 2, "Community Crime Prevention Grants /930–10/1/1980," box 126, JCPL; see also folders 7 and 8, "Community Anti-Crime Legislation," box 3, White Files, JCPL.

34. "Evaluation of the Urban Initiatives Anti-Crime Program: Baltimore, MD," 9; "Urban Initiatives Anti-Crime Program First Annual Report to Congress"; Morehouse, "FOCUS."

35. Memorandum for Honorable Anne Wexler, subj.: "Weekly Urban Policy Report, June 7, 1978, from John G. Kester, Special Assistant to the Secretary of Defense," Office of Anne Wexler, folder "Department of Defense: Program to Target Procurement to High Unemployment Areas," box 113, Jane Hartley's Urban Policy Files, JCPL; "Evaluation of the Urban Initiatives Anti-Crime Program: Baltimore, MD," 10.

36. "Evaluation of the Urban Initiatives Anti-Crime Program: Baltimore, MD," 11.

37. "New Orleans, LA Public Housing Agency," Office of Congressional Liaison Moore, folder "HUD Anti-Crime 9-25-79," box 80, Grants File, JCPL; "Detroit, MI Public Housing Agency," Office of Congressional Liaison Moore, folder "HUD Anti-Crime 9-25-79," box 80, Grants File, JCPL.

38. "Chicago, IL Public Housing Agency," Office of Congressional Liaison Moore, folder "HUD Anti-Crime 9-25-79," box 80, Grants File, JCPL.

39. Ibid.

40. "Urban Initiatives Anti-Crime Program First Annual Report to Congress."

41. "Evaluation of the Urban Initiatives Anti-Crime Program: Baltimore, MD," 38.

42. July 7, 1975, memorandum to Cannon from Aldrich, subj.: "Summer Urban Youth Project: New York City Trip," Parsons Collection, box 17, "Summer Jobs for Urban Youth," GFPL.

43. Moynihan noted that in New York City the fire alarm rate tripled from 69,700 alarms to 240,000 alarms between 1965 and 1969. January 16, 1970, memorandum, For the President from Daniel P. Moynihan, folder "'Black Vote'

(72)" (underline Moynihan's), box 10, Krogh Collection, Richard Nixon Presidential Library; Stephen E. Nordlinger, "Arson 'Epidemic' Stirs U.S. to Take Lead in Crackdown," *Baltimore Sun*, January 2, 1979, A1; Statement of G. R. Dickerson, Director, Bureau of Alcohol, Tobacco, and Firearms, April 28, 1979, Arson Problems in New York Hearings before the Subcommittee on Treasury, U.S. Postal Service, and General Government Appropriations, House Committee on Appropriations, 96th Cong., 1st sess., 10; May 2, 1979, letter to Congressman Addabbo from Stephen T. Boyle, Director, Office of Congressional Liaison, included in April 28, 1979 Hearings, 43.

44. "Arson and More Arson," *Washington Post*, April 20, 1979, A14; Lois Timnick, "'Spite' Blamed for Most of Arson in L.A. Last Year," *Los Angeles Times*, December 10, 1980, 3; May 2, 1979, letter to Congressman Addabbo; Nordlinger, "Arson 'Epidemic' Stirs."

45. January 16, 1970, memorandum for the president from Daniel P. Moynihan.

46. Manning Marable, "Miami and the Fire This Time," *In These Times*, May 28–June 3, 1980, 3; John Conyers Jr., "Police Violence and Riots," *Black Scholar* 12 (January–February 1981): 2–5; Bruce Porter and Marvin Dunn, *The Miami Riot of 1980: Crossing the Bounds* (Lexington, MA: Lexington Books, 1984).

47. Marable, "Miami and the Fire This Time"; Marable, "Small Changes Come to Dade County," *In These Times*, July 2–15, 1980, 6.

48. After Carter's first year in office, white unemployment dropped to 5.6 percent, while black unemployment rose to 12.5 percent. Chuck Stone, "Carter's Paternalistic Racism and the Inept Presidency," *Black Scholar* 9 (March 1978): 39–41. Leo R. Ribuffo, "Jimmy Carter: Beyond the Current Myths," *OAH Magazine of History* 3, no. 3–4 (Summer–Fall 1988): 19–23; Bruce J. Schulman, "Slouching towards the Supply-Side: Jimmy Carter and the New American Political Economy," in *The Carter Presidency: Policy Choices in the Post-New Deal Era*, ed. Gary M. Fink and Hugh Davis Graham (Lawrence: University Press of Kansas, 1998): 51–71.

49. Manning Marable, "The Fire This Time: The Miami Rebellion, May 1980," *The Black Scholar* 11 (July-August 1980): 2–18, 3; Marable, "Small Changes Come to Dade County," 6.

50. See Porter and Dunn, *Miami Riot of 1980*; Melissa Patterson and Robert Samuels, "McDuffie Riot Memories Fade in Liberty City, but Neighborhood Still Bears Deep Scars," *Miami Herald*, May 16, 2010; Briefing Summary, Justice System Improvement Act: Reorganization Proposal, August 28, 1979, folder 6, box 17, White Files, JCPL.

51. "South Bronx Fiasco," *New York Amsterdam News*, February 10, 1979, 18; Iwan Morgan, "Jimmy Carter, Bill Clinton, and the New Democratic Economies," *Historical Journal* 47, no. 4 (December 2004): 1015–1039; Kennedy quoted in

William E. Lechtenburg, *In the Shadow of FDR: From Harry Truman to Ronald Reagan*, rev. ed. (Ithaca, NY: Cornell University Press, 1985).

52. Ruth Wilson Gilmore, *Golden Gulag: Prisons, Surplus, Crisis, and Opposition in Globalizing California* (Berkeley: University of California Press, 2007); Judith Stein, *Pivotal Decade: How the United States Traded Factories for Finance in the Seventies* (New Haven, CT: Yale University Press, 2011). See also Jefferson Cowie, *Stayin' Alive: The 1970s and the Last Days of the Working Class* (New York: New Press, 2010); Daniel Rodgers, *Age of Fracture* (Cambridge, MA: Harvard University Press, 2011); Bruce Schulman, *The Seventies: The Great Shift in American Culture, Society, and Politics*, repr. ed. (New York: Da Capo, 2002); Robert O. Self, *All in the Family: The Realignment of American Democracy since the 1960s* (New York: Hill and Wang, 2013).

53. Police Foundation, "Evaluation of the Urban Initiatives Anti-Crime Program: Dade County, FL Case Study" (John F. Kennedy School of Government, prepared for Department of Housing and Urban Development, Office of Policy Development and Research, 1984), 18, 23, 33–34.

54. Bradford D. Hunt provides one of the best descriptions of this process in *Blueprint for Disaster: The Unraveling of Chicago Public Housing* (Chicago: University of Chicago Press, 2009). Patricia Roberts Harris, "A New Look at HUD," *Black Scholar* 9, no. 2 (October 1977): 15–21; Newman, *Design Guidelines for Creating Defensible Space*, 17.

9. FROM THE WAR ON CRIME TO THE WAR ON DRUGS

1. On the rise of conservatism during the 1960s and 1970s, see Gary Gerstle and Steve Fraser, "Introduction," in *The Rise and Fall of the New Deal Order, 1930–1980*, ed. Steve Fraser and Gary Gerstle (Princeton, NJ: Princeton University Press, 1989), ix-xxv; Matthew D. Lassiter, *The Silent Majority: Suburban Politics in the Sunbelt South* (Princeton, NJ: Princeton University Press, 2006); Lisa McGirr, *Suburban Warriors: The Origins of the New American Right* (Princeton, NJ: Princeton University Press, 2001); Robert O. Self, *American Babylon: Race and the Struggle for Postwar Oakland* (Princeton, NJ: Princeton University Press, 2003).

2. During the 1976 primary, Reagan asserted this view when discussing the law and order issue, appearing even tougher on crime than Ford. "What is the cause of crime in America?" Reagan asked during the campaign. "If one should listen to the Congress of the U.S., its most vocal voices, you will hear the old refrain, 'Poverty is the root cause of crime.' But time *has* proven these people wrong—dead wrong in too many cases." Thomas E. Cronin, Tamia Z. Cronin, and Michael E. Millakovich, *U.S. v. Crime in the Streets* (Bloomington:

Indiana University Press, 1981), 119. See Edward Banfield, *Moral Basis of a Backward Society* (New York: Free Press, 1967) and Edward Banfield, *The Unheavenly City: The Nature and Future of Our Urban Crisis* (New York: Little, Brown, 1970); Milton Friedman, *Capitalism and Freedom: Fortieth Anniversary Edition* (Chicago: University of Chicago Press, 2002); Oscar Lewis, *The Children of Sanchez: Autobiography of a Mexican Family* (New York: Vintage Books, 1979); Charles Murray, *Losing Ground: American Social Policy, 1950–1980* (New York: Basic Books, 1984). Scholarship on the so-called "underclass" includes Douglas Glasgow, *The Black Underclass: Unemployment and Entrapment of Ghetto Youth* (New York: Random House, 1980); Lawrence Mead, *Beyond Entitlement: The Social Obligations of Citizenship* (New York: Free Press, 1986); Herbert J. Gans, *The War against the Poor: The Underclass and Antipoverty Policy* (New York: Basic Books, 1995); Michael Katz, ed., *The "Underclass Debate": Views from History* (Princeton, NJ: Princeton University Press, 1993); and Katz, *The Undeserving Poor: From the War on Poverty to the War on Welfare* (New York: Pantheon, 1990). Ronald Reagan, *Remarks in New Orleans, Louisiana, at the Annual Meeting of the International Association of Chiefs of Police*, September 28, 1981, American Presidency Project, available at http://www.presidency.ucsb.edu/ws/?pid=44300.

3. Morris quoted in "Crime Fighters at the End of the Road," *Washington Post*, April 15, 1982, A23.

4. Katherine Beckett, *Making Crime Pay: Law and Order in Contemporary American Politics* (New York: Oxford University Press, 1999), 3; David Garland, *The Culture of Control: Crime and Social Order in Contemporary Society* (Chicago: University of Chicago Press, 2002), 14; see also Michael Tonry, *Malign Neglect: Race, Crime and Punishment in America* (New York: Oxford University Press, 1996).

5. Biden quoted in Mary Thornton, "Senate Votes to Toughen Federal Sentencing Law," *Washington Post*, October 1, 1982, A3; May 25, 1988, "Statement of Congressman Glenn English," press release, Williams Files, White House Conference Recommendations OA 19050, Ronald Reagan Presidential Library (hereafter, RRPL); Crime Control package, 1984 legislative chronology, *Congress and the Nation, 1981–1984*, 6 (Washington, DC: Congressional Quarterly Press, 1985), available at http://library.cqpress/congress/catn81-0011176010.

6. May 11, 1988, memorandum for Jim Miller from Wayne Arny and Alan Raul, subj.: "DOD Anti-Drug Program," Addington Files, Drugs (8) OA 16788, RRPL. See also Stuart Schrader, "American Streets, Foreign Territory: How Counterinsurgent Police Waged the War on Crime" (PhD diss., New York University, 2015).

7. N.d., George H. W. Bush, "National Law Enforcement: A Personal Perspective," Counterterrorism and Narcotics Files, National Narcotics Border Inter-

diction System (1), box 92258, RRPL; Stephen Graham, *Cities under Siege: The New Military Urbanism* (New York: Verso, 2011).

8. Bush, "National Law Enforcement;" May 23, 1984, "Briefing Book: DOJ for Administration Anti-Crime Legislation," To Meese from Attorney General William French Smith, subj.: "Anti-Crime Leg," Meese Files, Anti-Crime Legislation (2) OA 10246, RRPL; June 30, 1988, "Statement by the President," folder "Legislation-Anti Drug Abuse Act of 1988 [5 of 7]," box 4, MacDonald Files, RRPL; Keith B. Richburg, "Congress Approves Major Overhaul of the Nation's Anticrime Statutes," *Washington Post*, October 12, 1984, A21; Sam Enriquez, "Seized in Raids," *Los Angeles Times*, April 20, 1986, B1.

9. Bush, "National Law Enforcement"; May 18, 1988, "Remarks by the President at U.S. Coast Guard Commencement"; Enriquez, "Seized in Raids"; Christian Parenti, *Lockdown America: Police and Prisons in the Age of Crisis* (New York: Verso, 2000), 54; Eric Blumenson and Eva Nilsen, "Policing for Profit: The Drug War's Hidden Economic Agenda," *University of Chicago Law Review* 65 (1988): 64, 82; "FBI Drug Sting Probed after Agent's Arrest," *Washington Post*, March 16, 1985, A4; Michelle Alexander, *The New Jim Crow: Mass Incarceration in the Age of Colorblindness* (New York: New Press, 2011), 78, 80.

10. April 28, 1988, "Remarks by Donald Ian MacDonald, National Drug Policy Board," Williams Working-Legislative Initiative 1988 (2) OA 16690, RRPL.

11. Blumenson and Nilsen, "Policing for Profit," 64, 82; Victor Merina, "The Slide from Cop to Criminal," *Los Angeles Times*, December 1, 1993; "FBI Drug Sting Probed," A4.

12. Heather Ann Thompson, "The Prison Industrial Complex: A Growth Industry in a Shrinking Economy," *New Labor Forum* 21 (Fall 2012): 38–47; Leslie Maitland Werner, "Getting Out the Word on the New Crime Act," *New York Times*, November 16, 1984, A24; Bruce Western, Becky Pettit, and Josh Guetzkow, "Black Economic Progress in the Era of Mass Imprisonment," in *Invisible Punishment: The Collateral Consequences of Mass Imprisonment*, ed. Marc Mauer and Mede Chesney-Lind (New York: New Press, 2002), 167. See also Kimberly E. Gilmore, "States of Incarceration: Prisoners' Rights and United States Prison Expansion after World War II" (unpublished diss., New York University, 2005).

13. Between fiscal year 1981 and fiscal year 1982, the Reagan administration cut annual federal spending on social programs from $94.8 billion to $88.8 billion, including a decrease of $490 million from child nutrition programs, and a $341 million reduction in AFDC payments. The poverty rate itself also rose from 15 percent in 1975 to 23 percent by 1987. Margy Waller, "Block Grants: Flexibility vs. Stability in Social Services" (Brookings Institute, Center on Children and Families no. 34, December 2005), available at http://www .brookings.edu/es/research/projects/wrb/publications/pb/pb34.pdf; Andrew E.

Busch, *Ronald Reagan and the Politics of Freedom* (New York: Rowman and Lit-tlefield, 2001); Richard S. Williamson, "A New Federalism: Proposals and Achievements of President Reagan's First Three Years," *Publius* 16 (Winter 1986): 11–28; "Strengthening the Social Fabric," *Christian Science Monitor*, No-vember 15, 1988, 1; Leith Mullings, "Losing Ground: Harlem, the War on Drugs, and the Prison Industrial Complex," *Souls* 5, no. 2 (2003): 1–21; Ronald Reagan, *Radio Address to the Nation on Welfare Reform*, February 15, 1986, American Presidency Project, available at http://www.presidency.ucsb.edu/ws/?pid =36875.

14. May 18, 1988, "Remarks by the President at U.S. Coast Guard Commence-ment," Nitchem Field, New London, CT, Addington Files Drugs (7) OA 16788, RRPL.

15. See James Mills, *The Underground Empire: When Crime and Governments Embrace* (New York: Dell, 1986); Faye V. Harrison, "Drug Trafficking in World Capitalism: A Perspective on Jamaican Posses in the U.S.," *Social Justice* 16, no. 4 (Winter 1989): 115–131; "Strengthening the Social Fabric."

16. Resident quoted in "Just Saying No Is Not Enough: HUD's Inadequate Re-sponse to the Drug Crisis in Public Housing," 100th Cong., 2d sess., H.R. Rep. No. 100–702 (June 15, 1988); June 23, 1988, "Issue Paper for Discussion at the National Drug Policy Board," Counterterrorism and Narcotics Files, Policy Board Minutes (1) Richard Porter NSC Staff, box 92258, RRPL; March 3, 1988, letter to Mac from Dick (Williams) "Re: Crack Use in Inner Cities," Williams Files, Crack/Cocaine OA 19050, RRPL.

17. Between 1980 and 1984 alone, the FBI's antidrug allocation increased more than tenfold, from $8 million in 1980 to $95 million in 1984. March 21, 1987, "Radio Address by the President to the Nation," Camp David, Maryland, MacDonald Files, Anti-Drug Abuse Budget, 1987-Working Papers OA 16316, RRPL; January 21, 1987, memorandum to Donald T. Regan; Katherine Beckett, *Making Crime Pay: Law and Order in Contemporary American Poli-tics* (New York: Oxford University Press, 1999), 3, citing Executive Office of the President, Budget of the U.S. Government (1990), citing U.S. Office of the Na-tional Drug Control Policy, National Drug Control Strategy (1992); Marc Mauer and Meda Chesney-Lind, "Introduction," in Marc Mauer and Meda Chesney-Lind, *Invisible Punishment: The Collateral Consequences of Mass Imprisonment* (New York: New Press, 2003), 6.

18. The legislation also included provisions stipulating that any person caught in possession of small amounts of illegal drugs now faced a civil fine of up to $10,000. Individuals convicted of a drug-related murder or in federal court were now subject to the death penalty. January 21, 1987, memorandum to Donald T. Regan from Charles Hobbs and Richard L. Williams, subj.: "The

Anti-Drug Abuse Budget," MacDonald Files, Anti-Drug Abuse Budget, 1987–
Working Papers OA 16316, RRPL; George Bush, "National Law Enforcement:
A Personal Perspective"; November 18, 1988, "Fact Sheet: Anti-Drug Abuse Act
of 1988," White House, Office of the Press Secretary, Addington Files, Drugs
(1) OA 16788, RRPL; Parenti, *Lockdown America*, 57; "Congress Clears Massive
Anti-Drug Measure," *Congressional Quarterly Almanac*, vol. 42 (1986), 98. I
borrow "apartheid sentencing" from Parenti. Though in 1985 roughly 800,000
Americans faced drug-related charges; by 1989 the number had shot up to
roughly 1.4 million. Parenti, *Lockdown America*, 58; Richard M. Smith, "The
Plague among Us," *Newsweek*, June 16, 1986, 15; "Drugs: The Enemy Within,"
Time Magazine Special Report, September 15, 1986.

19. Alexander, *New Jim Crow*, 54, 58, 60; Lawrence D. Bobo and Victor Thompson,
"Racialized Mass Incarceration: Poverty, Prejudice, and Punishment," in
Doing Race: 21 Essays for the 21st Century, ed. Hazel R. Markus and Paula Moya
(New York: W. W. Norton, 2010): 322–355, 332; A. T. Callinicos, "Meaning of
Los Angeles Riots," *Economic and Political Weekly* 27, no. 30 (July 25, 1992):
1603–1606; Bruce Western, *Punishment and Inequality in America* (New York:
Russell Sage Foundation, 2006), 47; Glenn Loury, ed., *Race, Incarceration, and
American Values* (Cambridge, MA: MIT Press, 2008).

20. In urban areas like Oakland, the drug task force became so dependent on
federal drug fighting grants that by 1995 the commander of a special task force
within the Oakland Housing Authority began shifts by proclaiming, "Let's go
out and kick ass," as well as "Everybody goes to jail tonight for everything,
right?" George Bush, "National Law Enforcement: A Personal Perspective";
May 18, 1988, "Remarks by the President at U.S. Coast Guard Commencement"; Enriquez, "Seized in Raids; Parenti, *Lockdown America*, 54; Blumenson and Nilsen, "Policing for Profit," 64, 82; "FBI Drug Sting Probed,"
A4; quoted in Alexander, *New Jim Crow*, 78, 80.

21. March 21, 1987, "Radio Address by the President to the Nation," Camp David,
Maryland, MacDonald Files, Anti-Drug Abuse Budget, 1987– Working Papers OA 16316, RRPL; January 21, 1987, memorandum to Donald T. Regan; Katherine Beckett, *Making Crime Pay: Law and Order in Contemporary American
Politics* (New York: Oxford University Press, 1999), 3, citing Executive Office
of the President, Budget of the U.S. Government (1990), citing U.S. Office of
the National Drug Control Policy, National Drug Control Strategy (1992);
Marc Mauer and Meda Chesney-Lind, "Introduction," in Mauer and
Chesney-Lind, *Invisible Punishment: The Collateral Consequences of Mass Imprisonment* (New York: New Press, 2003), 6.

22. March 24, 1987, memorandum for the President from James Miller III, subj.:
"Proposed Executive Order Entitled 'National Drug Policy Board,'" Williams

Files, 3703: 0913011988 NDPB Issues, November 1988-WHC Responses (5) OA 19052, RRPL.

23. March 24, 1987, memorandum for the President; September 7, 1988, "Statement of Administration Policy: H.R. 5210—Omnibus Drug Initiative Act of 1988," Williams, Congressional Drug Proposals 1988 # 1 1300; OA 16900, RRPL.

24. The Drug Policy Board also worked to include the private sector in its narcotics control effort as much as possible. While the federally controlled nonprofit agency ACTION worked during the Carter administration to foster tenant patrols and security hardware in the nation's housing projects, by the late 1980s it was responsible for managing drug abuse activities. In 1987 alone, the year Reagan called the board, funding of ACTION increased by $5 million, giving the agency an unprecedented annual budget of $13 million. June 30, 1988, "Statement by the President," folder "Legislation-Anti Drug Abuse Act of 1988 [5 of 7]," box 4, MacDonald Files, RRPL; January 16, 1987, memorandum for Ed Meese from Joseph R. Wright Jr., subj.: "Funding in the 1988 Budget for Drug Abuse Activities," MacDonald Files, Anti-Drug Abuse Budget 1987 Working Papers A 16316, RRPL.

25. May 23, 1984, "Briefing Book: DOJ for Administration Anti-Crime Legislation"; February 19, 1988, "Statement of the Honorable Charles B. Rangel, Chairman—Select Committee on Narcotics Abuse and Control," Press Conference on the 1989 Drug Budget and International Drug Policy, Williams, Drug Abuse Budgets 1981–1987 (12) OA 19358, RRPL; November 18, 1988, "Remarks by the President at Signing Ceremony for the Anti-Drug Abuse Act of 1988"; March 24, 1988, "Proposed Remarks for Vice President George Bush, Hartford Country Bar Association, Hartford CT," Counterterrorism and Narcotics, National Narcotics Border Interdiction System, folder 1, box 92258, RRPL; May 24, 1988, "Legislative Initiative: High Risk Youth Committee," Williams Legislative Initiative 1988 1303 [3] OA 16690, RRPL; June 23, 1988, "Issue Paper for Discussion at the National Drug Policy Board," Counterterrorism and Narcotics Files, Policy Board Minutes (1) Richard Porter NSC Staff, box 92258, RRPL.

26. August 10, 1988, "Legislative Referral Memorandum," Executive Office of the President, MacDonald Files II Legislation—Anti Drug Abuse Act of 1988 [4 of 7] box 4; RRPL; Western, *Punishment and Inequality in America*, chap. 7.

27. Federal Bureau of Investigation, "Crips and Bloods: Drug Gang," Freedom of Information Act Document; "The Drug Gangs," *Newsweek*, March 28, 1988, 20–27; U.S. Department of Justice, National Institute of Justice, Division of Law Enforcement, Investigation and Enforcement Branch, Bureau of Crime and Criminal Intelligence, "Crips & Bloods Street Gangs," reproduced by California Department of Justice, Office of the Attorney General, Sacramento, CA, n.d. (likely 1988); Bernard Headley, "War Ina 'Babylon': Dynamics of the

Jamaican Informal Drug Economy," *Social Justice* 15, no. 3–4 1988: 61–86, 67; Harrison, "Drug Trafficking in World Capitalism."

28. "Crips & Bloods Street Gangs."

29. Federal Bureau of Investigation, "Crips and Bloods: Drug Gang"; "The Drug Gangs," *Newsweek*, March 28, 1988, 20–27; "Crips and Bloods Street Gangs"; Headley, "War Ina 'Babylon,'" 61–86, 67; Harrison, "Drug Trafficking in World Capitalism."

30. Street Terrorism Act, California Penal Code Section 186.20; ibid. See also Donna Murch, "Ferguson's Inheritance," *Jacobin Magazine*, August 5, 2015, available at https://www.jacobinmag.com/2015/08/ferguson-police-black-lives-matter/.

31. "Around the Nation," *Washington Post*, August 21, 1989, A4; "Pilot Project to Stem the Violence Set in East L.A.," *Los Angeles Sentinel*, July 20, 2000, A1; Norman quoted in Nieson Himmel, "L.A. Gang Killings Put at 236—Up 15% from '87," *Los Angeles Times*, December 16, 1988, C1.

32. The favorable statistics were directly tied to the increased gang reporting that resulted from the sweeps. By 1989, after a handful of weekend sweeps swooped up thousands more young Angeles, Community Gang Services estimated that 70,000 young men and women were gang members in Los Angeles, up from 30,000 in 1980. From "Youth Gang Programs and Strategies," Office of Juvenile Justice and Delinquency Prevention Summary, August 2000, available at https://www.ncjrs.gov/html/ojjdp/summary_2000_8/suppression.html; Ron Dungee, "Weekend Gang Sweep Results in 352 Arrests," *Los Angeles Times*, August 24, 1989, A1; Nieson Himmel, "L.A. Gang Killings Put at 236—Up 15% from '87," *Los Angeles Times*, December 16, 1988, C1; Robert Welkos, "700 Seized in Gang Sweep; 2 More Die in Shootings," *Los Angeles Times*, September 19, 1988, 21.

33. Scott Armstrong, "Sawhorses Enlisted in Drug War," *Christian Science Monitor*, June 15, 1990, 8; "What Is Operation Cul de Sac? Will It Help?," *Los Angeles Sentinel*, June 20, 1991, A1.

34. On the "criminalization of urban space," see Heather Ann Thompson, "Why Mass Incarceration Matters: Rethinking Crisis, Decline, and Transformation in Postwar American History," *Journal of American History* 97, no. 3 (December 2010): 703–758, 705. Quoted in Maurice Miller, "Drug Enforcement Barricades Not Accepted by All Residents," *Los Angeles Sentinel*, March 1, 1990, A1.

35. *California v. Acevedo*, 500 U.S. 565, 600 (1991), Stevens, J., dissenting; Alexander, *New Jim Crow*, 61, quoted on 103.

36. *McCleskey v. Kemp* Supreme Court majority opinion, Page 481 U.S. 316; *California v. Acevedo*, 500 U.S. 565, 600 (1991), Stevens, J., dissenting; Alexander, *New Jim Crow*, 61.

37. Alexander, *New Jim Crow*, 11, 113, 103; U.S. Department of Justice, Drug Enforcement Administration, *Operation Pipeline and Convoy* (Washington, DC, n.d.), www.usdoj.gov/dea/programs/pipecon.htm; Alexander, *New Jim Crow*, 70.

38. "Crips & Bloods Street Gangs."

39. Ibid.

40. According to the Census Bureau, the number of Americans who married outside their race increased from 149,000 in 1960 to 651,00 in 1980 to more than double that number—or 1,348,000—by 1990. U.S. Census Bureau, "America's Families and Living Arrangements," (2000), available at http://www.census.gov/population/socdemo/hh-fam/p20-537/2000/tabfg4.txt; Anita Kathy Foeman and Teresa Nance, "From Miscegenation to Multiculturalism: Perceptions and Stages of Interracial Relationship Development," *Journal of Black Studies* 29 (1999): 540–557. In addition to the police profiling interracial couples and black families, black-owned businesses were vulnerable to police investigations on suspicion of gang affiliation. With "tremendous amounts of cash on hand and no legitimate reasons for possessing it," the California Attorney General's Office warned that Crips and Bloods members used beauty salons, music shops, auto body shops, night clubs, limousine services, construction companies, pager services, restaurants, liquor stores, car washes, food markets, real estate companies, and other small businesses to launder and invest their profits from the black market. Under these terms, any black-owned business, particularly in segregated urban communities, could be subject to possible attack and surveillance under the pretext that it operated as a front for drug trades. "Crips & Bloods Street Gangs."

41. "Crips & Bloods Street Gangs."

42. Colton Simpson, author interview by telephone November 27, 2005; Stanley Tookie Williams, *Blue Rage, Black Redemption* (New York: Touchstone Books, 1997), 134; Yusuf Jah and Sister Shah'Keyah, *Uprising: Crips and Bloods Tell the Story of America's Youth in the Crossfire* (New York: Touchstone Books, 1997), 29.

43. "Around the Nation," *Washington Post*, August 21, 1989, A4; "Pilot Project to Stem the Violence Set in East L.A.," *Los Angeles Sentinel*, July 20, 2000, A1; Norman quoted in Himmel, "L.A. Gang Killings."

44. "A Sheriff's Office Makes Own Crack," *Chicago Tribune*, April 20, 1989, 29; Jeffrey Schmalz, "New Twist on Crack in Florida," *New York Times*, April 19, 1989, A12; ibid.

45. Sharon Jefferson, "NAACP Calls for Investigation," *Call and Post*, January 22, 1987, 1A.

46. Ray Zeman, "20 Youth Gang Heads Say They Want Jobs," *Los Angeles Times*, December 28, 1974, A1.

EPILOGUE: RECKONING WITH THE WAR ON CRIME

1. J. Phillip Thompson, *Black Mayors, Black Communities, and the Call for a Deep Democracy* (New York: Oxford University Press, 2005).

2. The severity of felon disenfranchisement laws corresponds directly to the number of black and Latino prisoners under criminal supervision in a given state. Christopher Uggen, Sarah Shannon, and Jeff Manza, "State-Level Estimates of Felon Disenfranchisement in the United States, 2010" (Washington, DC: The Sentencing Project, 2012), available at http://sentencingproject.org/doc /publications/fd_State_Level_Estimates_of_Felon_Disen_2010.pdf; see also The Sentencing Project, "Felony Disenfranchisement: A Primer" (Washington, DC: The Sentencing Project, 2014), available at http://sentencingproject.org/doc /publications/fd_Felony%20Disenfranchisement%20Primer.pdf. On the impact of the U.S. census counts on the general health of American democracy, see Heather Ann Thompson, "How Prisons Change the Balance of Power in America," *Atlantic Monthly*, October 2013, available at http://www.theatlantic .com/national/archive/2013/10/how-prisons-change-the-balance-of-power-in -america/280341/; Christopher Uggen and Jeff Manza, "Democratic Contraction? Political Consequences of Felon Disenfranchisement in the United States," *American Sociological Review* 67 (December 2002): 777–803; Erica Frankenberg, Chungmei Lee, and Gary Orfield, "A Multiracial Society with Segregated Schools: Are We Losing the Dream?," The Civil Rights Project, Harvard University (The Civil Rights Project, January 2003), available at http://civilrightsproject .ucla.edu/research/k-12-education/integration-and-diversity/a-multiracial -society-with-segregated-schools-are-we-losing-the-dream/frankenberg -multiracial-society-losing-the-dream.pdf.

3. In Baltimore, where officials declared community involvement a major priority but allocated only 2 percent of High Impact funds for such efforts, the Lock Haven Radio Watch equipped volunteers with walkie-talkies in order to assist the police department in monitoring several neighborhoods. Officials credited the auxiliary force with a 23 percent decline in burglaries and a 96 percent drop in auto thefts during the three months in which it operated. Eleanor Chelimsky, *High Impact Anti-Crime Program: National Level Evaluation Final Report, Vol. II* (Washington, DC: Department of Justice, National Institute of Law Enforcement and Criminal Justice, Law Enforcement Assistance Administration, 1976), 313.

4. H. R. Haldeman, *The Haldeman Diaries: Inside the Nixon White House* (New York: G. P. Putnam and Sons, 1994), 66.

5. In New York City, where 35 to 40 percent of its residents were people of color, only 7 percent of the police force was black. On the federal level during this

period, of the 2,200 agents working for the Drug Enforcement Agency, only 177 were black. And none of the ninety U.S. attorneys were of African descent, although the 3.3 percent of the lawyers working for the Justice Department itself were black. Lee P. Brown, "Bridge over Troubled Waters: A Perspective on Policing in the Black Community" in *Black Perspectives on Crime and the Criminal Justice System*, ed. Robert L. Woodson (Boston: G. K. Hall, 1977), 79–106, 88; Sterling Johnson, "Luncheon Speaker," in Woodson ed., *Black Perspectives*, 161–168, 162–163; James Baldwin, *Nobody Knows My Name* (New York: Dial Press, 1961), 65–67.

ACKNOWLEDGMENTS

This book evolved from the barbed wire, concrete, metal detectors, and watch-towers that define the American carceral landscape. At California's High Desert State Prison in Susanville, Riverside County Jail, and the Centinella Correctional Facility in El Centro, the conversations I had with friends, family, and loved ones serving time made uncovering the historical developments that gave rise to mass incarceration immediate and important. Tim K, Tike, Roger, Stone, Smoke, Rap, and Colton Simpson's insights and correspondence fueled my pursuit of answers and provided me with the strength to continue moving forward. Tim's comments and criticisms on early chapter drafts helped me grasp the twin processes of criminalization and incarceration, and his willingness to distribute my writing to others greatly enriched and emboldened my analysis.

I have been fortunate enough to cross paths with many phenomenal teachers over the years who deeply shaped my thinking and this book's content. Angela Dillard and Robin D. G. Kelley made me want to be a historian. They have both been formidable influences since my undergraduate days and continue to provide critical mentorship. Eric Foner nurtured my understanding of the contours of U.S. history and allowed me to reach for the seemingly impossible, stimulating my analysis and encouraging the progression of my ideas. I could not have asked for a more generous advisor. My perception of the nature of postwar liberalism and social policy grew out of conversations and feedback from Ira Katznelson, Mae Ngai, Alan Brinkley, Alice Kessler-Harris, and Premilla Nadasen. In addition, I remain grateful to Barbara Fields and Nikhil Pal Singh, who provided me comments in the early stages of this project that went on to shape my thinking through its duration. Finally, Manning Marable gave me a sense of the possibilities of history and theory. I am honored to have worked with Manning, and I will forever carry his legacy in my own work and praxis. I am further indebted to Leith Mullings for taking me under her wing in the context of an irreplaceable loss.

My views on the rise of the carceral state and the relationship between welfare and crime control policies came out of conversations with Heather Thompson. Heather's breadth of knowledge and commitment to enlightening fellow historians and the wider public on these issues have made my own work relevant. Her expertise can be felt on nearly every page of this book. In addition to Heather, a number of scholars working in the field of carceral studies have consistently offered wisdom and exchange that invigorated my understanding of American law enforcement and the politics of crime control. Vesla Weaver, Donna Murch, Julilly Kohler-Hausmann, and Khalil Muhammad gave me guidance on chapter drafts and controversial lines of reasoning. This book would not have materialized without their friendship and feedback. I am also grateful to Robert Chase, Alex Elkins, Max Felker-Kantor, Phil Goff, Kelly Lytle Hernandez, Marisol LeBrón, Logan McBride, Tracy Meares, Max Mischler, Jessica Neptune, Melanie Newport, Devah Pager, Peter Pios, Stewart Schrader, Megan Stubbendeck, and Bruce Western for their contributions.

Much of the writing of this book took place during my time as a postdoctoral scholar in the University of Michigan Society of Fellows, where I thrived in a vibrant community of intellectuals. Tiya Miles offered me meaningful advice and served as a source of inspiration, and I am beholden to Don Lopez for his mentorship and generosity. Thanks also to Martha Jones, Karen Lacey, Matthew Lassiter, Bill Novak, Sherrie Randolph, Margo Schlanger, Penny Von Eschen, and Stephen Ward for their time and counsel. The undergraduate researchers I was lucky enough to work with helped fill in critical gaps during my time in Ann Arbor. I very much appreciate the assistance Ross MacPherson, Salvatore Mancina, and Brittany Smith provided. I must also thank the Ford Foundation and the community of Ford Fellows for giving me the necessary support to complete this project.

My colleagues in the Departments of History and African and African American Studies at Harvard have been enormously encouraging through the completion of this book. Larry Bobo and Walter Johnson deserve special mention in this respect. I am also grateful to Emmanuel Akyeampong, David Armitage, Vincent Brown, Tomiko Brown-Nagin, Amanda Claybaugh, Genevieve Clutario, Lizabeth Cohen, Nancy Cott, Marla Frederick, Alejandro de la Fuente, Evelyn Brooks Higginbotham, Maya Jasanoff, Andrew Jewett, James Kloppenberg, Jill Lepore, Mary

Lewis, Sarah Lewis, Lisa McGirr, Tey Meadow, George Paul Meiu, Ian Miller, Ingrid Monson, Marcyliena Morgan, Sam Moyn, Laurence Ralph, Tommie Shelby, Dan Smail, Brandon Terry, Jonathan Walton, and Kirsten Weld. Henry Louis Gates Jr. has opened up new spaces within the academy and in public discourse where the questions at the center of this project could be considered. I value Professor Gates's fortitude and the incredible community he has built.

In many ways, I would not have survived the process of researching and writing without theorizing, commiserating, cavorting, and laughing with fellow scholars and friends. Our Black Historians Matter (BHM) cohort has served as an intellectual and psychological backbone for more than a decade. BHM members Samir Meghelli, Zaheer Ali, Kellie Jackson-Carter, Russell Rickford, Adrienne Clay, JT Roane, Amanda Alexander, Horace Grant, and Megan French Marcelin provided much-needed camaraderie, debate, and solidarity. In particular, this project developed out of the intellectual kinship I share with Megan. Thanks also to George Aumoithe, Lydia Barnett and Nick Valvo, Martha Biondi, Anmol Chadda, Jim Downs, Jenn Eaglin, Garrett Felber, Kendra Field, Reighan Gilliam, Thai Jones, Peniel Joseph, Lucas Kirkpatrick and Christine Hopkins, Erik and Sheela Linstrum, Michael Ralph, Bryan Rosenblithe, and Wes Alcenat. Vanessa Diaz and Ben O'Dell, Danny Grossman and Danny Reubens, Sophie Harris, Thierry Kehou and Emily Schiffer, Sabrina Luna, Loren Nunley, Mary Spooner and Jimmy Bendernagel, and Francophone are my chosen family and my rock. Thank you for loving me no matter what.

Without the vast knowledge of the staff at the National Archives and the presidential libraries of John F. Kennedy, Lyndon Baines Johnson, Richard Nixon, Gerald Ford, Jimmy Carter, and Ronald Reagan, I could have easily gotten lost in bureaucratic red tape while navigating federal manuscript collections and White House Central Files. Yet the knowledge of archivists at these sites helped make the project more manageable. At the end of a long day of sifting through files, the National Archives and Records Administration staff proved exceptionally accommodating with my relentless photocopying and considerate with key anecdotes when appropriate.

My editor, Brian Distelberg, had a vision for this book from the beginning. Brian always asked questions that elevated my analysis and pushed me in new directions. I could not have reached the final product without his patience, persistence, and extraordinary attention to tone and narrative structure. Brian solicited two anonymous reviewers whose suggestions vastly enhanced the book. I wish to thank them both for responses that sharpened my argument and scope in significant ways. Thanks also to Dave Prout, as well as the editors and staff at Harvard University Press, especially Joyce Seltzer, Michael Higgins, and Stephanie Vyce.

Finally, I would not be where I am today without unwavering love and grounding from my family. Mom, Adam, Melina, Lindsay, and Dad are my foundation and my biggest source of pride. And Matthew held me up at both my highest and lowest points through the process of writing this book. Every day, past and future, I look forward to growing, and to celebrating history, with him.

INDEX

———